CW00337137

Buying a Home
in
Australia
&
New Zealand

A Survival Handbook

by
Graeme Chesters

SURVIVAL BOOKS • LONDON • ENGLAND

First published 2006

Survival Books Limited
26 York Street, London W1U 6PZ, United Kingdom
☎ +44 (0)20-7788 7644, ▤ +44 (0)870-762 3212
✉ info@survivalbooks.net
🖳 www.survivalbooks.net
To order books, please refer to page 383.

British Library Cataloguing in Publication Data.
A CIP record for this book is available
from the British Library.
ISBN 1 901130 88 6

Printed and bound in Italy by Legoprint spa.

ACKNOWLEDGEMENTS

I would like to thank all those who contributed to the successful publication of this book, in particular Martin Kidd, Vivienne Peters and Dougal Robertson for their invaluable help, and Tourism New South Wales, Tourism Queensland, bigstockphoto.com, istockphoto.com, Vivienne Peters and Dougal Robertson for photographs. I would also like to thank Joe Laredo (editing), Catherine Wakelin (proofreading), Kerry Laredo (dtp) and, last but not least, Jim Watson for his great cartoons, maps and cover design.

TITLES BY SURVIVAL BOOKS

Alien's Guides
Britain; France

The Best Places To Buy A Home
France; Spain

Buying A Home
Abroad; Australia & New Zealand;
Cyprus; Florida;
France; Greece; Ireland;
Italy; Portugal;
South Africa; Spain;
Buying, Selling & Letting
Property (UK)

**Foreigners Abroad: Triumphs
& Disasters**
France; Spain

Lifeline Regional Guides
Brittany; Costa Blanca;
Costa del Sol; Dordogne/Lot;
Normandy; Poitou-Charentes;
Provence/Côte d'Azur

Living And Working
Abroad; America;
Australia; Britain; Canada;
The European Union;
The Far East; France; Germany;
The Gulf States & Saudi Arabia; Holland,
Belgium & Luxembourg;
Ireland; Italy; London;
New Zealand; Spain;
Switzerland

Earning Money From Your Home
France; Spain

Making A Living
France; Spain

Other Titles
Renovating & Maintaining
Your French Home; Retiring Abroad;
Shooting Caterpillars in Spain;
Surprised by France

Order forms are on page 383.

WHAT READERS & REVIEWERS

When you buy a model plane for your child, a video recorder, or some new computer gizmo, you get with it a leaflet or booklet pleading 'Read Me First', or bearing large friendly letters or bold type saying 'IMPORTANT – follow the instructions carefully'. This book should be similarly supplied to all those entering France with anything more durable than a 5-day return ticket. It is worth reading even if you are just visiting briefly, or if you have lived here for years and feel totally knowledgeable and secure. But if you need to find out how France works then it is indispensable. Native French people probably have a less thorough understanding of how their country functions. – Where it is most essential, the book is most up to the minute.

LIVING FRANCE

Rarely has a 'survival guide' contained such useful advice. This book dispels doubts for first-time travellers, yet is also useful for seasoned globetrotters – In a word, if you're planning to move to the USA or go there for a long-term stay, then buy this book both for general reading and as a ready-reference.

AMERICAN CITIZENS ABROAD

It is everything you always wanted to ask but didn't for fear of the contemptuous put down – The best English-language guide – Its pages are stuffed with practical information on everyday subjects and are designed to complement the traditional guidebook.

SWISS NEWS

A complete revelation to me – I found it both enlightening and interesting, not to mention amusing.

CAROLE CLARK

Let's say it at once. David Hampshire's **Living and Working in France** is the best handbook ever produced for visitors and foreign residents in this country; indeed, my discussion with locals showed that it has much to teach even those born and bred in l'Hexagone. – It is Hampshire's meticulous detail which lifts his work way beyond the range of other books with similar titles. Often you think of a supplementary question and search for the answer in vain. With Hampshire this is rarely the case. – He writes with great clarity (and gives French equivalents of all key terms), a touch of humour and a ready eye for the odd (and often illuminating) fact. – This book is absolutely indispensable.

THE RIVIERA REPORTER

A mine of information – I may have avoided some embarrassments and frights if I had read it prior to my first Swiss encounters – Deserves an honoured place on any newcomer's bookshelf.

ENGLISH TEACHERS ASSOCIATION, SWITZERLAND

HAVE SAID ABOUT SURVIVAL BOOKS

What a great work, wealth of useful information, well-balanced wording and accuracy in details. My compliments!

THOMAS MÜLLER

This handbook has all the practical information one needs to set up home in the UK – The sheer volume of information is almost daunting – Highly recommended for anyone moving to the UK.

AMERICAN CITIZENS ABROAD

A very good book which has answered so many questions and even some I hadn't thought of – I would certainly recommend it.

BRIAN FAIRMAN

We would like to congratulate you on this work: it is really super! We hand it out to our expatriates and they read it with great interest and pleasure.

ICI (SWITZERLAND) AG

Covers just about all the things you want to know on the subject – In answer to the desert island question about the one how-to book on France, this book would be it – Almost 500 pages of solid accurate reading – This book is about enjoyment as much as survival.

THE RECORDER

It's so funny – I love it and definitely need a copy of my own – Thanks very much for having written such a humorous and helpful book.

HEIDI GUILIANI

A must for all foreigners coming to Switzerland.

ANTOINETTE O'DONOGHUE

A comprehensive guide to all things French, written in a highly readable and amusing style, for anyone planning to live, work or retire in France.

THE TIMES

A concise, thorough account of the DOs and DON'Ts for a foreigner in Switzerland – Crammed with useful information and lightened with humorous quips which make the facts more readable.

AMERICAN CITIZENS ABROAD

Covers every conceivable question that may be asked concerning everyday life – I know of no other book that could take the place of this one.

FRANCE IN PRINT

Hats off to *Living and Working in Switzerland*!

RONNIE ALMEIDA

CONTENTS

IMPORTANT NOTE

Both Australia and New Zealand are diverse countries with myriad faces and many ethnic groups, religions and customs (Australia is also one of the largest countries in the world). Although ostensibly the same throughout each country, local property rules and regulations may vary in some regions and states, as do property-related taxes. **I cannot recommend too strongly that you check with an official and reliable source (not always the same) before making major decisions or undertaking an irreversible course of action.** Don't believe everything you're told or read, even, dare I say it, herein!

To help you obtain further information and verify data with official sources, useful addresses, references and websites have been included in most chapters and **Appendices A, B** and **C**. Important points have been emphasised throughout the book in **bold** print, some of which it would be expensive or even dangerous to disregard. **Ignore them at your cost or peril!** Unless specifically stated, the reference to any company, organisation, product or publication in this book doesn't constitute an endorsement or recommendation. Any reference to any place or person (living or dead) is purely coincidental.

THE AUTHOR

Graeme Chesters was born in Cheshire in 1963, finished his education at Bristol University and worked in the City of London for ten years before turning to writing full time. He has written for several newspapers and magazines, as well as writing and editing eight books, including *Living and Working in the Gulf States & Saudi Arabia* and *Living and Working in the Far East*. Graeme was based in Spain for several years and writes about subjects ranging from wine to football and travel to television. He is married to Louise, is child-free and lives on the border of Kent and London.

AUTHOR'S NOTES

- All times are shown using am (ante meridiem) for before noon and pm (post meridiem) for after noon. Most Australians and New Zealanders don't use the 24-hour clock. All times given are local, therefore you should check the time difference when making international telephone calls.

- Prices quoted should be taken only as estimates, although they were correct when going to print and usually don't change greatly overnight. Prices are quoted inclusive of tax (which is the method generally used in Australia and New Zealand) unless otherwise stated.

- His/he/him/man/men (etc.) also mean her/she/her/woman/ women. This is done simply to make life easier for the reader and, in particular, the author, and isn't intended to be sexist.

- British English is used throughout, but American English equivalents are given where appropriate.

- Warnings and important points are shown in **bold** type.

- The following symbols are used in this book: ☎ (telephone), ▤ (fax), 🖥 (internet) and ✉ (email).

- Lists of useful addresses, further reading and useful websites are contained in **Appendices A**, **B** and **C** respectively.

- For those unfamiliar with the metric system of weights and measures, Imperial conversion tables are included in **Appendix D**.

- Maps of Australia and New Zealand are contained in **Appendix E**.

INTRODUCTION

If you're planning to buy a home in Australia or New Zealand or even just thinking about it, this is THE BOOK for you! Whether you want a modern detached house, a townhouse, cottage or an apartment, a holiday or permanent home, this book will help make your dreams come true. The aim of *Buying a Home in Australia & New Zealand* is to provide you with the information necessary to help you choose the most favourable location and the most appropriate home to satisfy your family's requirements. Most importantly, it will help you avoid the pitfalls and risks associated with buying a home in Australia or New Zealand.

You may already own a home in another country; however, buying a home in Australia or New Zealand (or in any 'foreign' country) is a different matter altogether. One of the most common mistakes many people make when buying a home abroad is to assume that the laws and purchase procedures are the same as in their home country. This is almost certainly not true! Buying property in Australia or New Zealand is generally very safe, particularly when compared with some other countries. However, if you don't follow the rules provided for your protection, a purchase can result in disastrous financial loss, as some people have discovered to their cost.

For many people, buying a home in Australia or New Zealand has previously been a case of pot luck. However, with a copy of *Buying a Home in Australia & New Zealand* to hand you will have a wealth of priceless information at your fingertips – information derived from a variety of sources, both official and unofficial, not least the experiences of the author, his friends, colleagues and acquaintances. This book doesn't contain all the answers; what it will do is reduce the risk of making an expensive mistake that you may regret later, and help you make informed decisions and calculated judgements, instead of costly mistakes and uneducated guesses – forewarned is forearmed! *Buying a Home in Australia & New Zealand* will help you save money and will repay your investment many times over.

Before buying a home in Australia or New Zealand you need to ask yourself why you want to buy a home there? Is your primary concern a good investment or do you wish to work or retire there? Where and what can you afford to buy? Do you plan to let your home to offset the running costs? What about property, capital gains and inheritance taxes? *Buying a Home in Australia & New Zealand* will provide answers to these and many other questions. It won't, however, tell you where to live and what to buy, nor, once you've made your decision, whether you will be happy – that part is up to you!

Buying a home in Australia or New Zealand is a wonderful way to make new friends, broaden your horizons and revitalise your life – and it provides a welcome bolt-hole to recuperate from the stresses and strains of modern life. I trust that this book will help you avoid the pitfalls and smooth your way to many happy years in your new home, secure in the knowledge that you've made the right decision.

Good Luck!   **Graeme Chesters**
                                                    November 2005

1.

MAJOR CONSIDERATIONS

Buying a home abroad isn't only a major financial commitment, but it's also a decision that can have a huge influence on other aspects of your life, including your health, security and safety, your family relationships and friendships, your lifestyle, your opinions and your outlook. You also need to take into consideration any restrictions that might influence your choice of location and type of property, such as whether you will need (or be able) to learn another language, whether you will be able (or permitted) to find work, whether you can adapt to and enjoy the climate, whether you will be able to take your pets with you, and not least, whether you will be able to afford the kind of home (and lifestyle) that you want. In order to ensure that you're making the right move, it's advisable to face these and other major considerations before making any irrevocable decisions.

WHY AUSTRALIA OR NEW ZEALAND?

There are many excellent reasons for buying a home in Australia or New Zealand. They're two of the most beautiful countries in the world, with varied landscapes offering something for everyone, including magnificent beaches for sun-worshippers (although sunbathers must be aware of the dangers of excessive sun exposure); spectacular countryside for nature lovers; and mountains and seas for fans of adventure activities and sports. They also have vibrant, Mediterranean-style cities, great wines for connoisseurs, innovative Pacific Rim cuisine for gourmets, an abundance of culture for art lovers (which will come as a surprise to some people), a sophisticated sporting infrastructure and competitive sports leagues, and tranquillity for the stressed.

No longer are Australia and New Zealand regarded as isolated, rural backwaters located somewhere to the north of Antarctica, where men are men and sheep are worried. As for this sheep-related slur, neither country has such a massive ratio of sheep to humans as in the past. In the '70s, New Zealand was known as the country of 60 million sheep and 3 million people, but by mid-2004, the country's human population rose to over 4 million, while the sheep population had dropped to 39 million (compared with a peak of over 70 million in 1982 and the first time the number had fallen below 40 million for 60 years), the result of the elimination of farm production subsidies to maintain flock numbers and aid exports. Australia had 103 million sheep in mid-2004, which was also close to an historic low, and a human population of around 20 million.

Australians and New Zealanders have a zest for life and many love sport, the great outdoors and eating and drinking with friends *al fresco*. In both countries, the pursuit of the good life is a serious business and many people put their family and social lives before their career and the pursuit of success and wealth. The two countries enjoy an exhilarating mixture of natural beauty and a burgeoning sophistication and style, combining the best of the Anglo-Saxon tradition with Mediterranean flair and Asian and Pacific spice. In the past, they were said to be pale imitations of the UK and the USA, but in the 21st century, Australia and New Zealand are regarded as combining the best of the UK and the USA without many of their drawbacks. It's often said that when buying property in Australia or New Zealand you aren't buying a home but a lifestyle. As locations for a holiday, retirement or permanent home, the two countries 'Down Under' have few rivals and in addition to the incomparable choice of properties and excellent value, they offer a generally fine climate for most of the year, particularly along the coasts.

Nevertheless, it's important to ask yourself exactly why you want to buy a home in the Antipodes (a term used to describe Australia and New Zealand; its formal meaning is any two places or regions that are on diametrically opposite sides of the earth, which Australia and New Zealand are from the UK). For example, are you primarily looking for a sound investment or do you plan to work or start a business in Australia or New Zealand? Are you seeking a holiday or retirement home? If you're seeking a second home, will it be mainly used for two or three-week holidays or for lengthier stays? Do you plan to let it to offset the mortgage and running costs (and the cost of the flights to and from your home country)? If so, how important is the property income? You need to answer these and many other questions before deciding on the best (and most appropriate) place to buy a home in Australia or New Zealand.

Often buyers have a variety of reasons for buying a home Down Under; for example, some people buy a holiday home with a view to living there permanently or semi-permanently when they retire. If this is the case, there are many more factors to take into account than if you're 'simply' buying a holiday home that you will occupy for just a few weeks or months a year (when it might be wiser not to buy at all). If, on the other hand, you plan to work or start a business in Australia or New Zealand, you will be faced with a completely different set of criteria.

Can you really afford to buy a home in Australia or New Zealand? What about the future? Is your income secure and protected against inflation and currency fluctuations? In the past, some foreigners purchased holiday homes by taking out second mortgages on their family homes and stretching their financial resources to the limits. Not surprisingly, when a recession struck (as it did in the early '90s) many people had their homes repossessed or were forced to sell at a huge loss when they were no longer able to meet the mortgage payments.

You shouldn't expect to make a quick profit when buying property in Australia or New Zealand and should look upon it as an investment in your family's future happiness, rather than merely in financial terms. This is particularly true in the current uncertain property market. Property values in Australia and New Zealand increased (sometimes dramatically) in the early years of the 21st century, but the market slowed considerably in 2005, with falls in some regions. The 'experts' are predicting that 2006 and 2007 will be years of stagnation, or further price falls, particularly if interest rates increase; pessimistic voices see an even longer period of lower sales volumes and prices.

SURVIVAL TIP
Before making an irrevocable decision regarding buying a home in Australia or New Zealand, you should do extensive research (see page 136), study the possible pitfalls and be prepared to rent for a period before buying (see page 141).

Advantages & Disadvantages

There are advantages and disadvantages to buying a home in Australia and New Zealand, although for most people the benefits far outweigh any drawbacks. The two countries have many attractions: large areas of both enjoy a sunny and warm climate for much of the year, although there are more climatic variations many people imagine (see **Climate** on page 22) and south Victoria, Tasmania and parts of New Zealand's South Island have decidedly chilly winters and cool summers (similar to the British climate); access to your Antipodean home from home has never been easier or cheaper, especially from the UK, thanks mainly to the large volume of flights and the fierce competition between airlines; travel within the Antipodes is easy and relatively inexpensive, mainly thanks to increased competition on domestic air routes; and both countries have a stable political environment and are perceived as being removed from the terrorist threat that stalks much of the rest of the world.

Australia offers a variety of cultural, leisure, outdoor, sightseeing and sporting activities, and its people are invariably direct (sometimes to the point of bluntness), friendly, open and welcoming to foreigners, even whinging Poms, as the British are commonly known. The standard of living is generally high and the cost reasonable by Western European or North American standards, including good value homes (especially in less fashionable areas). Although prices have risen in many popular areas recently, property remains cheaper than its equivalent in the UK, for example, with the bonus that it's often accompanied by a sizeable plot of land (see **Cost Of Property** on page 29).

Australia

One of Australia's most notable attractions is its natural beauty, the landscape varying from tropical rainforest to rolling meadows and vineyards to vast, red deserts and deserted beaches (Australia has over 7,000). The Barossa Valley (north of Adelaide) is one of Australia's best-known wine producing regions, a beautiful, gently sloping valley with a flavour of Germany owing to the local population, many of whom descend from mid-19th century German settlers. By way of complete contrast, Uluru (the Aboriginal name for Ayers Rock) is a vast sandstone monolith (3.6km/2.2mi long) rising 348m/1,141ft from the flat desert in the centre of Australia. Other examples of Australia's natural beauty include the Freycinet Peninsula on Tasmania's east coast, a beautiful region of beaches and coves; the Flinders Ranges in eastern South Australia, an 800km/500mi mountain range regarded by some as the best expression of outback Australia, with gorges, mountains, salt lakes and sand ridges; the Great Barrier reef stretching offshore along much of the Queensland coast; Kakadu National Park in the far north, which is a World Heritage site, a vast area of varied landscapes, rock art and wildlife; the Kimberley, a frontier landscape of creeks and rivers with crocodiles, gum trees, red earth, craggy rocks and wallabies; and the Snowy Mountains, which are the centre of Australia's skiing industry, and an area of beautiful alpine scenery, caves, forests and lakes.

To the surprise of some (particularly the British), Australia is also a country of culture and has transcended the 'white-bread' (i.e. stodgy and unsophisticated) image that afflicted the it until the '80s. Noted Australian artists include Arthur Boyd, Sidney Nolan, Brett Whiteley and Fred Williams, while Gillian Armstrong, Bruce Beresford, George Miller and Peter Weir are prominent film directors. Even better known are some of Australia's actors, such as Russell Crowe, Mel Gibson and Nicole Kidman, who are among Hollywood's biggest stars (Russell Crowe is also one of its most controversial).

Australia is well represented in the world of fiction and famous Australian writers include Thea Astley, Peter Carey (a Booker Prize winner), Robert

Drew, Helen Garner, Rodney Hall, Elizabeth Jolley, Thomas Keneally (another Booker Prize winner), David Malouf, Frank Moorhouse, Christina Stead, Patrick White (a Nobel Prize winner) and Tim Winton. Australia has also produced a string of internationally successful pop and rock acts, including AC/DC, The Bee Gees, Nick Cave, Natalie Imbruglia, INXS, The Little River Band, Midnight Oil, Kylie Minogue and Silverchair.

New Zealand

Until recently, New Zealand was often regarded as Australia's poor relation (particularly by Australians!), but the early 21st century has seen the country forge a new identity and grow in confidence. Part of the credit for this must go to the huge amount of positive (and free) publicity generated by the multi-Oscar-winning *Lord of the Rings* film series. For anybody who's been on Mars and might have missed the news, much of this incredibly successful film trilogy was filmed in New Zealand, using the country's spectacular scenery as a memorable backdrop (post-production took place in Wellington). The success of the *Lord of the Rings* series propelled its Kiwi director Peter Jackson to fame and fortune, and made him the world's most famous New Zealander, noted for his scruffy appearance and corpulent frame as much as for his success as a director!

New Zealand is a greener, milder, more peaceful (some think duller) version of Australia, an enticing destination for those in search of deserted beaches (nowhere in New Zealand is more than 150km away from the sea), geysers, crystal-clear lakes, majestic mountains and whitewater rivers, and an outdoor lifestyle (whatever the weather). New Zealand has two marine, three maritime, 14 national and 20 forest parks, plus two World Heritage Areas: Te Waihipouna-mu in the South Island and the Tongariro National Park in the North Island. But the country has more to offer than natural beauty. Since the '90s, the easing of licensing regulations and loosening up of lifestyles have led to an increase in the number of bars, clubs and restaurants, giving New Zealand a more sophisticated nightlife than previously. It's no longer just a destination for bearded types who sport bobble hats, hiking boots and waterproofs, and spend their time bungee jumping over deep gorges, scrambling up mountains in driving rain and whiling away their evenings singing songs around the campfire.

New Zealand's people are another of the country's assets, their culture combining European and Maori traditions, and many are forward-thinking, friendly, helpful and independent. Contrary to a clichéd view of New Zealand, the country has more to offer than watching or playing rugby, although the sport is welded into the fabric of New Zealand life and often makes front-page news. As well as an increasingly lively bar, club and restaurant scene, the country offers theatre (particularly in Wellington) and some interesting art, much of it a blend of Maori, Melanesian and Pakeha (European) influences. Specialities include bone, shell, stone and wood carvings, as well as *tukutuku* (wood panelling) and jewellery made from pebbles and stones, much of it inspired by the local terrain. New Zealand also has a vibrant music scene, but the only pop and rock artists to reach international prominence are the (both now-defunct) Split Enz and (the much more successful) Crowded House.

Among the many other advantages of buying a home in Australia or New Zealand are (usually) good rental possibilities, decent local tradesmen and services (particularly in cities and resort areas), fresh, innovative food and fine wines at reasonable prices, a relaxed pace of life in rural areas (and in some of the towns and cities), good healthcare, plenty of open space (particularly in Australia, the vast majority of which is open space), and some of the most beautiful scenery in the world.

Last, but by no means least, Australia and New Zealand have the great advantage for native English speakers that most of their citizens speak English (or at least a form of English!) as a first language. This is a particular attraction for the British, who're renowned for their inability (or unwillingness) to learn other languages. Some Britons buying homes in sunnier, warmer countries (i.e. just about anywhere) have struggled to come to terms with the local language, particularly the many who've bought in France, Greece, Italy, Portugal and Spain. Buying in a country that speaks your language has many obvious practical and social advantages, and Australia and New Zealand score over the English-speaking alternatives of Canada, California, Florida and South Africa. They lack the severe winters of Canada; the high crime, racial tension and proximity to the San Andreas Fault of California (although New Zealand is seismically active); the crime and hurricanes of Florida; and the violence and instability of South Africa.

Naturally, there are also a few disadvantages, including bushfires, droughts and heatwaves in parts of Australia, 'leaking building syndrome' in some areas of New Zealand (see pages 169), earthquakes in New Zealand (around 14,000 are recorded annually, but only around 20 have a magnitude greater than five, and the last fatal earthquake was in 1968, which killed three people on the South Island's west coast), unexpected renovation and restoration costs (if you don't do your homework), a high rate of burglary in some areas, overcrowding in popular tourist areas during the peak season(s), and traffic congestion and pollution in some towns and cities. For many people, however, particularly those who live anywhere except Southeast Asia, the major drawback of owning a holiday home in Australia or New Zealand is the length of time and expense of getting to and from it. And for those emigrating Down Under, an emergency back in the mother country (for example, in Europe or North America) might entail a very expensive flight, particularly if booked last minute at a busy time of year.

CLIMATE

Australia

The biggest attraction of Australia for many immigrants, particularly those from the northern hemisphere, is its temperate climate and the lifestyle it affords. Australia is an 'upside down' country (weather-wise), with the warmest part (nearest the equator) at the top and the coldest at the bottom. It's less prone to climate extremes than other continents of comparable size because it's surrounded by oceans and has few high mountain masses. Australia's seasons are the opposite of the Northern Hemisphere, i.e. when it's summer in Europe it's winter in Australia and vice versa. The most pleasant seasons in most of Australia are spring and autumn, with the exception of Tasmania where summer is the most enjoyable season. Australia has climates to suit everyone (bar Eskimos), although it broadly has just two climatic zones. Some 40 per cent of Australia lies in the tropical zone, while the remaining regions (south of the Tropic of Capricorn) are in the temperate zone. The tropical zone has two seasons: wet (November to April) and dry (May to October), while the temperate zones have four seasons: spring (September to November), summer (December to February), autumn (March to May) and winter (June to August).

The average hours of sunshine per day in Australia's capital cities ranges from five in Hobart to eight in Perth. January is the hottest month in most southern regions, while February is hottest in Tasmania and southern Victoria. Average summer temperatures in January range from around 17°C (63°F) in Hobart to 29°C (84°F) in Alice Springs and Darwin. Temperatures exceed 30°C (86°F) in most areas during summer, and temperatures occasionally soar to 45°C (113°F) or higher. The hottest place in Australia is Marble Bar (WA), where the temperature from October to March usually averages 40°C (104°F) or more. The highest recorded temperature in Australia is 53.1°C (127°F), measured at Cloncurry (QLD) in 1889. If you cannot stand extreme heat, choose Adelaide, Hobart, Melbourne or Sydney rather than Brisbane, Darwin or Perth.

Australia has the lowest rainfall of any continent after Antarctica, with average annual rainfall for the capital cities varying from 1,536mm (60.4in) in Darwin, which is in the monsoon region, to 530mm (21in) in Adelaide. During the wet season in the north (particularly from January to March), roads can quickly become impassable as tracks turn into raging rivers after a downpour. In contrast, large arid inland areas get less than 250mm (10in) of rain per year. In winter, temperatures can fall below 10°C (50°F) on winter nights in most regions, and sleet can fall on the urban areas of Hobart and even in Adelaide and Canberra. Snow is rare except in the Australian Alps, straddling the New South Wales/Victoria border, where it's possible to ski between June and October.

Approximate average daily maximum/minimum temperatures for Australia's major cities are shown below in Centigrade and, in brackets, Fahrenheit. (A quick way to make a *rough* conversion from Centigrade to Fahrenheit is to multiply by two and add 30 – see also **Appendix D**.)

City	Spring	Summer	Autumn	Winter
Adelaide	22/11 (72/52)	28/17 (82/63)	22/12 (72/54)	16/8 (61/46)
Alice	30/14 (86/57)	35/21 (95/70)	18/13 (82/55)	20/7 (68/45)
Brisbane	26/16 (79/61)	29/21 (84/70)	26/16 (79/61)	21/10 (70/50)
Cairns	29/21 (84/70)	31/24 (88/75)	29/22 (84/72)	26/18 (79/64)
Canberra	19/6 (66/43)	27/12 (81/54)	20/7 (68/45)	12/1 (54/34)
Darwin	33/24 (91/75)	32/25 (90/77)	32/23 (90/73)	30/20 (86/68)
Hobart	17/8 (63/46)	21/12 (70/54)	17/9 (63/48)	12/5 (54/41)
Melbourne	20/9 (68/48)	25/14 (77/57)	20/11 (68/52)	14/7 (57/45)
Perth	22/12 (72/54)	29/17 (84/63)	24/14 (75/57)	18/9 (64/48)
Sydney	22/13 (72/55)	26/18 (79/64)	22/14 (72/57)	17/9 (63/48)

The weather forecast is available in daily newspapers, via the internet and TV teletext services, and on TV and radio broadcasts. Warnings of dangerous weather conditions affecting motoring are broadcast regularly on ABC national and local radio stations. Many newspapers devote a full page (often in colour) to the weather, and news programmes on radio and TV are usually followed by detailed weather forecasts and analyses. Forecasts are usually accurate, not least because of Australia's generally stable weather patterns.

ACT/Canberra

Canberra has four distinct seasons, with hot, dry summers and cold winters. It's situated inland, so the climate isn't moderated by the ocean as in Australia's coastal cities. Canberra is the coldest capital city in winter, with temperatures plunging to around freezing at night, although it rarely snows. Winter mornings are frosty but most days are bright and sunny, temperatures averaging around 12°C (54°F). Annual rainfall is low at around 660mm (26in). The ACT has an average of seven hours sunshine per day and summer temperatures average around 27°C (81°F). Canberra is noted for its clean air and isn't prone to pollution in summer.

Northern Territory/Darwin/Alice Springs

The Northern Territory has a tropical climate with just two seasons: wet from November to April (also known as the 'green' season) and dry for the remainder of the year. The weather is generally as hot as hell all year, with average daily temperatures in Darwin between 20 and 33°C (68 and 91°F) and reaching over 40°C (104°F) for weeks on end in the central desert regions (and Alice Springs). Rainfall is almost non-existent in Darwin from May to September, which is more than compensated for between December and March, when it's between 250 and 380mm (10 and 15in). The heat and humidity are often oppressive, with humidity as high as 95 per cent just before the start of the wet season. The Northern Territory is prone to cyclones and violent thunderstorms. Alice Springs has an average of 9.5 hours of sunshine a day, with warm winters and hot, dry summers. Summer evenings can be cool, while in winter the temperature often falls below freezing at night. Alice has low annual rainfall, with an average of around 40mm (1.5in) falling between December and February.

NSW/Sydney

New South Wales has a variety of weather, although it generally has an equable climate. Sydney has the highest rainfall of any Australian capital city at 1,140mm (45in), which is spread fairly evenly throughout the year, including summer. In Sydney it rains on some 150 days a year, the wettest months being April to June. It has mild winters, when daytime temperatures rarely fall below 10°C (50°F) and can reach 17°C (63°F). Summer temperatures average around 25°C (77°F), although the humidity sometimes makes the weather feel oppressive, particularly from January to

March. Occasionally, the temperature in Sydney exceeds 40°C (104°F) and can still be 30°C (86°F) at midnight, although this is rare, as cool sea breezes help lower temperatures during heatwaves. Sydney frequently has high pollution levels in summer.

Queensland/Brisbane

Queensland has a sub-tropical climate in the south and is tropical in the north, with wet and dry seasons. Summer is the wet season, when rainfall averages around 1,000mm (40in), particularly in the north, where violent thunderstorms and floods are common. The state has the wettest town in Australia, Tully, with over 4,000mm (160in) of rain per year (four times that of Brisbane). Extremes of flood and drought are common in country areas. Brisbane is one of the sunniest cities in Australia, with an average of over 7.5 hours per day and mild, sunny winters. Average temperatures are between 10°C (50°F) and 21°C (70°F) in winter and between 21°C (70°F) and 29°C (84°F) in summer. Summer temperatures can, however, exceed 38°C (100°F), and humidity can be very high, although it's usually tempered by cool sea breezes in coastal areas.

South Australia/Adelaide

South Australia has an almost Mediterranean climate, characterised by long, dry summers and short, mild winters, and is said to have the best year-round climate in Australia. Adelaide is noted for its low rainfall (the lowest of any state capital) at just 530mm (21in), which falls mainly between April and October. South Australia is the driest state and its northern regions are mostly desert. It's not too cold in winter, when average temperatures are between 8°C (46°F) and 16°C (61°F). There's an average of four hours sunshine per day in winter and seven hours in summer. Summers are hot with maximum temperatures averaging over 27°C (81°F), although nights aren't usually too hot and there's low humidity. It's very hot in the northern desert regions, where summer temperatures are frequently over 40°C (104°F).

Tasmania/Hobart

Tasmania has a temperate climate with four distinct seasons, but is without the extremes of the mainland cities. It's the coldest part of Australia and is occasionally hit by icy southerly winds from Antarctica, although it's still relatively mild by northern European standards. Nights can be cool throughout the year, although winters aren't as cold as in Canberra and Alice Springs. The average winter temperature in Hobart is between 5°C (41°F) and 12°C (54°F). It has around 620cm (25in) of rain per year (half that of Sydney and Brisbane), rain falling on around half the days of the year, mostly between July and October. In the west, rainfall is around four times that of Hobart. Hobart enjoys an average of around five hours of sunshine per day, maximum summer temperatures averaging around 21°C (70°F). Water temperatures are much lower than the rest of Australia, and it's generally too cold for sea bathing.

Victoria/Melbourne

The Victorian climate is somewhere between maritime and continental. The weather in Melbourne can be extremely changeable, and it's said that you can experience all four seasons in one day (rather like the UK). Victoria has a generally mild climate, although it can have very hot and cold periods. Melbourne experiences cold, wet and windy weather in autumn and winter, although temperatures rarely fall below 5°C (41°F), with highs of around 14°C (57°F). Mountainous regions have snow in winter, when temperatures remain below freezing for long periods. Melbourne has low rainfall of around 660mm (26in), half that of Sydney and Brisbane, which is fairly evenly distributed throughout the year (June and July are the wettest months). The city has mild autumns (the most pleasant season) and hot summers, when temperatures average 25°C (77°F) and occasionally soar to 40°C (104°F).

Western Australia/Perth

The southern areas of Western Australia enjoy a Mediterranean climate, while northern areas have a tropical climate with dry and wet seasons. Perth is the sunniest capital city in Australia with an average annual temperature of 18°C (64°F) and over eight hours sunshine per day. Spring and autumn are the most pleasant seasons. The average rainfall is low at 914mm (36in) per year (although it's over 1,500mm/60in on the south-west coast) and it falls mainly between April and October. The northern and eastern regions have very low rainfall and consist mostly of desert. Winters in Perth are mild and sunny but wet, with average temperatures of between 9°C (48°F) and 18°C (64°F), although frost is common away from the coastal areas. Summers are very hot, with daytime temperatures frequently between 30°C (86°F) and 40°C (104°F) and hot nights, although it's a dry rather than humid heat. The summer heat is mitigated by cool breezes that blow in off the sea from Fremantle (west of Perth), called the Fremantle Doctor for its soothing effect (some enterprising locals bottle it and sell it to tourists!).

Natural Disasters

Australia is hit by frequent natural disasters, including bush fires, cyclones, droughts, earthquakes, floods and tropical storms. Periodic droughts are a way of life and a constant worry for farmers. In many rural areas, rivers are sucked almost dry by the demand for water for irrigation, causing many to slow to a trickle and the water to become polluted by toxic algae (rivers are also polluted by salt and some are dying). There are frequent (sometimes permanent) water restrictions in most regions of Australia, even in the major cities. The Australian weather is periodically (e.g. in 1997) affected by *El Niño*, an ocean warming phenomenon where prevailing cold water currents along the west coast of South America become warmer, thus upsetting weather patterns and leading to floods in North and South America and droughts in Australia.

Bush fires are a constant threat in country areas (mainly in summer), which are often caused by lightning strikes (many are also deliberately lit). They often threaten country towns and occasionally major cities, and deaths among fire-fighters and homeowners are frequent (some people needlessly lose their lives because they refuse to abandon their homes). Lighting fires in a bush fire zone is strictly forbidden; even where it's permitted, you must ensure that every spark is extinguished before leaving and must *never* throw cigarette butts out of car windows. Earthquakes are rare in Australia, although in 1989 one struck Newcastle (NSW), killing 13 people, injuring 160 and causing damage costing $1.7 billion.

Cyclones (known as 'blows') are fairly common in the summer months (between November and April) in the northern regions of Australia (from Western Australia to Queensland). In 1974, cyclone Tracey flattened Darwin with gusts of up to 280kph (174mph). It killed 66 people and destroyed more than 5,000 homes, leaving fewer than 500 intact in what was the worst natural disaster in Australia's modern history. The city has since been completely rebuilt to 'withstand' cyclones. More recently, Exmouth in Western Australia was devastated by Cyclone Vance in 1999. Violent tropical and electrical storms are common in the north of Australia, particularly northern Queensland. In January 1998, for example, torrential rains in Townsville caused widespread flooding when 500mm (20in) of rain fell in just 12 hours.

Greenpeace Australia Pacific predicts that the Australian climate will become more in extreme in the 21st century. The average temperature of much of the country is expected to rise by up to 2°C by 2030 and by up to 6°C by 2070. Australia, already the world's second-driest continent (after Antarctica), is also expected to become even dryer. High temperatures and increasing dryness combined in 2003 to cause severe bushfires which burned for 59 days, a sign of what's to come. Rainfall in south-west Australia could decline by up to 60 per cent by 2070, and much of Australia can expect storms with greater maximum wind speeds and more sudden and extreme rainfall (but with a reduction of total rainfall).

New Zealand

Being an island nation, New Zealand's climate tends to be dominated by its ocean setting, although it experiences a variety of climatic patterns due to its mountainous terrain. Climatic conditions vary considerably and include sub-tropical, sub-Antarctic, semi-arid (mainly in the Northland region), super-humid, frost-free, and sub-Alpine with permanent snow and ice in the mountainous areas. The eastern regions experience a drier climate than the west, on account of prevailing westerly winds, the wettest area being the south-west (west of the Southern Alps). Being in the southern hemisphere, New Zealand's seasons are the opposite of those in the northern latitudes, i.e. summer (December to February), autumn (March to May), winter (June to August) and Spring (September to November). Unseasonal weather is rare.

The most important characteristic of New Zealand weather is its changeability. The North Island tends to be warmer and drier than the South Island, although the highest mountain peaks often have snow year round. The average rainfall in the North Island is around 1,300mm. Daytime temperatures in Auckland average 23°C (73°F) in summer and 14°C (57°F) in winter, while in Wellington they range from 26°C (79°F) in summer to as low as 2°C (35°F) in winter. Wellington is renowned for its extremely windy weather, which can also make the sea crossing between the two islands rough. Variations in weather and temperature in the South Island are more pronounced, and the Southern Alps have 'wet' (west) and 'dry' (east) sides. On the east side of the Southern Alps rainfall can be as low as 300mm (droughts are fairly common) and temperatures a lot warmer than on the west side. Snow is a permanent feature on the highest peaks. Christchurch averages temperatures of around 22°C (72°F) in summer and 12°C (54°F) in winter, while Dunedin averages 19°C (66°F) in summer and 10°C (50°F) in winter.

Average temperatures, rainfall levels and sunshine hours for the main towns and cities are shown below. Bear in mind that the temperatures are averages and it can be much warmer or colder on individual days:

Town/City	Average Temp (°C) Summer	Winter	Average Annual Rainfall (mm)	Annual Hours' Sunshine
North Island				
Bay of Islands	25	15	1,648	2,020
Auckland	23	14	1,268	2,140
Rotorua	23	12	1,511	1,940
Napier	24	13	780	2,270
Wellington	20	11	1,271	2,020
South Island				
Nelson	22	12	999	2,410
Christchurch	22	12	658	1,990
Queenstown	22	8	849	1,940
Dunedin	19	10	772	1,700
Invercargill	18	9	1,042	1,630

COST OF PROPERTY

Australia

Property prices vary considerably throughout the country and in the various suburbs of the major cities. Not surprisingly, the further you are from a town or city, the lower the cost of land and property. Properties in central and popular beach locations cost anywhere between two and four times as much as similar properties in less fashionable or convenient outlying city suburbs. For many buyers it's a choice between a small apartment in an inner city and a large detached family home in the outer suburbs – in recent years the average Aussie battler (commuter) has had to move further and further into the outer suburbs of major cities in order to find affordable accommodation.

A two or three-bedroom, single-storey home in most city outer suburbs costs between $110,000 and $185,000; four-bedroom, two-storey homes cost from around $150,000 to $375,000. On the other hand, waterfront properties in Sydney can be astronomically expensive and a reasonable two-bedroom apartment in an attractive building with water views costs over $900,000 (2 million dollar homes are commonplace in Sydney and Melbourne and on the White Sunshine Coast). There's a high demand everywhere for waterfront properties, which have generally been an excellent investment, particularly in NSW where the government plans to preserve the coastline from further development (canal developments are already banned). In the current sluggish market, however, some may be overpriced.

After a period of large annual house price increases in the later '90s and early 21st century, the Australian residential property market experienced a 'correction' in 2005. According to *The Economist* magazine's house-price index, between 1997 and 2004, Australian residential property prices rose by 113 per cent (in the major cities, rises were closer to 200 per cent), with prices generally reaching their zenith in the third quarter of 2003. By the end of 2004, average house prices in the capital cities were around $550,000 in Sydney, $383,000 in Canberra, $330,000 in Brisbane, $319,000 in Melbourne, $280,000 in Hobart and Perth, $270,000 in Adelaide and $260,000 in Darwin.

An interest rate rise in March 2005 contributed to a market slowdown and some reductions in the above average figures. The remainder of 2005 is expected to see static house prices, with falls in some areas and sectors of the market. Analysts expect property oversupply and further interest rate rises to cause residential property prices to be sluggish or in decline in 2006 and perhaps also in 2007, before an upturn in the market. These predictions are to be taken with a pinch of salt: predicting the movement of any market (e.g. the art, currency, property or stock market) is notoriously difficult, there being several (sometimes unpredictable) factors to take into account. If, however, the predictions are correct, the forthcoming two or three years will be a good time to enter the Australian residential property market. This is particularly the case in Sydney, where prices are predicted to fall the most. The property market in NSW has been depressed more than average by news of the introduction of a vendor duty tax from July 2005. Other Australian cities are expected to experience softer landings, with some analysts still seeing room for further price increases, especially in parts of Canberra, Melbourne and Perth.

Selling at auction has been popular in recent years, particularly when prices were rising. Around 25 to 30 per cent of homes in Melbourne are sold at auction compared with around 20 per cent in Sydney, 15 per cent in Brisbane and 10 to 15 per cent in Adelaide.

A few kilometres can make a huge difference to the price of a property, with apartments in central areas costing up to $2,500 per square metre more than those in harbour-side developments a few kilometres further out. Land prices also reduce considerably from around 15km/9mi outside a city and are at their lowest around 25km/16mi from city centres. The cost of land varies from as little as $40,000 for an average size suburban house at least 25km/16mi from cities such as Adelaide, Hobart and Perth to over $350,000 for a similar plot within 15km/9mi of central Sydney (if you can find one). The cost of building a home varies depending on the location and the quality of materials used. Brick veneer costs from around $800 to $900 per m^2, depending on the location. The cost of building a home increased considerably after the introduction of GST in July 2000.

In the last few years, there have been few bargains when it comes to buying property and, although you might have been able to negotiate a reduction of 5 or possibly 10 per cent, it was a seller's market. That has changed and buyers today can undercut asking prices more substantially and pick up bargains. There's usually a good reason, however, when a property is substantially cheaper than other similar properties. Although it's sometimes unwise to look a gift horse in the mouth, you should generally be suspicious of a bargain that appears too good to be true. On the other hand, most sellers and estate agents still price properties higher than the market price or the price they expect to receive, knowing that buyers will try to drive the price down, so always haggle over the price asked (even if you think it's a bargain). This is, in fact, one of the few occasions in Australia when you're expected to bargain, although you should try to avoid insulting an owner by offering a derisory price, even in the current uncertain market.

If you're buying a home for a limited period or as an investment, you should buy one that you hope will sell quickly and at a profit. Homes that sell best are exceptional period houses of character with lots of original features, and water and beach-front homes (particularly in Queensland, although sales of apartments in Brisbane hit a six-year low in the first quarter of 2005), which are in high demand and can be let for most of the year to holidaymakers if required. Luxury units in central Brisbane, Melbourne and Sydney have also been a good investment, but some are currently overpriced. Buying property in Australia is usually a long-term investment and isn't recommended for those seeking a short-term gain (this was particularly true in late 2005). You must pay capital gains tax on the profit made on the sale of an investment property (see page 253).

You can find out the price of homes in any Sydney suburb through the *Sydney Morning Herald Home Price Guide*, which lists all the sales results (both auction and private treaty) in Sydney suburbs for the last 12 months (it can be ordered via the internet from Australian Property Monitors, 🖳 www. apm.com.au). A similar service is provided by newspapers in other major cities, and you can also peruse property advertisements in a number of publications on the internet (e.g. 🖳 www.sydneyproperty.com.au).

The following table shows the average house and unit (apartment) prices for auction sales in autumn 2005. **Note that the housing market was volatile in 2005 and prices are intended as a rough guide only.**

City	Average Price ($'000s)	
	House	Unit (flat)
Adelaide	270	200
Brisbane	310	245
Canberra	355	300
Darwin	280	200
Gold Coast	395	290
Hobart	260	200
Melbourne	365	300
Perth	300	210
Sydney	495	380

New Zealand

In general, property prices in New Zealand are slightly lower than in Europe because of its small population (i.e. relatively low demand), low cost of land and generally low construction costs. There is, however, a huge gulf between Auckland and the rest of the country. Property is much more expensive in Auckland, mainly because most of the best paid jobs are to be found there. Auckland also has one of the better climates in New Zealand, and prices are further increased because a majority of immigrants make Auckland their first choice. Wellington is the country's second most expensive area for property purchase. Price variations are less marked throughout the rest of the country.

After some years of large annual increases in house prices, 2005 saw a slowdown in the property market, although certain commentators dismiss this as a blip and in summer 2005 (winter in New Zealand) there's no consensus as to what the market will do. The national average house price in New Zealand in December 2004 was $260,000, increasing to $265,000 in January 2005, but at the time the second figure was released, the president of the Real Estate Institute advised caution because reduced sales volumes and decreases in prices in some regions indicated that the market would begin to turn. For example, in the Auckland Metropolitan area, prices fell from $355,000 to $340,000 from December to January, while in Auckland City, the average fell from $412,500 to $385,000. In Wellington, price falls were much more modest, down from $276,250 to $275,000, but in Hawke's Bay, for example, the average price rose, from $225,000 to $245,050.

By early spring 2005 (autumn in New Zealand), areas which had seen some of the largest price increases in previous months, e.g. Nelson and Tasman, began to see falls. The Bank of New Zealand economist predicted that a housing downturn was imminent, and when it arrived, prices would drop between 5 and 10 per cent over a two to three year period. The Reserve Bank was more precise, predicting that average house prices would fall 4.8 per cent in 2006 and a further 1.9 per cent in 2007 (after having risen 56 per cent between 2001 and 2004).

But in summer 2005 (winter in New Zealand), figures showed that the national average house price had risen to $275,000 (after a record figure of $280,000 in March and a fall to $272,000 in April) surprising the many economists who thought a downturn was about to begin, following April's fall. Prices had fallen slightly in a couple of regions, but in most they had continued to rise, with a notable narrowing of the gap in house prices between urban and provincial areas. This last trend was put down to jaded city dwellers escaping to life in the country.

The table below shows average house price figures in spring and summer 2005 (from the Real Estate Institute):

	Spring 2005 (autumn locally)	Summer 2005 (winter locally)
Northland	$230,000	$251,000
Auckland	$369,000	$370,000
Taranaki	$162,637	$213,750

Waikato/BoP/Gisborne	$244,000	$245,000
Hawke's Bay	$230,000	$249,500
Manawatu/Wanganui	$155,000	$160,000
Wellington	$275,000	$285,000
Nelson/Marlborough	$269,000	$265,000
Canterbury/Westland	$242,000	$247,500
Otago	$216,100	$201,750
Southland	$144,500	$150,000

Apartments are often as expensive as houses and townhouses (or even more so), as they're invariably located in city centres, whereas most houses are in suburbs or in the country. Advertised prices are usually around 3 to 8 per cent above a property's true market value and substantially above its rateable value (see **Property Taxes** on page 256).

When calculating your budget, you should also allow for lawyer's fees (see **Conveyance** on page 209) and bear in mind that banks charge a mortgage processing fee equal to 1 per cent of the mortgage amount and require a deposit (usually $500 minimum) on application.

BUYING FOR INVESTMENT

With prices now generally stagnant or even falling in many parts of Australia and New Zealand, property is an interesting investment proposition: some 'experts' are advising that people buy in 2005 and 2006, before the market recovers, while others advise that buyers wait because prices have further to fall. There are various kinds of property investment. Your family home is an investment, in that it provides you with rent-free accommodation. It may also yield a return in terms of increased value (a capital gain), although that gain may be difficult to realise unless you trade down or move to another region or country where property is cheaper. Of course, if you buy property other than for your own regular use, e.g. a holiday home, you will be in a position to benefit from a more tangible return on your investment. There are four main categories of investment property:

● A holiday home, which can provide your family and friends with rent-free holiday accommodation while (hopefully) maintaining or increasing its value; you may also be able to let it to generate an income.

● A home for your children or relatives, which may increase in value and could also be let when not in use to provide an income.

● A business property, which could be anything from a private home with bed and breakfast or guest accommodation to a shop or office.

● A property purchased purely for investment, which could be a capital investment or provide a regular income, or both. In recent years, many people have invested in property to provide an income on their retirement.

A property investment should be considered over the medium to long term, i.e. a minimum of five and preferably 10 to 15 years, as you need to recoup the purchase costs (see **Fees** on page 161) when you sell. You also need to take into account income tax if a property is let and capital gains tax (see page 253) when you sell a second home. Bear in mind that property isn't always 'as safe as houses' and property investments can be risky over the short to medium term.

When buying to let, you must ensure that the rent will cover the mortgage (if applicable), running costs and periods when the property isn't let. Bear in mind that rental rates and 'lettability' vary according to the region and town, and that an area with high rents and occupancy rates one year may not be so fruitful the next. Gross rental yields (the annual rent as a percentage of a property's value) are from around 5 to 10 per cent a year in most areas (although gross yields of 15 per cent or more are possible); net yields (after expenses have been deducted) are 2 to 3 per cent lower.

Before deciding to invest in a property, you should ask yourself the following questions:

● Can I afford to tie up the capital for at least five years?

● How likely is it that the value of the property will rise during this period, and will it outstrip inflation?

● Can I rely on a regular income from my investment? If so, how easy will it be to generate that income, e.g. to find tenants? Will I be able to pay the mortgage if the property is empty and, if so, for how long?

● Am I aware of all the risks involved and how comfortable am I with taking those risks?

● Do I have enough information to make an objective decision?

See also **Location** on page 100, **Mortgages** on page 197 and **Chapter 9 (Letting)**.

COST OF LIVING

Australia

No doubt you'd like to know how far your dollars stretch and how much money (if any) you will have left after paying your bills. The standard of living in Australia has increased considerably for all income levels in the last 20 years, although incomes have increased much faster for the rich than the poor. However, in recent years, many people in 'middle Australia' reckon that life is becoming more expensive. Australia's inflation rate is based on the consumer price index (CPI), which gives an indication of how prices have risen (or fallen) over the past year. The CPI, which skeptics believe stands for 'con people incessantly', is calculated from a basket of basic goods and services.

In stark contrast to Australia's international image of affluence and plenty, poverty is widespread and there's a widening gap between the rich and poor, the richest 20 per cent of the population earning some 13 times as much as the poorest 20 per cent. Over 50 per cent of Australian families struggle to pay their bills, and many people receive assistance from their families. Some 40 per cent of children live in families with very low incomes, including many one-parent families, and over 2 million adults and children are dependent on government allowances (over 2 million Australians also live in households with an income below the poverty line). Many elderly people also struggle on state pensions (or no pensions) – elderly women are among the poorest sections of society. Many immigrants with families strive to live on $350 to $450 per week, low-income families in major cities paying half or more of their weekly wage in rent. In recent years, low-income families have been deserting inner-city suburbs in droves for cheaper outer suburbs and rural areas.

In a survey conducted by Mercer Human Resource Consulting in 2004, Sydney was rated the most expensive city in the southern hemisphere and ranked 20th in the world. Perth was the second most expensive Australian city (but not in the world top 50) and Melbourne the third. Sydney had a similar cost of living to Rome and Vienna and was more expensive than Berlin, San Francisco and Singapore. Although most surveys agree that Sydney is Australia's most expensive city, most don't agree on the position of other Australian cities. There's little difference in the cost of living between

Adelaide, Brisbane and Perth. The cost of living in rural areas is, not surprisingly, lower than in major cities (particularly housing).

It's difficult to calculate an average cost of living, as it depends on an individual's circumstances and lifestyle. What is important to most people is how much money they can save (or spend) each month. Manufactured goods tend to be expensive in Australia, particularly imported goods, including automobiles, clothes and other manufactured items, which are generally more expensive than in Europe or North America. If you do a lot of travelling, transport costs are high owing to the large distances involved, although petrol is much cheaper than in Europe.

Your food bill naturally depends on what you eat and is similar to the USA and around 25 per cent less than in most European countries. Approximately $400 should be sufficient to feed two adults for a month in most areas (excluding alcohol, caviar and fillet steak). The prices of staple foods in Australia's capital cities are listed in the monthly British newspaper *Australian Outlook* (see **Appendix A**) and a free Commonwealth Bank Property Value Guide is published annually by the Commonwealth Bank of Australia. Even in the most expensive cities (e.g. Sydney), the cost of living needn't be astronomical. If you shop wisely, compare prices and services before buying and don't live too extravagantly, you may be pleasantly surprised at how little you can live on. It's possible to save a considerable sum by shopping for certain items overseas, e.g. via the internet.

The approximate *minimum* monthly major expenses for an average person or family in a typical town or suburb are shown in the table below. **These are 'ball park' figures only and depend on your lifestyle, extravagance or frugality, and where you live in Australia – almost everyone will agree that they're either too low or too high!** When calculating your cost of living, deduct the appropriate percentage for income tax (see page 236) and other deductions from your gross salary.

ITEM	MONTHLY COSTS (A$)		
	Single	Couple	Couple with 2 children
Housing **(1)**	400	600	800
Food	325	400	650
Utilities **(2)**	100	150	200
Leisure **(3)**	100	175	350
Car/travel **(4)**	200	250	350

Insurance (5)	75	150	150
Clothing	150	200	300
Rates	50	75	100
TOTAL	**1,400**	**2,000**	**2,900**

1. Rental or mortgage on a modern apartment or semi-detached house in an 'average' small town or outer city suburb. The cost for a single person is for a studio (bedsitter) or sharing accommodation. Other costs are for a two (couple) or three-bedroom property (couple with two children). They don't include subsidised housing.

2. Includes electricity, gas, telephone and water, plus heating bills.

3. Includes all entertainment, holiday and sports expenses, plus newspapers and magazines (which could of course be much higher than the figure given).

4. Includes running costs for an average family car, plus petrol, road tax, servicing and third party insurance, but not depreciation or credit costs.

5. Includes all 'voluntary' insurance, except for comprehensive car insurance and expensive private health insurance.

New Zealand

The inflation rate in New Zealand is low (around 2.4 per cent in 2004) and the government is committed to maintaining it at around this rate or lower. Prices of many imported goods have fallen in real terms in recent years, particularly cars and electrical appliances. In general, New Zealanders enjoy a high standard of living, although salaries are lower than in Australia, North America and many European countries.

It's difficult to estimate an average cost of living in New Zealand, as it depends on where you live as well as your lifestyle. If you live in Auckland, drive a BMW and dine in expensive restaurants, your cost of living will be much higher than if you live in a rural part of the South Island, drive a small Japanese car, and live on lamb and kiwi fruit. You can live most economically by buying New Zealand produce when possible and avoiding expensive imported goods, which are more expensive not only because of the distance they must travel but also because they're considered fashionable.

The following table gives a *rough* idea of the weekly cost of living for two people in New Zealand. Note that the list doesn't include 'luxury' items such as alcohol, and if you live in Auckland the cost of living is around 20 to 30 per cent higher.

Item	Amount (NZ$)
Housing	125
Transport (including a car)	50
Food	100
Utilities and furniture	40
Other goods	25
Health	25
Leisure	50
Clothes	40
Total	455

Examples of typical salaries, housing costs and the price of many everyday items can be obtained from Statistics New Zealand (💻 www.stats.govt.nz), the statistical office of the New Zealand government.

PERMITS & VISAS

Before making any plans to buy a home in Australia or New Zealand, you must ensure that you have a valid passport and the appropriate visa which will allow you to use the home as you wish. Nationals of Australia and New Zealand can live and work in either country with no more official documentation than their passport. All other nationalities (with some exceptions) must apply for permission to stay in Australia or New Zealand, either temporarily or permanently, *before* their arrival.

The information in this chapter is intended as a guide only and the rules and regulations concerning permits and visas change frequently, as well as sometimes being ambiguous, confusing and vague. It's important to check the latest regulations with an Australian or New Zealand mission or an immigration consultant (such as The

Emigration Group – see 🖥 www.emigration.uk.com) before making a visa application.

For more information about permits and visas, see *Living and Working in Australia* and *Living and Working in New Zealand* (Survival Books).

Visas

Australia

With the exception of New Zealanders, anyone wishing to enter Australia requires a visa (or a visa waiver), which must be obtained before arrival in the country. New Zealanders receive a special category visa on arrival and nothing is stamped in their passports. There are no formalities and they can live and work in Australia for as long as they wish. **If you need a visa and arrive without one, you will be sent back to your home country at your own expense.** The type of visa issued depends on the reason for your planned trip to Australia, which may be anything from a few weeks holiday or a short business trip to permanent residence.

There are three main categories of Australian visas: migration, temporary residence and visitors. Multiple-entry visas are issued to those who need to visit Australia frequently over a long period, such as businessmen, entertainers, the parents of children living there and sportsmen. There are fees for almost all visas. The processing of visa applications in some categories can take a considerable time in some countries due to the large number of applications to be processed, and approval can take anything from a few weeks to many months.

Information about visas, charges and forms can be obtained from offices of the Department of Immigration and Multicultural and Indigenous Affairs (DIMIA) in Australia (🖥 www.immi.gov.au) and Australian missions overseas. General information about visa applications is contained in *making and processing Visa applications* (form 1025i). It's important to obtain and complete the correct form, pay the correct fee and satisfy other requirements such as being inside or outside Australia, as required. You must be careful to indicate the visa class under which you wish to be considered, as your application cannot be considered under any class other than the one noted on your application form. An *Application for Migration to Australia* form (47) must be completed by all applicants wishing to travel to Australia to live permanently and applications must be sent or delivered to a DIMIA office or an Australian diplomatic mission overseas with all relevant documentation and the fee.

Family members who apply at the same time can usually apply on the same form and pay just one fee (a child born after an application is made, but before it has been decided, is included in the parents' application). In certain circumstances, a spouse or dependent child can be added to an application. Applications for some visas, such as visitors' visas, may be decided while you wait. In this case, if you're granted a visa you're usually given a visa label in your passport. If your application for a visitors' visa is refused, you're given a notice of refusal. For all other visas, you're notified of the decision by letter. If you're refused a visa, you're notified why and, if applicable, where you can apply for a review of the decision and the time limit for doing so.

If you plan to travel to or from Australia while your visa application is being considered (assuming this is possible), you should inform the DIMIA, as a visa will be refused if you're in the 'wrong place' when a decision is made. For most visas where an application is made overseas, you must be outside Australia when a decision is made and for visa applications in Australia, you must be in Australia when the decision is made. If you make a visa application in Australia, you must ensure that you have a visa to return *before* leaving the country, otherwise if your application is refused you may have no right of review. If you apply for a visa in Australia, you're usually granted a bridging visa to remain within the law if your current visa expires while a decision is being made regarding your application.

New Zealand

If you plan to visit New Zealand for a short period (e.g. for a holiday, business trip or to assess the country before applying for residence), you must apply for a visitor's visa, if applicable. Australian citizens don't need a visa to travel to New Zealand, and nationals of certain countries can use a 'visa waiver scheme', which allows you to travel to New Zealand without a visitor's visa and obtain a visitor permit on arrival. Countries that qualify under the visa waiver scheme are: Andorra, Argentina, Austria, Bahrain, Belgium, Brazil, Brunei, Canada, Chile, Denmark, Finland, France, Germany, Greece, Hong Kong, Hungary, Iceland, Indonesia, Ireland, Israel, Italy, Japan, Korea (South), Kiribati, Kuwait, Liechtenstein, Luxembourg, Malaysia, Malta, Mexico, Monaco, Nauru, the Netherlands, Norway, Oman, Portugal, Qatar, San Marino, Saudi Arabia, Singapore, Slovenia, South Africa, Spain, Sweden, Switzerland, Tuvalu, the United Arab Emirates (UAE), the UK, Uruguay, the USA (except for nationals from American Samoa and Swains Island), Vatican City and Zimbabwe. **Everyone else**

needs a visitor's visa to travel to New Zealand and you won't even be allowed to board a plane to New Zealand without one.

A visitor's visa is an endorsement in your passport that allows you to travel to New Zealand. The visa may be for a single or multiple journeys, but doesn't necessarily allow you to remain in New Zealand. Those who travel to New Zealand with a visa or visa waiver must complete an arrival card on their outgoing journey, which serves as an application for a visitor permit that is processed on arrival. A visitor permit allows you to stay for a short period (usually three months, or six months if you're a UK citizen) as a tourist, to see friends or relatives, study, take part in sporting and cultural events, undertake a business trip or undergo medical treatment. It doesn't state on the permit that you may use it to look for a job or visit New Zealand with a view to living there, although many people use it for this purpose (and it's perfectly legitimate).

Travellers under the visa waiver scheme must have a valid return ticket, sufficient money to support themselves (usually around $1,000 per month or $400 if staying with friends or relatives) and a passport valid for three months beyond the date they intend to leave New Zealand. They must also intend to stay in New Zealand for no longer than the period of the permit. If you comply with these requirements, you may travel to New Zealand and should be granted a visitor permit on arrival. Visitors may stay for a maximum of nine months (which can be made up of a number of shorter periods) in an 18-month period. Once you've reached the maximum, you're required to remain abroad for nine months before returning to New Zealand as a visitor. Visitor permits can be extended by a further three months on application to the NZIS, although this is at their discretion, and you may be required to be able to support yourself financially without working.

You can be refused a visitor permit (and also a visitor's visa) if you don't meet the above requirements or are someone to whom Section 7 of the Immigration Act 1987 applies. This includes those who:

● have been deported from any country;

● are the subject of a New Zealand 'removal order';

● have committed a criminal offence which resulted in imprisonment of 12 months or more;

● are believed to have criminal associations or are suspected of constituting a danger to New Zealand's security or public order.

The above restrictions also apply to Australians, who don't need a visa or visitor permit to visit New Zealand.

Visitor's visas can be applied for at NZIS offices and New Zealand diplomatic missions. Like Australia, New Zealand operates a system whereby applications for visas in major cities such as London and New York can be cleared almost instantly via an electronic link with the NZIS computer in New Zealand. Fees are usually charged for visas and permits, and vary depending on the country where you apply. They must be paid in local currency by bank draft, money order or in cash (if you're applying in person). Personal cheques and credit cards aren't usually accepted. Fees aren't refundable, even if a visa isn't granted.

The authority responsible for controlling entry to New Zealand is the New Zealand Immigration Service (NZIS, also called Immigration New Zealand, but hereafter referred to as NZIS), or *Te Ratonga Manene* in Maori, a service of the Department of Labour (🖳 www.immigration.govt.nz). A list of NZIS offices, branches and agencies in New Zealand and worldwide can be found on the website. New Zealand embassies, consulates and high commissions (see **Appendix A** for a list) also provide information about immigration.

Note that as a visitor to New Zealand you aren't entitled to use publicly funded health services unless you're a resident or citizen of Australia, a UK national or hold a permit valid for at least two years (e.g. long-term business visa). Unless you come under one of these categories, it's strongly recommended that you have comprehensive medical insurance for the duration of your visit (see **Health Insurance** on page 265 and **Holiday & Travel Insurance** on page 272).

Work Visas & Permits

Australia

To be eligible to work in Australia you must meet the personal and occupational requirements of the category for which you're applying, and be of good health and character. Qualification is based on a points system. The Australian migration programme (often spelled program) is divided into two main categories: migration and humanitarian (see *Living and Working in Australia* by Survival Books for details). Migration is divided into the following main categories:

● A family migration stream, where people can be sponsored by a relative who's an Australian citizen or a permanent resident.

● A skill migration stream, which includes those with particular business or work skills or 'outstanding talents'.

- Special eligibility migrants, who are former citizens or residents wanting to return to Australia, and also certain New Zealanders.

The form *Migrating to Australia – Who can migrate?* (957i) contains general information about migration and the various categories. An *Application for Migration to Australia* form (47) must be completed by all applicants wishing to travel to Australia to live permanently. There's a fee (e.g. around £5 in the UK) for this form and the information package. The Department of Immigration and Multicultural and Indigenous Affairs (DIMIA) has an enquiry telephone service in Australia (☎ local call rate 13-1881 or 🖳 www.immi. gov.au). The Emigration Group (see see 🖳 www.emigration.uk.com) can also advise you and help you make an application.

Don't make any firm plans (such as travel arrangements, selling your home or resigning your employment) in the expectation that a visa application will be granted. Even when an application appears to be going smoothly it can still be delayed or even rejected at the last minute, e.g. on health grounds.

New Zealand

A work visa allows you to travel to New Zealand in order to undertake a period of temporary work. It isn't usually applicable to those intending to take up permanent residence in the country and applies mostly to contract workers and other short-term employees. Work visas are granted to foreigners when no suitable New Zealand citizen or resident is available to do a job. Their issue isn't based on a points system and each case is treated on its merits, taking into account the availability of local labour. To obtain a work visa you must have a firm offer of a job in writing and apply to the NZIS, which can be done outside or within New Zealand (if, for example, you arrive as a visitor and then wish to work). The visa fee is between around $150 and $290 (depending on where it's issued) and isn't refundable, even if your application is rejected. On arrival in New Zealand you will be issued with a work permit, which applies to a particular job only and for a specified period, usually a maximum of three years (but often for a much shorter period).

Retirement

Australia

An Investor Retirement visa (which is a temporary visa) was introduced in July 2005 and is designed to allow retired business people with significant assets (at least $500,000 or $750,000, depending on the region where they settle) to come to live in Australia and invest their money there. The visa requires sponsorship from the Australian state or territory government where you plan to live. The primary applicant must be at least 55 and there must be no dependants except a spouse. You must have sufficient assets to support yourself in Australia (a net annual income of between $50,000 and $65,000, depending on the region where you settle) and must maintain private health insurance for the duration of your stay. The visa holder can work for up to 20 hours per week.

The visa is initially valid for four years, with a further period of the same duration allowed. The investor retirement visa is only temporary and doesn't lead to permanent residence or citizenship, and confers no right to Medicare or social security benefits. The Department of Immigration and Multicultural and Indigenous Affairs (DIMIA) website (🖥 www.immi.gov.au) has a list of the areas of Australia currently deemed to be regional/low population growth areas, which attract lower income requirements for this visa.

New Zealand

There's no special immigration category for those wishing to retire to New Zealand and those aged over 55 aren't eligible to apply for residence under the Skilled Migrant category. Most retirees seek residence under the Family stream, although those with business experience and capital may qualify under the Skilled/Business stream (below). See *Living and Working in New Zealand* (Survival Books) for more information.

LANGUAGE

If you want to make the most of the Antipodean way of life and your time in Australia or New Zealand, it's essential to learn English as soon as possible. For people living in either country permanently, learning English isn't an option, but a necessity and you should take evening classes or a language course before you leave home, as you will probably be too busy for the first few months after your move, when you most need the language.

SURVIVAL TIP
**Your business and social enjoyment and success
in Australia and New Zealand will be directly related to
the degree to which you master English.**

If you come to Australia or New Zealand without being able to speak English, you will be excluded from everyday life and will feel uncomfortable until you can understand what's going on around you (and you won't be allowed to stay permanently).

However bad your grammar, however poor your vocabulary and however terrible your accent, an attempt to speak English will be much better appreciated than your fluent Arabic, Danish, Serbo-Croat or whatever, which only people from that community will understand anyway. Like most native English speakers, few Australians and New Zealanders learn other languages.

HEALTH

One of the most important aspects of living in Australia or New Zealand (or anywhere else for that matter) is maintaining good health, and both the countries Down Under are among the world's 'healthiest'. Despite the common stereotype of the Aussies and Kiwis as beer-swilling sports watchers stuffing themselves with barbecued meats, many have become health freaks in recent years. Fitness and health centres flourish in most towns, and even jogging (*footing*) has become fashionable in recent years. Smoking has declined considerably and is now a minority habit.

Australia

Australia is among the most advanced countries in the field of medicine and is noted for its highly-trained medical staff and modern hospitals equipped with the latest high-tech apparatus. Healthcare services in Australia are provided by both government (including Commonwealth, state, territory and local governments) and private organisations. The country spends around 9.5 per cent of its GDP on healthcare (compared with around 7 per cent in the UK and some 15 per cent in the USA), which is about average for OECD countries. Despite the rising cost of modern medicine, including astronomically expensive equipment to diagnose and treat illnesses such as cancer and heart disease, costs have largely been contained in the last 15 years. Recently, there's been a growing emphasis on preventive medicine and community care, including education programmes to promote a healthy lifestyle. Two yardsticks widely used to measure the quality of a country's healthcare are the infant mortality rate (around five deaths for every 1,000 live births) and life expectancy (82.6 years for women and 77.4 for men), both of which are among the 'best' in the world.

Australia has a national health system called Medicare, which provides free or subsidised medical care and free hospital treatment in public hospitals for all permanent residents (plus certain visitors) irrespective of their age, health status or income. The public health system is supplemented by a wide variety of private clinics, hospitals and practitioners, plus a range of voluntary agencies and non-profit organisations. Alternative medicine and natural remedies are popular in Australia, where acupuncture, chiropractic, homeopathy, naturopathy, osteopathy and physiotherapy thrive. Health facilities and doctors are unevenly distributed in Australia, the major cities and urban areas having a surplus of GPs, while in most country areas there's a shortage, particularly in the Northern Territory and Western Australia. Trying to encourage doctors to relocate from the cities to remote country and outback areas is a major problem, which the government is trying to address by importing doctors specifically to work in country areas. The Royal Flying Doctor Service provides medical services in remote country areas and evacuates urgent cases to hospital.

Australians are generally healthier than they were 20 years ago, owing to a decrease in smoking and drinking and an improved diet (although Australia's love affair with junk food and red meat is largely undiminished). Nevertheless, the amount of exercise Australians take is generally low, and over half the adult population is either overweight or obese; many children have eating disorders, and a quarter are classified as obese. Stress-related problems (often due to over-work or lack of sleep) are on the increase in Australia's cities, and the country has a relatively high suicide rate, particularly among the young and the over 65s. Voluntary euthanasia is a topical subject in Australia, particularly since the world's first voluntary euthanasia law was passed in 1995 in the Northern Territory. This was subsequently overturned in 1997 by the federal government after four people had been medically assisted to die. In most states, patients can refuse life-sustaining treatment, but doctors cannot assist them to die (although in reality many doctors do 'assist' terminally-ill patients).

The biggest killers in Australia are cancer (the cause of some 30 per cent of deaths), heart disease and stroke, and smoking-related illnesses. Alcoholism is fairly widespread, as is drug addiction, which is a serious and increasing problem. The country has an unusually high level of diabetes: in 2004, there were an estimated 940,000 sufferers (around 4.7 per cent of the population). There are special health programmes in Australia for Aborigines and Torres Strait Islanders, many of whom have acute health problems (often related to alcohol abuse and a poor diet) and a much lower life expectancy than other Australians.

Virulent flu (influenza) strains are a widespread problem and directly or indirectly kill some 1,500 people a year and affect as many as 30 per cent of the population (flu vaccinations are recommended for those aged over 65). Miscellaneous health problems in recent years have included outbreaks of dengue fever, hepatitis C (a life-threatening infection transmitted mostly by intravenous drug users), legionnaire's disease, meningococcal disease and salmonella poisoning (from cooked meat). Air pollution caused by high smog levels is an increasing problem in Australia's cities, particularly Sydney (where pollution is higher than in London, New York or Tokyo) and Melbourne, where asthmatics, bronchitis sufferers and the elderly are particularly at risk. Sydney is reportedly the allergy capital of the world on account of the numerous plants that send out pollens on breezy spring days.

Australia has the highest rate of melanoma in the world. Although cases are reducing as people heed warnings, some 850 people die annually from skin cancer. If you aren't used to Australia's fierce sun, you should limit your exposure and avoid it altogether during the hottest part of the day (between around 10am and 3pm), wear protective clothing (including a hat) and use sunscreen. Those with fair skin should take extra care, as you can burn in just 15 minutes on a hot summer day. The government's slogan in the battle against skin cancer is 'Slip, Slop, Slap', i.e. slip on a shirt, slop on sunscreen and slap on a hat. This is backed by a 'SunSmart' campaign begun in 1987, which is particularly targeted at teenagers. It's important to use a sunscreen with a high protection factor, e.g. a pH 15+ broad-spectrum, water-resistant sunscreen (sunscreens with a protection factor of 30+ are now available).

Too much sun and too little protection dry your skin and cause premature ageing, so care should be taken to replace the skin's natural oils (many Australian women in their 20s and 30s have the skin of people 20 to 30 years older). Medical experts recommend the wearing of good quality sunglasses, e.g. with UV400 polycarbonate lenses, to protect against eye cancer and other eye problems caused by the sun. Hikers should wear legionnaire or Arab-style hats with neck flaps. Children are particularly vulnerable and should wear wide-brimmed hats in the sun and a T-shirt when swimming. Those who live the outdoor life (such as sportsmen) are also especially at risk and should follow the example of Australian cricketers by wearing total block-out zinc cream on exposed areas when spending a long time in the sun. Drink plenty of water when in the sun to prevent dehydration (in extreme heat you should drink a litre every hour), and avoid excess alcohol and over-exertion, particularly if you're elderly. Other problems associated with too much sun include fungal infections, heat exhaustion, prickly heat, sunburn and sunstroke.

Australia has some of the deadliest creatures in the world, including catfish, crocodiles, jellyfish, scorpions, sharks, a plethora of poisonous snakes (e.g. death adder, sea snakes and western taipan), venomous spiders (e.g. the funnel-web, red-back and trap-door), and stonefish, many of which can deliver a fatal bite or sting. Although you're unlikely to have a close encounter with most of Australia's wildlife (unless you venture into the bush or the sea off unprotected beaches), poisonous snakes and spiders can be found in suburban parks and gardens and near water courses. You should avoid undergrowth and country areas unless you're wearing protective clothing, i.e. not thongs (flip flops) or shorts, and try to avoid disturbing wildlife. Insects (e.g. mosquitoes, ticks and wasps) are also a problem in many areas, although they're unlikely to kill you. Children are taught at school to recognise dangerous wildlife.

Australia provides better than average facilities for the disabled, but accommodation and support services for the disabled are relatively poor. All capital cities and most regional centres produce maps showing accessible parking, paths and toilets for those with mobility difficulties, and nationwide facilities are listed in *Easy Access Australia* (available from 🖥 www.easyaccessaustralia.com.au). Many councils provide a directory of services for people with disabilities and for older residents. General information is available from the National Information Communication Awareness Network (NICAN), PO Box 407, Curtin, ACT 2605 (☎ 02-6285 3713, 🖥 www.nican.com.au).

You can safely drink the tap water in Australia, although the wine tastes much better and, taken in moderation, even does you good (if you believe the winemakers!). Water supplies are fluoridated in most parts of Australia in order to help prevent tooth decay.

New Zealand

The quality of healthcare in New Zealand is excellent and comparable with other developed countries. Most illnesses and chronic conditions can be treated in New Zealand hospitals, with the exception of a few highly specialist areas (such as certain transplants), when it may be necessary to travel abroad. The standard of public health is generally high, although there are some differences between racial groups, with Maoris in particular suffering ill health more often than people of European origin. New Zealanders tend to suffer more from alcohol-related diseases than Europeans, but less from smoking-related diseases. A disturbing trend in recent years has been that diseases associated with poverty, such as rickets and TB in children, are on the increase after being virtually wiped out. The infant mortality rate is 5.96 deaths per 1,000 live births (around average for OECD countries) and average life expectancy at birth is 78.49 years.

New Zealand provides 'free' or subsidised healthcare to its citizens, permanent residents and certain visitors. The system is comparable to those in European countries such as France or Germany, where the state covers the bulk of the cost of medical treatment but expects most patients to make a contribution. 'Free' care isn't as comprehensive as under the British National Health Service, which aims to provide free care to almost everyone, including emergency treatment for visitors. On the other hand it's nothing like that in the USA, where every last pill, potion and sticking plaster must be paid for.

The New Zealand Ministry of Health (💻 www.moh.govt.nz) is responsible for funding and providing state healthcare, which it delegates to District Health Boards (DHBs) whose job is to meet the government's health objectives by spending their budgets in the most cost-effective way. DHBs use their funding to 'buy' healthcare services from various 'suppliers', including family doctors, hospitals, nursing homes and other health organisations. This system has been in existence since 1993 and introduced the commercial market into the public healthcare sector. It has seen most hospitals reformed as Crown Health Enterprises (CHEs or 'cheeses' in local slang), which are effectively in competition with each other to provide the best healthcare at the lowest cost. As each of the 21 DHBs has substantial freedom to adopt its own system and framework, there tends to be a lack of national consistency in the health system.

The state healthcare system has come under huge pressure in recent years due to an increasing demand for services amid severe financial constraints, as politicians have sought to reduce the spiralling health budget to fund tax cuts. A number of hospitals have been closed and the number of people on waiting lists for non-emergency treatment, once unknown in New Zealand, has sometimes soared to almost 100,000. There has also been disruption to healthcare as successive governments have experimented with various measures aimed at providing a better service for less money (a formidable task). The latest healthcare innovation is the Health Information Strategy for New Zealand – launched in August 2005 – which aims to deal with current challenges, including the ageing population, the rising incidence of chronic diseases such as diabetes and cardiovascular disease, the emergence of new infectious diseases such as SARS, and the high cost of new technology and treatments.

The New Zealand public and media are concerned at a perceived lack of funds behind the country's state healthcare, and medical staff generally feel they're underpaid and obliged to work with over-stretched resources. There have been several high-profile cases of people needing urgent treatment having to wait too long. The New Zealand Medical Association (NZMA,

🖳 www.nzma.org.nz) also highlights the shortage of rural GPs and professionals in some specialist areas, such as psychiatry, as well as the 'brain drain' of doctors from New Zealand who have accumulated vast student debts and are attracted by salaries and working conditions abroad.

Although you won't be denied medical attention in New Zealand (assuming you don't mind waiting), alternative treatments are also popular. A recent survey by *Consumer* magazine claimed that half of New Zealanders have tried alternative therapies, usually for conditions for which they had been seeing a 'traditional' doctor. The most popular alternative therapies are chiropractic, herbal medicine, homeopathy and osteopathy. New Zealand doctors are generally sympathetic to these therapies and occasionally refer patients to alternative practitioners.

PETS

Australia

Pets can be imported into Australia from most countries, although there are rigorous controls and it's expensive. All imports are subject to quarantine, and an import permit must be obtained before shipment. Applications should be made at least two months before the intended date of importation, to the Australian Quarantine and Inspection Service (AQIS, 🖳 www.aqis.gov.au) in the state where you will be living. The application fee is $80 (plus an additional assessment fee of $20 or more) and the import permit takes up to four weeks to be issued and is valid for two months. Dogs and cats must have been continuously resident for six months (or since their birth if less than six months old) in the country of origin immediately prior to shipment to Australia and must not have been in quarantine or under quarantine restrictions during the 30 days before export. Dogs and cats must be aged at least 12 weeks at the time of export. Certain breeds of dog that are considered dangerous aren't eligible for importation, including dogo Argentino, fila Brazileiro, Japanese tosa and the pitbull terrier or American pitbull. The importation of birds and small mammals such as hamsters is also prohibited.

Imported dogs and cats must be identified by a microchip. All dogs aged over three months must be registered annually with your local council. If your dog has been microchipped and 'desexed', the charge is $20; if it still has its reproductive organs intact, you must pay $40!

All imported cats and dogs must have current vaccinations. Dogs must have vaccinations for distemper, hepatitis, para-influenza and parvovirus, and must also test negative for canine brucellosis, canine tropical pancytopenia and leptospirosis within 30 days of export. Cats must have vaccinations for calicivirus, feline enteritis and rhinotracheitis. Vaccinations must have been given at least 14 days before shipment and not more than 12 months previously. All dogs and cats must be treated for internal parasites within 14 days of shipment and for external parasites within 96 hours of export, and must pass a clinical examination within 48 hours of shipment. If dogs and cats exported to Australia don't meet the pre-export and post-arrival testing, certification, health and vaccination requirements, they may need to be re-exported, treated or destroyed, or remain in quarantine until any disease concerns have been resolved.

Quarantine

Dogs and cats from the Cocos (Keeling) Islands, New Zealand and Norfolk Island aren't required to undergo quarantine. Dogs and cats from approved rabies-free countries and territories, including Cyprus, Hawaii, Ireland, Japan, Malta, Norway, Singapore, Sweden, Taiwan and the UK, are quarantined for 30 days. Dogs and cats from countries and territories where rabies is considered to be well controlled (including Austria, Belgium, Canada, Denmark, Finland, France, Germany, Greece, Hong Kong, Israel, Italy, Luxembourg, Malaysia, the Netherlands, Portugal, Spain, Switzerland and the USA) are quarantined for a minimum of 30 days and a maximum of 120. Pets from certain other approved rabies-free countries (mostly Pacific islands) must spend 60 days in quarantine. The import of dogs and cats from countries and territories where dog-mediated rabies is endemic is permitted only indirectly via an approved country, where the animal must be resident for at least six months prior to export to Australia. Many pet owners decide that the cost and strain of quarantine on their pets (and themselves) is too much to bear and find their pets new homes.

Pets must be shipped by air to Australia in an International Air Transport Association (IATA) approved container, available from pet shipping agents such as Airpets Oceanic (UK ☎ 01753-685571, 💻 www.airpets.com) and Par Air Services Livestock Limited (UK ☎ 01206-330332, 💻 www.parair.co.uk) in the UK. Animals are inspected at airports by a veterinary surgeon before shipment and can only arrive at the following airports in Australia: Kingsford Smith Airport (Sydney), Perth Airport and Tullamarine Airport (Melbourne). Other entry points require AQIS (see below) consent. On arrival in Australia, dogs and cats are quarantined in an approved animal quarantine station at Byford (Western Australia), Eastern Creek (NSW) or Spotswood (Victoria). Quarantine costs are around $12 per day for a cat and

$16 for a dog. Weekly visits are permitted during the quarantine period. Other charges include $35.50 for document clearing, $71 for the examination of the animal and $95 or $120 for transport (depending on the time of day). For further information contact the Australian Quarantine Inspection Service (AQIS), PO Box 858, Canberra, ACT 2601 (☎ 02-6272 4455, 💻 www.affa.gov.au). AQIS publish a leaflet *The Importation of Dogs and Cats into Australia* (AQIS information sheet 2) as well as providing comprehensive information and forms online.

New Zealand

New Zealanders are enthusiastic animal lovers and many people keep dogs and cats. However, cats have received a 'bad press' in recent years, as they're believed to be responsible for the decimation of New Zealand's wildlife. Cats aren't indigenous to New Zealand and flightless birds such as the kiwi had few natural predators until the first European settlers landed their pets on the country's shores. If you plan to take a pet to New Zealand, it's important to check the latest regulations, which are complex. Given the distance (unless you're travelling from Australia) and container regulations, it's best to entrust the transportation of pets to a specialist shipping company.

New Zealand has strict regulations regarding the import of animals in order to prevent animal diseases entering the country, and pets and other animals cannot be imported without authorisation from customs. You must obtain an import permit, which is available from the Executive Co-ordinator, Biosecurity New Zealand, PO Box 2526, Wellington (☎ 04-470 2754, 💻 www.biosecurity.govt.nz). Note that if your pet needs to undergo a period of quarantine, the import permit will be approved only when accompanied by a letter from a MAF-approved quarantine establishment (there are only three) confirming that your cat or dog has a reserved place. You require a 'zoo-sanitary certificate' and a health certificate from a veterinary surgeon in your home country, and your pet will need to undergo a period of quarantine after its arrival in New Zealand (except as described below).

All animals must be vaccinated against rabies and must have had a Rabies Neutralising Antibody Tritation test no less than six months before they enter quarantine. A repeat test must be done within 30 days of the start of quarantine. Cats and dogs imported from Australia, Hawaii, Norway, Singapore, Sweden and the UK needn't be quarantined, provided they're microchipped, are older than 16 weeks and have been resident in the exporting country for a minimum of six months before travel. The cost of transporting a cat or small dog from Europe or the USA, including all necessary paperwork, is likely to be at least $650, with quarantine accommodation costing from around $40 per day.

For further information contact the Ministry of Agriculture and Forestry, PO Box 2526, Wellington (☎ 04-474 4100, 🖥 www.maf.govt.nz), a New Zealand diplomatic mission or NZ Customs (☎ freephone 0800-428 786 or 09-300 5399 from abroad). Customs also have a comprehensive website (🖥 www.customs.govt.nz) or you can contact one of the following offices: Auckland International Airport, PO Box 73-003 (☎ 09-275 9059), Christchurch, PO Box 14-086 (☎ 03-358 0600) or Wellington, PO Box 2218 (☎ 04-473 6099).

2.

THE BEST PLACE TO LIVE

Once you've decided to buy a home in Australia or New Zealand, your first task will be to choose the region and what sort of home. Deciding where to live can be difficult and the choice can be overwhelming if you're seeking a holiday, investment or retirement home.

SURVIVAL TIP
If you're unsure where and what to buy, the best decision is to rent for a period (see page 141).

The secret of successfully buying a home in Australia or New Zealand (or anywhere else for that matter) is research, research and more research, preferably before you even set foot there. You may be fortunate and buy the first property you see without doing any homework and live happily ever after. However, a successful purchase is much more likely if you thoroughly investigate the towns and communities in your chosen area, compare the range and prices of properties and their relative values, and study the procedure for buying property. It's a lucky person who happens upon the ideal home, and you have a much better chance of finding your dream home if you do your homework thoroughly.

Australia is a huge country (a continent, in fact) with a wide range of landscapes, including desert, semi-desert, scrub, temperate and tropical forests, farmland, wetlands and even the odd mountain range (see **Geography** below). It also has several climatic zones as well as numerous micro-climates (see **Climate** on page 22), making your choice of location less than straightforward. New Zealand is much smaller than Australia, around the same size as the UK, and has a smaller variation of landscape, including a variety of mountain ranges, extensive subtropical and temperate forests, and a limited amount of grasslands. Unlike most Western countries, vast areas of Australia and New Zealand are still largely uninhabited.

GEOGRAPHY

Australia

Australia is one of the world's oldest land masses (some of its rock was formed over 3 billion years ago) and its largest island. Separated from other land masses, it evolved in partial isolation, resulting in its unique flora and fauna, and the development of the Aboriginal race, with a culture stretching back between 40,000 and 60,000 years. The country extends 3,200km/1,988mi from north to south and 4,000km/2,485mi from east to west, covering an area of 7,682,300km^2 (2,966,144mi^2), including Tasmania, with a coastline of 36,738km (22,826mi). It's the world's sixth-largest country (after Russia, Canada, China, the USA and Brazil) and is around the same size as the continental USA (minus Alaska), one and a half times the size of Europe (excluding Russia) and more than 30 times the size of the UK. Almost 40 per cent of the country lies north of the Tropic of Capricorn.

Australia lies in the southern hemisphere, south-east of Asia and between the Indian and Pacific oceans. Its nearest neighbour is Papua New Guinea (PNG), which is some 200km (125mi) north of Cape York in the north-west. Bali and other Indonesian islands lie off the north-west coast, and the French island of New Caledonia is situated to the north-east. New Zealand is around 1,700km (1,050mi) from the south-east coast, and to the south lies Antarctica. Australia is surrounded by four seas (Arafura, Coral, Tasman and Timor) and three oceans (Indian, South Pacific and Southern).

The Great Barrier Reef lies between 50 and 300km (31 to 186mi) off the north-east coast and stretches from the Torres Strait to Gladstone. It's the largest coral reef in the world, extending some 2,000km (1,260mi) and encompassing an area of around 200,000km^2 (77,226mi^2). The reef is the world's largest living entity and an important marine ecosystem containing many rare life forms (it's also a World Heritage site).

Australia is the world's flattest continent, with an average elevation of less than 500m/1,640ft (the world's average is 700m/2,296ft) and only some 5 per cent of it is more than 600m/1,968ft above sea level. The Great Western Plateau covers most of Western Australia, a large part of the Northern Territory and South Australia, and part of Queensland. East of the plateau are the Central Eastern Lowlands, extending from the Gulf of Carpentaria in the north to eastern South Australia and the western Victorian coast. The Great Dividing Range (or Eastern Highlands) follows the east coast southwards from northern Queensland to southern Tasmania, separating a narrow fertile strip of land on the coast from the arid inland. The vast, flat inland plain is broken only by a few low mountain ranges such as the Flinders and Macdonnell Ranges, the Olgas and Uluru (or Ayers Rock, the largest rock on earth, 9.4km/5.8mi in circumference – if you're tempted to climb it, bear in mind that it's Aboriginal sacred ground and many people have died of heart attacks in the attempt!). Other mountain ranges include the Hamersley Range, the Kimberleys and the Stirling Range in Western Australia, and the Snowy Mountains (Australian Alps) in Victoria, where Mount Kosciusko is the highest point (2,230m/7,316ft) in Australia.

Australia has the lowest rainfall of any continent after Antarctica and evaporation exceeds rainfall in 70 per cent of the country. Surface water is scarce and most lakes (with memorable names such as Lake Disappointment) and rivers are dry most of the year. Much of the centre and west of the country consists of desert (some 1.5 million km^2/579,195mi^2). A third is desert or arid lands, some 55 per cent semi-arid and shrub lands, and only around 6 per cent is cultivated for crops or used for grazing. Australia has three main deserts, the Great Sandy, the Great Victoria and the Gibson, and several smaller ones. Lush forests are found on the east coast, particularly in the far north. The country's longest rivers are the Murray, Darling, Ord and Swan. The main river is the River Murray which, with the River Darling, has a catchment area covering New South Wales, Queensland and Victoria. Severe salting has occurred in recent years due to indiscriminate land clearing for agricultural use, which has reduced irrigation potential and lowered the quality of drinking water (if nothing is done, the Murray-Darling basin will be dead in 40 to 50 years).

Australia comprises six states (New South Wales, Queensland, South Australia, Tasmania, Victoria and Western Australia) and two territories (the Australian Capital Territory and the Northern Territory). The island of Tasmania (also called the Apple Isle) is larger than Denmark or the Netherlands and was founded by the Dutchman Abel Tasman in 1642 and originally named Van Dieman's Land (changed to Tasmania in 1856). External territories include the Australian Antarctic Territory, Christmas Island, the Cocos (Keeling) Islands and Norfolk Island (the territory of Ashmore and Cartier Islands). Macquarie Island (around 1,600km/994mi south-east of Tasmania) is administered by Tasmania.

New Zealand

New Zealand lies in the South Pacific Ocean south-east of Australia and comprises two main islands, called the North Island and the South Island (they were named in the 19th century by the British, who obviously exercised a great deal of imagination in christening them), plus numerous smaller islands (of which Stewart and Chatham are the most important). Associated with New Zealand are Ross Dependency (in Antarctica) and Niue, Tokelau and the Cook Islands (in the Pacific Ocean). The capital of the country is Wellington, although Auckland is the largest city. Contrary to popular belief (and much to the relief of most New Zealanders), New Zealand isn't just off the coast of Australia, but some 2,000km (1,250mi) away across the Tasman Sea. New Zealand covers an area of 270,534km^2 (104,461mi^2), which makes it comparable in size to the UK.

New Zealand is a mountainous country, some 60 per cent of which is between around 200m (655ft) and 1,070m (3,500ft) above sea level, including over 220 mountains above 2,000m (6,550ft). The principal mountain ranges in the North Island extend along the eastern side, where the north central region has three active volcanic peaks: Mount Ruapehu (2,797m/9,176ft), the highest point on the island, Mount Ngauruhoe (2,291m/7,516ft) and Tongariro (1,968m/6,456ft). Mount Taranaki (2,518m/ 8,261ft), a solitary extinct volcanic cone, is situated near the western extremity of the island. The North Island has numerous rivers, most of which rise in the eastern and central mountains, including the Waikato River (435km/270mi), the longest river in New Zealand. It flows north out of Lake Taupo (606km²/233mi²), the country's largest lake (where mineral springs are also found), into the Tasman Sea in the west. The North Island has an irregular coastline, particularly on its northern extremity, the Auckland Peninsula, where it's just 10km/6mi wide.

The South Island has a more regular coastline than the North Island and in the south-west is characterised by deep fjords. The chief mountain range of the South Island is the Southern Alps, a massive range extending from the south-west to the north-east for almost the entire length of the island (17 peaks in the range are over 3,000m/9,842ft high). Mount Cook (3,754m/12,316ft) is the highest point in New Zealand and rises from the centre of the range, which also contains a number of glaciers. Most of the rivers of the South Island, including the Clutha River (338km/210mi long), the longest river on the island, rise in the Southern Alps. The largest lake is Lake Te Anau (342km²/132mi²) in the southern part of the Southern Alps. The Canterbury plains in the east and the Southland plains in the extreme south are the only extensive flat areas on the South Island.

The islands of New Zealand emerged in the Tertiary period and contain a complete series of marine sedimentary rocks, some of which date from the early Paleozoic era. Much of the topography of New Zealand has resulted from warping and block faulting, although volcanic action has also played a part in its formation, particularly that of the North Island, where it continues to this day. Geysers and mineral hot springs occur in the volcanic area, particularly around Rotorua. New Zealand is within an earthquake zone and minor (usually unnoticeable) tremors occur almost monthly, although records show that serious earthquakes occur, on average, only once every 210 years.

Much New Zealand plant life is unique, and of the 2,000 indigenous species some 1,500 are found only here, including the golden kowhai and the scarlet pohutukawa. The North Island is home to predominantly subtropical vegetation, including mangrove swamps in the north. The forest, or so-called bush, of the North Island is mainly evergreen with a dense undergrowth of mosses and ferns. Evergreen trees include the kahikatea, kauri (the traditional wood used for house building in New Zealand), rimu and totara, all of which are excellent timber trees. The only extensive area of native grassland in the North Island is the central volcanic plain. The eastern part of the South Island is, for the most part, grassland up to an elevation of around 1,500m, while most forests are situated in the west (consisting mainly of native beech and Alpine vegetation at high altitudes).

With the exception of two species of bat, New Zealand has no indigenous mammals. The first white settlers (who arrived early in the 19th century) found a kind of dog and a black rat, both of which had been introduced by the Maoris around 500 years earlier and are now almost extinct. All other wild mammals are descended from deer, ferrets, goats, opossums, pigs, rabbits and weasels, all of which were imported by early western settlers. No snakes and few unusual species of insects inhabit New Zealand (unlike Australia, which is infested with them), although it does boast the tuatara, a lizard-like reptile with a third eye believed to be a distant relative of the dinosaurs. New Zealand has a large population of wild birds, including 23 native species which include the songbirds bellbird and tui and flightless species such as the kakapo, kiwi (from which New Zealanders take their colloquial name), takahe and weka. The survival of flightless birds is attributed to the absence of predatory animals (with the exception of domestic cats). The blackbird, magpie, myna, skylark, sparrow and thrush are among the most prevalent imported species.

New Zealand's rivers and lakes contain a variety of native edible fish, including eel, freshwater crustaceans (particularly crayfish), lamprey and whitebait. Trout and salmon have been introduced and are found in waters throughout the country. The surrounding ocean waters are the habitat of blue cod, flounder, flying fish, hapuku, shark, snapper, swordfish, tarakihi and various species of whales, in addition to a variety of shellfish including mussels, oysters and toheroas.

CITIES

Australia and New Zealand boast an impressive seven cities between them in a 2005 list of the world's top 55 cities, ranked according to quality of life (source: Mercer Consulting, 1166 Avenue of the Americas, New York 10036, USA, ☎ 212-345 7000, 💻 www.mercer.com). Auckland and Sydney were the top Antipodean cities, ranked joint 8th with Bern and Copenhagen. Melbourne and Wellington were joint 14th with Berlin, Luxembourg,

Stockholm and Toronto. Perth was ranked joint 20th with Ottawa. Adelaide slipped a place from 2004, to joint 25th, tied with Calgary, Hamburg, Helsinki, Honolulu and San Francisco. Brisbane was ranked joint 31st in 2005 with Oslo and Paris, which was a drop of seven places from its 2004 ranking. In contrast, a 2005 survey by the Economist Intelligence Unit assessing the 'liveability' (for British expatriates) of 127 cities worldwide, rated Australia's and New Zealand's cities much higher. Melbourne was ranked joint second, with Adelaide, Perth and Sydney in joint 5th place, and Brisbane just below in joint 11th place. Auckland and Wellington were also in the top 20.

Australia

Adelaide

Adelaide is the capital of South Australia, named after Queen Adelaide, the consort of King William IV. It's situated on the Fleurieu Peninsula, overlooking Gulf St. Vincent, with the low lying Mount Lofty Ranges sitting to the east. Adelaide is the main interim point of the Indian Pacific railway between Sydney and Perth, and the terminus of the Overland to Melbourne and The Ghan via Alice Springs to Darwin. Its population is 1.2 million, the fifth-largest of Australia's capital cities, and its inhabitants are known as Adelaideans.

Adelaide is a beautiful city but it has lagged behind Australia's other cities over the last 20 years or so. Some people regard this as an advantage because it means that the city is less frenetic than most of Australia's other main centres. Others see it as negative and view Adelaide as a dull place, with few of the cultural and social attractions and little of the vibrancy of Australia's other cities, which is unfair. Adelaide has long had a reputation as a religious city – it's called the City of Churches – but this is more a reflection of the past than the present and it's rumoured that for every church built in the city a pub was also built to see to the needs of the less holy. Adelaide in the 21st century has rather more nightlife than previously and enjoys its fair share of bars, cafés and restaurants. It's also beautifully situated, with many parks and a backdrop of hills, as well as attractive beaches, galleries, historic houses and museums. In a 2005 survey of the world's best cities in which to live, carried out by the Economist Intelligence Unit, Adelaide was ranked joint fifth with Perth and Sydney.

One of Adelaide's major attractions for potential immigrants is its inexpensive property. This is a particular draw for people working in vocational (and modestly paid) professions such as nursing and teaching, who can enjoy a higher standard of living in Adelaide than in Melbourne or Sydney. Adelaide's climate is also reputed to be one of the best of Australia's cities. The city is on the same latitude as Sydney, but its weather is quite different, more classically Mediterranean, with cooler, wetter winters, and hotter, drier summers – 'proper' weather.

Adelaide (and the rest of South Australia) was hamstrung financially following the 1992 collapse of the State Bank, which led to a debt of around $4 billion. This has recently been reduced, making the economic outlook for the next decade better than for the last. The major components of Adelaide's economy are the defence, manufacturing and research industries. The city has General Motors Holden and Mitsubishi car manufacturing plants and the main government research institution, DSTO (the Defence Science and Technology Organisation). Other industries include electronic component production and ore refining.

Adelaide hosts a number of annual events (as well as being called the Wine State, Australia's best-known wine region – the Barossa Valley – is located just outside the city, South Australia is known as the Festival State) including the Adelaide Festival of Arts, the Adelaide Film Festival, the Barossa Music Festival and the Fringe Festival. It's also a respected seat of learning, with Flinders University, the University of Adelaide and the University of South Australia all noted research and teaching institutions.

Alice Springs

Alice Springs lies at almost the exact centre of Australia, around 1,500km (935mi) from the nearest major cities, Adelaide and Darwin. Often called simply 'Alice', it's the second-largest settlement in the Northern Territory, with a population of around 30,000. Alice is best-known for two things: its proximity to Uluru (Ayers Rock), one of Australia's best-known landmarks, and as the setting for Nevil Shute's novel *A Town Like Alice*.

Alice was established as a frontier settlement for the north-to-south camel trains that trekked across Australia's desert interior, and today it's the mid-point of the Adelaide to Darwin railway. During the '60s, Alice became an important defence centre with the establishment of the joint Australian/USA Pine Gap satellite monitoring base, 19km (12mi) south-west of Alice. The base gives the city an American air (with a population of around 2,000 Americans).

By far the major industry is tourism, which developed because of Alice's proximity to Uluru, 400km (250mi) to the west. But with the creation in the '80s of Yulara resort and airport near Uluru, some tourists no longer visit Alice, heading straight for Yulara. However, it has plenty of other attractions including an arts centre, ballooning, camel tours, a casino, the Desert Park wildlife centre, a museum, plenty of nightlife and a number of tourist resorts. To serve its 500,000 visitors per year, Alice has plenty of backpacker lodges, caravan parks and hotels.

The economy of Alice is booming and it's one of Australia's wealthiest cities, its major sources of income including tourism, Pine Gap and high government funding directed towards the local Aboriginal population (Aborigines make up 17 per cent of Alice's population and 29 per cent of the Northern Territory's).

Alice's climate is extreme with summer temperatures often reaching 40 to 42°C (and sometimes 48°C) and winter lows dropping to -7°C. There are also the large diurnal ranges (differences in temperature within a period of 24 hours) typical of deserts, with hot days and cold nights. There's often little or no rain in Alice Springs, but the amount received can vary greatly from year to year.

Brisbane

Brisbane (pronounced BRIZ-buhn, with locals called Brisbanites) lies in the south-east corner of Queensland, an hour's drive north of the Gold Coast. The city straddles the Brisbane River and its eastern suburbs look out over Moreton Bay. The greater Brisbane region sits on the coastal plain east of the Great Dividing Range, although parts of the city are very hilly.

Brisbane has a population of around 975,000, and 1.85 million people live in the greater metropolitan area. It has a lower population density than most Australian cities because much of the housing is detached homes on large plots of land, often with lush gardens. Pre-1950 houses are often built in the Queenslander architectural style, with large verandahs and built on stilts to maximise the circulation of cool air in this nearly tropical city (it's situated just a few degrees south of the Tropic of Capricorn). An important consideration for those thinking of buying property in Brisbane is the discovery in 2001 of an infestation of fire ants in some suburbs. The state government is trying to eradicate the insects, but property in affected areas can prove difficult to sell.

Brisbane used to be regarded as a backwater, but is currently one of Australia's major growth cities. It attracts a lot of migrants, both from within Australia and internationally, many drawn by its balmy, dry winter climate, when temperatures rarely drop below 21°C (70°F). On the downside, summers and autumns can be humid, rainy and stifling, with conditions particularly steamy between November and April. Summer thunderstorms are common and Brisbane is also prey to cyclonic winds and hailstorms.

However, despite the usually humid summers with violent rainstorms, recent years have seen sometimes severe summer droughts.

Brisbane used to be seen as a 'branch office' city, as many major financial institutions and businesses have their headquarters in Sydney or Melbourne. To compensate for this, the Queensland state government has been developing science and technology industries throughout the state (particularly in Brisbane) as part of its 'Smart State' campaign. Brisbane has a diverse economy, with a wide range of blue and white collar industries. The former include metalworking, paper milling, petroleum refining and stevedoring, while the latter encompass financial services, higher education, information technology and public sector administration. Tourism is also important.

As well as its wide range of employment opportunities, Brisbane offers competitively-priced property (it has the lowest cost of living of any Australian city) and an attractive street café scene, but its most obvious drawback is its rather shabby city centre, which is well below the standard of Australia's other major cities. Some people also consider parts of Brisbane to be tacky, particularly some of the tourist arcades, but the city also boasts some elegant architecture and impressive galleries, museums and parks.

In a 2005 survey of the world's best cities in which to live, carried out by the Economist Intelligence Unit, Brisbane was ranked joint eleventh.

Cairns

Cairns is in the far north of Queensland, 1,700km (1,060mi) from Brisbane. It was originally established as a port to export gold and other precious metals from the mines west of the city. Situated in the tropical north, Cairns used to be viewed as a frontier country backwater, but in the 21st century the city is booming thanks to tourism, the population has swelled to 125,000 and it has developed a more sophisticated image.

Cairns is successfully selling itself as a year-round tourist destination and is Australia's third most popular tourist venue, after Sydney and Brisbane. It's greatly assisted by having a wealth of natural wonders on its doorstep, including the Great Barrier Reef (an hour and a half away by boat), and Cape Tribulation and the Daintree National Park (both areas of tropical rainforest). Cairns is also the jump-off point for those visiting the Atherton Tablelands, Cape York Peninsula and Cooktown.

As part of the drive to modernise Cairns, the foreshore was redeveloped in 2003, with lagoons and the Pier Marketplace giving the city a more upmarket feel. The warm, tropical climate, with monsoon rains between November and March, is said to be similar to Hawaii, mention of which also adds to the city's desired upmarket image. The climate, however, has its downside: cyclones sometimes arrive during the wet season and flooding of the Barron and Mulgrave Rivers can cut the city off from all road traffic.

Cairns's economy relies heavily on tourism, which contributes around 40 per cent of the city's income. Agriculture is also important and sugar is by far the largest crop. Fruit and tobacco are grown in the cooler, higher areas of the Atherton Tablelands west of Cairns, while fishing, manufacturing and mining also contribute to the economy.

Canberra

Canberra is Australia's largest inland city (population around 330,000, making it the eighth most populous Australian city), lying at the northern end of the Australian Capital Territory (population around 345,000). It's the smallest state/territory capital, with the exception of Hobart.

Canberra is located near the Brindabella Ranges, around 150km (95mi) inland from the east coast, at altitudes between 550m (1,800ft) and 700m (2,300ft) above sea level. Its inland setting and height give it a more continental, colder climate than the stereotypical image of Australia and it has four distinct seasons. Winters can be cold but summers conform to the Australian norm – hot and dry – and skies are clear for much of the year. Being an inland city, Canberra doesn't have beaches close by, but the surrounding countryside is noted for its beauty and in winter ski resorts are only a couple of hours drive to the south.

Like Adelaide, Canberra has a reputation for dullness (it's often described as boring by Australians who haven't been there), primarily because it's a government city (it isn't a popular destination for foreign migrants because most of the city's jobs are in federal government and public service, for which Australian citizenship is required). The ACT authorities are trying to remedy this by attracting other industries to the city. A number of Australian Defence Force establishments are located in or near Canberra, although tourism is the city's second largest industry (after government), visitors being attracted by Canberra's large number of national institutions and monuments.

Canberra was a planned city (rather than one which grew organically), originally designed by Walter Burley Griffin (although it has been altered significantly) and created specifically as the country's seat of government. It's situated roughly halfway between Melbourne and Sydney (it's closer to Sydney) because neither could agree on which city should be the seat of government, thereby necessitating an alternative!

The pre-planning explains why Canberra is so orderly, tidy and easy to navigate (unlike most cities, the roads were designed with motor traffic very much in mind, giving quick access and minimal congestion), but also why it's rather soulless, and nothing like as lively as Melbourne or Sydney. That said, Canberra does have some excellent bars, cafes and restaurants, and it's a picturesque city, with some interesting galleries and museums.

Darwin

Darwin, the capital of the Northern Territory, lies in the far north-west of Australia on the coast of the Timor Sea, and is home to 115,000 people. It has a diverse multicultural population, with over 75 nationalities represented. Nearly a quarter of Darwin's population describe themselves as Aboriginal or Torres Strait Islanders. Darwin's geographical position (facing south-east Asia) gave it the distinction of being the only Australian city to have come under substantial attack during the second world war (by Japanese aircraft).

Until recently, Darwin was regarded by many Australians as a sweaty tropical backwater stuck at the top of the country, but it's currently one of Australia's fastest growing cities. This is because of its physical proximity to the economic powerhouses of Asia (Darwin is closer to Jakarta than Sydney, and closer to Singapore than Melbourne, and is known as the Gateway to Asia), the building of the Alice Springs to Darwin railway line and fuel extraction in the Timor project. Its isolation, however, means that the cost of living is higher than in most other parts of the country.

The Northern Territory's modest economy and small population mean that the job market in Darwin isn't as broad-based as elsewhere in Australia. But if you're looking for an exciting and unusual place to live, Darwin is worth considering. Mining and tourism are the largest economic sectors. The most common minerals are bauxite, gold and manganese, along with natural gas and oil from the Timor Sea. There's also a significant military presence in Darwin (and some other parts of the Northern Territory), which is an important source of employment.

Darwin should grow in importance as a port, the result of the increasing petroleum exploitation in the Timor Sea and growing trade with Asia. Tourism is also important and is increasing as more visitors come during the wet season (November to March or April) as well as the dry season (most of the rest of the year).

Darwin has a 'new' feel, mainly because much of it had to be rebuilt after the 1974 'visit' of Cyclone Tracy, which flattened a lot of the city. If you don't like hot, humid, tropical weather, however, Darwin isn't for you. The wet season can be particularly taxing for those who don't like stifling conditions and the city is also prey to cyclones and tropical thunderstorms.

Geelong

Geelong is Victoria's largest regional city, a port of 205,000 people on Corio Bay, 70km (45mi) south-west of Melbourne. It's the gateway to the tourist resorts of the Bellarine Peninsula and the Great Ocean Road. Although linked to nearby Melbourne by motorway, Geelong feels like a place apart, mainly because it's surrounded by large areas of farmland. The surrounding region is also noted for its wineries and surfing beaches.

Geelong's main industries are aluminium smelting, a Ford Motor company engine plant and a Shell refinery, and the nearby town of Torquay is home to surfing equipment and clothing manufacturers. Geelong hosts some notable events, including the annual Bells Beach Surfing Classic and the Australian International Airshow. The city has been rejuvenated in recent years by a programme of urban landscaping and the building of new accommodation, galleries, museums, restaurants and a university. The latest stage of this is the installation of new artworks, paving and planting.

The Gold Coast

The Gold Coast is a coastal strip in the south-east of Queensland 70km (45mi) south of Brisbane, along which a number of modest settlements have gradually merged into a city of around 480,000 people. It has become Australia's sixth-largest city and largest tourist resort, the sub-tropical climate, impressive surf beaches and some clever marketing having combined to attract domestic and international tourists, and a fair number of retirees. As well as tourism, construction, manufacturing and retailing are important sectors of the Gold Coast's economy.

The Gold Coast is Australia's equivalent of a Spanish holiday Costa, a narrow coastal strip densely covered with bars, high-rise apartments, hotels, nightclubs, restaurants (over 500) and a plethora of shopping centres and retail establishments catering largely to tourists. Its most impressive feature is its 50km (31mi) of beaches, the most famous of which is Surfers Paradise. The hinterland of the Gold Coast is very different from the coastal strip, an impressive region of mountains, national parks, rainforest and valleys.

Hobart

Hobart lies on the Derwent River estuary in south-east Tasmania and is home to around 195,000 people (taking in the Greater Hobart area). It's a small, picturesque city and a busy seaport, the home port for Australia's (and

France's) Antarctic activities. Hobart is famous in the yachting world as the finish of the Sydney to Hobart yacht race, which begins in Sydney on Boxing Day (26th December). Hobart is Australia's most southerly capital city, noted for its atypical climate, which is cooler and cloudier than the tourist brochure image of Australia: temperatures rarely exceed the mid-20s Celsius (mid-70s Fahrenheit), even during the height of summer. Conditions are similar to northern France and southern England, and Hobart and its surrounds appeal to people who enjoy this type of weather and the presence of plenty of rugged, unspoiled greenery on their doorstep.

Finding a job can be difficult in Hobart, however, unless you have specific skills that are currently in demand, and wages tend to be lower than in the rest of Australia, but so are property prices, and the island offers a superb lifestyle. The city's vibrant tourist industry is an important source of employment and other employers include the Cascade Brewery, a high-speed catamaran factory and a zinc smelter.

Hobart is a small, manageable city, which adds to its charm, as do its riverside location, busy harbour, impressive Georgian architecture, parks, mountain backdrop and surrounding vineyards. It reminds some people of Ireland, with its slower pace of life and slight air of melancholy, and backdrop of lush green countryside.

Launceston

Launceston (pronounced LON-ces-ton) sits at the junction of the North Esk, South Esk and Tamar Rivers in north-east Tasmania and is the state's second-largest centre, after Hobart, with which it has a strong (but friendly) rivalry. Launceston has a population of 100,000 and is the regional centre for commerce, culture, education, health, recreation, retail and tourism.

It's an attractive, low-rise, quiet city, with many gardens and parks. As Australia's third-oldest city (after Sydney and Hobart) it has lots of historical buildings and sights, and offers good local hiking and swimming spots. Launceston has rather less nightlife than some cities (some people think there isn't much to do) but is a stone's throw from one of Tasmania's natural wonders, the Cataract Gorge. The nearby Tamar Valley has excellent vineyards, and Launceston's Boags Brewery produces some of Australia's best beers.

Launceston's key industries are community services, manufacturing, retailing and wholesale. Important secondary industries include agriculture, fishing, forestry and tourism.

Melbourne

Melbourne (pronounced MEL-buhn) is situated on the south coast of Victoria in the far south-east of Australia and is the most southerly mainland capital city. It's a large commercial and industrial centre, with plenty of large Australian companies and multinational corporations (around a third of the 100 largest multinationals operating in Australia are located here). Melbourne also has Australia's largest seaport, seven universities (it has one of the highest numbers of international students studying in its universities, after London, New York and Paris) and much of the country's automotive industry, among many other manufacturing industries.

Sometimes overlooked in favour of glamorous, high profile Sydney, Melbourne is often described as a more 'liveable' city, with a much better road system and cheaper property (around a third less). Melbourne is Australia's second-largest city, with a population of around 3.5 million, and was the capital between 1901 and 1927.

Melbourne's main disadvantage (for some people) is probably its climate, which is less reliable than Sydney's, with a consequent effect on lifestyle, which is less *al fresco* in Melbourne. Winter, spring and autumn are quite a lot cooler and greyer in Melbourne than in Sydney, but Melbourne's summer climate is sometimes better than Sydney's because it's nearly as warm but less humid. Melbourne's summers can be changeable, however, with temperatures swinging from a fresh 19°C (66°F) one week to a sweltering 40°C (104°F) the next and then back again, depending on the prevailing wind.

Melbourne more than compensates for its unpredictable climate, however, and it often ranks highly in surveys of the world's best cities in which to live (twice, in 2002 and 2004, it's was first in the survey by *The Economist*, and was placed second in 2005, after Vancouver).

Melbourne is reputed to have the best food in Australia (there are plenty of restaurants) and also offers elegant Victorian architecture, attractive parks and a large, lively arts and cultural life (including the annual Melbourne International Comedy Festival and Melbourne International Film Festival, and a rock and pop scene that Melburnians regard as the country's liveliest). Rather than culture, however, Melbourne is known as one of the world's most sports-mad cities. It hosts nine of the 16 teams in the Australian Football League (Australian Rules Football, not soccer) and hosts the Australian Open Tennis (one of the four Grand slam tournaments), the Melbourne Cup (one of the world's most prestigious handicap horse races), top cricket matches and the Australian Formula One Grand Prix.

Newcastle

Little-known outside Australia, Newcastle in New South Wales is the country's sixth-largest city, with a population of 485,000 in the metropolitan area (which includes the Cessnock, Lake Macquarie, Maitland, Newcastle and Port Stephens local government areas). Residents of Newcastle call themselves (slightly clumsily) Novocastrians.

Newcastle lies 160km (100mi) north of Sydney, at the mouth of the Hunter River. The river's north side is dominated by river channels, sand dunes and swamps, so most of the city is on the hilly southern bank. Newcastle is the economic centre for the resource-rich Hunter Valley and much of northern New South Wales. It's the world's busiest coal export port and Australia's oldest and second-largest throughput port (whatever that means), and also has an important shipbuilding industry. As well as its industrial side, Newcastle has a vibrant youth culture. The University of Newcastle has over 20,000 students and the city has a thriving music scene: Silverchair, one of Australia's most successful rock bands, hail from Newcastle.

Unfortunately, the city is prey to occasional earthquakes. A 1989 earthquake measuring 5.5 on the Richter scale killed 13 people, the first Australian tremor known to have claimed human lives. On the plus side, Newcastle enjoys an almost subtropical climate and has some spectacular beaches.

Perth

Perth is a sprawling city cited on the Swan River in the south-west of Western Australia. To the east of the city lies a low escarpment, the Darling Scarp, but Perth is generally flat. Perth's western suburbs fringe the city's fine beaches, which are less (over)developed than in some Australian cities. The Perth Metropolitan Area has a population of 1.45 million, making it Australia's fourth-largest city.

Perth has become popular with foreigners wishing to buy property in Australia, particularly the British. It has the highest proportion of British-born residents of any Australian city, and there has also been substantial immigration from South Africa, mainly of European-descended South Africans. Perth also has large immigrant communities from south-east Asia.

Perth has something of the air of southern California (without the high crime, racial tension and alarming proximity to the San Andreas Fault!) and many people think it has the best climate of Australia's cities, with short, mild winters, long, hot, dry summers and plenty of sunshine all year. However, the climate has changed in recent years, with less rainfall. This, combined with the city's population growth, has led to concerns that Perth might soon run out of water. As a result, household sprinkler restrictions have been introduced and the State Government is building a seawater desalination plant at Kwinana, due to be finished in late 2006. The authorities are also considering piping water from the tropical Kimberley in the north of the state.

Perth boasts a vibrant economy, splendid beaches and parks, and modestly-priced property. It has a large middle class and offers a suburban lifestyle, meaning that nightlife is relatively limited. The locals are usually friendly and relaxed, but they can be rather parochial, particularly towards east coasters (who view Perth as an isolated backwater). Perth's main disadvantage (to some people) is its isolation, tucked away in the south-west of the country, with its nearest large neighbour (Adelaide) three and a half hours away by air. Perth isn't just Australia's most isolated city but, along with Honolulu, lays claim to be the world's most isolated.

In a 2005 survey of the world's best cities in which to live, carried out by the Economist Intelligence Unit, Perth was ranked joint fifth with Adelaide and Sydney.

Sydney

Sydney is Australia's oldest and largest city. It's also the largest city in the southern hemisphere by area and has around 4.7 million inhabitants. The majority of Sydneysiders are of British or Irish origin, with notable populations hailing from Asia, Greece, Italy and the Lebanon. Sydney is the larger of Australia's two main cultural, financial, trade and transport centres, the other being Melbourne. It has a magnificent location in a coastal basin, with the Pacific to the east and the Blue Mountains to the west. It has the largest natural harbour in the world, Port Jackson, and over 70 beaches, of which Bondi is the most famous. Sydney's urban area is similar in size to Greater London, but has only half the population.

Sydney overshadows Australia's other cities, sometimes unfairly. But it's undoubtedly an enticing place, a noted world tourist destination and regularly voted one of the world's most beautiful cities, noted for its stunning waterside location, iconic attractions, trendy ambience, great restaurants, sophisticated outdoor lifestyle, abundant shopping, friendly locals, cosmopolitan culture, vibrant economy and warm climate. Its international profile was significantly increased by hosting the 2000 summer Olympics, which were widely regarded as the best of recent times.

Despite all these attractions, Sydney isn't for everybody. If you're childless (or child-free), sociable and relatively wealthy, it's a wonderful place to live, but if you have children and a modestly paid job, the city's high property prices (it's much more expensive than the rest of Australia, even in the outer suburbs) make it difficult to find decent, affordable accommodation anywhere which isn't a long, tortuous commute to the city centre, and you might be happier and more solvent in Adelaide, Brisbane or Perth.

Sydney's climate isn't to everybody's taste either, with quite high rainfall throughout the year (its generally wetter than London, for example, although there have been recent droughts) and regular periods of windy and humid weather. It's hit by hailstorms and windstorms every few years and water shortages are an increasing problem. Sydney doesn't suffer from cyclones and its earthquake risk is low, but many areas which border bushland have been affected by bushfires, notably in 1994 and 2002.

In a 2005 survey of the world's best cities in which to live, carried out by the Economist Intelligence Unit, Sydney was ranked joint fifth with Adelaide and Perth.

Townsville

Townsville is a city of around 160,000 in the central section of the stretch of Queensland coast opposite the Great Barrier Reef. It's the largest city and capital of tropical Queensland. The Townsville area is sometimes called the 'Twin Cities' because it includes the cities of Thuringowa and Townsville.

Townsville has some notable attractions, including a long beach and garden area known as 'The Strand', an impressive tropical aquarium, the Museum of Tropical Queensland and nearby Magnetic Island (20 minutes across Cleveland Bay), mostly comprising national park and some excellent beaches.

Tourism has helped Townsville to grow in recent years and it's also an industrial port for exporting minerals from Cloncurry and Mount Isa, beef and wool from the western plains, and sugar and timber from the coast. Townsville also has a number of manufacturing and processing industries, and refines copper, nickel and zinc. There's a large army base at Lavarack Barracks and an airforce base at Garbutt.

Wollongong

Wollongong is an industrial city 82km/50mi (by rail) south of Sydney. Its name comes from an Aboriginal term meaning 'sound of the sea' and the city is sometimes referred to simply as 'The Gong'.

Wollongong has an impressive setting, on a narrow coastal plain, with the Tasman Sea to the east and a steep sandstone precipice to the west. The city has a population of 185,000, but the wider metropolitan area is home to around 260,000. Wollongong has a high proportion of residents with a Mediterranean background, with a prominent Macedonian community and plenty of immigrants from Italy, Greece and Turkey.

In recent years, Wollongong has attracted a lot of people moving from Sydney to escape the capital's high property prices, traffic congestion and increasing crime. Wollongong's cheaper property and good transport links with the capital have seen some people move to the outer suburbs while keeping their jobs in Sydney. The city's major employers include construction, education, health, manufacturing and retailing.

New Zealand

Auckland

Auckland and its neighbouring cities (Manukau, North Shore and Waitakere) make up the Auckland urban area (Auckland, or Auckland City, is the territorial authority covering the Auckland isthmus, which is less than 2km/1.25mi wide at its narrowest point). Although it isn't the country's capital, Auckland is most new arrivals first introduction to New Zealand, with most flights from Europe and North America landing there. It's also New Zealand's most prominent city and home to almost a third of the country's population (around 1.3 million people live in the Auckland area).

Auckland isn't simply New Zealand's largest city, it's also, geographically, one of the world's largest cities, nearly twice the size of London, but with only a seventh of the population. The Auckland area is the country's fastest growing region and around 70 per cent of New Zealand's overseas migrants settle there. The population is set to reach 1.6 million in the next 30 years. The majority of Aucklanders (around 60 per cent) claim European (mainly British) descent, although there are also large Maori and Pacific Island communities (the city has the largest Polynesian population of any city in the world).

Auckland is regularly acclaimed as one of the world's best cities in which to live, with plenty of attractions, including a mild climate, lots of jobs, good educational opportunities, many leisure facilities and a modest cost of living. It's known as The City of Sails (appropriately, it hosted the America's Cup in 1999 and 2003), with an abundance of beaches and offshore islands, and a lifestyle centred on the sea. It's also the country's economic centre: the Auckland area is home to around a third of New Zealand's workforce and nearly 40 per cent of all business enterprises. Most of the major international corporations operating in New Zealand have their head offices in Auckland and the city's main industries include distribution (45 per cent of New Zealand's wholesalers are based there), education, manufacturing and services.

Auckland is particularly well situated, spread out on a narrow stretch of the North Island. The Pacific surrounds much of the city, complimented by the lush, subtropical forests of the nearby hills and islands. It has a temperate climate, with warm, humid summers and cool, damp, sometimes quite long winters. The climate varies somewhat across the city due to the local geography, particularly hills and trees.

The term Jafa is a (mainly) joke term of abuse for Aucklanders. The people of Auckland and other New Zealanders have a generally jovial love-hate relationship. The stereotypes dictate that Aucklanders see the rest of the country's inhabitants as unsophisticated bumpkins, while other New Zealanders see Aucklanders as arrogant yuppies.

The Quarter Acre bungalow (a three or four-bedroom house or bungalow, sitting on around a quarter of an acre of land) is the most common type of home in Auckland, which is one of the reasons why the city has grown so large and has an over-reliance on the motor car. The regional council is trying to address this issue by building more apartments and townhouses and by banning the subdivision of properties on the city fringes. In order to curb Auckland's severe traffic congestion, recent investment has been made in local rail services to try to encourage people out of their cars. Some Aucklanders commute by ferry to avoid the increasing traffic congestion, particularly on the Harbour Bridge.

Christchurch

Christchurch lies on the east coast of the South Island and has a population of around 375,000. It's the main city of the Canterbury region and is known as the Garden City due to its abundance of public parks and residential gardens. Christchurch derives its name and existence from a colonisation programme operated by members of Christchurch College, Oxford, which not surprisingly has given it a distinctly English feel. It used to have a reputation as a dull place, but in recent years it has been livened up by an influx of Asian students and tourists. Christchurch now has a wide selection of bars, karaoke bars and sushi restaurants, is increasingly popular with young people and apparently has the liveliest gay Japanese nightlife outside Tokyo (which is quite a boast).

Christchurch is a very flat city, only a few metres above sea level, with a generally temperate climate and summer temperatures which are often kept in check by a north-east breeze. A regular feature of the weather is the Norwester, a hot wind that can reach gale force and cause substantial property damage. Christchurch is subject to smog in winter and this sometimes gives air pollution readings higher than World Health Organisation recommendations. Winters can be quite cold, with regular frosts and snow a few times a year.

Agriculture, new technologies and tourism are important to Christchurch's economy, with the latter boosted by the city's proximity to ski resorts and the Southern Alps. Christchurch has also played an important role in the history of Antarctic exploration.

Dunedin

Sitting at the far south end of the South Island, Dunedin is the largest city in Otago and the second-largest in the South Island. It's situated on the hills and valleys around the head of Otago harbour and has a population of around 125,000. Dunedin was settled by Scots in the mid-19th century, giving it a distinctive air, with some beautiful Edwardian and Victorian architecture (some of it a legacy of Dunedin's gold-rush affluence).

The city was the site of New Zealand's first botanical garden, newspaper and university (the University of Otago), and is surrounded by spectacular scenery. It still has a slightly staid image, but that's changing, driven by a vibrant music scene, a growing boutique fashion industry, an increasing population of artists and a growing number of students. Dunedin College of Education, Otago Polytechnic and the University of Otago are the major educational institutions. Dunedin's climate is moderate. Winter can be frosty and there's significant snowfall every few years. Spring weather can be very changeable, but between November and April, the weather is usually mild and settled.

The city offers the advantages of a metropolitan lifestyle without the drawbacks of a high cost of living, traffic jams, long commutes and a high crime rate. It also has plenty of natural attractions close by, including miles of white beaches, golf courses, excellent fishing and good trekking country. Dunedin is famous as a centre for ecotourism, and the world's only mainland royal albatross colony and several penguin and seal colonies lie within the city boundaries. Employment is provided by Dunedin's vibrant niche industries, including biotechnology, engineering, fashion and software engineering, and its deep-water port.

Dunedin has two minor claims to fame: it has the world's most southern motorway, a 10km (6mi) section of State Highway One; and is home to Baldwin Street which, according to the *Guinness Book of Records*, is the steepest street in the world with an incline of an alarming 1:2.9.

Gisborne

Gisborne is New Zealand's most easterly city, situated on the east coast of central North Island. It's the closest city to the international dateline, making it the first city in the world to see the sun each day. Gisborne lies at the confluence of three rivers, the Taruheru, Turanganui and Waitamata, hence its nickname 'City of Bridges'.

The Gisborne district has a population of 45,000 (with around 30,000 in the city) and a pleasant climate, with warm summers and mild winters. It's one of the sunniest places in New Zealand, with around 2,200 hours per year. Gisborne is surrounded by rich farmland, producing beef, citrus, kiwi fruit, lamb, mutton, pork, wine and wool. It's also a decent surfing spot (60 per cent of locals are estimated to surf) and noted for its parks and recreational facilities.

Agriculture, forestry and associated manufacturing businesses are the backbone of Gisborne's economy, which is also one of New Zealand's three major grape growing areas, particularly for Muller Thurgau and Chardonnay. Wood processing is growing in importance, as are food processing, light manufacturing and tourism related industries.

Hamilton

Hamilton is New Zealand's fifth-largest city (and fourth-largest metropolitan area) and largest inland metropolitan area, with a population of around 125,000, including 25,000 students. It sits by the spectacular Waikato River in the Waikato district of the North Island, an hour and a half's drive south of Auckland, at a major rail and road terminus. The region has some of New Zealand's best agricultural land and Hamilton used to be primarily an agricultural service centre, but now has a diverse economy.

Education and research are important to the city's economy, notably through the University of Waikato and the agricultural research centre at Ruakura, the sources of much agricultural innovation in New Zealand. Hamilton hosts the annual National Agricultural Fieldays at Mystery Creek, the southern hemisphere's largest agricultural trade exhibition.

Mystery Creek is New Zealand's largest event centre, hosting events such as the National Boat Show and the National Car Show. Manufacturing and retail are also important to Hamilton's economy, as is the provision of health services, particularly at the Waikato Base Hospital. Hamilton is home to New Zealand's only aircraft-manufacturing business and also has its largest concentration of trailer-boat manufacturers.

Hamilton city centre is lively but some people find the city's newer suburbs bland and lacking in character. The city has a growing problem with traffic congestion.

Invercargill

Invercargill lies on the Southlands Plains on the Oreti (or New) River, bordered by large swathes of conservation land and marine reserves. It's the southernmost city in New Zealand and one of the world's most southerly settlements. Invercargill has a population of around 50,000 and is the commercial centre of the Southland region. The city has been regenerated in recent years, with the opening of many new bars, cafés, restaurants and shops.

Invercargill has a reputation as a friendly city and is a pleasant spot, with wide streets, historic buildings, good shopping and plenty of gardens and parks. It stresses the fact that it offers urban living without most of the drawbacks and has affordable housing and a welcome lack of traffic jams.

Farming, especially dairy and sheep, is key to the local economy. Invercargill is the gateway to New Zealand's southern coastline and Stewart Island, the only place in the world where you can see kiwis living in their natural environment. Its climate is temperate oceanic, similar to that of the UK (which might not be an attraction to potential British migrants!). Owing to its southerly latitude, the city enjoys 16 hours of daylight on the summer solstice in late December.

Napier

Napier is an important port city on Hawke's Bay on the east coast of the North Island, with a population of around 55,000. It lies 332km/210mi (by road) north-east of Wellington and is renowned for its '30s Art Deco architecture and its variety of entertainments. It's a popular year-round holiday destination and a retirement centre, enjoying a Mediterranean-like climate of long, warm summers and short, mild winters. The weather is relatively dry and Napier has some of the highest sunshine hours in New Zealand, although it's prone to the tail end of tropical cyclones from the central Pacific, which are sometimes still storm strength when they reach Hawke's Bay.

Napier claims to be the Art Deco Capital of the world. A huge earthquake (7.9 on the Richter scale) in 1931, along with the subsequent fires, destroyed much of Napier and the city was rebuilt in the styles of the era. As a result, it has one of the world's best range of '30s architecture, including Spanish

Mission, Stripped Classical and, above all, Art Deco. Napier's Art Deco has its own flavour, including Maori motifs and the Frank Lloyd Wright-influenced buildings of Louis Hay.

Napier is the largest city in the Hawke's Bay region, which is the most significant crossbred wool centre in the southern hemisphere and one of New Zealand's largest apple, pear and stone fruit producing areas. The region is also noted for its vineyards and wines, and Napier has one of New Zealand's busiest ports, shipping fruit, meat, pulp, timber and wool worldwide. Other local industries include electronics and fertiliser manufacturing.

Nelson

Nelson sits on the eastern side of Tasman Bay at the north end of the South Island. The combined population of Nelson and (adjoining) Richmond is around 55,000, ranking it as New Zealand's tenth most populous city. The geographical centre of New Zealand allegedly lies in Nelson, but the true centre is actually 35km (22mi) to the south-west.

Nelson is a centre of adventure tourism, ecotourism and caving, and is close to lakes, mountains and a national park. It also enjoys good beaches and a sheltered harbour. As if these natural advantages weren't enough, it's also reckoned by many to have New Zealand's best climate and regularly tops the statistics for sunshine hours, averaging over 2,400 per year.

The economy is based on forestry, horticulture, seafood and tourism (Nelson is a resort and retirement city), with Port Nelson the largest fishing port in Australasia. Other local growth industries include arts and crafts (there are over 350 working artists in Nelson), aviation, engineering and information technology.

New Plymouth

New Plymouth is the port and main city of the Taranaki region on the west coast of the North Island and is the only deep water port on New Zealand's west coast. It has a population of 50,000 and is a service centre for the region's main economic activities, which include dairy farming and gas, and oil and petrochemical exploration and production.

New Plymouth has a variety of attractions, including its excellent botanical gardens, a controversial 45m-high artwork (the Wind Wand) and views of Taranaki mountain (also called Mount Egmont). Locals also boast that, because New Plymouth is a coastal city with a mountain close by, you can waterski and ski on the same day.

Palmerston North

Palmerston North sits at the foot of the spectacular Tararua Mountain Range, on the banks of the Manawatu River in the centre of the Manawatu Plains in the Wanganui-Manawatu region of the North Island. It's around 140km (87mi) north of the capital, Wellington, and is home to around 80,000 people, including a large student population. Palmerston has one of the lowest costs of living of New Zealand's cities.

Palmerston North, known simply as 'Palmy' by the locals, is a major rail and road junction and the service centre for the surrounding region. The climate is noted for being windy, especially in spring, and it has some of the largest electricity generating wind farms in the southern hemisphere. Nearly 45 per cent of the workforce is employed in education, government and research, reflecting the important influence of the tertiary education centre. A quarter of the workforce is employed in the retail and wholesale sector.

Palmerston North's population has been falling in recent years, possibly because it isn't on the coast, which is where many people want to live. As a result of the population decline, the city has been trying to attract more residents, including a drive to persuade the British Lions rugby supporters who visited the city for a rugby match in summer 2005 to consider emigrating there!

Rotorua

Rotorua lies on the south shore of Lake Rotorua in the Bay of Plenty region of the North Island. It has a population of around 55,000 and a strong Maori heritage, claiming to be the heartland of New Zealand's Maori culture. Tourism is crucial to Rotorua (it attracts over 1.3 million visitors per year) and the city is a spa resort, famous for its geothermal activity, geysers and hot mud pools. It also has botanical gardens, some interesting historic architecture and is one of New Zealand's prime trout fishing spots.

Farming and forestry are important to the local economy and manufacturing is growing in significance, focusing on food, engineering and timber products. Rotorua's climate is temperate, cooled slightly by its relatively high altitude (290m/950ft). The weather is often sunny, rain is distributed fairly evenly throughout the year and it's less windy than much of the rest of the country.

Tauranga

Tauranga is a city in the Bay of Plenty region of the North Island, 105km (65mi) east of Hamilton and 85km (53mi) north of Rotorua. It's located on a large harbour, protected by Matakana Island, and this sheltered position gives it a warm, dry climate, making it a popular retirement and holiday destination.

Tauranga has a population of 106,500 and is the fastest-growing city in New Zealand, mostly due to the influx of retirees and sun and surf seekers. Mainstays of the local economy include beef and dairy farming, construction, the production of food, drink and tobacco, and manufacturing (especially machinery and metal products).

Wanganui City

Wanganui City is located on the South Taranaki Bight, close to the mouth of the Whanganui River (which is spelt differently, presumably to confuse everybody) in the south-west of the North Island. It has a temperate climate with slightly above the national average sunshine hours (2,100 per year).

Wanganui city is home to 40,000 people and its economy is based on the fertile land which surrounds the city. There's also some engineering and port facilities.

Wellington

Wellington is well sited on an impressive harbour at the southern end of the North Island, roughly in the centre of New Zealand. Although sometimes overshadowed by Auckland (partly because, apart from Air New Zealand and Qantas, few international airlines fly to Wellington), it's the country's financial and political capital, and the seat of the national government. It has boomed over the last five years, with thriving arts, culture and cafe and restaurant scenes (there are over 300 cafes and restaurants in Wellington). At 185,000, its population is only around a seventh of Auckland's.

In recent years, Wellington has been best known as the production base for the hugely successful and lucrative *Lord of the Rings* film trilogy.

Appropriately, the city is the centre of New Zealand's creative and film industries, and over half the country's software developers are based there. Those who work in the fields of biotechnology, information technology and telecommunications will also find plenty of job opportunities.

On the downside, some people find Wellington's weather not to their taste: summers are cool, with an average temperature of around 20°C (68°F), and the average minimum in winter is 6°C (43°F). However, the main drawback is the wind; along with Chicago, Wellington is dubbed the Windy City. Gales are prevalent in the summer and when autumn turns into winter, although winters are often calm. The wind in Wellington is sometimes so strong that it threatens the ferries that ply the waters between the North and the South Islands. In 1968, 50 people died when the car ferry Wahine sank during a particularly violent storm.

Whangarei

Whangarei is the largest urban area in the Northland region of the North Island, with a population of 50,000. It's the northernmost city in New Zealand, with a damp, subtropical climate, situated between forested hills and a spectacular deep water harbour, surrounded by fertile farmland, orchards and plenty of beaches.

Whangarei is a lively harbour town and the commercial and service centre for the Northland region, particularly the farming and forestry practised in the hinterland. Other industries include fishing, the oil refinery at Marsden Point, a luxury yacht building operation, tourism and a developing wine industry. Whangarei is the site of Parahaki, New Zealand's largest Maori Pa (fortified village).

REGIONS/STATES/TERRITORIES

Australia

Australian Capital Territory

The Australian Capital Territory occupies, by Australian standards, a tiny area (2,358km²/910mi²), and is wholly surrounded by New South Wales. It's dominated by Canberra, Australia's capital city, and has a population of around 345,000, the vast majority of whom live in and around Canberra.

Small towns in the ACT include Hall, Naas, Tharwa and Williamsdale. There's a modest amount of agricultural land (dairy cattle, sheep and some vineyards) and a large area of national park (Namadgi National Park), much of it forested and mountainous.

The ACT has internal self-government, but doesn't have the legislative independence of the Australian states. Its major industries, by far, are government and public service, and others include advanced technology (including communications, computing and electronics), hospitality, research and development, and tourism.

New South Wales

New South Wales is Australia's oldest and most populous state, covering 809,444km^2 (312,445mi^2), and is home to over 6.8 million people. It lies in the south-east of Australia, north of Victoria and south of Queensland. Its three main cities, from north to south, are Newcastle, Sydney and Wollongong, all on the coast. Sydney is by far the most significant city (not just in New South Wales, but in Australia). Important New South Wales towns

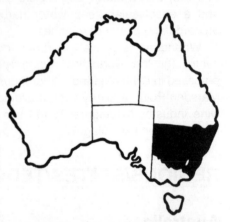

include Albury, Armidale, Broken Hill, Coffs Harbour, Dubbo, Lismore, Nowra and Tamworth.

New South Wales contains two Federal enclaves: the Australian Capital Territory (see above) and the Jervis Bay Territory. Jervis Bay (pop. around 750) was purchased from New South Wales so that Canberra would have access to the sea. It's a natural harbour, situated 150km (95mi) south of Sydney, and is a separate territory from the ACT, but is treated as part of it for most practical purposes.

New South Wales is divided geographically into four sections: a narrow coastal strip, with climates ranging from cool temperate in the south to subtropical towards the Queensland border; the mountainous Great Dividing Range, with many peaks over 1,000m (3,280ft) and the highest, Mount Kosciuszko, reaching 2,229m (7,308ft); the agricultural plains that cover much of the state, with a much lower population than the coastal strip; and the thinly populated dry plains of the north-west.

New South Wales's economy is based around agricultural and pastoral industries, large coal reserves, a varied manufacturing sector and sophisticated service industries. The agricultural and mining sectors earn almost half of the state's export revenues. The major manufacturing products are chemicals, electrical goods, fertilisers, machinery, metal products and processed foods.

The Northern Territory

The Northern Territory lies in the central northern part of Australia and has only 1 per cent of the country's population (around 200,000, often known as Territorians), despite covering a sixth of the Australian continent, 1,420,968km^2 (548,495mi^2). Sizeable settlements are rare and include the capital Darwin, nearby Palmerston, Katherine (near the bottom of the Top End, see below) and Alice Springs, in the desert 1,500km (935mi) to the south. Small  settlements are scattered around much of the Northern Territory, but the larger centres are all found on the state's one sealed road, the Stuart Highway (known locally as 'the track'), linking Darwin to South Australia.

The Northern Territory is home to some spectacular rock formations and scenery, which are major tourist attractions. Uluru (Ayers Rock) and Kata Tjuta (The Olgas) are the most famous rock formations, while the Kakadu National Park in the north of the state contains some remarkable wetlands and wildlife. Most of the Northern Territory (around 80 per cent) lies within the tropics and the 6,200km (3,870mi) coastline is generally flat, backed by mangroves, mudflats and swamps, while much of the interior is plateau with some mountain ranges. The northern quarter of the state is known as the 'Top End', a region of savannah, woodlands and pockets of rainforest.

The isolation and frontier spirit of the Northern Territory are an attraction for some people, but conditions can be harsh, particularly the gruellingly hot climate, and the Northern Territory's alcohol consumption is one of the highest in the world, estimated to be an impressive (or appalling) 1,120 standard drinks per person per year.

The Northern Territory's economy is based on cattle (the state has some huge cattle stations, covering thousands of square kilometres), mining (including bauxite, copper, diamonds, gold, manganese, silver and zinc) and seafood. The state also has reserves of natural gas, oil and uranium.

Queensland

Queensland covers 1,852,642km^2 (715,120mi^2) of the north-east of Australia and is home to around 3.8 million people. The northernmost part of the state is the Cape York Peninsula, a huge triangular area that tapers towards New Guinea. To the west of Queensland lies the Northern Territory, to the east is the Pacific Ocean and to the south is New South Wales.

Queensland's population is less centralised than the rest of Australia, with Brisbane having only 45 per cent of the state's population, against a national average for state capitals of around 64 per cent. The state is home to the largest city (by area) in the world, Mount Isa, which covers over 40,000km^2 (15,440mi^2). The year-round warm climate of Queensland is an attraction for many immigrants (but puts off others, as does the humidity that often accompanies the heat) and another draw is the fact that Brisbane has the lowest cost of living of Australia's state and territory capital cities.

Queensland's major industries are agriculture (especially bananas and pineapples, along with a wide range of other tropical and temperate fruit and vegetables), cattle, cotton, mining (including bauxite, coal and copper), sugar cane and wool. Retail and tourism are also important to the economy. The Great Barrier Reef is a major tourist draw for Queensland. It's the world's largest coral reef, over 2,000km (1,250mi) long, and can be seen from space. The reef is sometimes inaccurately described as the world's largest living organism, although it's actually many separate coral colonies.

South Australia

South Australia is situated in the southern central part of the country, along the Southern Ocean. It covers an area of 984,377km² (379,970mi²) and has a population of around 1.575 million, most of whom live in the fertile coastal areas and in the Murray River valley. South Australia has borders with all mainland states and territories except for the Australian Capital Territory. It consists mainly of arid and semi-arid rangelands, with several low mountain ranges. In the west of the state is the thinly-populated Nullarbor Plain.

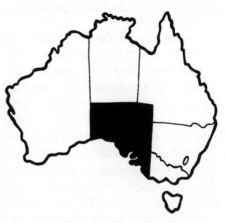

South Australia's economic growth has lagged behind the rest of Australia for some time (partly because of the collapse of the State Bank in 1992), although its performance is improving. The state's main industries and exports are wheat, wine and wool, and over half of Australia's wines are produced in South Australia. German immigrants fleeing religious persecution brought with them the vine cuttings that founded the famous wineries of South Australia's Barossa Valley. Clare Valley, Coonawarra and McLaren Vale are other noted South Australian wine areas. Manufacturing is also important to the state's economy, generating 15 per cent of GDP, particularly car and component manufacturing, defence technology and pharmaceuticals. South Australia is known as the Festival State (because of the annual festivals held in Adelaide – see **Adelaide** on page 63) and as the Wine State.

Tasmania

The island state of Tasmania is situated 240km (150mi) south of the south-east corner of the Australian mainland, separated from it by the Bass Strait. It's thought that Tasmania was joined to the mainland until the end of the last ice age, around 10,000 years ago. The state covers 68,332km²

(26,383mi^2) and has a population of around 460,000. It's the only Australian state with any land to the south of the 40th parallel and is known as the apple state due (unsurprisingly) to the large amount of apples grown there.

Tasmania's capital and largest city is Hobart, which comprises the cities of Clarence, Glenorchy and Hobart. Other major population centres include Launceston in the north and Burnie and Devonport in the north-west. The sub-Antarctic Macquarie Island is under Tasmania's administration.

Tasmania is a rugged island with a temperate climate, regarded by some early English colonists as so similar to pre-Industrial England that they dubbed it 'Southern England'. Geographically, much of Tasmania is similar to New Zealand (which isn't something that would impress the average Aussie!), but because it hasn't been volcanically active in recent geological times, its mountains are softer and more rounded than New Zealand's.

The island's most mountainous region is the Central Highlands, which covers much of the central western parts of Tasmania. The Midlands (the central eastern area) is flat by comparison and is mainly used for agriculture. The west coast has high rainfall, sufficient to power hydro-electric schemes, and the area is also important for mineral production. The south-west of Tasmania is particularly densely forested and the National Park has some of the southern hemsiphere's last temperate rainforests. Most of Tasmania's population lives on and around the coastal rivers, the Derwent and Huron in the south, and the Mersey and Tamar in the north.

Tasmania has the smallest revenue of Australia's states, with an annual budget similar to Brisbane's. The island's economy has, for a long time, been temperamental. This has been attributed to different reasons at different times, including: not having a gold rush; a lack of federal infrastructure; too small a population; a decline in the mineral and wool markets; and a lack of foreign investment. A significant drain on the state's economy is the continuing exodus of people, particularly the young, to the mainland seeking better job opportunites.

Tasmania's main industries are agriculture, forestry, mining (including copper, iron, tin and zinc) and tourism. Major employers on the island include the government, the Federal Group (which owns Tasmania's two casinos) and Gunns Limited, the state's largest forestry company. Some Australian companies have also moved their call centres to Tasmania. Manufacturing has declined greatly in recent years, adding to the exodus of people to the mainland, in this case experienced, trained workers.

Tasmania's economic ups and downs, as well as the relative isolation of life on an island, have made some Tasmanians see themselves and the world differently from the majority of mainlanders. This is reflected in the island's large arts community and strong environmental movement. But the environmental community has often had a divisive effect in Tasmania because its work has led to large areas of the island being conserved as national parks and other protected areas. This has severely limited economic development in these areas, most notably for the forestry and mining industries. Environmentalists argue that this is more than compensated for by the fact that a pristine environment attracts more tourists and retirees to Tasmania. There may be something to this: the island's historic sites, unspoiled environment and temperate climate have made Tasmania an increasingly popular choice with retirees, keen to escape the mainland's bushfires, coastal (over)development, droughts and heat.

Victoria

Victoria lies in the far south-east of the country and is Australia's smallest mainland state by area (csovering 237,629km²/91,725mi²). Its northern border is the south bank of the Murray River, the river itself being part of New South Wales. South Australia lies to the west and there's ocean to the east and south.

Victoria has a population of around 5 million, making it Australia's most densely populated state. The capital, Melbourne, is home to some 70 per cent of the state's population and dominates Victoria's culture, economy and media. But Victoria has many other attractions, including the Budj Bim National Heritage Landscape, skiing in the Victorian Alps and tours around the state's wine producing areas. Victoria is also the base of a particular local passion, Australian Rules Football, and is home to ten of the 16 major league clubs.

Historically, Victoria's economy relied on brown coal mining, gold mining and offshore oil drilling, and still does, to some extent. In 1851, gold was discovered at Ballarat, then at Bendigo and subsequently at sites all over Victoria, triggering one of the world's largest gold rushes.

Melbourne is an important manufacturing and service centre, but agriculture dominates Victoria's economy, boosted by the fact that the state has reasonably rich soils and a temperate, wet climate, compared with the rest of Australia. Major agricultural exports include beef and dairy cattle, sheep products (lamb and wool) and wheat (mainly from the drier western half of the state). Wine grape production is becoming more important, particularly as some of Australia's wine makers are seeking favoured cooler regions of the country in order to make more sophisticated, subtle wines.

Victoria's climate varies from the wet, temperate conditions of Gippsland in the south-east, to the alpine climate of the snow-covered mountains (Mount Bogong is the state's highest peak, at 1,986m/6,515ft) and the extensive semi-arid plains of the west and north-west. Owing to its reasonably high rainfall, Victoria has an extensive network of rivers.

Western Australia

Western Australia is Australia's largest state, covering the westernmost third of the Australian mainland. It covers 2,645,615km^2 (1,021,205mi^2) and borders South Australia and the Northern Territory. Western Australia's population is around 1.95 million, many of whom live in the state capital Perth and the surrounding area. Western Australia is the country's fastest growing state and has the lowest unemployment rate. In recent years it has had the  highest rate of overseas migration (the majority from the UK), outnumbered only by arrivals from other Australian states.

Perth lies on the south-west coast of the state (and the country), and the Perth Metropolitan area has grown to include the port of Fremantle and the town of Rockingham. Other important centres in Western Australia include Albany, Broome, Bunbury, Geraldton, Kalgoorlie and Port Hedland, but all are small. The south-west coastal area of the state is the best suited to human habitation, being relatively temperate and forested, while much of the rest of Western Australia is very hot and semi-arid or desert, and lightly populated. One exception, weather-wise, is the northern tropical region, especially the Kimberley.

Western Australia's economy has long been largely based on the extraction and export of mining and petroleum commodities, especially alumina, gold, iron ore, natural gas and nickel. The state is a leading alumina extractor and produces over 20 per cent of the world's aluminium. Western Australia is the world's third-largest iron ore producer, with around 16 per cent of global output, and extracts around 75 per cent of Australia's 240 tonnes of gold each year.

Agricultural exports are important to Western Australia, especially barley, sheep products (meat and wool) and wheat. Tourism is growing in importance, with most of the state's visitors coming from the UK, Ireland, Singapore, Japan and Malaysia.

New Zealand – The North Island

The regions/unitary districts of the North Island described below are arranged geographically, roughly from north to south, rather than alphabetically.

Northland

Northland is (unsurprisingly) the northernmost of New Zealand's administrative regions, located in what Kiwis sometimes call the Far North or the Winterless North (because of the kind climate, with warm, humid summers and mild winters.). It occupies the top 80 per cent (285km/178mi) of the North Auckland Peninsula, encompassing just over 5 per cent of New Zealand's total area. To the west is the Tasman Sea and to the east the Pacific Ocean. Much of the terrain is rolling hill country and farming and forestry (the region's main industries) occupy over half the land.

The west coast of Northland is dominated by several long straight beaches, the most famous os which is the inaccurately named (80km/50mi) Ninety Mile Beach. The west coast has two large inlets, Kaipara Harbour and Hokianga Harbour. The east coast is more rugged, with bays, peninsulas and several large natural harbours. Northland is still home to kauri forests (the kauri is a coniferous tree native to the northern North Island, which grow up to 50m/165ft tall), although many of the forests were decimated in the 19th century.

Northland is New Zealand's least urbanised region, with only around half of the population of 150,000 living in urban areas. Whangarei is the region's largest population centre, home to around 50,000 people, and seven other centres have populations of over 1,000. Around a third of the population is Maori, most of the rest being of European descent. Pacific Islanders are under-represented, compared with the rest of New Zealand.

Northland's economy is based on agriculture (particularly beef cattle), fishing, forestry and horticulture (particularly citrus fruit). Wood and paper manufacturing are also important and the region is a popular tourist destination, especially the Bay of Islands. Northland has New Zealand's only oil refinery, at Marsden Point near Whangarei.

Auckland

Auckland is the second-smallest region (after Nelson), set on and around the isthmus of Auckland in the north of the North Island. Its coastline is bordered by the Tasman Sea and the Pacific, and the region has many fine beaches. Despite its small size, the Auckland region is by far the most populous, home to around 1.3 million people, roughly a third of New Zealand's population.

The region encompasses the cities of the Auckland metropolitan area, smaller towns, rural areas and the islands of the Hauraki Gulf. It's very much dominated by the city of Auckland, which comprises much of the region.

Waikato

Waikato is situated in the northern central area of the North Island. The coastal area is mainly rough hill country, bounded by the Tasman Sea, with three large natural harbours: Aotea, Kawhia and Raglan. The area around Ragland is noted for its volcanic black sand beaches and fine surfing, and Waikato has some spectacular subterranean caverns.

East of the coastal hills is the Waikato River floodplain, with a wet, temperate climate and rich farmland, home to most of the region's population. Waikato's economy is heavily reliant on agriculture and is intensively farmed with crops and livestock, while the upper reaches of the Waikato river are used for hydroelectricity and the northern region produces good wines. Other industries include business services, communications and tourism, but these are less highly developed than in many other parts of New Zealand.

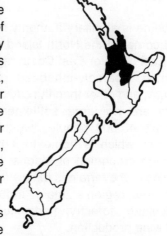

The city of Hamilton is the region's main centre (population 125,000) and the towns of Cambridge, Te Awamutu and Tokoroa each have between 10,000 and 15,000 inhabitants. The people of Waikato sometimes use the nickname Mooloo for themselves or their province, but nobody seems to know why.

Bay of Plenty (BoP)

The Bay of Plenty is a region situated around a body of water of the same name. The population is around 260,000 and the region is dominated by two cities: Tauranga (population 106,500) and Rotorua (population 55,000). As a compromise between the two, the town of Whakatane was chosen as the seat for the Bay of Plenty Regional Council (rather like the choice of Canberra as Australia's capital, which was a compromise between Melbourne and Sydney). Agriculture and tourism are the region's economic mainstays, with the geothermal region around Rotorua being one of New Zealand's most popular tourist destinations.

Gisborne

Gisborne is a unitary authority in the north-east corner of the North Island, also called the East Cape or East Coast region. It's an isolated, sparsely-inhabited part of the country, and other than the city of Gisborne, there are no large settlements. Of the region's 45,000 people, two-thirds live in the city, which is home to a higher than average proportion of Maoris. Inland from the coast, the terrain is mainly forested hills and the region's main industries are agriculture, forestry, horticulture, tourism and wine production.

Hawke's Bay

Hawke's Bay is a region on the east coast of the North Island, bearing the name of what is now Hawke Bay, a 100km (62mi) circular bay. To add to the slight confusion regarding names, the region is often referred to as 'The Hawke's Bay', and the use of the apostrophe seems to have become optional.

The region comprises hilly coastal land around the bay, the Wairoa River floodplains in the north, the Heretunga Plains around Hastings in the south and a mountainous interior. The population is 145,000, of whom 55,000 live in the city of Napier. Hawke's Bay has a significant Maori population (around 20 per cent). The climate is temperate and dry, and the region is known for its horticulture, with extensive orchards and vineyards, while in the more hilly areas, cattle and sheep farming and forestry are important sectors.

Taranaki

Taranaki is situated on a peninsula on the west coast of the North Island. Mount Taranaki is the region's dominant feature, the second-highest mountain on the North Island. The region covers a modest area of 7,258km² (2,800mi²) and has a population of 105,000, just under half of whom live in the city of New Plymouth.

Taranaki is very fertile due to its rich volcanic soil and high rainfall. Dairy farming is dominant and the milk factory outside Hawera is the second-largest in the southern hemisphere. Taranaki also has on and offshore gas and oil deposits; the Maui gas field off the north coast provides most of New Zealand's gas and supports two methane plants. The region has some excellent surfing and windsurfing areas, some of which are world-class.

Wanganui-Manawatu

As well as being something of a mouthful, Wanganui-Manawatu is a region towards the bottom of the North Island. It's dominated by and named after the two river catchments of Manawatu and Wanganui, the latter of which is the longest navigable river in New Zealand. Wanganui-Manawatu's population of 225,000 is New Zealand's fifth-largest. The two major urban areas are Palmerston North (population 80,000) and Wanganui (population 40,000). Half of the region's population lives outside a large urban area.

Wanganui-Manawatu is the North Island's second-largest region and the sixth-largest in New Zealand, covering 22,215km²/8,575mi² (8.1 per cent of the country's total land area). The region has a range of low, medium and high terrains, including a series of mountain ranges (notably the Ruahine and Tararua Ranges) and includes the three main active volcanoes on the North Island.

The region's soils are productive if fertilised and it's one of New Zealand's most important pastoral areas. Manufacturing has also become important to the economy, although most businesses are agriculturally-based. The region has areas of great ecological significance and a seventh of its land is part of New Zealand's conservation estate. The rugged interior is an important training area for New Zealand's defence forces, which have three bases in the region.

Wanganui-Manawatu's climate is relatively mild, but more extreme inland. Chateau Tongariro 'boasts' New Zealand's lowest recorded temperature (-13.6C, in 1937). Sunshine hours in much of the region are around the national average (1,900 hours per year), but Palmerston North is often cloudy, with an average of 1,725 hours.

Wellington

Wellington is a region in the very south of the North Island, bordered to the west, south and east by water. To the west lies the Tasman Sea, to the east the Pacific, which are connected by the Cook Strait, a narrow, unpredictable stretch between the North and South Islands, only 28km (17mi) wide at its narrowest.

Over three-quarters of the region's 450,000 people live in the four cities in the south-west corner of the region, especially the capital, Wellington. The region of Wellington has some fine beaches on the narrow coastal strip, while the inland area comprises undulating hills and rough hill country. The economy is largely dependent on the government sector along with business services (many of which work with the government sector).

New Zealand – The South Island

The regions/unitary districts of the South Island described below are arranged geographically, roughly north to south, rather than alphabetically.

Tasman

Tasman is a region at the northern tip of the South Island. Its northern corner includes the prominent, narrow peninsula, Farewell Spit, and the Kahurangi

National Park. The south and east of the region are dominated by undulating countryside. Tasman has three national parks, which comprise almost 60 per cent of the total area. The population is around 45,000, only 1.1 per cent of New Zealand's total, and most of Tasman's urban population (around 11,000) lives in the Richmond area. Tasman has the country's highest percentage of people of European background, nearly 97 per cent. Community spirit is important in the region and Tasman has a higher proportion of people involved in voluntary work than any other region.

The Tasman region's major industries are agriculture (it's New Zealand's main hop growing area), fishing and forestry, and there's a significant population of artists and craftspeople (more than in any other region of New Zealand). It's also a popular place to retire and has a growing viticultural sector.

Nelson

The region of Nelson mostly comprises, and is dominated by, the city of Nelson. Geographically, the region is split into five areas: the alpine lakes and rivers around Nelson Lakes; the parks around Golden Bay; the coastline of the Abel Tasman National Park; the horticultural land of Mapua, Motueka and Moutere; and the urban centres of Nelson and Richmond. The economy is based on agriculture and natural resources.

Marlborough

Marlborough is a region in the north-east of the South Island. The southern section is mountainous, while the central area contains extensive plains, in the middle of which is the town of Blenheim. This area, which is where the majority of the region's population lives, has a temperate climate and fertile soils, and it has become the centre of New Zealand's highly successful wine production industry. The north coast of Marlborough is very attractive, as it's made up of the 'drowned' valleys of the Marlborough Sounds. Agriculture and the exploitation of natural resources are the mainstays of the region's economy.

West Coast

The West Coast is a long, thin region, 600km/375mi in length, covering much of the west coast of the South Island. It seems a land apart to many New Zealanders, being remote, although beautiful, and inhabited by people with a peculiar (in the proper sense of the word) identity. The region is often known simply as 'The Coast' and its inhabitants are called Coasters.

To the west of the West Coast region lies the Tasman Sea, and to the east are the Southern Alps. Much of the region's land is rugged and most of the population lives on the coastal plains. West Coast is noted for its beautiful, varied terrain, with wild coastlines, mountains and native bush, some of which is temperate rain forest. West Coast has very high rainfall (hence the rain forest) due to the prevailing north-west winds and the proximity of the Southern Alps.

The West Coast region has a small population (around 32,000), and the main towns are Greymouth, Hokitika and Westport. Local industries include farming, fishing, forestry, mining for alluvial gold and coal, tourism and wood processing. The region is home to one of New Zealand's last independent dairy co-operatives, the Westland Dairy Company, which remained independent when most farmer-owned dairies merged to form Fonterra, the world's largest, farmer-owned dairy co-operative.

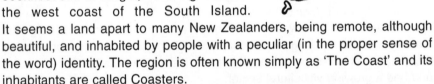

Canterbury

Canterbury is New Zealand's largest region, covering 42,200km² (16,290mi²) and the majority of the east coast of the South Island. The Canterbury Plains make up much of the region of Canterbury and the land is suitable for reasonably intensive agriculture, but prone to droughts.

Much of Canterbury's population lives in a series of large and small settlements spread north-east to south-west along the plains, joined by State Highway 1. Canterbury is the region's main city. The economy is dependent on various manufacturing industries, particularly beverages, food and tobacco, and tourism is also important.

Otago

The Otago region is in the south-east of the South Island. It covers 32,000km² (12,350mi²), making it New Zealand's second-largest region, with a population of 185,000. The major centre is Dunedin. Kaitangata is a major coal source, but the economy is heavily reliant on agriculture and its related manufacturing industries, especially food and tobacco. Tourism is also important to the economy, as is Otago University.

Southland

Southland is (unsurprisingly) New Zealand's most southern region. It's an area of physical contrast, including Fiordland, a rugged area of fiords, lakes and mountains; rolling hills and plains; and Stewart Island across the Foveaux Strait, which is rich in native bush and wildlife. Southland also has a variety of climates, wet in Fiordland and drier in the north. The air quality in the region is better than in much of the rest of the country.

Southland has long been the centre of New Zealand's sheep farming industry and has recently diversified into beef production, dairy farming, deer farming, forestry and horticulture. Other major industries are dairy processing, fertiliser production, fishing, manufacturing, meat processing and tourism. Southland also has a vibrant cottage industry producing carvings, pottery and sculptures, and the region is rich in raw materials, including 65 per cent of New Zealand's coal reserves.

Southland has one city, Invercargill, and many of the region's people have Scottish ancestry. Its farming success is mainly the result of Scottish agricultural experience.

LOCATION

The most important consideration when buying a home anywhere is usually its location – or, as the old adage goes, the three most important considerations are location, location and location! If you're looking for a good investment, a property in reasonable condition in a popular area is likely to be greatly preferable to an exceptional property in an out-of-the-way location. Even if you aren't concerned with making money from your property, there's little point in buying a 'dream home' if it's right next to a motorway or a rubbish dump or is so inaccessible that a trip to the baker is a major expedition. Australia and New Zealand offer almost everything that anyone could want, but you must choose the right property in the right spot. The wrong decision regarding location is one of the main causes of disenchantment among foreigners who have purchased property in Australia and New Zealand.

Many people's choice of location is based on previous holidays, friends' recommendations, accessibility or simply an area's reputation. However, if you're likely to be spending the rest of your life in your new home, and even if you will only be spending the occasional holiday there, it's worth taking the time and trouble to consider every aspect of its location first hand. When choosing a permanent home, don't be too influenced by where you've spent an enjoyable holiday or two. A place that was acceptable for a few weeks' holiday may be far from suitable for year-round living.

The 'best' place to live in Australia or New Zealand obviously depends on your preferences and it's impossible to specify a best location for everyone. The important thing is to identify the positive and possible negative aspects of each of your selected locations in order to help you to choose the one that suits you and your family best.

If you have a job in Australia or New Zealand, the location of a home will probably be determined by its proximity to your place of employment. Obtain a map of the area and decide the maximum distance you're prepared to travel to work, then draw a circle of the appropriate radius with your workplace in the middle. If you intend to look for employment or start a business, you must live in an area that allows you the maximum scope. Unless you have reason to believe otherwise, you would be foolish to rely on finding employment in a particular area. If, on the other hand, you're seeking a holiday or retirement home, you will have a huge choice of areas.

If you have little idea about where you wish to live, read as much as you can about the different cities and regions of Australia and New Zealand (see page 83) and spend time investigating your areas of interest. Note that the climate, lifestyle and cost of living can vary considerably from region to region (and even within a particular region). Before looking at properties, it's important to have a good idea of the kind of home you're looking for and the price you wish to pay, and to draw up a shortlist of the areas or towns of interest. If you don't do this, you're likely to be overwhelmed by the number of properties to be viewed. Estate agents usually expect serious buyers to know where they want to buy within a 30 to 40km (20 to 25mi) radius and some even expect clients to narrow it down to specific towns and villages.

Don't, however, believe the times and distances stated in adverts and by estate agents. According to some agents' magical mystery maps, everywhere in New South Wales is handy for Sydney and all homes in New Zealand's North Island are convenient for Auckland. Check distances and ease of access yourself.

If possible, you should visit an area a number of times over a period of a few weeks, both on weekdays and at weekends, in order to get a feel for the neighbourhood (don't just drive around, but walk!). A property seen on a balmy summer's day after a delicious lunch and a few glasses of chilled wine may not be nearly so attractive on a subsequent visit without sunshine and the warm inner glow.

You should also try to visit an area at different times of the year, e.g. in both summer and winter, as somewhere that's wonderful in summer can be forbidding and inhospitable in winter (or vice versa). If you're planning to buy a winter holiday home (yes, they do ski in Australia and New Zealand), you should also view it in the summer, as snow can hide a multitude of sins! In any case, you should view a property a number of times before deciding to buy it. If you're unfamiliar with an area, most experts recommend that you rent for a period before deciding to buy (see **Renting Before Buying** on page 141). This is particularly important if you're planning to buy a permanent or retirement home in an unfamiliar area. Many people change their minds after a period and it isn't unusual for families to move once or twice before settling down permanently.

When house hunting, obtain large scale maps of the area where you're looking. These make it easy to mark off the places that you've seen. You could do this using a grading system to denote your impressions. If you use an estate agent, he will usually drive you around and you can return later to those that you like most at your leisure (provided you've marked them on your map!).

You should also check the medium-term infrastructure plans for the area, with both the local and national authorities, particularly with regard to planned road and railway construction. Although a rural plot may seem miles from anywhere today, there could be plans for a motorway passing along the boundaries within the next five or ten years.

Foreign buyers aren't welcome everywhere, particularly when they 'colonise' a town or area (see **Community** below). However, foreigners are generally welcomed by the local populace (even whingeing Poms!), not least because they boost the local economy and bring work skills that are in short supply. Permanent residents in rural areas who take the time and trouble to integrate with the local community are invariably warmly welcomed.

The 'best' place to live in Australia or New Zealand depends on a range of considerations, including the following:

Accessibility

Is the proximity to public transport, e.g. an international airport, port or railway station, or access to a motorway important? Bear in mind that outside the main cities public transport in Australia and New Zealand is often thin on the ground. And don't believe all you're told about the distance or travelling times to the nearest motorway, airport, railway station, port, beach or town, but check it for yourself.

SURVIVAL TIP
Although it isn't so important if you're buying a permanent home in Australia or New Zealand and planning to stay put, one of the major considerations when buying a holiday home is communications (e.g. air links and links to airports) with your home country.

If you buy a remote country property, the distance to local amenities and services could become a problem, particularly if you plan to retire to Australia or New Zealand. If you're buying a home with a view to retiring there later, check the local public transport, as you may not always be able (or wish) to drive. See also **Getting Around** on page 117.

Although budget and smaller airlines have recently made accessible previously remote parts of Australia and New Zealand, such services are notoriously fickle and it isn't wise to buy in a particular area purely because it's served by cheap flights; airlines create and cancel routes (and are bought and sold) at the drop of a hat and you could be left stranded.

Amenities

What local health and social services are provided? How far is the nearest hospital with an emergency department? What shopping facilities are provided in the neighbourhood? How far is it to the nearest town with good shopping facilities, e.g. a supermarket? How would you get there if your car was out of commission? If you live in a remote rural area you will need to be much more self-sufficient than if you live in a town.

Don't forget that Australia is a huge country, and New Zealand can also seem quite large if you live in a remote area, and those living in rural areas will need to use the car for everything. It has been calculated that it costs some $10,000 a year (including depreciation costs) to run a new small car doing around 15,000km (9,300mi) a year (which is less than average). Note also that many rural villages have few shops or facilities and aren't usually a good choice for a retirement home.

Climate

For most people the climate (see page 22) is one of the most important factors when buying a home in Australia or New Zealand, particularly a holiday or retirement home. Bear in mind both the winter and summer climate as well as the position of the sun and the direction of the prevailing wind. The orientation or aspect of a building is vital and you must ensure that balconies, terraces and gardens face the right direction.

Community

When choosing the area, decide whether you want to live among your own countrymen and other foreigners in a largely expatriate community, such as in parts of Perth, or whether you prefer (and are prepared) to integrate into an exclusively Australian or New Zealand environment.

However, unless you speak English fluently or intend to learn it, you should think twice before buying a property in a village. Note that the locals in some villages resent 'outsiders' moving in, particularly foreigners, although those who take the time and trouble to integrate into the local community are usually warmly welcomed.

If you're buying a permanent home, it's important to check out your prospective neighbours, particularly when buying an apartment. For example, are they noisy, sociable or absent for long periods? Do you think you will get on with them? Good neighbours are invaluable, particularly when buying a second home in Australia or New Zealand.

Crime

What is the local crime rate? In some areas the incidence of burglary is extremely high, which not only affects your security but also increases your insurance premiums. Is crime increasing or decreasing? Note that professional crooks like isolated houses, particularly those full of expensive furniture and other belongings, which they can strip bare at their leisure. You're much less likely to be a victim of theft if you live in a village, where strangers stand out like sore thumbs. See also **Crime** on page 292.

Employment

How secure is your job or business and are you likely to move to another area in the near future? Can you find other work in the same area, if necessary? What about your partner's and children's jobs? If there's a possibility that you will need to move in some years' time, you should rent or at least buy a property that will be relatively easy to sell.

Garden

If you're planning to buy a country property with a large plot of land, bear in mind the high cost and amount of work involved in its upkeep. If it's to be a second home, who will look after the house and garden when you're away? Do you want to spend your holidays mowing the lawn and cutting back the undergrowth? Do you want a home with a lot of outbuildings? What are you going to do with them? Can you afford to convert them into extra rooms or guest accommodation?

Local Council

Is the local council well run? Unfortunately, some are profligate and simply use any extra income to hire a few more of their cronies or spend it on grandiose schemes, and some councillors abuse their positions to further their own ends. What are the views of other residents? If the municipality is efficiently run, you can usually rely on good local social and sports services and other facilities.

Natural Phenomena

Check whether an area is particularly susceptible to natural disasters, such as bush fires, cyclones, droughts, earthquakes, floods and violent storms. If a property is located near a waterway, it may be expensive to insure against floods, which are a constant threat in some areas. See also **Inspections & Surveys** on page 172.

Noise

Noise can be a problem in some cities, resorts and developments. Although you cannot choose your neighbours, you can at least ensure that a property isn't located next to a busy road, industrial plant, commercial area, discotheque, night club, bar or restaurant (where revelries may continue into the early hours). Look out for objectionable neighbouring properties which may be too close to the one you're considering and check whether nearby vacant land has been 'zoned' for commercial use. In community developments (e.g. apartment blocks) neighbouring properties may be second homes which are let short-term, which means you may need to tolerate boisterous holidaymakers as neighbours throughout the year (or at least during the summer months).

Don't assume, however, that rural life is necessarily tranquil. Other kinds of noise can disturb your peace and quiet, including chiming church bells, barking dogs, crowing cockerels and other farmyard animals, and aircraft if you live near a civil or military airfield. On the other hand, those looking to buy a rural property should note that there may be times when noisy activities such as lawnmowing are prohibited (e.g. at lunchtime on Saturdays and all afternoon on Sundays).

Parking

If you're planning to buy in a town or city, is there adequate private or free on-street parking for your family and visitors? Is it safe to park in the street? In some areas it's important to have secure off-street parking if you value your car. Parking is a problem in many towns and most cities, where private garages or parking spaces can be very expensive. Bear in mind that an apartment or townhouse in a town or community development may be some distance from the nearest road or car park. How do you feel about carrying heavy shopping hundreds of metres to your home and possibly up several flights of stairs? Traffic congestion is also a problem in many towns and tourist resorts, particularly during the high season.

Position

New Zealanders tend to place a great deal of importance on the position and orientation of their homes. Properties in positions that catch the sun usually sell at a premium over those in shady spots because they tend to be not only brighter but also warmer in winter. In Wellington, for example, any property that's sheltered from the wind and isn't forever in the shadows cast by the surrounding hills is likely to be worth significantly more and will also be more pleasant to live in. Also bear in mind that many areas of New Zealand, particularly in the North Island, are susceptible to flash floods after torrential rain. It's therefore wise to avoid properties located near rivers and streams (which can quickly become raging torrents) or situated in hollows.

By contrast, in the hotter, sunnier parts of Australia some buyers prefer properties that aren't bathed in sunshine all the time and are especially keen to buy homes whose gardens and/or swimming pools receive a lot of shade and therefore protection from the punishing sun.

Property Market

Do houses sell well in the area, e.g. in less than six months? Generally you should avoid areas where desirable houses routinely remain on the market for six months or longer (unless the market is in a slump and nothing is selling).

Schools

Consider your children's present and future schooling. What is the quality of local schools? Are there any bi-lingual or international schools nearby? Note that, even if your family has no need or plans to use local schools, the value of a home may be influenced by the quality and location of schools.

Sports & Leisure Facilities

What is the range and quality of local leisure, sports, community and cultural facilities? What is the proximity to sports facilities such as a beach, golf course, ski resort or waterway? Bear in mind that properties in or close to ski and coastal resorts are considerably more expensive, although they also have the best letting potential. If you're interested in a winter holiday home, which area should you choose?

Termites

Termites or white ants are a problem in many areas of Australia. According to Archicentre, the building advisory service of the Royal Australian Institute of Architects, 650,000 homes in Australia have been damaged by termites. They also estimate that the average cost of treatment for a home with termites by a pest controller is $1,500, and the average cost of repair for a home with termite damage is $4,500.

Tasmania is the only state free of 'economically significant' termite attacks on buildings. Parts of all the other states and territories (particularly coastal regions and their hinterlands, i.e. where most people live) have a high risk from termites. The highest risk is in Queensland and the Northern Territory, the lowest in Western Australia. New Zealand has a much lower risk from termites, although some areas have had infestations, for example Otorohanga (south of Hamilton and south-west of Rotorua) has been stigmatised following termite problems. New Zealand has had strict border controls since the '40s to prevent the arrival of termite-infested material from Australia, and they've generally been successful.

The risk of termite infestation is a good reason to have a full survey before buying property in Australia. Obvious signs of termite or other borer problems include pin holes in architraves, small piles of fine dust on the floor and deterioration of floor joists and timber beams. Ways to avoid becoming a victim of termites include not storing firewood or timber under a property, not stacking wood against timber walls, not raising garden beds by piling earth against walls and by making sure that there's no termite-affected furniture in the house.

Archicentre provides a termite and borer fact sheet on its website (🖳 www.archicentre.com.au/survival_kit/termites_borers.pdf).

Tourists

Bear in mind that if you live in a popular tourist area, you will be inundated with tourists in summer and all year in warmer regions or those with skiing. They won't only jam the roads and pack the public transport, but may even occupy your favourite table at your local cafe or restaurant! Although a 'front-line' property on the beach or in a marina development may sound attractive and be ideal for short holidays, it isn't usually the best choice for permanent residents. Many beaches are hopelessly crowded in the high season, streets may be smelly from restaurants and fast food outlets, parking impossible, services stretched to breaking point, and the incessant noise may drive you crazy. You may also have to tolerate water restrictions in some areas.

Town Or Country?

Do you wish to be in a town or do you prefer the country? Bear in mind that if you buy a property in the country, you will probably have to put up with poor public transport (or none at all), long travelling distances to a town of any size, solitude and remoteness. You won't be able to pop along to the local shop, drop into the local bar for a glass of your favourite tipple with the locals, or have a choice of restaurants on your doorstep. In a town or large village, the weekly market will be just around the corner, the doctor and chemist close at hand, and if you need help or run into any problems, your neighbours will be close by.

On the other hand, in the country you will be closer to nature, will have more freedom (e.g. to make as much noise as you wish) and possibly complete privacy, e.g. to sunbathe or swim *au naturel*. Living in a remote area in the country will suit nature lovers looking for solitude who don't want to involve themselves in the 'hustle and bustle' of town life (not that there's much of this in Antipodean rural towns). If you're after peace and quiet, make sure that there isn't a busy road or railway line nearby or a local church within 'donging' distance (see **Noise** above).

Note, however, that many people who buy a remote country home find that the peace of the countryside palls after a time and they yearn for the more exciting night-life of a city or tourist resort. If you've never lived in the country, it's wise to rent first before buying. Note also that, while it's cheaper to buy in a remote or unpopular location, it's usually much more difficult to find a buyer when you want to sell.

GETTING THERE

Although it isn't so important if you're planning to live permanently in Australia or New Zealand and stay put, one of the major considerations when buying a holiday or part-time retirement home is the cost of getting to and from Australia or New Zealand, and you should ask yourself the following questions:

● How long will it take to get to a home in Australia or New Zealand, taking into account journeys to and from airports, ports and railway stations?

● How frequent are flights at the time(s) of year when you plan to travel?

● Are direct flights available?

● What is the cost of travel from your home country to the region where you're planning to buy a home in Australia or New Zealand?

● Are off-season discounts or inexpensive charter flights available?

You should bear in mind that it may take you up to a week to recover from the journey Down Under (if you've come from Europe, for example), especially if you suffer badly from jet-lag. Obviously, the travelling time and cost of travel to a home in Australia or New Zealand will be more significant if you're planning to spend frequent holidays there rather than one long visit a year.

```
SURVIVAL TIP
Allow plenty of time to get to and from airports,
ports and railway stations, particularly when travelling
during peak hours, when traffic congestion can be
horrendous, and also to take into account the
extra time that security checks may take.
```

Airline Services

Australia

Air travel is the fastest way to get around Australia, and around 80 per cent of domestic long-distance trips are made by air. Australian airlines are strict about safety and it's one of the safest places in the world to fly (Qantas has regularly been rated as one of the safest airlines in the world by IATA, who in 2000 also named Airservices Australia the world's best provider of air traffic control services). Australia is served by around 50 international airlines operating scheduled passenger services. Australia's national airline is Qantas (Queensland and Northern Territory Aerial Service), formed in 1920 (only KLM is older) and privatised in 1995. It's one of the best (noted for the excellence of its food and wines) and most profitable airlines in the world. Qantas (🖥 www.qantas.com.au) has a fleet of around 196 aircraft and carries over 30 million passengers per year (over 21 million on domestic routes) to 120 destinations in 40 countries. It has partnership agreements with several other airlines, including American Airlines and British Airways, whereby partners can buy seats on Qantas flights and vice versa. There are Qantas Club lounges at all major airports in Australia and shared lounges in many other countries. Qantas has its own terminals at Australia's major airports, and caters for disabled passengers and passengers in wheelchairs. Smoking is prohibited on all flights operated by Australian airlines, both domestic and international, with a maximum $500 fine for offenders (so don't try smoking in the toilet!).

For many years, Qantas and the defunct Ansett monopolised the domestic flight market. The cooperation between them meant that domestic air travel remained relatively expensive. But Ansett went into administration in March 2002 and the regional airlines that it owned either went out of business or are currently operating only a limited service. This had the effect of shaking up the market and new airlines have been formed which are taking on Qantas, creating welcome competition (for the consumer).

Regional Express (or Rex, 🖥 www.regionalexpress.com.au) is Australia's largest independent regional airline, connecting 29 metropolitan and regional centres across New South Wales, South Australia, Tasmania and Victoria. It was formed in August 2002 and in 2005 had a fleet of 27 aircraft. Virgin Blue (🖥 www.virginblue.com.au) is a leading low-cost airline, currently offering the most competition to Qantas, serving 23 destinations in Australia, two in New Zealand and Fiji, and the Cook Islands and Vanuatu. Regional airlines in Australia include Airlines of South Australia, Skywest (Western Australia) and Sunstate (Queensland).

Flying times between Sydney and other state capitals are: Canberra (236km/147mi) 30 minutes; Brisbane (746km/464mi) and Melbourne (708km/440mi) around one hour 15 minutes; Adelaide (1,166km/725mi) and Hobart (1,039km/646mi) around two hours; and Perth (3,284km/2,041mi) around five hours. Qantas flies to almost 60 destinations in Australia.

There are many flights each day between Australia's major cities (although some journeys require a number of stops), but on less travelled routes there are just one or two flights a week. You should always book a domestic flight as far in advance as possible, particularly during holiday periods (this also allows you to take maximum advantage of reduced fares). Many regional and local airlines operate small aircraft, which are generally booked well in advance and consequently don't offer discounts or low fares. Many domestic airlines also offer a variety of air tours lasting from two to 14 days.

New Zealand

New Zealand is served by some 25 international airlines, most of which fly to Auckland or Christchurch. New Zealand's main domestic airline (and also its international airline) is Air New Zealand (☎ freephone 0800-737 000, 🖥 www.airnz.co.nz), which was previously state-owned but is now privatised and regularly acclaimed as one of the world's best airlines. In 2001 Air New Zealand (ANZ) came near to bankruptcy when it attempted to buy the remaining 50 per cent of Ansett Australia (it already owned 50 per cent), which went into liquidation in mid-2001. The New Zealand government, in an attempt to save the airline, announced a $500 million rescue package, which effectively makes the government the majority shareholder in the company. (Many New Zealanders believe that the airline shouldn't have been privatised in the first place). ANZ has a comprehensive route network, with over 470 flights per day to 25 domestic destinations, and flights to a wide range of destinations in Asia, Australasia, Europe and North America (and two in Mexico).

ANZ's main domestic competitors are Freedom Air, Origin Pacific and Qantas (🖥 www.qantas.com.au). Freedom Air (🖥 www.freedomair.co.nz) serves Auckland, Christchurch, Dunedin, Hamilton, Palmerston North and Wellington (as well as Australia and Fiji). Origin Pacific (🖥 www.origin pacific.co.nz) is a relative newcomer, operating only since 1997, serving Auckland, Blenheim, Christchurch, Hamilton, Napier, Nelson, New Plymouth, Palmerston North and Wellington.

Mount Cook also operates domestic services, although it's a partner airline to ANZ (operating services on their behalf), as are Air Nelson and Eagle Air, rather than real competitors. A number of other competitors have started up or been proposed over the years, including the inappropriately named Kiwi Air (considering that the kiwi is a flightless bird!), although most have fallen by the wayside. Many domestic services provide in-flight bar facilities, which is something of an innovation in New Zealand where the sale of alcohol is subject to strict licensing hours. Smoking isn't permitted on the domestic services of any airline. Surprisingly, however, the health-conscious New Zealanders haven't banned that other risk to the well-being of air travellers – airline food!

There are also a number of mini-airlines serving minor destinations, often using aircraft with as few as four seats. Great Barrier Airlines (☎ freephone 0800-900 600) and Mountain Air (☎ freephone 0800-922 812) both operate a service to Great Barrier Island (a paradise-like island, likened to Fiji or Tahiti) in the Hauraki Gulf off Auckland.

Airports

Australia

The main airports in Australia are Adelaide, Brisbane, Cairns, Darwin, Melbourne, Perth, Port Hedland, Sydney and Townsville. Sydney and Melbourne are Australia's two largest international airports, while Adelaide, Brisbane, Cairns, Darwin, Hobart, Perth and Townsville also have a limited number of international flights. The capital, Canberra, doesn't have an international airport and is served by domestic flights from other Australian cities (Sydney is only half an hour away by air). Most of Australia's major airports are owned and controlled by the Federal Airports Corporation (FAC), although they're gradually being privatised. When minor airports and country landing strips are included, Australia has a total of around 445 'airports'. Most Australian airports are deserted much of the time and come to life for only a few hours a day, when international flights arrive and depart. Terminals may open for only a few hours before arrivals or departures and close for the day after the last flight has arrived or left. International terminals are usually separate from domestic buildings and the two may be located some distance apart. There are bus and taxi services from all major airports to local city centres.

Sydney: Sydney's international airport is called Kingsford-Smith (after Australia's pioneering aviator) and is located in the suburb of Mascot, 10km/6mi south of the city centre. The international and domestic terminals are located 4km/2.5mi apart on either side of the runway. It's Australia's busiest airport and handles around 26 million passengers per year. It was refurbished and modernised in 1998 in time for the 2000 Olympics, including an underground railway link to the city centre. A second Sydney airport is planned, although the state government is finding it difficult to find a suitable site owing to concerns over aircraft noise (the 'not in my back yard' problem).

Melbourne: Melbourne's Tullamarine airport is located 23km/14mi north-west of the city centre and is Australia's second-largest airport (after Sydney), handling over 19 million passengers a year. Melbourne has tried (with some success) to attract airlines by reducing airport charges and now serves many more international destinations than previously. The Airtrain rail link joins the airport with the city and to the Gold Coast. Melbourne has a second airport at Essendon, between the city and Tullamarine, which operates local flights within Victoria and to Tasmania.

Adelaide: Adelaide airport is just 6km/4mi south-west of the city centre and has both international and domestic terminals, five minutes' walk apart. It is Australia's fourth-largest domestic and sixth-largest international airport, handling around 4.2 million passengers a year. Five airlines, Cathay Pacific, Garuda Indonesia, Malaysia Airlines, Qantas and Singapore International, have direct international flights to Adelaide, although many airlines provide free connecting flights to Melbourne, Sydney and even Singapore in order to attract passengers.

Brisbane: Brisbane airport is 10km/6mi from the city centre and has separate international and domestic terminals some 12 minutes apart by road. There are international flights to Europe, Hong Kong, Japan, New Zealand, North America, Papua New Guinea and Singapore. In 2004, Brisbane airport handled around 14 million passengers.

Darwin: Darwin airport (located 8km/5mi south of the city centre) has the longest runway in the country and operates international flights to Bali, Brunei, Dili, Singapore and Timika. There are domestic flights (from the same terminal as international flights) to most major cities once a day or less frequently. Darwin handles around 1.4 million passengers per year.

Perth: Perth airport (21km/13mi east of the city centre) is a gateway for services from Asia and Europe. It has international and domestic terminals on opposite sides of the runway, some 10km/6mi apart by road. Changing flights can be a chore, although many international flights arrive after midnight when there are no connecting domestic flights anyway. Fares to Europe are lower from Perth than elsewhere in Australia and there's a lively market in international tickets. Perth handled just under 6 million passengers in 2004.

Other Airports: Alice Springs airport is 7km/4mi south of the town centre, from where most flights are to Darwin or Adelaide. Cairns and Townsville have international airports which are also connected to Brisbane and other major cities by regular domestic flights. Tasmania has four main airports: Devonport, Hobart, Launceston and Wynyard (or Burnie), served by domestic flights from the mainland. The only international flights are from Hobart to New Zealand (Christchurch).

New Zealand

New Zealand's main international airport is Auckland, which is connected by direct flights to most main cities in Asia, several cities in the USA and

Europe (particularly London), plus several Polynesian destinations. The airports at Wellington and Christchurch also dub themselves 'international', but offer a much smaller number of international flights, mainly to Australia, although Christchurch serves some other countries, including the UK. Wellington is the country's domestic air hub, as many flights from all points north and south stop at Wellington to allow passengers to change planes. There are also domestic airports at Blenheim, Dunedin, Gisborne, Hamilton, Hastings, Hokitika, Invercargill, Kaitaia, Te Anau, Mount Cook, Napier, Nelson, New Plymouth, Palmerston North, Queenstown, Rotorua, Taupo, Tauranga, Wanganui, Whakatane and Whangerei. These serve mainly domestic flights and private planes, and their facilities range from a modest but modern terminal building to a motley collection of huts.

Auckland International airport is 21km (13mi) south of the city at Mangere and has three separate terminals. There's an AirBus shuttle connecting the airport with the city centre every 20 or 30 minutes costing $13 single and $22 return. The privately operated Johnston's Shuttle Link and the SuperShuttle also run to the city centre, taking 35 minutes and costing around $15 one way. Airport information is available on ☎ 09-256 8899 or at 💻 www. auckland-airport.co.nz.

Wellington International Airport is 7km (5mi) south of the city at Rongotai. It has been designated a 'low noise' airport and may be used only by the quietest planes, which, even so, aren't permitted to arrive or depart at night. Wellington's airport is notoriously windy and renowned among pilots as a difficult place to land or take off. As with Auckland, there are three terminals. The two airport shuttle buses, again privately operated by Johnston's Shuttle Link and SuperShuttle, cost $8 and take 20 minutes to reach central Wellington. Airport information is available on ☎ 04-385 5100 or at 💻 www. wellington-airport.co.nz.

Christchurch International Airport, whose facilities have recently been greatly improved, is 11km (7mi) north of the city centre and is easily reached by bus for a fare of $2.70 (half price at off-peak times). For information, ☎ 03-358 5029 or visit 💻 www.christchurch-airport.co.nz.

Fares

Australia

The Australian airline industry was deregulated in 1990, before which there was a duopoly operated by Qantas and the now-defunct Ansett, who charged the same (very high) fares and offered virtually the same services. Deregulation heralded the arrival of a number of new domestic carriers who quickly forced Qantas and Ansett to reduce fares, e.g. the cost of a Sydney-Perth ticket was immediately halved! Random discounting is now common on domestic flights, although there are often conditions such as advance booking, flying at weekends only or between fixed dates. A variety of discount fares is available when flying to Australia from some countries (e.g. the UK), although Australia's isolated position in the world means that international travel is invariably expensive. Domestic air travel is also relatively expensive because of the long distances involved. If you're migrating to Australia, you should book as far ahead as possible (but never before you've received your visa!).

Air fares are high from most countries to Australia, as there's a relatively low volume of traffic on most routes and little competition. The main exception is between the UK and Australia (the 'kangaroo route'), one of the most competitive routes in the world on which airlines regularly indulge in price wars, offering cut-price tickets on selected flights. The low season return fare is around GB£600 from London to Sydney between April and June, rising to between GB£1,000 and GB£1,500 during the high season of December to January (when fares vary little between airlines). Fares during the shoulder season of July to November and February to March are usually between GB£650 and GB£800. Fares from London to Melbourne or Brisbane are usually more expensive than to Sydney. From Europe, fares vary depending on whether you're flying east via Asia or west via North America. It's usually cheaper to fly via America between November and February.

Flights in the weeks immediately prior to Christmas are usually fully booked months in advance, and delaying your flight a few days until after the Christmas period can result in a considerable saving. Expect to pay GB£100 to GB£200 or more for return flights with British Airways, Qantas or Singapore Airlines than with other airlines, which may be worthwhile if you take advantage of their domestic fare deals. Fares are higher if you break the journey, although most travellers find that it's worthwhile taking advantage of stopover deals and it helps avoid or reduce jet lag. It may be worthwhile buying a round-the-world (RTW) ticket, which doesn't cost a lot more than a full fare economy ticket from the UK to Australia (or New Zealand) and allows for up to around 15 stopovers.

Fares from the USA aren't as good value as from Europe, although excursion and promotional fares are available which are much lower than full-fares, e.g. apex and promotional return fares from Los Angeles to Sydney/Melbourne are around US$900 in the low season and US$1,500 in the high season. Regular tickets are valid for 12 months, so it may pay to buy your ticket well in advance of your trip. There's not a lot of choice from the USA, from where a limited number of airlines fly non-stop to Australia. Many airlines stop at Honolulu, Papeete or Auckland, or a combination of these. When flying from Sydney to Los Angeles, you leave Sydney in the afternoon and arrive in LA in the morning of the same day! An 'open-jaw' ticket (flying into one airport and out of another) is usually no more expensive than an ordinary return.

Major airlines offer economy, business and first class fares. Full fare tickets allow you to change the date and time of travel at a moment's notice and offer a full refund should you decide not to travel. When buying apex and other discounted tickets, always make sure that you fully understand any ticket restrictions. Return fares from Australia to Europe are higher than when travelling in the opposite direction. The best deals are from Sydney, although bargains can be found from Melbourne and Perth (discount fares are advertised in the major daily newspapers). A departure tax of $38 is incorporated into the ticket price for passengers aged 12 or over. Departing passengers must also complete an *Outgoing Passenger Card*.

Charter flights are sometimes available from the UK to Australia between November and April. Flights cost from around GB£400 return. However, charter flights have severe restrictions, including no stopovers, a minimum stay of two weeks and a maximum of eight.

New Zealand

ANZ's services were notoriously expensive until the now-defunct Ansett arrived on the scene, which prompted more competitive pricing. However, standard fares are still high, and it's necessary to shop around and compare prices to obtain the best deal. For example, Origin Pacific have special offers on aircraft repositioning flights. The cheapest fares are to be had by booking at least seven days ahead. Sample fares are Auckland to Wellington one way for between $100 and $240, Auckland to Christchurch one way for between $105 and $285, and Wellington to Christchurch one way for between $80 and $190. International flights cost from around 10 per cent more than the prices quoted for Australia above.

A departure tax of $25 is levied on passengers on departing international flights, which must be paid before you pass through immigration. At Auckland International Airport it can be paid at the Bank of New Zealand offices on the ground and first floors.

GETTING AROUND

Australia

Public transport in Australia varies from region to region and town to town. In most cities and large towns services are good to excellent and relatively inexpensive, although some suburbs and areas are poorly served. Most Australian cities have a relatively small suburban rail network and many regions aren't served by trains at all, which is one of the reasons most Australians are so attached to their cars (only Americans are more devoted to their cars). However, it isn't *always* essential to own a car in Australia, particularly if you live in a city (where parking is often impossible). On the other hand, if you live in the country or a suburb off the main rail and bus routes, it's usually essential to have your own transport. Bus and rail services in most areas are also severely curtailed on Sundays and in some cases on Saturdays as well.

Bear in mind when travelling interstate that Australia is a huge country (nearly as big as Europe or the USA and over 30 times the size of the UK) with vast distances between capital cities. Flying saves you a lot of time and the loss of sleep associated with long-distance bus and train journeys, although you see little of Australia when flying around the country. Book early if you plan to travel long distance on public holidays or at the beginning or end of school holidays. Despite the vast distances involved in travelling in Australia, many Australians prefer to travel by private car.

In cities, trains are much faster than buses, particularly during rush hours, even where new faster roads have been built. Most cities have an integrated public transport system, and tickets usually allow transfers between buses, ferries, trains and trams (as applicable), fares being calculated on a zone system, e.g. travelpasses in Sydney. Buses and trams carry around 65 per cent of passengers in the major cities, where there's a range of daily, weekly, monthly, quarterly and annual tickets, plus discounted books of ten tickets offering savings on single fares. Many cities have free downtown shuttle buses. Passengers found travelling without tickets can be fined up to $200.

Sydney

Australia's largest city has an integrated service that includes buses, ferries, suburban trains and City Rail's 'underground' system (a conventional railway that runs underground in the city centre). Sydney also has a monorail and light railway, although they're expensive and mainly a novelty for tourists rather than a serious form of public transport. Sydney has the most expensive public transport of any Australian city, but it's still relatively cheap by international standards. In 2000, Sydney received some much-needed transport improvements, including expanded rail and ferry lines, and an underground railway linking the airport to the city centre.

Melbourne

Melbourne has an inexpensive and efficient public transport network consisting of buses, trains and trams, which has recently been privatised. Trams form the backbone of the public transport system and the city's network is one of the most extensive in the world and the only one remaining in Australia (unlike Sydney, Melbourne was wise enough to retain its trams). The network covers 325km/202mi and is served by some 750 trams operating up to 20km/12mi outside the city centre. The Melbourne public transport system is called the 'Met', which is the collective name for bus, rail and tram services (a free 'Get around on the Met' map is available – ☎ local call rate 13-1638). Tickets can be purchased at train stations, on board buses and trams, and from retail outlets such as newsagents and cafés. An unpopular automated 'Metcard' ticketing system has recently been introduced.

New Zealand

Although the population of New Zealand is dispersed over a wide area, the country has a decent public transport service, which is centred around road, rail and air links, plus the essential umbilical ferry link connecting the North and South Islands. Unless you live in a remote country area, you shouldn't find it too difficult to get around without your own transport. Probably the most impressive feature of New Zealand's public transport is that the different elements are closely integrated and if you start a journey by bus, continue by rail and then take to the air, you usually find that services are planned and timed to connect.

Although car ownership and usage in New Zealand is high, this shouldn't be taken as a sign that public transport is unreliable (although it does have a few shortcomings, such as finishing too early in some cases), but rather that the roads are relatively uncongested and therefore driving still has many advantages over public transport. Even in metropolitan Auckland and

Wellington, commuters travelling into the centre often drive (although traffic jams are encouraging more drivers to consider public transport).

All public transport timetables in New Zealand use the am/pm time system rather than the 24-hour clock. If your luggage is lost, stolen or damaged on public transport in New Zealand, you should make a claim to the relevant authority, as you may receive an ex-gratia payment.

Like many countries, New Zealand has started to take the needs of disabled travellers seriously only within the last decade or so. Domestic airlines and trains cater fully for disabled travellers, but you should tell them that you need special assistance when booking. As most taxis are simply converted saloon cars, you can use them only if you can gain access to a standard car. There are wheelchair-accessible taxis in cities, although you need to book in advance (particularly for the return journey), as their number is limited. There are no special facilities for the disabled on coach and bus services, although discount fares are widely available. Further information can be obtained from the Disability Information Service, 314 Worcester Street, Christchurch (☎ 03-366 6189).

Domestic Rail Services

Australia

Australia offers some of the most spectacular long-distance rail journeys in the world, although the unchanging scenery in some regions can begin to pall after a few hours, unless you're unnaturally keen on flat, red terrain. Interstate rail travel has been overtaken by the age of air travel and (apart from suburban services in the major cities) is mainly of interest to tourists and travellers with plenty of time on their hands (the average speed of Australian trains is around 65kph/40mph). There's an interstate railway service serving all states except Tasmania. Trains don't stop at all intermediate stations, e.g. those within a few hours of major terminals.

Long-distance trains have evocative names such as the *Ghan* (Adelaide-Melbourne-Sydney-Alice Springs-Darwin), the *Great South Pacific Express* (Sydney-Brisbane-Cairns), *Indian Pacific* (Sydney-Adelaide-Perth), the *Prospector* (Perth-Kalgoorlie) and the *Spirit of the Outback* (Brisbane-Longreach). The *Indian Pacific* crosses Australia and takes its name from its route from the Pacific Ocean (Sydney) to the Indian Ocean (Perth), a journey of 4,348km/2,700mi taking around 65 hours. It includes the longest stretch of straight track (478km/300mi) in the world, across the Nullabor Plain in Western Australia. The *Indian Pacific* is one of the world's longest trains, with up to 25 carriages plus a bar and music room with piano, observation lounge and restaurant. The *Great South Pacific Express* is 'the first five-star hotel on wheels' in Australia and the country's answer to Europe's Orient Express. Cars are carried on the *Queenslander*, the *Spirit of the Outback* and between Adelaide and Alice Springs, Melbourne and Perth, and on the Melbourne-Mildura goods line. The *Prospector* (Perth-Kalgoorlie) provides only first-class, air-conditioned accommodation and maintains the fastest average speed (around 110kph/68mph) of any train in Australia, taking 7.5 hours for the 655km/407mi journey.

Adelaide: Long-distance trains stop at the Adelaide Rail Passenger Terminal in Keswick, 2km south-west of the city centre. There's an overnight service to Melbourne taking around 12 hours and a day coach/train service taking 11 hours. The *Ghan* to Alice Springs (19 hours) leaves at 2pm on Thursdays with an additional service on Mondays in winter, and it continues on to Darwin. There are five weekly trains to Perth (none on Tuesdays and Thursdays) taking around 36 hours, possibly requiring a change of train at Port Pirie. There's a small network of suburban trains in Adelaide operated by the State Transport Authority. Tickets must be purchased before entering platforms or boarding trains.

Alice Springs/Darwin/Northern Territory: Alice is served by the *Ghan*, which departs from Adelaide at 2pm on Mondays and Thursdays (see above) and arrives in Alice at 12.30pm the following day. The return leaves Alice at 5.10pm and arrives in Adelaide at 4.30pm the next day (although it's often early). The fare is from $215 for an adult one-way. The station in Alice is a 15-minute walk from the edge of the town (taxis meet trains). The north of the Northern Territory has recently joined the rail network, and the one-way fare from Adelaide to Darwin (already touted as one of the world's great train journeys) is from $440.

Brisbane/Queensland: There's a fast Citytrain service in Brisbane with seven lines, and the Airtrain, connecting the airport to the city and the Gold Coast has recently been opened. The 640km/398mi stretch between Brisbane and Rockhampton is electrified and served by modern 'tilt' trains (fast trains which run along narrow-gauge lines, sometimes at seemingly precarious angles – hence the name!).

Queensland has the most extensive rail network of any Australian state, covering over 10,000km/6,200mi of lines on narrow gauge tracks (trains in Queensland are slower than buses due to the narrow gauge, with the exception of tilt trains). All trains are operated by Queensland Rail (☎ local call rate 13-1617, 🖥 www.qr.com.au), whose 'flagship' train (where all passengers travel first class with sleeping berths) is the *Queenslander*, taking a leisurely 30 hours between Brisbane and Cairns. The *Westlander* operates from Brisbane to Charlesville (777km/482mi), taking 16 hours, and the *Inlander* links Townsville with Mount Isa. The only rail link from outside the state is from NSW (served by XPT trains), on which northbound trains run overnight and southbound trains during the day. Seat or sleeper reservations are compulsory on long-distance trains, known as 'Traveltrains'. Most services are air-conditioned and provide sleeping cars and sitting cars with bar and meal services. Many trains stop at small stations on request and some trains are mixed freight and passenger trains (usually mainly freight with one passenger car). Vehicles can be transported on the *Queenslander* and the *Spirit of the Outback* (Brisbane-Longreach) services.

Local 'tourist' trains include the *Kuranda Scenic Railway* and the *Spirit of the Tropics*, designed for budget travellers and incorporating a non-stop disco car (Club Loco)! The vintage *Gulflander* train operates between Normanton and Croydon in the west of the state. There are 'plans' for a regional rail line on the Sunshine Coast (the existing track is sited 20km/12mi inland from the heavily-populated coastal area).

'Sunshine' rail passes offer unlimited economy class travel on most routes, including the Brisbane suburban network. Ordinary one-way tickets allow unlimited stopovers and 14 days to reach your destination, while return tickets are valid for two months. Stop-offs must be stated when buying tickets and reservations made for all journeys. You can change your travel plans, but a re-booking fee may be charged. Day rover tickets in Brisbane cost around $9 and are valid after 9am and at weekends.

Canberra: Australia's capital city is served by the main Sydney-Melbourne line, which passes through Wodonga to the north-east of Canberra; from there you must take a bus, the whole journey taking around nine hours. It's usually better to fly when travelling to Canberra.

Melbourne: The Victorian State Railway, the V/Line, was recently privatised and is now on lease to the British travel company National Express. V/Line operates all rail and associated coach routes within Victoria, including day and overnight, high-speed (XPT) services to Sydney (Melbourne-Sydney during the day and Sydney-Melbourne overnight) taking 13 hours. V/Line supersaver fares offer a 30 per cent discount when travelling off-peak, i.e. on Tuesdays, Wednesdays and Thursdays arriving in Melbourne after 9.30am and leaving Melbourne at any time except between 4pm and 6pm. In recent years, new, air-conditioned, 'high-speed' Sprinter trains have been introduced on some routes. The Canberra Link involves taking a train to Wodonga on the border with NSW and a bus from there to Canberra. There are *Overland* daily night services to Adelaide taking 12 hours (change to the *Indian Pacific* in Adelaide for Perth). The city centre 'City Loop' forms an underground railway around the centre.

Perth/Western Australia: The *Indian Pacific* takes 65 hours to travel from Perth to Sydney and runs three times a week, on Sundays, Mondays and Thursdays. The cheapest adult fare in 2005 was $513. There are also suburban lines (operated by Westrail) between Perth and Armadale, Fremantle, Joondalup and Midland. The only other rail services in Western Australia are the Perth-Bunbury line and the Perth-Kalgoorlie route operated by the *Prospector*. Tickets should be purchased from vending machines at train stations before boarding. Multi-ride tickets can be validated at stations. Seven-day advance purchase fares are available in the low season offering a 30 per cent discount. A car-train service is available between Adelaide and Perth.

Sydney/NSW: Sydney has the most extensive suburban rail network in Australia, although even here many suburbs have no rail services. Most routes are served by old, mostly double-decker trains (Sydney was the first city in the world to introduce double-decker electric trains), on which seats can usually be reversed to face in either direction (these are being replaced by ultra-modern Tangara trains). Yellow stripes on platforms indicate where half-length, four-carriage trains stop (you must stand behind the yellow line). Doors open and close automatically, although the doors on old trains are rarely closed during hot weather, so keep clear of the doorways (or hold on tight). Trains operate from around 5am until midnight – violence, although rare, has caused the cancellation of trains after midnight on some suburban routes. After dark there are special 'Night Safe' areas (marked on the platform in blue) where you should wait for trains. After 8pm, only two carriages are in use (next to the guard's compartment, indicated by a blue light), and a help button is positioned near the door which can be used to alert the guard or driver.

The NSW Countrylink network (🖳 www.countrylink.nsw.gov.au) operates the most comprehensive state rail service in Australia using Xplorer trains, on which seats must be booked in advance. There are commuter trains between Sydney and Goulburn, Katoomba, Lithgow, Newcastle and Wollongong. For information, call ☎ 13-2232 between 6.30am and 10pm any day.

Other Services: There are no regular passenger railways in Tasmania, although there's a freight rail service throughout the island and several steam railways for tourists (e.g. Ida Bay to Deep Hole). Elsewhere in Australia a few small private railways serve mainly agricultural and industrial areas, e.g. the iron-ore mining developments in the north-west of Western

Australia and an extensive tram network in Queensland connecting the sugar cane fields to the mills in sugar-producing areas.

New Zealand

New Zealand's rail network is operated by Tranz Scenic, the country's only passenger rail company (🖳 www.tranzscenic.co.nz). The network is limited, mainly due to the mountainous terrain in many parts of the country and, of course, by the fact that lines cannot cross the Cook Straits (until a bridge or tunnel is built). The service itself is modern and comfortable (part of the Auckland-Wellington line has recently been electrified), but neither frequent nor fast, although stops at many small stations on long-distance lines have been eliminated making journey times shorter. As a result, rail services are widely promoted as a tourist attraction rather than a day-to-day amenity. In this regard the rail service is excellent, as many lines pass through native forests, past volcanic peaks and through alpine passes providing spectacular, panoramic views. There are four main railway routes, each with a colourful name, as follows:

The Overlander	Auckland-Wellington
Capital Connection	Palmerston North-Wellington
TranzCoastal	Christchurch-Picton
TranzAlpine	Christchurch-Greymouth

There are many special fare offers, including (in mid-2005) from around $20 one way on the Capital Connection route and around $109 return on the TranzAlpine route. If you're a student or disabled, you qualify for a 50 per cent discount off the standard fare. You must provide proof of identity and must book in advance. There's only one class of travel whichever service you choose.

Some services provide free refreshments and/or a free lunch, and there are also buffet cars selling more substantial meals and a bar on some services. Some trains have guided tourist commentaries (whether you're a tourist or not). If you wish to take a bicycle on a train, check when booking, as they aren't allowed on many services and only limited space is available when they are. Smokers may also have a tough time travelling by train in New Zealand, as smoking isn't permitted on any train, even though some of the journeys are long.

There are no underground services anywhere in New Zealand, but there are fast and reliable commuter rail networks in Auckland and Wellington. Auckland's commuter rail network is operated by Rideline (⌨ www.ride line.co.nz), which also operates buses and ferries. There are two lines running from the railway station, one to Waitakere in the west and the other to Papkura in the south. The website has extensive details of fares, offers and routes. Wellington's commuter rail network is run by Tranz Metro, which has four lines to Johnsonville, Paraparaumu, Melling and Wairarapa. Tranz Metro services are popular with commuters and offer frequent trains, with full details on their website (⌨ www.tranzmetro.co.nz).

Domestic Bus Services

Australia

There are comprehensive bus services in Australia's major cities and an extensive network of long-distance interstate buses, usually referred to as coaches. Bus services in rural areas are less frequent, and it may be necessary to have your own transport if you live in the country. Melbourne is the only Australian city with an extensive tram network, although other cities are planning new tram lines.

Buses are the cheapest form of public transport in Australia, both within cities and over long distances, and provide a far more comprehensive network than the railways, encompassing almost every corner of Australia.

Each city and region has its own bus companies providing town and country services. In large towns and cities, most bus services start and terminate at a central bus station, which is generally modern and clean. Most are equipped with luggage lockers or a left luggage office, shops, showers, a snack bar or restaurant, and toilets. They have little in common with the seedy places inhabited by drug addicts, drunks and assorted derelicts found in many other countries. Smoking is prohibited on all buses and trams in Australia. If you need assistance, ask at the bus station information office. Most bus companies provide free timetables and route maps, and in some cities comprehensive timetables and maps are available that include all bus services operating within their boundaries.

In most cities in Australia there are a number of local bus companies, sometimes operated by the local railway company or the state or city authorities. There's a comprehensive bus network in all Australian cities, and services are frequent, including a night bus service in the major cities. Buses are slow but fairly frequent in most cities, where they're often the only option for getting to most suburbs. Major cities usually have an integrated public transport system, the same ticket being valid on buses, suburban trains, trams (Melbourne) and ferries (Sydney). In stark contrast to the cities, in country areas there's usually only one bus company and services are sparse and infrequent. In remote areas there may be only school buses, which usually carry other passengers, but aren't obliged to.

Buses on most routes operate from around 6am until 11pm or midnight (but possibly only until 7pm on Sundays). Buses run frequently during the weekday rush hours, e.g. every 10 or 15 minutes on the main routes. Outside rush hours there's usually a half hour service on most routes during weekdays, although services are often severely restricted at weekends and on public holidays (there may be no service at all on some routes on Sundays and public holidays). In major cities there's usually an express bus service (called 'rockets' in some cities) operating between the outer suburbs and the major centres on routes to city centres (express bus numbers are usually prefixed with an X). Night services operate in the major cities from around midnight until 6am, some of which have radio links with taxi operators, so that you can arrange to have a taxi meet you at your destination (very civilised). There are free buses in most major cities covering a circular (loop) route within the city centre.

It's usual to board a bus by the front door and disembark from the centre doors. You must normally ring a bell to inform the driver that you want him to stop at the next stop (a buzzer sounds in the cab) and stand by the centre door. When the bus stops, a green light is illuminated which signals that you must push the handle or press a button to open the door, which doesn't usually open automatically. In most cities, bus stops have numbers, which are often quoted by people when giving directions (they may be colour-coded). Buses also display their route number, although in some cities numbers may vary according to whether they're running to or from the city centre. All bus companies publish route maps, and there are comprehensive city travel guides in most cities, and state bus directories in some states.

Long-distance interstate buses are generally cheaper, easier to book and faster than trains, and there's a more comprehensive network. However, they're also less comfortable and more restrictive than trains. Long-distance buses are particularly popular among independent travellers (e.g. backpackers), 80 per cent of whom use them almost exclusively. Travelling by bus is around a third of the cost of travelling by air. There are numerous daily departures on the most popular routes, although some services operate only a few times per week and, in the Northern Territory, northern Queensland and northern parts of Western Australia, some routes are interrupted for weeks at a time during the wet season (November to May). There are unsociable arrival hours on some long-distance routes.

Greyhound (🖳 www.greyhound.com.au) is Australia's only national coach operator, formed in 2000 when McCaffertys bought Greyhound Pioneer Australia. The main operator in the southern part of Western Australia is the state rail company, Westrail, while Tasmanian Redline Coaches (🖳 www.tasredline.com.au) provides express services throughout Tasmania.

New Zealand

Most towns and cities have a good public bus service, and some cities operate double-decker buses, like those in the UK. Bus services have been deregulated and privatised to some extent in recent years, although in many cases the original public bus company is still the largest operator on a majority of routes. One of the drawbacks of the public bus service is that it ends early, and on Saturdays and Sundays the last services leave at around 5pm. Even during the week in Auckland (where the main operator is Rideline) you won't find a public bus running after 11.30pm (many routes finish much earlier) and some services are discontinued altogether at weekends. Auckland bus services include the Link, which runs at ten-minute intervals around the main parts of the city in a loop.

In Wellington the bus system is run by Stagecoach and has frequent services, including an after-midnight service from the entertainment district to outlying suburbs. Timetables and other information are available from ☎ freephone 0800-8017000. Christchurch buses are among the best in the country, with cheap and frequent services, and a free Shuttle runs around the city centre at ten-minute intervals. Information is available from Bus Info (☎ 03-366 8855). On New Zealand buses you usually buy your ticket from the driver as you enter the bus. Some buses accept the exact fare only.

One benefit of bus deregulation is that small private firms have been allowed to enter the public transport business, and some operate services late into the evening and at weekends when the main operators have suspended their services. Some services, using minibuses and cars, can be ordered by telephone when required. As several companies now operate in most towns, there's no centralised place where you can obtain timetable information. Check your telephone directory for details of where to obtain information about services and a copy of timetables. In larger cities there's more than one bus station serving the different companies and routes. In Wellington, the main stations are at Waterloo Quay and

Courtenay Place. In Auckland, buses use the Downtown and Midtown terminals (although Midtown is only a series of lay-bys rather than a purpose-built terminal).

Trams operate in several cities in New Zealand, including Wellington, where they're called trolley buses and operate on several routes in the city centre and inner suburbs. The cost is the same as for buses (see above), and the Daytripper pass issued for buses can also be used on trams. Wellington also has a cable car operating between Lambton Quay and the Botanic Gardens in Kelburn. This is a popular tourist attraction, but is also used daily by commuters, as it's an easy way to travel up one of Wellington's steepest hills. Trams operate on a city centre loop in Christchurch, stopping at nine points along the way, and mostly attract tourists but are also handy for commuters and shoppers in the city centre. You can buy a one hour, half-day or full day ticket from the conductor on board (the service operates between 9am and 6pm).

New Zealand has a comprehensive and reliable long-distance coach service, which is the main way of travelling long distances for those who don't have a car or who cannot afford or don't want to fly. Services are provided by two major companies: InterCity Group (NZ) Limited (operating as InterCity

Coachlines (🖥 www.intercitycoach.co.nz) serves 600 destinations, while Newmans, its main competitor, also serves an impressive number of destinations (🖥 www.newmanscoach.co.nz). There are also around a dozen smaller companies, such as Northliner Express Coachlines.

Coach services, even of competing companies, are well co-ordinated so that they connect not only with other coach services but also with other modes of transport. So, for example, if you take the train from Auckland to Wellington, the Interislander ferry across the Cook Strait and then a coach to Christchurch, it's possible to plan a route which connects smoothly allowing just enough time to get from one terminus to another. Unlike trains, there are several coach services per day on the main routes such as Auckland-Wellington.

Coaches are modern and provide facilities such as toilets, reclining seats and air-conditioning. On routes that are popular with tourists the driver usually provides a commentary on sights and places of interest. On services operating in more remote areas, you may find that half the coach is given over to freight and parcels. Snacks and drinks aren't available on board coaches but they stop regularly for refreshments, although drivers tend to choose the more expensive places (so it pays to take your own snacks with you). Smoking isn't permitted on coach services.

Ships & Ferries

Australia

The only regular maritime passenger service in Australia is the car ferry operating between Melbourne and Devonport on the north coast of Tasmania. It's served by the *Spirit of Tasmania* (🖳 www.spiritof tasmania.com.au), a luxury 467-cabin ship of 31,356 tonnes, with a capacity of around 1,300 passengers plus vehicles. The trip is often rough, so poor sailors should take seasickness pills (or a plane). In fact, the ferry isn't much cheaper than flying and takes around 14 hours, compared with less than an hour by air from Melbourne to Hobart. Ferries run three times weekly in either direction on Mondays, Wednesdays and Fridays from Melbourne's Station Pier, and on Tuesdays, Thursdays and Saturdays from Devonport (although there are seasonal variations). Departures are at 6pm or 7.30pm to Tasmania and at 4pm or 6pm in the other direction. Cabins and hostel-style accommodation are available.

Fares vary with the season from around $100 single, including an evening buffet dinner and continental breakfast. There are three fare rates, depending on the time of year: bargain (late April to mid-September), holiday (Christmas to March) and shoulder (the rest of the year). There's a 25 per cent discount for students in cabin accommodation and occasional mid-week discounts. Vehicle transportation is heavily subsidised by the Tasmanian government and costs between $10 and $96 (depending on the season) one way.

Travelling by ferry is one of the joys of living in Sydney, where many people use them to commute to work. The city has eight main ferry routes and 33 ferry wharves, all served from the main Circular Quay ferry terminal. In addition to regular (slow) ferries, there's also a catamaran (RiverCat) service from Circular Quay to Parramatta (via the Parramatta River) and a JetCat service to Manly. Most ferries operate from around 6am until midnight, although times vary with the route, and services are restricted at weekends, when ferries may not stop at all wharves. Most services run every 50 minutes during the day and more frequently during rush hours, e.g. every 15 or 20 minutes. Regular commuters can buy a book of ten tickets (called a 'Ferry Ten') and weekly, quarterly and annual commuter tickets, which offer even greater savings, and can be combined with other modes of public transport such as buses and suburban trains.

Special tickets are available for trips to major attractions (such as Taronga Zoo), which include the return ferry trip from Circular Quay and the entrance fee, and are cheaper than buying separate tickets. Special ferries are also available to follow sailing races such as the famous Sydney-Hobart race, which starts on Boxing Day (26th December).

There are ferries in Victoria operating between Cowes on Philip Island and Stony Point on the Mornington Peninsula, from Stony Point to Tankerton on French Island, and from Sorrento to Queenscliff. Brisbane has a fast and efficient ferry service along and across the Brisbane river operating every 20 minutes from dawn until around 11pm, Mondays to Saturdays (operating hours are reduced on Sundays). In Perth there's a ferry service across the Swan River from the Barrack Street jetty to the Mends Street jetty. Ferries also operate from Fremantle to Rottnest Island. Darwin harbour ferries make daily crossings to Mandorah on the Cox peninsula. A ferry service also operates from Woodbridge on the south-east coast of Tasmania to Roberts Point on Bruny Island.

New Zealand

As a country consisting mainly of two large islands, the North and the South, separated by the Cook Strait, New Zealand is highly reliant on the ferry service between the two. In addition to the Interislander, there are several smaller ferry services linking the two main islands, as well as serving smaller islands.

The Interislander ferry service is highly efficient and employs two roll-on roll-off ferries most of the year, the Arahura (the larger) and the Aratere (the newer), which carry passengers, vehicles and railway carriages. They sail between Wellington in the North Island and Picton in the South Island, taking around three hours. (The ferry route is 96km/60mi, although the Strait is only 20km/12mi wide at its narrowest point). Purbeck, a freight vessel, also operates across the Strait, as does a fast ferry, The Linx.

The number of daily sailings varies between summer and winter. In summer (December to April) there are five daily sailings (but only four on Sundays and Mondays), but in winter the service is usually reduced to two or three crossings per day, as one of the vessels is taken out of service for maintenance. Summer timetables vary only slightly from year to year: ships leave Wellington at 8am, 9.30am, 3.30pm and 5.30pm, and Picton at 5.30am, 11.30am, 1.30pm, 7pm and 9pm.

It isn't essential to book ahead for the Interislander ferry except at busy times, such as the beginning of school holidays, although it's cheaper, as discounted tickets can only be purchased in advance. If you turn up without a ticket, you must pay the full fare, even if you're travelling off-peak. Reservations can be made up to six months in advance (☎ freephone 0800-802 802 or visit 🖥 www.interislander.co.nz) and there's a wide range of fares, offers and conditions that apply to ferry travel. Children under two travel free and groups of 20 or more may be eligible for a group discount. The Saver Charge fare is $50 per adult and $30 per child, the Easy Change fare is $60 for an adult, $40 for a child. A group of two adults, two children and a vehicle weighing under 2,500kg pays family rates. For example, the one-way fare between Wellington and Picton in August 2005 for two adults, two children over two and a small car was between $270 and $320.

Interislander ferries depart from the Interisland terminals in Wellington and Picton, both of which are well signposted. There are terminal buildings at both terminals where tickets can be purchased and where foot passengers can check in their luggage for the journey rather than carry it on board. There are also car parks and car hire facilities, and if you have a hire car or are staying on the other island for a short time only, it's cheaper to leave your car on one island and hire another when you arrive. A free bus service (the Interislander Shuttle Bus) runs between Wellington railway station and the Interisland terminal. A bus departs from the Interisland terminal and arrives at the railway station in time to catch the evening train to Auckland. At Picton, shuttle buses operate from the Interisland terminal to the station to meet the arrival and departure of trains, which run directly to Christchurch.

The latest check-in time is 30 minutes before departure for foot passengers and one hour for those with vehicles. Foot passengers may take only two pieces of luggage weighing a maximum of 30kg and no more than 200 'linear' centimetres in size (a combination of the height, width and breadth).

Interislander ferries are well equipped, with a cinema, telephones, several bars, children's nursery and play areas, Visitor Information Network (VIN) centres and a number of eating places, including fast food outlets. There are also fruit machines, something of a novelty in a country where gambling is tightly controlled. For a supplement you can also use the club class lounge which provides free drinks and snacks, newspapers and an oasis of peace before boarding the ship (children under 18 aren't permitted!).

Roads

Australia

There are some 813,000km (over 500,000mi) of roads in Australia, varying in quality from eight-lane highways to rutted dirt tracks which are impossible to negotiate in anything less than a four-wheel-drive (4WD) vehicle. Only some 40 per cent of roads are sealed, including nearly 19,000km (12,000mi) of the National Highway System linking the capital cities plus Brisbane and Cairns in Queensland, and Hobart and Burnie in Tasmania. Roads are usually classified as primary or secondary routes. Primary routes are the major roads that link the states and territories, together with those serving the principal centres of population and industry within them. Secondary routes include those which allow the carriage of produce from farms and mines, forest roads serving tourist resorts, and most streets in towns and cities. Lighting is good on major urban roads and usually adequate on other urban roads.

Generally, the roads between major cities and state capitals are excellent, with dual carriageways (divided highways) in metropolitan areas, particularly in the eastern coastal areas of Brisbane, Newcastle and Sydney, although it's generally felt that investment in roads hasn't kept pace with the growth of traffic, especially in metropolitan areas. In rural areas, where traffic density isn't high and there are vast distances between towns, roads may have only two lanes, and in the outback dirt roads are common. In general, the quality of Australian roads is excellent, although some main roads are in a poor condition from being constantly chewed up by juggernauts and the heavy volume of traffic.

New Zealand

Roads in New Zealand are divided into three main categories: motorways, state highways and secondary roads. Motorways are found only in the major cities, where they provide a direct route from the suburbs into the centre. They consist of two or more lanes in each direction, although motorways entering Auckland have three lanes in each direction, and are known by names rather than numbers: for example, in Auckland the Northern, Southern and North-western motorways radiate from the city centre in their respective directions, and the Wellington Urban Motorway runs northwards from the city centre.

Motorways are identified by signs with white lettering on a green background, and junctions are numbered. In 2004 a new system was introduced which numbers junctions according to their distance in kilometres from a given point of the motorway (usually the start), rather than in numerical order. For example, junction ten would be 10km (6mi) from the given point. State highways are major trunk roads with usually just one lane in each direction, on which you can expect to average around 55 to 65kmh when travelling cross-country. They're marked in red on maps and identified by a shield symbol, both on road signs and maps.

Secondary routes are marked in yellow on most maps and by a shield symbol on maps and road signs. They're identified by a two-digit number and in most cases the first digit indicates that the road starts or finishes (as the case may be) on the state highway with the same number. All other roads are unclassified and unnumbered and indicated by white lines on most maps, but have no special identification or road signs. They're usually of reasonable quality and sealed (tarmacked), unless they're specifically marked on a map or signposted as 'unsealed' or 'not tar sealed', which means that they're gravel or compacted earth. They're passable by standard two-wheel-drive cars in good weather and four-wheel-drive vehicles at any time.

3.

<u>YOUR DREAM HOME</u>

Once you've considered possible locations for your dream home in Australia or New Zealand, you must decide on the type of property that will best suit your requirements, weigh up the purchase options and assess the fees associated with buying. There's an overwhelming choice of property for sale and in late 2005 it was a buyers' market in many areas. As when buying property anywhere, it's never wise to be in too much of a hurry. Have a good look around in your chosen region and obtain an accurate picture of the types of property available, their relative values and what you can expect to get for your money. However, before doing this you should make a comprehensive list of what you want (and don't want) from a home, so that you can narrow the field and save time on wild goose chases.

To reduce the chances of making an expensive error when buying in an unfamiliar region, it's often prudent to rent a house for a period (see **Renting Before Buying** on page 141), taking in the worst part of the year (weather-wise). This allows you to become familiar with the region and the weather, and gives you plenty of time to look around for a home at your leisure.

Wait until you find something you fall head over heels in love with and then think about it for a week or two before rushing headlong to the altar. One of the advantages of buying property in Australia or New Zealand is that there's usually another 'dream' home around the next corner – and the second or third dream home is often even better than the first. However, don't dally endlessly, as good properties at the right price don't remain on the market for ever.

RESEARCH

A successful purchase is much more likely if you thoroughly investigate the various regions, the types of property available, prices and relative values, and the procedure for buying property Down Under.

SURVIVAL TIP
The secret of successfully buying a home
in Australia or New Zealand is research,
research and more research.

It's all too easy to fall in love with the beauty and ambience of Australia or New Zealand and to sign a contract without giving it sufficient thought. If you're uncertain, don't allow yourself to be rushed into making a decision, by fears of an imminent price rise (unlikely at the moment) or because someone else is supposedly interested in a property (estate agents sometimes maintain that this is the case, whether it is or not, in order to panic you into a purchase). Although many people dream of buying a home in Australia or New Zealand, it's vital to do your homework thoroughly and avoid the 'dream sellers' (often fellow countrymen) who will happily prey on your ignorance and tell you anything in order to sell you a property. Many people make expensive (and even catastrophic) mistakes when buying homes in the Antipodes, usually because they do insufficient research and are in too much of a hurry, often setting themselves ridiculous deadlines such as buying a home during a short holiday, although they wouldn't dream of acting so rashly when buying a property in their home country!

It isn't uncommon for buyers to regret their decision after a few months or years and wish they had purchased a different kind of property in a different region (or even in a different country!).

If possible, you should take advice from people who already own a house in Australia or New Zealand, from whom you can usually obtain invaluable information (often based on their own mistakes). Much of this advice is included in this book, but you will really believe it if you hear it 'from the horse's mouth'! You should also read books especially written for those planning to live or work in Australia or New Zealand (such as *Living and Working in Australia* and *Living and Working in New Zealand*, also published by Survival Books). It helps to study specialist property magazines and newspapers (see Appendix B for a list), and to visit property exhibitions such as those organised in the UK. There are also a number of websites where you can obtain information and advice from other expatriates (see **Appendix C**).

```
SURVIVAL TIP
Bear in mind that the cost of investing in a few
books or magazines (and other research) is tiny
compared with the expense of making a big mistake.
Nevertheless, don't believe everything you read!
```

AVOIDING PROBLEMS

The problems associated with buying property abroad have been highlighted in the last decade or so, during which the property market in many countries has gone from boom to bust and back again. From a legal viewpoint, Australia and New Zealand are two of the safest places in the world in which to buy a home, and buyers have a high degree of protection under local law, irrespective of whether they're citizens or foreign non-residents. Nevertheless, you should take the usual precautions regarding offers, agreements, contracts, deposits and obtaining proper title to a property.

The most common problems experienced by buyers Down Under include:

● Buying in the wrong place: Do your homework (see **Regions** on page 83, **Location** on page 100 and **Research** above) and rent first (see **Renting Before Buying** on page 141). The wrong decision regarding location is one of the main causes of disenchantment among foreigners who have purchased property in Australia and New Zealand.

● Buying a home that's difficult or impossible to sell: If there's a chance that you will need to sell (and recoup your investment) in the short to medium term, it's important to buy a home that will be easy to sell. A property with broad appeal in a popular area (particularly a waterside property) usually fills the bill; it will need to be very special to sell quickly in less popular areas. A modest, reasonably priced property is likely to be much easier to sell than a large, expensive home, particularly one needing restoration or modernisation. In most areas there's a small market for renovated rural property. There are usually many buyers in the lower price ranges, but they become much scarcer at around $500,000+ unless a property is exceptional, i.e. outstandingly attractive, in a popular area and with a superb situation. In some areas, even desirable properties remain on the market for many months or even years.

● Buying a house and land that's much larger than you need because it seems to offer such good value. Although buying a house with umpteen rooms and several acres of land may seem like a good investment, bear in mind that, should you wish to sell, buyers may be thin on the ground (see above), particularly if the price has doubled or trebled after the cost of renovation (see below). You should think carefully about what you're going to do with a large house and garden. Both will require a lot of maintenance, and your heating costs might be high if the property is in a cool region (i.e. Tasmania and Victoria in Australia and much of New Zealand's South Island). After you've installed a swimming pool, tennis court and croquet lawn, you still have a lot of change left out of even a couple of acres. Do you like gardening or are you prepared to live in a jungle? Can you afford to pay a gardener? Of course you can always plant an orchard or vineyard, create a lake or take up farming!

Don't, on the other hand, buy a property that's too small; when you have a home in Australia or New Zealand, you will inevitably discover that you have many more relatives and friends than you realised!

● Paying too much. Foreign buyers, particularly the British, are often tempted to pay more than the true market value of a property because it's so cheap compared to a similar property in their home country and they're reluctant to negotiate for fear of losing it. Some Antipodean vendors and agents take advantage of this tendency by asking inflated prices.

SURVIVAL TIP
Before buying a property from an agent advertising
in the foreign press, check the prices of similar properties
offered by Australian or New Zealand agents to ensure
that it's good value.

See **Cost Of Property** on page 29 and **Negotiating The Price** on page 158.

● Grossly underestimating restoration and modernisation costs. A tumbledown house for $100,000 can seem a steal, but renovation can cost as much as a new building, as well as taking time and creating headaches.

● Buying a property for business, e.g. to convert to holiday flats, and being too optimistic about the income. The letting season can be just 20 weeks or less in some areas, which means that it's difficult or impossible to cover the cost of maintaining a home, let alone make a living (see **Chapter 9**).

● Not having a survey done on an old property. As surveys aren't a matter of course in Australia and New Zealand, many people assume they aren't necessary – often with disastrous consequences (see **Inspections & Surveys** on page 172).

● Not taking legal advice. Another common assumption among foreign buyers Down Under is that the estate agent handling a sale will look after their interests and ensure that they don't run into problems, which isn't necessarily the case (see **Legal Advice** below).

● Not including the necessary conditional clauses in a contract. As above, the agent or seller's solicitor handling the sale won't necessarily safeguard your interests by inserting provisos in the purchase contract (see **Contracts** on page 208).

● Taking on too large a mortgage: Lenders are offering larger and longer mortgages, which can tempt buyers into borrowing more than they can afford to repay (see **Chapter 4**).

Legal Advice

Many people who buy homes in Australia and New Zealand don't obtain independent legal advice, and most of those who experience problems have taken no precautions whatsoever. Of those that do take legal advice, many do so only after having paid a deposit and signed a contract or, more commonly, after they've run into problems.

SURVIVAL TIP
The most important thing to do
before buying property in Australia or New Zealand
(or indeed anywhere) is to obtain expert,
independent legal advice from someone who's
familiar with local law.

As when buying property in any country, you should never pay any money or sign anything without first obtaining legal advice from an experienced lawyer in a language in which you're fluent. You will find that the small cost (in comparison to the price of a home) of obtaining legal advice is excellent value, if only for the peace of mind it affords. Trying to cut corners to save a few dollars on legal costs is foolhardy in the extreme when a large sum of money is at stake.

You may be able to obtain a list of lawyers who speak your language and are experienced in handling Australian or New Zealand property sales, either in Australia or New Zealand or in your home country, e.g. British buyers can obtain a list from the Law Society in the UK. Specialist lawyers advertise in international property newspapers and magazines.

There are professionals speaking various languages in all areas of Australia and New Zealand (reflecting the cultural melting pot that both countries are), and many expatriate professionals (e.g. architects and surveyors) also practise there. However, don't assume that because you're dealing with a fellow countryman he will offer you a better deal or do a better job than a local person (the contrary may be true). It's wise to check the credentials of all professionals you employ, whether Aussie, Kiwi or foreign.

It's never wise to rely solely on advice proffered by those with a financial interest in selling you a property, such as a builder or estate agent, although their advice may be excellent and totally unbiased.

Finance

You should have your finance in place before you start looking for a property and, if you need a mortgage, obtain a mortgage guarantee certificate from a lender that guarantees you a mortgage at a certain rate, which is usually subject to a valuation (see **Mortgages** on page 197). If you're buying a property for restoration, most lenders won't make a loan against a property that they consider is uninhabitable (e.g. lacking access or sanitation) and they may require 'proof' that the restoration costs won't exceed 40 per cent of the purchase price (in which case a little inventiveness may be required on your part!); you might also be required to use local-registered builders, which is recommended in any case. You will also need a 10 per cent deposit plus the fees and taxes associated with buying (see **Fees** on page 161).

RENTING BEFORE BUYING

Renting is particularly important for those planning to establish a business in Australia or New Zealand, when it isn't advisable to buy a home until you're sure that your business will be a success.

SURVIVAL TIP
Unless you know exactly what you're looking for
and where, it's best to rent a property for a period to
reduce the risk of making a costly mistake, particularly
when you're planning to buy in an unfamiliar area.

Renting long-term before buying is particularly prudent for anyone planning to live in Australia or New Zealand permanently. If possible, you should rent a similar property to the one you're planning to buy, during the time(s) of year when you plan to occupy it. The advantages of renting include the following:

● It allows you to become familiar with the weather, the amenities and the local people, to meet other foreigners who've made their homes in Australia or New Zealand and share their experiences, and to discover the cost of living for yourself.

● It 'buys' you time to find your dream home at your leisure.

- It saves tying up your capital and can be surprisingly inexpensive in many regions. You may even wish to consider renting a home in Australia or New Zealand long-term (or 'permanently'). Some people let their family homes abroad and rent one in Australia or New Zealand for a period (you may even make a profit!).

On the other hand, the disadvantages of renting should be taken into consideration, including the following:

- Annual property price increases in many areas are higher than interest rates (although this is much less certain in the current property market), which means that you may be better of putting your money into a property than investing it while you rent.

- Taking a long-term rental before buying means in effect moving house twice within a year or two, which is one of life's most stressful experiences.

- You may not find the type of rental property you are searching for, which may influence your experience of living in a particular area and possibly in Australia or New Zealand generally. For example, most rental properties are apartments, and rural homes are rarely available for rent.

   If you're looking for a long-term rental property, you may need to rent a holiday apartment for a week or two to allow yourself time to find one that suits you.

Rented Accommodation

Renting rather than buying a home is usually the better choice for anyone who's staying in Australia or New Zealand for a few years or less, when buying isn't usually practical, and for those who don't want the expense and restrictions involved in buying and owning a home. If you're a migrant, it's also sensible to rent for a period before buying, particularly if you're unsure of where you will be living or working. There's also a likelihood that you will change jobs or states within your first few years in Australia or New Zealand (a common occurrence) or even decide to return home. Renting also allows you to become familiar with the neighbourhood, the people and the weather before deciding whether you want to live there permanently.

Australia

There isn't as strong a rental market in Australia as in some other countries (although it's becoming more popular in the major cities). Most people own their own homes and renters are sometimes made to feel like second-class citizens. Rented accommodation has traditionally been scarce in most major cities, particularly in Sydney and Melbourne, where houses in the inner suburbs were rare and you might have had to settle for an apartment or a house in an unpopular outer suburb.

The early years of the 21st century saw more rental property available (with speculators buying properties in the healthy market and then renting them to tenants), but by the summer of 2005 the amount available was declining, e.g. Sydney's rental vacancy rate had dropped to its lowest level for five years. The shortage of rental properties has led to predictable increase in rents.

Furnished accommodation is more expensive than unfurnished and is even more difficult to find, which can be a problem if you're waiting for your furniture to arrive from overseas. Short-term accommodation can usually be arranged before arrival, but you shouldn't rent a property long term without inspecting it first. If you're planning to rent for more than a few weeks, it's wise to investigate the rental market in your chosen area before arriving in Australia, e.g. by studying the advertisements in Australian newspapers (which can be done on the internet) and contacting agents. Some landlords don't allow pets or smokers, so check whether any restrictions apply in advance.

New Zealand

Rental property of all sizes and descriptions is available in New Zealand, although only some 25 per cent of property is rented (including just 10 per cent of new properties). However, in recent years there's been an increased tendency among New Zealand households to rent rather than buy, particularly in Auckland (which accounts for nearly 40 per cent of the rental market), where rented properties can be in short supply. Rented property in towns and cities consists mainly of apartments and flats, although houses are available to rent. Unless a newspaper advertisement specifically states that a property is a house or cottage, you should assume that it's an apartment. Two-bedroom apartments are the most highly sought-after property in the main towns and cities.

Finding A Rental Property

Australia

Your success or failure in finding a suitable rental property depends on many factors, not least the type of property you're looking for (a one-bedroom apartment is easier to find than a four-bedroom detached house), how much you want to pay and the area where you wish to live. Good rental accommodation is in short supply in major cities, particularly Sydney and Melbourne, with the possible exception of luxury homes with astronomical rents. There are sometimes 20 to 30 applicants for each vacant property in popular suburbs, particularly homes with three or more bedrooms, and you may have to take what you can get. Most people settle for something in the outer suburbs and commute to work. However, if you need to travel into a city centre (particularly Sydney) each day, you should be prepared to spend at least an hour or longer travelling each way from the outer suburbs. There are a number of ways to find a rental property, including the following:

- Ask your acquaintances, friends and relatives to help spread the word, particularly if you're looking in the area where you already live. A lot of rental properties are found by word of mouth, particularly in Sydney and Melbourne, where it's difficult to find somewhere with a reasonable rent unless you have connections (many rental properties change tenants without even coming onto the open market).

- Check the advertisements in local newspapers and magazines. The best day for advertisements is Saturday.

- Visit estate agents and letting agents. All cities and large towns have estate agents who also act as letting agents for owners (look under 'Real Estate Agents' in the yellow pages). Obtain rental lists from agents or have them emailed or faxed to you at your workplace. You can also contact agents via the internet.

- Look for advertisements in shop windows and on notice boards in company offices, shopping centres, supermarkets, and universities and colleges.

- Check newsletters published by churches, clubs and expatriate organisations, and their notice boards.

To find accommodation through advertisements in local newspapers, you must be quick off the mark, particularly in the cities. Buy the newspapers as soon as they're published, if possible the night before, and start telephoning 'at the crack of dawn' – even then you're likely to find a queue when you arrive to view a property in Sydney or Melbourne. You must be available to inspect properties immediately or at any time. Finding a property to rent in Sydney is like trying to find one in London or New York, where the best properties are usually found through personal contacts. Some people go to any length to rent a property, including offering to pay above the asking price (bidding wars sometimes break out), pay six months' rent in advance and sign a contract for two or three years.

Most properties in Australian cities are let through agents, whose main task is to vet prospective tenants. Always dress smartly when visiting agents in order to create a good impression. When registering with an agent, you need two forms of identification (e.g. driving licence and passport), written references from your employer and/or previous landlord, and character references. Agents usually contact all referees and may ask why you left your previous accommodation. If you have a pet, you may need a reference from your previous landlord stating that it was clean and well-behaved, but animals aren't usually permitted in rental apartments. You need to complete a registration form and should ensure that it's complete and correct in every detail, or you might jeopardise your chances. Single parents, students, the unemployed and young people have a tough time finding anywhere at an affordable rent and, if you're on a low income or are unemployed, you need to prove that you can pay the rent. If you're acceptable, you may be given the keys to view a property in return for a $50 deposit and proof of identity.

New Zealand

You can find property for rent through specialist rental agents, estate agents (who also handle rentals) and by perusing the small ads in local newspapers. If you see anything advertised in a newspaper, you should arrange to view it straight away, as the best properties are snapped up quickly. You should never rent anything without viewing it first. New Zealand landlords and agents are notoriously inventive in their descriptions (although legislation has been introduced to try to curb this) and they can make even the shabbiest, most tumbledown 'villa' sound like the poshest place in town. If you use an agency or estate agent to find a rental property, he will usually charge at least one week's rent as commission.

It's possible to arrange to rent a house or flat before your arrival in New Zealand, and several immigration consultants (and even some travel agencies) can arrange rentals for you. Bear in mind that properties obtained through these sources are often more expensive than those obtained locally. Another drawback of renting from abroad is that it's difficult to assess a property accurately from thousands of miles away and the location may prove to be inconvenient (although it may look ideal on a map).

Rental Costs

Australia

Rental costs vary considerably depending on the size (number of bedrooms) and quality of a property, its age and the facilities provided. Not least, rents depend on the region, city and neighbourhood. Rents are also lower in rural than urban areas. As a general rule, the further a property is from a large city or town, public transport or other facilities, the cheaper it is. Average rents tend to be highest in Sydney, Melbourne and Darwin. Approximate weekly rents for unfurnished properties are shown below:

Type of Property	Weekly Rent ($)
Studio/bedsit	140-200
1-bedroom apartment	150-275
2-bedroom apartment	200-400
3-bedroom apartment	275-500
2-bedroom house	225-500
3-bedroom house	325-650

The lower rents quoted above apply to modest homes in the less expensive outer suburbs of cities such as Adelaide and Perth. The upper prices apply to outer suburbs in more expensive cities such as Sydney, Melbourne, Brisbane and Darwin. They don't include properties located in the central business district (CBD) of major cities or in exclusive residential areas, for which the sky's the limit: you can easily pay $2,000 per week for a swanky two-bedroom apartment in a smart part of Sydney. It may be possible to find cheaper, older apartments and houses for rent, but they're rare, generally small, and don't contain the standard fixtures and fittings of a modern home.

Most letting agencies and estate agents charge tenants a fee of two weeks' rent for a one-year lease and one week's rent for a six-month lease, which are legal maximums. Usually, you're expected to pay one month's rent in advance, depending on the type of property and the rental agreement, plus a bond (see below) which is held against damages. Tenants must also pay a fee for the lease document, plus a deposit for electricity and gas. Beware of hidden extras such as a fee for connecting the electricity, gas or telephone (or a refundable deposit).

New Zealand

The main divide in rental costs is between Auckland and Wellington on the one hand and the rest of the country on the other. In these two cities you pay significantly more to rent a property, particularly in the better areas. There's not a great deal of difference elsewhere and the national average rent of around $200 per week has remained unchanged in the last few years. Apart from location, the size and facilities of a property are the main factors affecting the rent. The typical rent for a two-bedroom unfurnished apartment ranges from $150 per week in less expensive areas such as Dunedin and Rotorua, to between $350 and $500 per week in central Auckland and Wellington. The weekly rent for a three-bedroom unfurnished apartment ranges from $200 in Dunedin to between $450 and $650 in central Auckland. Anything with a sea view will cost up to 50 per cent more, particularly in Auckland (there are lots of glorious views in New Zealand, but sea views are the only ones for which landlords charge extra). Basic properties are at a premium in any town with a university and may actually cost more than a good quality property elsewhere.

Most landlords prefer to let their properties for at least 12 months at a time and some won't let for less than this period; those who do tend to charge a higher rent, particularly for lets of less than six months. If you find a rental property through an estate agent or rental agency, you must usually pay a fee equal to one week's rent. Approximate weekly rents for unfurnished properties are shown below:

City	2-Bedroom Flat	3-Bedroom House
Auckland	310	385
Christchurch	215	310

Dunedin	185	265
Gisborne	145	195
Hamilton	185	260
Napier	180	250
Nelson	190	260
Otago	260	300
Palmerston North	160	210
Tauranga	205	270
Wellington	240	310

Rental Contracts

Australia

When you find a suitable house or apartment to rent, you should insist on a written contract with the owner or agent, which is called a tenancy agreement. In some states, such as NSW and Victoria, a standard form must be used by law, and in others there are usually minimum conditions which cannot be reduced by landlords. The Agreement for Tenancy states the responsibilities of both parties and provides a fair balance between the landlord and tenant, although you should read it carefully before signing it. Apart from self-catering holiday accommodation, renting a house or apartment usually requires a commitment of six or 12 months with an option to renew.

The owner is responsible for property rates (taxes) and unit service charges, and the tenant for utility costs, unless otherwise agreed. Tenants must take good care of the property, although the landlord is required to maintain it in a habitable condition and ensure that basic services such as water and sewerage are in order. If the landlord refuses to carry out urgent and necessary repairs within a reasonable period of time, you can arrange to have them done and send him the bill, although you mustn't deduct the cost from the rent. If you rent a house with a garden and swimming pool, maintenance costs may be included in the rent.

If you wish to vacate a property before your lease expires, you're liable to pay the rent up to the end of your lease period, although you may be able to find someone to take over the lease and repay your bond (check whether this is possible with your agent or landlord). If you give the landlord adequate notice of termination (usually 21 days), he should try to minimise his loss by advertising and re-letting the property. If you have a verbal contract (termed a periodic tenancy) on a weekly or monthly basis, a week's or a month's notice is sufficient. If you're a tenant with a verbal or written agreement, you cannot be evicted or be forced to leave unless your landlord obtains an eviction order. In order to be evicted you must be in breach of your lease, e.g. by damaging the property, failing to pay the rent, refusing the landlord entry, renovating without permission or sub-letting. A landlord cannot evict you by removing your belongings and changing the locks, or forcing you to leave by cutting off services. At the end of a fixed-term residential tenancy agreement, the landlord can terminate the agreement by giving 60 days' notice before the end of the agreement. The landlord may repossess a property for his own use or to sell it with vacant possession. He isn't required to state his reason for terminating the contract, although there may be grounds for a tenant to appeal to the local Residential Tenancy Tribunal, e.g. your age, lack of alternative accommodation or poor health.

A renting guide is available from estate agents explaining the rights and responsibilities of tenants and landlords. Some people (e.g. Africans, Asians and students) may encounter discrimination, although it's illegal under the Federal Discrimination Act. Most states have a Residential Tenancy Tribunal to investigate complaints by landlords and tenants, and disputes over bonds, evictions, excessive rents and repairs. You can also obtain advice at a Citizens' Advice Bureau, community legal centre, consumer affairs office, Legal Aid Commission or tenants' advice centre. Most large cities also have a tenants' union hotline. The local Office of Fair Trading in many states publishes a *Renting Guide* or *Tenants' Rights Manual* (in NSW see 🖳 www. fairtrading.nsw.gov.au).

New Zealand

When renting property in New Zealand, it's usual to sign a tenancy agreement, although the Department of Building and Housing issues a standard agreement for landlords and tenants. If your landlord uses this agreement and you're happy with the details, it isn't usually necessary to have it checked by a lawyer, as the terms and conditions are simple and written in non-legal language (other countries please take note!). Most tenancy agreements are on a periodic basis, which means that the tenancy continues indefinitely until either party gives notice. A tenant is required to give 21 days' notice to end a tenancy, but a landlord must give 90 days notice, except in exceptional circumstances, such as when he wishes to move into the property himself (in which case he need only give 42 days notice). It's also possible to have a tenancy agreement for a fixed period, in which case the tenancy lasts for the period agreed at the outset only, although it can be extended by mutual agreement.

When you take up a tenancy, you must pay a bond to the landlord, which is usually the equivalent of one or two weeks' rent, although legally it can be up to four weeks. The bond isn't held by the landlord but by the Bond Processing Unit of the Tenancy Services Centre (Department of Building and Housing) and the landlord must pay your bond to the Unit within 23 working days of receiving it. At the end of the tenancy, the Bond Processing Unit refunds your bond less the cost of any damage (for which you're responsible under the standard tenancy agreement). Rent is usually paid fortnightly. The landlord must pay rates and home insurance, although your belongings may not be covered under the landlord's policy and you may need to take out separate insurance for these (see page 263).

If you have a dispute with your landlord, the Tenancy Services Centre will advise you on your rights and responsibilities and help resolve the problem. The biggest causes of disputes in rented property, apart from tenants' failure to pay the rent on time, are landlords who don't maintain their premises (although they're legally required to) and problems with neighbours (who may also be the same landlord's tenants) in, for example, an apartment block or units.

ESTATE AGENTS

Australia

Most property in Australia is bought and sold through estate agents, who sell property on commission for owners. When buying property in Australia, always use a licensed agent. The Real Estate and Business Agents Act imposes obligations and requirements on licensed agents, which protect both buyers and sellers by creating a source of legal redress in the event of error, loss, misrepresentation or negligence. The act protects deposits paid by buyers and prevents conduct which could be misleading or prejudicial to buyers, and is backed by disciplinary procedures and a

Fidelity Guarantee Fund. However, the act doesn't apply to private sales where no agent is involved.

The Real Estate Institute of Australia, Level 1, 16 Thesiger Court (PO Box 9068), Deakin, ACT 2600 (☎ 02-6282 4544, 💻 www.reiaustralia. com.au) is the umbrella organisation for state real estate organisations, e.g. the Real Estate Institute of New South Wales, and you should check with them that an agent is a member. In July 2000, the Property Agents and Motor Dealers Act came into force, whereby estate agents are obliged to adhere to a code of conduct and incur harsher penalties for false or misleading representations. Estate agents must adhere to a code of ethics (of which you can request a copy) and must have professional indemnity insurance. Clients also have access to a Tribunal and Complaints Fund.

There's a multi-listing service in all states, whereby homes are advertised in estate agents' offices throughout the state, which costs vendors nothing until their home is sold. However, some agents may only show you, or at least try to push, properties for which they have an exclusive listing (when they don't need to share the commission with anyone else).

Estate agents usually act for the seller and it's their job to obtain the highest price they can for a property, so don't expect impartial advice if you're a buyer. If they offer to make a considerable reduction on the advertised price, it probably means that it's overpriced and has been on their books for a long time. An estate agent usually tries to get you to view as many properties as possible (irrespective of whether they fit your requirements or price range), as this shows sellers that he's doing a good job. You should try to sort out the possibles from the improbables before making any appointments to view and, if you're shown properties that don't meet your specifications, tell the agent immediately. You can also help the agent narrow the field by telling him exactly what's wrong with the properties you reject.

Don't see too many properties in one day, however anxious you are to find somewhere, as it's easy to become confused as to the merits of each property. Many vendors hold an 'open house' at weekends (possibly with a 'home open' sign outside), although the total inspection period may be just a few hours. Otherwise, it's essential to make an appointment with an owner or agent to inspect a property. It's possible to inspect Australian properties on the internet from anywhere in the world, as most large estate agents, builders and developers now have websites.

New Zealand

When looking for a house to purchase, you can visit local estate agents (known as real estate agents in New Zealand), look for a private sale in the small ads in local newspapers, or tour the area looking for 'For Sale' signs. The easiest option is to visit an estate agent (or a number). There are 'family' estate agents and a number of large national chains, including Bayleys (🖳 www. bayleys.co.nz) and Harcourts (🖳 www.harcourts.co.nz). If you wish to see what's available before you arrive in New Zealand, the vast majority of agents have websites. The Real Estate Institute of New Zealand includes details on its website (🖳 www.reinz.org.nz) from a number of agents in different parts of the country. The larger estate agents also publish property newspapers or magazines advertising properties for sale. For example, Harcourts publish a 'Blue Book' series, which you can buy in a number of countries or download from their website (see above).

All estate agents in New Zealand must be licensed and registered with the Real Estate Agents Licensing Board. You can check by contacting them at PO Box 1247, Wellington (☎ 04-520 6949). Don't deal with anyone who isn't registered, because if they cannot meet the standards for registration it's unlikely that they will abide by any other standards either. However, the fact that an agent is licensed shouldn't be taken as a guarantee that he's reputable. It's illegal for an estate agent to mislead you deliberately, but as in other countries, there are lots of 'tricks of the trade' which are perfectly legal, such as exaggerating the desirability of the local area or suggesting that other people are clamouring to buy a house that has been up for sale for months.

In New Zealand, estate agents' fees are entirely the responsibility of the vendor, and the buyer doesn't pay anything (although of course the fees are in effect 'built in' to the price of a property). This underlines the fact that the agent is working for the seller, not for you, so you cannot expect him to do you any favours. (In fact, most estate agents are working for themselves, i.e. trying to earn as much money as possible!).

Before visiting an agent, you should have a good idea of the kind of property you're looking for (e.g. a house or an apartment), the price you can afford to pay and where you wish to live. The agent should then be able to give you a list of properties which fit that description. You should avoid the temptation to look at properties which are outside the areas you've chosen or which cost more than you can afford (agents will *always* send you details of properties outside your stated price range!). If a property you view seems suitable, you will be pressed to make a decision quickly.

When you see a property you like, don't hesitate to haggle over the price, which is standard practice, even when the seller or an agent suggests the price is firm or gives the impression that other buyers are keen to snap up a bargain. Usually, an offer of between 3 and 8 per cent under the asking price is 'acceptable', but there's nothing to say you cannot offer less if you think the price is too high or the vendor is anxious to sell. To get an idea of whether asking prices are realistic, you can check with Quotable Value (🖳 www.qv.co.nz), New Zealand's largest valuation and property information company, which publishes monthly tables of average property prices on a region-by-region basis. Some estate agents also publish regular surveys and reports on the state of the New Zealand property market and current prices. For information, contact the Real Estate Institute of New Zealand (🖳 www.reinz.org.nz).

Purchase Restrictions

If you're a permanent resident of New Zealand, there are no restrictions on the home you can buy in New Zealand. If you aren't a permanent resident, you're sometimes limited by the Overseas Investment Act 1973 (OIC Act) to buying a home on less than five hectares (12.5 acres) of land. If the land is on, or next to, a sensitive area (e.g. an island or reserve), overseas buyers and those with work permits are sometimes limited to buying less than 0.4 hectares (one acre) of land. Buying apartments, houses and land in urban areas isn't generally affected by OIC Act restrictions. Your solicitor will advise whether you need to seek agreement from the Overseas Investment Commission (OIC, i.e. the government body that oversees foreign investment policies) for a particular purchase. If you do, your solicitor will insert a condition in the contract making the purchase conditional on obtaining OIC consent.

Viewing

If possible, you should decide where you want to live, what sort of property you want and your budget before visiting Australia or New Zealand. Obtain details of as many properties as possible in your chosen area and make a shortlist of those you wish to view (it's also wise to mark them on a map). Most Antipodean agents expect customers to know where they want to buy within a 30 to 40km (20 to 25mi) radius and some even expect them to narrow their choice down to certain towns or villages. If you cannot define where and what you're looking for, at least tell the agent, so that he knows that you're undecided. If you're 'window shopping', say so. Many agents will still be pleased to show you properties, as they're well aware that many people fall in love with (and buy) a property on the spot.

Agents vary enormously in their efficiency, enthusiasm and professionalism. If an agent shows little interest in finding out exactly what you want, you should go elsewhere. You should make an appointment to see properties, as agents don't like people simply turning up. If you make an appointment, you should keep it or call and cancel it. If you're on holiday, it's acceptable to drop in unannounced to have a look at what's on offer, but don't expect an agent to show you properties without an appointment. If you view properties during a holiday, it's best to do so at the beginning so that you can return later to inspect any you particularly like a second or third time.

You should try to view as many properties as possible during the time available, but allow sufficient time to view each property thoroughly, to travel and get lost between houses, and for breaks for sustenance. Although it's important to see enough properties to form an accurate opinion of price and quality, don't see too many in one day (between four and six is usually enough), as it's easy to become confused about the merits of each property. If you're shown properties that don't meet your specifications, tell the agent immediately. You can also help the agent narrow the field by telling him exactly what's wrong with the properties you reject.

It's wise to make notes of both the good and bad features and take lots of photographs of the properties you like, so that you're able to compare them later at your leisure (but keep a record of which photos are of which house!). It's also shrewd to mark each property on a map so that, should you wish to return, you can find them without getting lost (too often). The more a property appeals to you, the more you should look for faults and negative points; if you still like it after stressing all the negative points, it must have special appeal.

PROPERTY PRICES

Australia

Property prices (see also **Cost of Property** on page 29) vary considerably throughout the country and in the various suburbs of the major cities. Not surprisingly, the further you are from a town or city, the lower the cost of land and property. Properties in central and popular beach locations cost anywhere between two and four times as much as similar properties in less fashionable or convenient outlying city suburbs. For many buyers it's a choice between a small apartment in an inner city and a large detached family home in the outer suburbs – in recent years the average Aussie battler (commuter) has had to move further and further into the outer suburbs of major cities in order to find affordable accommodation.

A two or three-bedroom, single-storey home in most city outer suburbs costs between $110,000 and $185,000; four-bedroom, two-storey homes cost from around $150,000 to $375,000. On the other hand, waterfront properties in Sydney can be astronomically expensive and a reasonable two-bedroom apartment in an attractive building with water views costs more than $900,000 (2 million dollar homes are commonplace in Sydney, in Melbourne and on the White Sunshine Coast). There's a high demand everywhere for waterfront properties, which have generally been an excellent investment, particularly in NSW where the government plans to preserve the coastline from further development (canal developments are already banned). In the current sluggish market, however, some may be overpriced.

After a period of large annual house price increases in the later '90s and early 21st century, the Australian residential property market experienced a 'correction' in 2005. According to *The Economist* magazine's house-price index, between 1997 and 2004, Australian residential property prices rose by 113 per cent (in the major cities, rises were closer to 200 per cent), with prices generally reaching their zenith in the third quarter of 2003. By the end of 2004, average house prices in the capital cities were around $550,000 in Sydney, $383,000 in Canberra, $330,000 in Brisbane, $319,000 in Melbourne, $280,000 in Hobart and Perth, $270,000 in Adelaide and $260,000 in Darwin.

An interest rate rise in March 2005 contributed to a market slowdown and some reductions in the above average figures. The remainder of 2005 is expected to see static house prices and maybe falls in some areas and sectors of the market. Analysts expect property oversupply and further interest rate rises to cause residential property prices to be sluggish or to decline in 2006 and perhaps also in 2007, before there's an upturn in the market. These predictions are to be taken with a pinch of salt: predicting the movement of any market (e.g. the art, currency, property or stock market) is notoriously difficult, there being a number of (sometimes unpredictable) factors to take into account. If, however, the predictions are correct, the forthcoming two or three years will be a good time to enter the Australian residential property market. This is particularly the case in Sydney, where prices are predicted to fall the most. The property market in NSW has been depressed more than average by news of the introduction of a vendor duty tax from July 2005. Other Australian cities are expected to experience softer landings, with some analysts still seeing room for further price increases, especially in parts of Canberra, Melbourne and Perth.

Selling at auction has been popular in recent years, particularly when prices were rising. Around 25 to 30 per cent of homes in Melbourne are sold

156 Your Dream Home

at auction compared with around 20 per cent in Sydney, around 15 per cent in Brisbane and 10 to 15 per cent in Adelaide.

A few kilometres can make a huge difference to the price of a property, with apartments in central areas costing up to $2,500 per square metre more than those in harbour-side developments a few kilometres further out. Land prices also reduce considerably from around 15km/9mi outside a city and are at their lowest around 25km/16mi from city centres. The cost of land varies from as little as $40,000 for an average size suburban house at least 25km/16mi from cities such as Adelaide, Hobart and Perth to over $350,000 for a similar plot within 15km/9mi of central Sydney (if you can find one). The cost of building a home varies depending on the location and the quality of materials used. Brick veneer costs from around $800 to $900 per m², depending on the location. The cost of building a home increased considerably after the introduction of goods and services tax (GST) in July 2000.

In the last few years, there have been few bargains and it has been a sellers' market, although you might have been able to negotiate a reduction of 5 or possibly 10 per cent. That has changed and buyers today can undercut asking prices more substantially and pick up a 'bargain'. There's usually a good reason, however, when a property is substantially cheaper than other similar properties. Although it's sometimes unwise to look a gift horse in the mouth, you should generally be suspicious of a bargain that appears too good to be true. On the other hand, most sellers and estate agents still price properties higher than the market price or the price they expect to receive, knowing that buyers will try to drive the price down, so always haggle over the price asked (even if you think it's a bargain). This is, in fact, one of the few occasions in Australia when you're expected to bargain, although you should try to avoid insulting an owner by offering a derisory price, even in the current uncertain market.

If you're buying a home for a limited period or as an investment, you should buy one that you hope will sell quickly and at a profit. Homes that sell best are exceptional period houses of character with lots of original features, and water and beach-front homes (particularly in Queensland, although sales of apartments in Brisbane hit a six-year low in the first quarter of 2005), which are in high demand and can be let for most of the year to holidaymakers if required. Luxury units in central Brisbane, Melbourne and Sydney have also been a good investment, but some are currently overpriced. Buying property in Australia is usually a long-term investment and isn't recommended for those seeking a short-term gain (this is particularly true at the moment). You must pay capital gains tax on the profit made on the sale of an investment property (see page 253).

You can find out the price of homes in any Sydney suburb through the *Sydney Morning Herald Home Price Guide*, which lists all the sales results (both auction and private treaty) in Sydney suburbs for the last 12 months (it can be ordered on the internet from Australian Property Monitors, 🖥 www. apm.com.au). A similar service is provided by newspapers in other major cities, and you can also peruse property advertisements in a number of publications on the internet (e.g. 🖥 www.sydneyproperty.com.au). See also **Cost of Property** on page 29.

New Zealand

In general, property prices in New Zealand are slightly lower than in most of Western Europe due to its small population and relatively low demand, low cost of land and generally low construction costs. There is, however, a huge gulf between Auckland and the rest of the country. Property is much more expensive there, mainly because most of the best paid jobs are to be found there. Auckland also has one of the best climates in New Zealand and prices are further inflated as it's the first choice of the majority of immigrants. Wellington is the country's second most expensive area for property purchase. Price variations are less marked throughout the rest of the country.

After some years of large annual increases in house prices, 2005 has seen a relative slowdown in the property market, although certain commentators dismiss this as a blip. In summer 2005 (winter in New Zealand), there's was little consensus regarding what the market would do. The national average house price in New Zealand in December 2004 was $260,000, increasing to $265,000 in January 2005, but at the time the second figure was released, the president of the Real Estate Institute advised caution because reduced sales volumes and decreases in prices in some regions indicated that the market would begin to turn. For example, in the Auckland Metropolitan area, prices fell from $355,000 to $340,000 from December to January, while in Auckland City, the average fell from $412,500 to $385,000. In Wellington, price falls were much more modest, down from $276,250 to $275,000, but in Hawke's Bay, for example, the average price rose, from $225,000 to $245,050.

By spring (northern hemisphere) 2005, areas that had seen some of the largest price increases in previous months, e.g. Nelson and Tasman, began to see falls. The Bank of New Zealand economist predicted that a housing downturn was imminent, and when it arrived, prices would drop between 5 and 10 per cent over a two to three year period. The Reserve Bank was more precise, predicting that average house prices would fall 4.8 per cent in 2006 and a further 1.9 per cent in 2007 (after having risen 56 per cent between 2001 and 2004).

But in summer (northern hemisphere) 2005, figures showed that the national average house price had risen to $275,000 (after a record figure of $280,000 in March and a fall to $272,000 in April) surprising many economists who thought that a downturn was about to begin, following April's fall. Prices had fallen slightly in a couple of regions, but in most they had continued to rise, with a notable narrowing of the gap in prices between urban and provincial areas. This last trend was put down to jaded city dwellers escaping to life in the country.

Apartments are often as expensive as houses and townhouses (or even more so), as they are invariably located in city centres, whereas most houses are in suburbs or the country. Advertised prices are usually around 3 to 8 per cent above a property's true market value and substantially above its rateable value.

When calculating your budget, you should also allow for lawyer's fees (see **Conveyance** on page 209) and bear in mind that banks charge a mortgage processing fee equal to 1 per cent of the mortgage amount and require a deposit (usually $500 minimum) on application.

See also **Cost of Property** on page 29.

NEGOTIATING THE PRICE

When buying a property, it usually pays to haggle over the price, even if you think it's a bargain. Don't be put off by a high asking price, as most sellers are willing to negotiate. In fact, sellers generally presume buyers will bargain and rarely expect to receive the asking price for a property (although some vendors ask an unrealistic price and won't budge a cent). In popular areas, asking prices may be unrealistically high (up to double the real market price), particularly to snare the unsuspecting and ignorant foreign buyer. It's a good idea for your peace of mind to obtain an independent valuation (appraisal) to determine a property's market value. If a property has been realistically priced, you shouldn't expect to obtain more than a 5 or 10 per cent reduction.

Timing is of the essence in the bargaining process. Generally the longer a property has been for sale and the more desperate the vendor is to sell, the more likely a lower offer will be accepted. Some people will tell you outright that they must sell by a certain date and that they will accept any reasonable offer. You may be able to find out from neighbours why someone is selling, which may help you decide whether an offer would be accepted. If a property has been on the market for a long time, e.g. longer than six months in a popular area, it may be overpriced (unless it has obvious defects). If there are many desirable properties for sale in a particular area or developments that have been on the market a long time, you should find out why, e.g. there may be a new road, railway or airport planned.

Before making an offer, you should find out as much as possible about a property, such as the following:

● When it was built;

● Whether it has been used as a permanent or a holiday home;

● How long the owners have lived there;

● Why they're selling (they may not tell you outright, but may offer clues);

● How keen they are to sell;

● How long it has been on the market;

● The condition of the property;

● The neighbours and neighbourhood;

● Local property tax rates;

● Whether the asking price is realistic.

For your part, you must ensure that you keep any sensitive information from a seller and give the impression that you have all the time in the world (even if you must buy immediately). All this 'cloak and dagger' stuff may seem unethical, but you can be assured that if you were selling and a prospective buyer knew you were desperate and would accept a low offer, he certainly wouldn't be in a hurry to pay you any more!

If you make an offer that's too low you can always raise it, but it's impossible to lower an offer once it has been accepted (if your first offer is accepted without haggling, you will never know how low you could have gone!). If an offer is rejected, it may be worth waiting a week or two before making a higher offer, depending on the market and how keen you are to buy a particular property.

If you make a low offer, it's wise to indicate to the owner a few negative points (without being too critical) that merit a reduction in price. Note, however, that if you make a very low offer, an owner may feel insulted and refuse to do business with you!

```
┌─────────────────────────────────────────────────────────┐
│                      SURVIVAL TIP                         │
│       Be prepared to walk away from a deal rather than    │
│                    pay too high a price.                  │
└─────────────────────────────────────────────────────────┘
```

If you want to buy a property at the best possible price as an investment, shopping around and buying a 'distress sale' from an owner who simply must sell may result in the best deal. Obviously you will be in a better position if you're a cash buyer and able to close quickly. Cash buyers in some areas may be able to negotiate a considerable price reduction for a quick sale, depending on the state of the local property market and how urgent the sale is. However, if you're seeking an investment property it's wise to buy in an area that's in high demand, preferably with both buyers and renters. For the best resale prospects, it's usually best to buy in an area or community (and style) that's attractive to local buyers.

An offer should be made in writing, as it's likely to be taken more seriously than a verbal offer.

BUYING AT AUCTION

If you have an eye for a bargain or enjoy the thrill of the auction room, you may wish to consider buying a property at auction. Before doing so you should:

- Ascertain the true market value of the property. The best way to do this is to check on the selling prices of similar properties in the immediate area.

- Pre-arrange your finance. You will probably be expected to pay a 10 per cent deposit as soon as your bid is successful and sign a contract within a day or two (if not immediately).

- Inspect the property thoroughly. Never buy unseen no matter how low the price. If it seems too good to be true, it probably is!

If the property seems genuine, you could consider making a pre-auction bid of around 20 to 30 per cent less than its market value. Prices fetched at auction are notoriously unreliable, and sellers who are 'jittery' may (legally) agree to a deal before the auction, in which case you could have yourself a bargain!

Australia

An alternative to buying from an agent is to buy at auction, although this method is generally used for properties at the upper end of the market. Auctions have become increasingly popular in the last few years, as sellers can sell quickly and buyers can usually save money (it's most common in Melbourne and Sydney). However, it's absolutely vital to do your homework before buying at auction, particularly regarding the market value of properties. Many agents quote a price 10 or 20 per cent below a property's expected sale price in order to attract more interest at auctions, although in a sellers' market many properties sell for much more than their reserve price. Property auctions are advertised in local newspapers and may be held on site.

You can engage a buyer's representative to find a house, bid for it at auction and negotiate the sale. Agents may charge as little as a few hundred dollars to bid at an auction or up to 3 per cent of the price if they conduct a search and secure a property. However, this can save you a lot of money, time and trouble. It isn't wise to bid yourself unless you know the ropes and are confident of what you're doing. It's necessary to have your finance in place in advance when buying at auction, as you're required to pay the deposit on the spot (usually 10 per cent) and close within a reasonable period. **Cooling-off rights don't apply when buying at auction.**

New Zealand

Only a small proportion of domestic properties in New Zealand are offered for sale at public auction, although it's becoming more popular. These are usually properties whose value isn't easily determined, such as unique luxury properties and those requiring major renovation. Properties repossessed from those who've failed to meet their mortgage repayments are also sold at auction.

FEES

In addition to the fees listed below, if you're buying a new home you may need to pay an architect and other fees. You also usually need to pay utility connection, reconnection, registration or transfer fees for electricity, gas, telephone and water. Although not a fee as such, removal costs must also be taken into account. In addition to the fees associated with buying a property, you must also consider the running costs, which include a caretaker's or management fees if you leave a home empty or let it, community fees for a unit or other communal garden, pool and property maintenance, contents insurance (see page 263), local property taxes, and standing charges for utilities (electricity, gas, telephone, water). Annual running costs usually average around 2 to 3 per cent of the cost of a property.

Australia

The fees associated with buying a home in Australia usually total 4 to 5 per cent of the purchase price, which is lower than in many other countries. Most fees are calculated as a percentage of the value of the property you're buying, so the more expensive the property, the higher the fees. Even removal costs are higher if you have a large house (unless you have a lot of empty rooms). If you're buying *and* selling, you must consider the cost of both transactions. The main fees are as follows (although they change regularly and, in the current slow market, there are calls to reduce or abolish some of them):

- **Stamp Duty:** Stamp duty varies considerably depending on the state or territory and averages around $2,000 (on a $100,000 property), $4,600 ($200,000 property) and $14,000 ($400,000 property). Stamp duty also varies according to the type of buyer and price of the property. In some states, it's lower for first-time buyers or is waived altogether. For example, in May 2004 NSW introduced the First Home Plus scheme, under which first-time buyers are exempt from paying stamp duty on homes costing up to $500,000. First-time buyers also receive a discount on stamp duty for homes costing between $500,000 and $600,000. Victoria introduced similar legislation in March 2004, with first-time buyers receiving a cash grant of up to $5,000 to help pay towards stamp duty. The ACT has abolished stamp duty for first-time buyers for homes costing up to $273,000, and first-time buyers with modest incomes can apply for stamp duty discounts. See 🖳 www.stampoutstampduty.com.au/rates for the latest situation in each state.

- **Land Transfer Registration:** This fee is for recording a change of owner at the Land Titles Office and is payable each time a property is sold. It's either a flat fee or a variable fee based on the price paid. The fee on a $100,000 property, for example, is $56 in New South Wales (fixed fee) and around $460 in South Australia (variable fee – around $960 on a $200,000 property).

- **Legal Fees:** Legal fees are usually between 1 and 2 per cent of the purchase price, but may vary according to the work involved. Legal fees vary considerably from state to state, e.g. from around $550 in Adelaide, Perth and Hobart to around $1,750 in Brisbane for a property costing over $100,000. The fees in most states are within the $550 to $1,100 range.

- **Solicitor's or Conveyancer's Fees:** These are the fees for the documentation necessary for a property purchase (see **Conveyance** on page 209). There isn't a fixed charge and the cost of conveyance can range from around $500 to $1,700.

- **Government Taxes:** There are federal and state taxes on financial transactions that vary according the state or territory.

- **Mortgage Fees:** A range of fees is associated with mortgages, including a mortgage application or establishment fee, a valuation fee, legal fees, maintenance fees and a loan registration fee (for mortgage information see page 197).

- **Termite & Pest Inspection:** This is compulsory in some states, while in others it's sufficient to certify that a property is free of termites and pests. However, a termite inspection is always recommended when buying property, whether it's required by law or not. The inspection costs from around $150 to $250 and may be paid by the vendor or buyer, or shared.

- **Strata Inspection:** When you're buying an apartment (unit), it's wise to have a strata inspection (relating to the Strata Titles Act), which tells you whether there have been any administrative or structural problems with the building. Strata inspections cost from around $180 to $250.

- **Inspection or Survey Fee:** Although it isn't compulsory to have a building inspection or a structural survey carried out, it's often wise, particularly when you're buying an old detached house. You should allow from $400 to $500 for a structural survey.

- **Building Insurance:** It's invariably a condition of lenders that properties are fully insured against structural and other damage. It may be necessary to insure a property from the day you sign the purchase contract.

New Zealand

As is the case in Australia, purchase costs are modest in New Zealand, rarely more than around 4 or 5 per cent of the purchase price. The main fees are as follows:

- **Land Transfer Registration Fee:** This is around $130 and is sometimes included in the legal fees (see below).

- **Solicitor's Fees:** There's no fixed scale of conveyance charges and conveyance by a lawyer (the only professional allowed to charge for conveyance) normally costs between $600 and $2,000, so it's worth shopping around and haggling over the cost. It's possible to find a lawyer who will do the job for as little as $400.

- **Mortgage Fees:** Banks charge a mortgage processing fee equivalent to 1 per cent of the mortgage amount.

- **Land Information Memorandum (LIM):** This is obtained from the local council and contains information about a property's zoning, boundaries, building consents etc. Costs vary greatly, from around $2 to $1,500.

- **Inspection or Survey Fee:** Although it isn't compulsory to have a building inspection or structural survey carried out, it's often wise, particularly when you're buying an old detached house. You should allow from $500 to $750 for a structural survey.

- **Building Insurance:** It's invariably a condition of lenders that properties are fully insured against structural and other damage. It may be necessary to insure a property from the day you sign the purchase contract.

TYPES OF PROPERTY

Australia

Modern Homes

Over three-quarters of Australia's eight million homes are detached houses, some 15 per cent are apartments, and around 10 per cent are row homes, semi-detached, terrace homes or townhouses. The most common Australian family home is a detached, single-storey bungalow (ranch style) on a quarter or third of an acre plot. It has three or four bedrooms, a combined lounge/dining room, kitchen (possibly eat-in), bathroom (or two), separate toilet, laundry room, possibly a family or rumpus room (which may be an extension of the kitchen), and a garage or car port. Bathrooms usually include a bath and separate shower and there may also be a shower room. Larger houses, e.g. from four bedrooms, have two or more bathrooms, with the master bedroom having an en suite bathroom or shower. Larger homes may also have a study and other rooms. The mild climate allows year-round, outdoor living, and most detached homes have terraces or patios with a barbecue, and around half have a swimming pool (which must be completely fenced off and childproof).

The quality of modern Australian homes is generally excellent. Construction may be brick (the most expensive and generally reserved for luxury homes), brick veneer (the most popular), or weatherboard and fibre cement known as fibro (the cheapest but no longer common). Brick veneer has the outward appearance of a full brick construction, except that the inner frame is made of timber and the inside is lined with plaster board or similar material. It costs less than a full brick home and is particularly suited to Australia's climate. A fibro house is a timber frame covered with fibre cement on the outside and plasterboard on the inside. Roofs are generally made of terracotta or cement tiles, although galvanised steel decking or fibre cement sheeting is often used in contemporary style homes. In remote country areas (e.g. the outback and the bush), mains electricity, running water, sewerage and telephone lines are a luxury, and dirt roads, generators, rain water tanks and septic tanks are common. Houses are raised on stilts in some tropical areas or those subject to flooding, where the garage may be located below the living area.

When you buy a new home, bathroom, kitchen and light fittings, curtains and fitted carpets are usually included in the price. Bedrooms have built-in wardrobes, and kitchens are fully fitted with a cooker and possibly even a dishwasher. Fly screens are common on external doors and all windows, and allow you to leave the doors and windows open without inviting insects in. Good insulation helps keep homes cool in summer and warm in winter; in the southern states, homes may have a fireplace or a heating unit in the lounge. Air-conditioning may be fitted as standard in up-market homes. Wallpaper is rare in Australia, where interior walls are generally painted. Most semi-detached and detached houses have single or double garages included in the price. In major cities, there are home display villages where you can view the latest designs from Australia's largest builders. New properties have a builder's warranty.

Apartments

Apartments (flats), called units or home units in Australia, are common in inner city and beachside areas because of the high cost of land, although they aren't as widespread as in European cities. Apartment blocks are usually purpose-built with up to 20 storeys and are rarely conversions of old large houses. Blocks may contain split-level apartments and penthouses (which traditionally occupy the whole top floor of a high-rise building) and usually have underground parking. Many modern apartment blocks have communal pools and other facilities such as gymnasiums, saunas and tennis courts. Queensland's Gold Coast is popular among retirees, who buy apartments in retirement villages which include billiards rooms, bowling greens, croquet lawns, swimming pools and tennis courts, and are served by village buses. Units in Australia are sold freehold under the Strata Titles Act. Apartments, particularly older apartments, aren't usually built or designed to the high standards found in North America or many European countries. Many older apartments are tiny, with poor storage and inadequate parking, and are lacking in quality fixtures and fittings.

Period & Older Homes

There are many period homes in the inner suburbs of the major cities, most of which have been modernised and are now relatively (or very) expensive. Terraced housing is found in some older inner-city suburbs, e.g. in Sydney, where decorative wrought ironwork is a feature of early homes, particularly in suburbs such as Paddington and Darlinghurst. Federation (early 19th century) houses made of wood and sandstone are also attractive and highly prized. In Queensland, there are elevated timber and iron houses with balustrades and verandas (known appropriately as 'Queenslanders'), which allow cooling breezes to permeate homes. However, there's also a vast amount of housing stock with no architectural merit or heritage value. Many homes built in the '50s and '60s building boom reflect the less sophisticated and enlightened ideas of that era and are entirely unsuited to today's lifestyle. In many cases, the plots they occupy are worth much more than the properties built on them.

If you need to modernise or renovate a property, you should expect to pay at least 20 per cent more than your original budget. Many old homes have problems such as damp, insect infestations, and poor electricity and plumbing installations.

Mobile Homes

Mobile homes (also called transportable or manufactured homes because they're factory-built in two or more sections and erected on site, usually in around six weeks) are popular in Australia, particularly among retirees. Many mobile homes look like conventional homes and include features such as bay windows, built-in wardrobes, skylights, verandas and even brick finishes. They cost between $70,000 and $140,000 and, at the top end of the market, aren't much cheaper than conventional homes. However, mobile homes are likely to depreciate over the years, rather than appreciate like a conventional home.

Mobile homes are usually sited in caravan parks or specially built estates. Sites must usually be leased, e.g. on a weekly or monthly basis, and you should beware of spiralling rents, which are an issue in most states (although some parks have rent controls). There are also a number of restrictions in parks, e.g. overnight fees for guests, and in some states owners even require the permission of park owners to sell. For further information contact the Manufactured Housing Industry Association, PO Box H114, Harris Park, NSW 2150 (☎ 02-9615 9999), which publishes an information booklet. The Queensland Government Office of Fair Trading publishes an online *Going Mobile – A Guide to Mobile Home Living* (🖳 www. consumer.qld.gov.au).

New Zealand

Most New Zealand families live in detached homes set on their own plot of land, known as a 'section'. This dates back to the pioneering days when the authorities divided great tracts of land into sections for house building. Each section was a quarter of an acre and the phrase 'quarter-acre paradise' was coined to describe the typical New Zealand home as well as the country itself. A quarter-acre section (or its metric equivalent, approximately 1,000m^2) is still the standard plot size in New Zealand, although many sections have been subdivided and a second property built in the garden, or in some cases the original house has been demolished and several new properties built in its place. At one point this sub-division threatened to get out of hand, and there are minimum plot sizes in some areas.

Most New Zealand properties are single-storey bungalows (although they're usually called 'houses'), although two-storey houses are becoming more popular. If a property is described as a 'villa', don't expect a palace complete with columns, marble floors and a sunken bath worthy of

Cleopatra, as they're usually quite modest homes made of wood with a corrugated iron roof (see below)! Semi-detached properties, terraced houses (known as townhouses) and apartments aren't as common as detached properties in most of New Zealand. The suburbs of most main cities have large townhouses from the Victorian area, many of which have been lovingly restored, and in recent years new smaller townhouses have been built. Apartments are largely confined to city centres. Apartment living went out of fashion in the '80s when many people moved out to the suburbs, although it's becoming fashionable again and apartments in the central areas of Auckland and Wellington are highly sought-after. Thankfully, there are hardly any high-rise apartment blocks in New Zealand, which does, however, boast a unique type of housing called a 'unit'. This is a single building containing a number (often four or six) of smaller properties, each having its own plot and therefore being part house, part apartment.

New Zealand homes aren't usually built to the same standards as is common in Europe, and construction methods are similar to those used in Australia and many parts of the USA. Brick and stone are less common, except in more expensive properties, although cheaper properties may have a single wall in brick or stone to add a touch of 'elegance'. Older properties are built of wooden weather-boards (often Kauri wood) with corrugated iron roofs (instantly identifiable from the noise when it rains!). As hardwood has become more expensive and environmentally unfriendly, construction of new properties is usually a timber frame filled by plywood panels, which are sprayed with fibre cement and painted to give the impression of rendered brickwork. Modern roofs tend to be made of textured steel or concrete tiles, rather than corrugated iron.

Although many new arrivals from Europe regard New Zealand home construction as 'flimsy', the materials used are adequate for the climate. An advantage of this type of construction is that there's a significant cost saving over brick and stone properties, and repair and maintenance costs are also lower. In addition, New Zealand is officially situated within an earthquake belt (it has been affectionately dubbed the 'shaky isles' or 'quakey isles'), where 'flimsier' construction has the benefit of being more flexible in the event of a quake, easier to repair, and also less likely to cause you serious injury if it comes tumbling down around your ears! Earthquakes, or rather tremors, are fairly frequent throughout New Zealand, although most are too minor to be noticed and on average a serious earthquake happens only once every 210 years.

The design and layout of New Zealand properties is fairly standard throughout the country. A typical home has a hall, kitchen, living area, dining area (which may be combined with either the living area or kitchen), bathroom and three bedrooms. Unless you're buying an individual, architect-designed property (rare, except at the top end of the market) the layout of the homes is monotonously predictable – it often seems as if every house in New Zealand was built from the same set of plans! The homes will, however, be functional and quite spacious. New Zealand homes are, on average, a little smaller than American homes, but roomier than properties in most of Europe.

Most homes, except for the oldest, unrenovated properties, are well equipped and fitted. Fitted kitchens with cupboards and built-in appliances are standard, and many newer properties also have a utility or laundry room. Newer properties are also likely to have a bathroom attached to the principal bedroom as well as a main bathroom (often known as a family bathroom). Bedrooms often have fitted furniture, and some homes also have walk-in wardrobes. Some modern builders proudly boast that all you need to bring with you when you move in is a lounge suite and a bed! If you find an older property that hasn't been renovated, it will be in stark contrast to a modern home: leaky tin roofs, gaps in the windows and even holes in the weather-boarding are fairly common. It's wise to tread warily if you're offered a house at a tempting price that's described as 'needing TLC' (tender loving care), which is usually a euphemism for a dump!

Leaky Building Syndrome

This sounds like a joke, but is far from being one. Leaky building syndrome is the name of the problems affecting anywhere between 30,000 and 90,000 houses built in New Zealand in the last decade or so, particularly those built in a 'Mediterranean style'. This involves flat or sloping roofs with minimal eaves and a white or beige plaster finish, designed to give a hint of Greece or Spain. Unfortunately, a lot of examples of this style of building are taking in water through the exterior finish. The finish is known in the building trade as monolithic plaster, but although it looks like plaster, it's actually a synthetic material which is sprayed on the outside of timber-framed houses.

The leaking monolithic plaster is only the beginning of the problem. After water has penetrated the 'plaster', it can soak into the wooden structure of the house. The timber in modern houses is untreated, which ties in with New Zealand's 'clean and green image', but is proving to be a disadvantage as a building material because when the wood gets wet, it rots. As a result of these problems, some experts recommend that people avoid buying or renting buildings with a monolithic plaster finish.

BUYING OFF-PLAN OR WITHOUT LAND

New Zealand

Buying 'off plan' means buying a property that hasn't yet been built, which involves certain risks (as in other countries). The practice is becoming more common in New Zealand, but you should always check the procedure with a lawyer. (See also **Renovation, Restoration & Building** on page 179).

One practice that's rare outside Australia and New Zealand is that of buying a house without land. In some cases, where developers have purchased a quarter-acre plot complete with a house, they will remove the house and put it up for sale without land. All you need to do is find yourself a plot and have your new home delivered to the site and installed there. This method of buying a house is much less common than it used to be, but it's still used and can be a way of buying a home cheaply. The main points to be aware of are not to buy a house until you have somewhere to site it, and to make sure that the plot has services (e.g. water and electricity) available. Also confirm the cost of moving the house and reinstalling it, which may exceed the cost of the house itself! The job needs to be done by specialist builders and hauliers who will literally cut the house into two or three sections and move it to your plot.

In New Zealand, the term 'lifestyle plot' or 'block' refers to a kind of smallholding – a plot of (often) undeveloped land, usually in the country. Buyers of lifestyle plots tend to be independent, rustic types who yearn for a more rural (back to nature) way of life. They often build their own home on the plot (or have one built) and may keep horses or ponies or a few farm animals in addition to growing their own vegetables. Lifestyle plots are available in many areas and are usually temptingly cheap. When buying a lifestyle plot, the main points to check are that mains services are available nearby and the cost of connecting them, and that the land is suitable for agricultural purposes, e.g. the quality of the soil and whether water is available for irrigation. If you plan to keep animals, good fencing (preferably post and rail) should be included, as the cost of fencing a large plot can be high. Finally, you should check any development plans for the area, as there have been a number of cases where buyers planning a life of seclusion have found some years later that their plot adjoins an industrial park or is divided by a main road. You can expect to pay around $275,00 for a small lifestyle plot (around 5 acres/2ha) or up to $750,000 if it's within commuting distance of Auckland (the practice of working in Auckland and commuting to a 'farm' in the country has become popular in the last few years).

RESALE HOMES

Buying 'new' doesn't necessarily mean buying a brand new home where you're the first occupant. There can be many advantages in buying a modern resale home rather than a brand new one, including better value, an established development with a range of local services and facilities in place, more individual design and style, no 'teething troubles', furniture and other extras included in the price, a mature garden and trees, and a larger plot. With a resale property you can see exactly what you will get for your money and the previous owners may have made improvements or added extras such as a swimming pool that may not be fully reflected in the asking price. The disadvantages of buying a resale home depend on its age and how well it has been maintained. They can include a poor state of repair and the need for refurbishment, redecoration or new carpets; inferior build quality and design, no warranty (i.e. with a home that's more than ten years old), termite or other infestations, and (in the case of a community property) the possibility of incurring high assessments for repairs.

RETIREMENT HOMES & SHELTERED HOUSING

For those who are retired or nearing retirement age (e.g. over 55), purpose-built retirement homes and sheltered housing are available in most areas of Australia and New Zealand (there are around 2,500 retirement villages in the former). Villages vary in size and offer different levels of accommodation, from self-contained independent living apartments, cottages or townhouses, to serviced apartments, hostels and nursing homes. Most villages offer a luxurious lifestyle, safety and security, a supportive environment, and some are more like country estates or luxury hotels with prices starting at over $500,000. Before buying a retirement home, you should visit a number of villages and talk to residents, as they vary enormously in quality, the variety of amenities and styles, and the cost. There's a large demand for homes in retirement developments and villages and they usually sell quickly.

Retirement homes offer special features, facilities and convenience for the elderly and retired (most residents are in their late 60s or older), including guest suites that can be booked for visitors. Facilities may include a billiards room, bowling green, craft room, croquet lawn, garage, heated outdoor or indoor swimming pool (or both), landscaped gardens, library service, lifts, lounge/dining area, open fire, private bar, private gardens, restaurant, spa complex, sun room and tennis courts. In some villages, all home cleaning is included and meals may also be provided (called 'assisted living'). One of the most important features of retirement homes is that help is on hand 24 hours a day, either from a live-in warden or caretaker or via an alarm system linked to a control centre. A nurse and maintenance man are usually on call and there are visiting doctors and dentists. Many retirement villages provide 24-hour, seven days a week emergency care and some also have their own nursing homes.

Initial (ingoing) costs of buying a retirement home include the purchase of a unit or lease, fees such as stamp duty and legal fees, and costs associated with agreements or contracts. Running (ongoing) costs include weekly/monthly fees for facilities, insurance, maintenance, rates and services. A deferred management fee may be payable on leaving a retirement village, which is usually a percentage of the original purchase price. When a unit or lease is put up for sale, fees must usually be paid until it's sold. This leaves owners (or their families) open to abuse, and some retirement villages deliberately allow units to remain empty so that they can charge fees (of up to $1,250 a month!) without providing any services. Other common problems include access to services, compliance with codes of practice, financial disputes and quality of management.

In Australia, state governments oversee the retirement village industry and most have a code of practice that aims to regulate the development, operation and promotion of villages. Check with the state authorities and the state retirement Village Residents Association. All states also have a Council of the Ageing (COTA) which provides information and advice about retirement villages (go to 🖥 www.cota.org.au).

INSPECTIONS & SURVEYS

It isn't compulsory or usual in Australia and New Zealand to have a building inspection or structural survey carried out, but when you've found a property that you like, you should not only make a close inspection of its condition, even if it's a fairly new building, but also ensure that 'what you see is what you get'. In many rural areas, boundaries aren't always clearly drawn – often because title deeds haven't been changed to match recent changes in local topography, e.g. the growth or clearance of woodland. If you're shown a property with a large plot of land, the vendor or agent may wave his arms and declare airily: 'This is all yours; it's included in the price'. The truth may be rather more complicated!

There are various ways you can carry out an inspection, and which one you choose will depend largely on whether the property is derelict and in need of complete restoration, partly or totally renovated, or a modern home. You should ensure that a property over ten years old is structurally sound, as it will no longer be covered by a warranty. Although Australia and New Zealand have good building standards, you should never assume that a building is sound, as even relatively new buildings can have serious faults (although rare).

Doing Your Own Checks

There are a number of checks you can carry out yourself, including the following:

- While considering boundaries, check the condition of any walls, fences or hedges and find out who they belong to and therefore who's responsible for their upkeep.

- If you're planning to make extensions or alterations (e.g. the addition of a swimming pool or stables) that may require planning permission, therefore you should make enquiries whether such permission is likely to be granted.

- When it comes to examining the building itself, check the outside first, where they may be signs of damage and decay, such as bulging or cracked walls, damp, missing roof tiles and rusty or insecure gutters and drainpipes, dry or wet-rot in beams and other woodwork, and doors and windows that no longer hinge, lock or fit properly. Plants growing up or against walls can cause damp, and the roots of trees or shrubs close to a building can damage foundations (look for telltale cracks). Use binoculars to inspect the roof and a torch to investigate the loft, noting any cracks or damp patches using a camera and notepad. If you see a damp patch on the outside, check whether it runs right through the wall when you go inside.

- In the case of a property that has been restored, if work has been carried out by registered local builders, ask to see the bills. If the current (or a previous) owner did the work himself, it's essential to consult an expert. You should also make sure that any major changes or additions have planning permission.

- If the property has a swimming pool, check that planning permission was granted for its construction, as it isn't unusual for owners to construct pools without permission, in which case you could be obliged to demolish it or fill it in. Check also the type of pool structure, which is rarely specified in purchase documents, its condition and that the filtration and other cleaning systems work as they should. If you know little or nothing about swimming pools, it's worthwhile getting an expert to make the checks for you. The small cost of an inspection should be set against the potentially astronomical cost of repairing an unsound pool and, if repairs are required, these may be paid for by the vendor or covered by a reduction in the price of the property. Make sure that a pool has an approved safety system, especially if you plan to let the property (see **Swimming Pools** on page 178); if there isn't a safety system, take into account the cost of its installation.

More generally, consider the location of the pool, the local climate and your inclinations, and ask yourself how often you're likely to use it and whether its maintenance will be more trouble and expense than it's worth.

- Test the electrical system, plumbing, mains water, hot water boiler and central heating systems as applicable. Don't take anyone's word that these work, but check them for yourself and, at the same time, find out how these systems work.

- If the property doesn't have electricity or mains water, check the nearest connection point and the cost of extending the service to the property, as it can be very expensive in remote rural areas (see **Utilities** on page 320). If a property has a well or septic tank, you should have it tested (see **Septic Tanks** on page 177). Also check whether a property is due to be (or could be) connected to mains drainage and sewerage.

- Check the quality of the water in the area of the property; for example, is it hard or soft and what is the nitrate content? (See **Water** on page 326.)

- Locate the stop cock for the mains water supply, if there is one, and test the pressure (preferably in summer during a dry spell). Ask where the meter is and check it.

- If a building has a 'ventilation space' beneath the ground floor, check that this hasn't become blocked by plants or been filled with debris; if it has, this could have caused ground-level wooden floors to rot and damp to rise up walls.

- In an area that's liable to flooding, storms and subsidence, it's wise to check an old property after heavy rainfall, when any leaks should come to light.

- If you buy a waterside property, you should ensure that it has been designed with floods in mind, e.g. with electrical installations above flood level and solid tiled floors.

- If the soil consists of clay, the ground surrounding a house can 'shrink' after a long dry period. Large trees can create the same effect by drawing water out of the soil (eucalyptus are notably adept at this). This shrinkage can cause cracks in walls and, in extreme cases, subsidence.

- Check whether there are any airfields nearby – public or private; you don't want your rural idyll spoiled by droning light aircraft or, worse, buzzing microlights.

- Check the local crime rate by asking your neighbours and contacting the nearest police station in order to assess whether any existing security measures, such as shutters and locks, are likely to be adequate or whether you will need to install additional systems, such as an alarm or window bars, which will affect not only your budget but also the appearance of your property. However, bear in mind that neighbours may be reluctant to tell you if burglary and vandalism is prevalent, and the local police may have different standards of comparison from your own!

It's strongly recommended that, if possible, you visit a property or area in the winter, as not only do some house prices fall when the tourist season ends, but media images rarely hint at how cool and damp it can be in the winter in parts of Tasmania, Victoria and New Zealand, and even in parts of New South Wales and South Australia. Such a visit may also reveal problems that weren't apparent at another time (e.g. that the DIY shop you were banking on for materials and tools is closed until the spring, which can be the case in remote areas).

Note, however, that although you can make basic checks yourself, they are no substitute for a professional inspection, the cost of which is a small price to pay for the peace of mind it provides.

SURVIVAL TIP
If you would have a survey carried out if you were buying the same property in your home country, you should have one done in Australia or New Zealand.

Professional Survey

Although a survey isn't legally required as part of the purchasing process in Australia and New Zealand, except for mandatory termite and pest inspections in some Australian states, it's strongly recommended before committing to a purchase. Some local buyers simply ask a builder friend to come along with them when visiting a property, or ask a local builder for a quote before buying (perhaps the cheapest and easiest way), but as a foreigner you're recommended to commission at least a valuation and preferably a full survey, especially if you're planning to buy an old building.

If you decide that you will need a survey before buying a property, it's worth making enquiries at an early stage to ascertain who's best qualified to help you, what type of survey reports they offer and how much they charge. You can expect that a competent surveyor won't be available immediately.

Survey Report

You should receive a written report (within a couple of weeks of the survey) on the condition of a property, including anything that could affect its value or your enjoyment of it in the future, and an estimate of its current and possibly future value. Some surveyors will allow you to accompany them and they may produce a video of their findings in addition to a written report.

You may be able to make a 'satisfactory' survey a condition of the preliminary purchase contract, although a vendor may refuse or insist that you carry out a survey before signing the contract. If serious faults are revealed by the survey, a conditional clause should allow you to withdraw from the purchase and have your deposit returned. You may, however, be able to negotiate a satisfactory compromise with the vendor.

Discuss with your surveyor in advance exactly what will be included in his report and, more importantly, what will be excluded (you may need to pay extra to include certain checks and tests). A home inspection can be limited to a few items or even a single system only, such as the wiring or plumbing in an old house.

The report should first identify and establish that the property and land being offered for sale are, in fact, in the vendor's name and that the land 'for sale' matches the land registry plan. Although this is normally the role of the lawyer, your valuer or surveyor has a duty to check it carefully, as a greater or lesser amount of land can affect a valuation.

In the case of an old property, perhaps the most important part of a valuation and survey is to ensure that, once any necessary repairs have been done, you won't be spending more than the property will be worth if you need or want to sell it. This involves determining what essential work needs to be carried out, the likely cost of such work and the estimated value of the property once it has been done; the difference between the two figures is the correct purchase price for the unrenovated property. If no essential work is necessary, the valuation is made on the property as it stands.

Septic Tanks

If the property is connected to a mains sewerage system, you're fortunate! Most rural properties and many in small towns aren't on mains drainage and therefore have individual sewerage systems, which normally consist of a septic tank. Before committing yourself to a purchase, have the septic tank checked or, if there isn't one, ask a specialist to assess your requirements and the likely cost of installing a system. Contact your town hall for a list of approved specialists authorised to carry out an inspection or a feasibility study. Even if they don't need replacing, old septic tanks may be in need of drainage, repair, or new pipes. Modern regulations demand, for example, considerably lengthened overflow pipes, which may need to be extended by up to 10m (33ft). This may not be possible within the property's boundaries, and you may need to enter negotiations with a neighbour.

If the property has neither mains drainage nor a septic tank, you must check that one can be installed. If you need to install a septic tank, you should check the following:

● That there's enough available land, bearing in mind that the drains for a septic tank must be installed a certain minimum distance from the boundaries of a property (e.g. 3 to 5m/10 to 16ft), and must cover a certain area depending on the size of the tank (generally at least 85m^2/915ft^2);

● Whether there are rivers, canals or other water courses (including underground springs and waterways) that might affect the siting of the tank and soak-away and the type of soak-away – for example, a septic tank mustn't be less than 35m from a well;

● Whether the ground is marshy or rocky, in which case installation could be difficult and/or expensive;

● Whether the land slopes upwards away from the house, which may mean that waste water must be pumped up to the soak-away – another additional expense;

- Whether there's access to the site for a lorry (delivering the tank and subsequently emptying it) and a digger to install the soak-away;

- Check with the local council and/or regional authorities regarding septic tank legislation – you might need to obtain approval for the installation and have it checked once installed.

The cost of installation can be between $3,000 and $7,000, depending on the size of tank and the type of installation, and must be provided for in your budget. Make sure that a tank is large enough for the property in question, e.g. 2,500 litres for two bedrooms and up to 4,000 litres for five bedrooms. It's essential to check these things before purchasing a property.

SWIMMING POOLS

It's common for foreign buyers to install a swimming pool at a home in Australia and New Zealand, which will greatly increase your rental prospects and the rent you can charge if you plan to let. Note that many self-catering holiday companies won't take on properties without a pool. There are many swimming pool installation companies Down Under or you can even buy and install one yourself.

There are various types of pool, each with advantages and disadvantages. Above-ground pools are the cheapest but can be unsightly. A 15m long oval pool can be installed for as little as $3,500, and smaller 'splasher' pools can cost less than $750, although more elaborate fibreglass or wooden pools can cost $8,500 or more.

In-ground pools come in three general types: moulded fibreglass (or 'one-piece') pools, which can simply be 'dropped' into a hole in the ground and cost around $13,000 for a reasonable size moulding; panelled pools, which can be bought in kit form and put together without professional help and cost from around $7,000; and concrete block pools, which normally require professional installation and are therefore usually the most expensive option, costing from around $25,000 for a 10m x 5m pool.

Note that you sometimes need planning permission to install a pool and need to comply with any local safety regulations. Details of requirements can be obtained from any recognised pool installation company, but also check yourself with your local and/or state authorities.

Pools require regular maintenance and cleaning, which is also expensive (heating a pool, particularly an outdoor one, can cost a fortune, especially in cooler regions). If you have a holiday home or let a property, you will need to employ someone to maintain your pool (you may be able to get a local family to look after it in return for using it).

RENOVATION, RESTORATION & BUILDING

Australia

Building a new home or having a new home built is common in Australia and usually takes from four to 12 months. It's generally cheaper and better to have a new home built than to buy and renovate an older home, as you don't need to make compromises for old building standards and the existing dimensions or plot restrictions. You also don't need to match new work to old or make good any damage to existing structures. New homes are generally built to a much higher standard than older homes. However, building code performances, the introduction of GST in 2000 and new regulations for insurance have led to a sharp increase in the price of building materials and therefore the cost of a new home.

Many Australians design and even build their own homes and, if you're up to it, you can do much of the work yourself, although plumbing and electrical work can be done only by qualified tradesmen. **Building a home isn't for the faint-hearted, as it's fraught with problems.** Alternatively, you can buy a plot and hire a builder or purchase a plot from a builder/developer with exclusive rights to develop a particular estate (called project or estate homes). Builders' project homes are popular and cheaper than building a home to your own design or having it designed and built by an architect, and land plus house packages are cost effective. All builders maintain show homes which can usually be visited without an appointment at weekends. The cost per square metre of building a home depends on the type of construction and the location; the following costs are for homes in an average location:

Construction Type	Project Home Cost (per m^2)	Architect Built Home Cost (per m^2)
Full brick	$1,450-1,750	$1,800-2,500
Brick veneer	$800-900	$1,600-1,700
Weatherboard	$750-825	$1,350-1,500

Fibre cement prices are subject to demand. Brick veneer is the most popular, while full brick is reserved for luxury homes; weatherboard and fibre cement are rarely used nowadays. Timber cladding is popular in some cities, e.g. Brisbane. Note that the quality of fixtures and fittings used makes a huge difference to the price.

The cost of land varies considerably depending on the city or region and the distance from a city centre. For example, a plot around 8 to 15km/5 to 9mi from Sydney centre costs at least $425,000, while a similar plot in Perth costs from around $100,000. Plots over 30km/19mi from city centres range from a high of around $140,000 in Sydney to around $50,000 in Adelaide and Perth. Most land and property in Australia is owned freehold, the only exception being the Australian Capital Territory (ACT), where most land is sold on a 99-year lease (after 99 years, leases must be re-applied for).

New properties built by a professional builder are always covered by a warranty, and most lenders won't make a loan on a new house without one. A standard contract for a new home usually provides that the builder rectifies any defects notified by the purchaser for a limited period, e.g. three months. It's important to choose your builder carefully, as building disputes are common and it can be expensive if you need to seek legal redress.

New Zealand

Property renovation and restoration is a major pastime in New Zealand, where tens of thousands of people spend their evenings and weekends rebuilding, extending or redecorating their home (when they've finished rebuilding, extending or redecorating their holiday home, that is!). It may be something you wish to consider – there are plenty of older properties in need of renovation in New Zealand, and they're often offered at tempting prices.

It isn't particularly expensive to renovate a property in New Zealand, as the basic materials (weather-boarding and corrugated iron) are plentiful and cheap. The main difficulty is likely to be finding somebody who will do the renovation for you. As most New Zealanders are avid 'DIYers', there's a shortage of people to do odd jobs and small property repairs. On the other hand, if you're keen on DIY yourself, it could be the ideal solution. However, you should note that property in need of renovation is sometimes in a serious state of decline, with a rotten wooden frame or weather-boarding and a leaking tin roof. **Therefore, even if you intend to do much of the work yourself, you should take advice from a surveyor or**

builder as to whether a house is worth saving before committing yourself to a purchase. Don't, whatever you do, believe an agent who says that a property will 'make a charming home with a little work'. Also bear in mind that you're unlikely to make a profit if you decide to sell a property you've renovated, but you could make a substantial loss, as it's easy to spend more than you could ever hope to recoup in 'added value'.

Any new building or significant addition to an existing building must comply with town planning regulations. Consent for the work can be obtained from your local council, who will send a building inspector to advise you on what you can and cannot do and monitor the work. If you intend to buy an old building, you should check that it isn't registered with the Historic Places Trust, as extensions and renovations to such properties are strictly controlled. Even many timber buildings which appear to have little or no historical interest are protected in this way, as they're considered part of New Zealand's heritage.

If you decide to build a house or renovate or extend an existing one, you should hire a builder who's a member of the Registered Master Builders Federation (☎ 0800-269 119, 🖳 www.masterbuilder.org.nz). Federation members offer a 7-year guarantee. The Certified Builders Association of New Zealand also guarantees that its members are qualified builders (☎ freephone 0800-237 843, 🖳 www.certifiedbuilders. co.nz). Both associations strongly advise customers against paying any builder before work has been completed.

4.

<u>MONEY MATTERS</u>

One of the most important aspects of buying a home in Australia or New Zealand is finance, including transferring and changing money, opening a bank account and obtaining a mortgage, all of which are dealt with in this chapter. Whether or not you plan to live Down Under, you may also incur local taxes, which are covered in **Chapter 7**.

If you're planning to invest in property or a business in Australia or New Zealand that's financed with funds in a foreign currency (e.g. GB£ or US$), it's important to consider both the present and possible future exchange rates. If you need to borrow money to buy property or for a business venture Down Under, you should carefully consider where and in what currency to raise finance. Bear in mind that if your income is paid in a foreign currency it can be exposed to risks beyond your control when you live in Australia or New Zealand, particularly regarding inflation and exchange rate fluctuations. On the other hand, if you live and work in Australia or New Zealand and are paid in local currency, this may affect your financial commitments abroad.

If you own a home in Australia or New Zealand, you can employ a local accountant or tax adviser to look after your financial affairs there and declare and pay your local taxes. You can also have your financial representative receive your bank statements, ensure that your bank is paying your standing orders (e.g. for utilities and property taxes) and that you have sufficient funds to pay them. If you let a home in Australia or New Zealand through a local company, they may perform the above tasks as part of their services.

SURVIVAL TIP
You should ensure that your income is (and will remain) sufficient to live on, bearing in mind devaluations (if your income isn't paid in local currency), rises in the cost of living (see page 36), unforeseen expenses such as medical bills and anything else that may reduce your income (such as stock market crashes and recessions!).

It's wise to have at least one credit card when visiting or living in Australia or New Zealand (Visa and MasterCard are the most widely accepted). Even if you don't like credit cards and shun any form of credit, they do have their uses, for example no-deposit car rentals; no pre-paying hotel bills (plus guaranteed bookings); obtaining cash 24 hours a day; simple telephone, mail-order and internet payments; greater security than cash; and, above all, convenience. Note, however, that not all Antipodean businesses accept credit cards.

CURRENCY

Australia

The Australian unit of currency is the Australian dollar (A$). The Australian economy has been fairly strong in recent years thanks to steady growth and low inflation (2.6 per cent in 2000, expected to rise to 3 per cent by the end of 2006); however, the A$ fell to an 11-year low against the US$ in 1997 owing to the turmoil in Asian money markets and collapsing Asian currencies. It took some time to recover, but by 2004 was generally strong, particularly against the US$.

The Australian dollar is divided into 100 cents, and coins are minted in values of 5 cents, 10 cents, 20 cents, 50 cents (all silver-coloured cupronickel coins), and $1 and $2 (gold-coloured bronze coins with irregular milling on the edge). The $1 and $2 coins are smaller than the 20 cents coin, which can cause confusion. Keep a supply of 20 cents and 50 cents coins handy for parking meters and other machines. Although the smallest coin is 5 cents, prices are still shown in single cents and rounded up or down to the nearest 5 cents. Australian banknotes have lurid designs and are printed in values of $5 (blue/mauve), $10 (blue/green/khaki), $20 (grey/red), $50 (blue/gold/orange) and $100 (green/orange). The $50 and $100 bills are treated with suspicion by some people and may not be accepted by small businesses, taxi drivers, etc.

Forgery used to be a problem in Australia, but it was the first country in the world to have a complete set of banknotes based on plastic (polymer). These notes offer much greater security against counterfeiting and last four times as long as conventional paper (fibrous) notes. According to the Reserve Bank of Australia, the rate of counterfeiting decreased in 2003 to around nine notes passed for each million in circulation, compared to 14 counterfeits per million in 2002.

It's sensible to obtain some Australian coins and banknotes before arriving in Australia and to familiarise yourself and your family with them. You should have some dollars in cash, e.g. $50 to $100 in small bills, when you arrive, but should avoid carrying a lot of cash. This saves you having to queue to change money on arrival at an Australian airport (where exchange rates are usually poor and there are often long queues). It's best to avoid $50 and $100 notes (unless you receive them as a gift!). There's no limit on the amount of Australian or foreign currency that can be imported into Australia, but amounts of $10,000 or more (or the equivalent in foreign currency) must be declared on arrival (see **Importing & Exporting Money** below).

New Zealand

The New Zealand unit of currency is the New Zealand dollar, affectionately know as the 'Kiwi dollar' or just the 'Kiwi' (New Zealanders gave up the British-style pounds, shillings and pence in 1967). It hasn't always been one of the world's strongest currencies but has a reputation for stability, although it fell to a 12-year low against the US$ in 1998 as a result of the crisis in world (particularly Asian) financial markets. But its fortunes have revived recently and it strengthened against the US$ every year between 2001 and 2005. You cannot spend foreign currency in New Zealand, although there are a few duty-free and tourist shops that accept Australian and US dollars (at an unfavourable exchange rate).

The New Zealand dollar is divided into 100 cents. Banknotes are issued in denominations of 5, 10, 20, 50 and 100 dollars (there's no $1 bill in New Zealand), and coins are minted in 1 and 2 dollars, 50, 20, 10 and 5 cents. (The 5 cent coin is colloquially known as the 'pest'.) The cent is identified by the symbol ¢, although occasionally you will see it expressed as a decimal, e.g. $0.75, or values in dollars expressed as cents, e.g. 115¢, neither of which is officially correct. Until 1992, Her Majesty Queen Elizabeth II appeared on all New Zealand banknotes, but she was 'retired' (despite protests from many people) and now appears only on the $20 note. Famous New Zealanders have been installed on other notes: Lord Rutherford ('Father of the Atom') on the $100, Apirana Ngata (a Maori statesman) on the $50, Kate Sheppard (a suffragette) on the $10 and Sir Edmund Hillary (one of the first men to climb Mount Everest) on the $5 note.

It's wise to obtain some New Zealand currency before your arrival in the country. However, because international *bureaux de change* don't usually handle coins, the smallest unit of currency you will be able to obtain outside New Zealand is $5. Ask for a selection of $5, $10 and $20 notes, which are the most useful. Many shops, taxi drivers and small businesses are reluctant to accept $50 and $100 notes; legally they cannot legally reject any notes or coins, but if you proffer a $100 note, they're likely to have no change. These notes also attract most scrutiny, as they're more likely to be the target of forgers, although counterfeit currency isn't a serious problem in New Zealand.

IMPORTING & EXPORTING MONEY

Australia

Australia has no currency restrictions and you may import or export as much money as you wish, in practically any currency. Currency refers to notes (including foreign currency) and doesn't include travellers' cheques or other monetary instruments. However, amounts of $10,000 or more in Australian or foreign currency must be declared to customs on arrival. This is to combat tax evasion and organised crime. Forms for reporting currency transfers are available from customs officers at ports and airports. Forms should be addressed to the Cash Transaction Reports Agency, c/o The Treasury, Langton Crescent, Parkes, ACT 2600 (☎ 02-6263 2111, 🖳 www.treasury. gov.au). For further information contact the Australian Transaction Reports and Analysis Centre, PO Box 5516, West Chatswood, NSW 1515 (☎ freecall 1800-021037, 🖳 www.austrac.gov.au).

Major Australian banks change most foreign banknotes (but not coins), but offer a better exchange rate for travellers' cheques (see below). When buying or selling foreign currency in Australia, beware of excessive charges. Apart from the difference in exchange rates, which are posted by all banks and *bureaux de change*, there may be a significant difference in charges. Most banks and building societies buy and sell foreign currency, although you usually need to order it a few days in advance, as only the major branches in capital cities keep foreign currency in stock. It pays to shop around for the best exchange rates, particularly when changing a lot of money (it's possible to haggle over rates in some establishments). Most banks have a wide spread (e.g. 5 to 10 per cent) between their buying and selling rates for foreign currencies. The A$ exchange rate against major international currencies is listed in banks and in the major daily newspapers.

Travellers' cheques are widely accepted in Australia in all major international currencies. The commission for cashing travellers' cheques varies with the bank, e.g. of the big four banks, ANZ charges $7 for cheques in foreign currency, WBC charges $7.50 for all foreign currency cheques, and the National charges $5 and the Commonwealth $7 per transaction (irrespective of the number of cheques cashed or their value). No fee is charged when cashing American Express or Thomas Cook travellers' cheques at their own branches. Australia Post charges $7.70 for a maximum of ten cheques per transaction (with a maximum payment of $1,000 per person per day), and other banks and travel agents 1.5 to 2 per cent or a flat fee of $5 to $10 (plus a stamp duty of 20 cents per cheque). Banks in rural areas (if you can find any) usually levy the highest fees for cashing travellers' cheques. You can also cash travellers' cheques at luxury hotels and some businesses, although exchange rates are usually poor. You need your passport to cash cheques.

Most banks charge a commission of 1 per cent of the face value when you're buying travellers' cheques, sometimes with a minimum charge of around $10. If you're planning to take up residence or spend some months in Australia, it's worthwhile buying A$ travellers' cheques, as you avoid exchange rate fluctuations and save on commission and fees. When travelling outside Australia, it's best to buy travellers' cheques in £GB or US$, which are the most widely accepted (US$ cheques should always be used when visiting the USA). Lost or stolen travellers' cheques can be replaced in Australia and most countries overseas (the easiest to replace are American Express, ☎ freecall 1800-688022, and Thomas Cook, ☎ freecall 1800-127495) and you should always keep a record of your cheque numbers separate from your cheques.

If you have money transferred to Australia by banker's draft or a letter of credit, bear in mind that it can take up to two weeks to be cleared. You can also have money sent to you by international money order (via a post office), a cashier's cheque or telegraphic transfer, e.g. via Western Union (the quickest, safest and *most expensive* method). You usually need your passport to collect money transferred from overseas or to cash a banker's draft or other credit note.

Postal orders can be sent to Commonwealth countries and a giro post office transfer can be made to most countries. If you're sending money overseas, it's best to send it in the local currency, so that the recipient won't need to pay conversion charges. Some countries have foreign exchange controls limiting the amount of money that can be sent overseas. Insured post is the only safe way to send cash, as the insured value is refunded if it's lost or stolen.

You can send money direct from your bank to another bank via an interbank transfer. Most banks have a minimum charge for international transfers, which makes it expensive for small sums. Overseas banks may also deduct a percentage (e.g. 1 or 2 per cent) of the amount transferred as their fee (everybody wants a cut!).

New Zealand

Exchange controls operated in New Zealand between 1938 and 1984 but have since been abolished and there are now no restrictions on the import or export of funds. A New Zealand resident is permitted to open a bank account in any country and to export unlimited funds from New Zealand. It's also possible to transmit funds to New Zealand without being hindered by bureaucratic procedures.

When transferring or sending money to (or from) New Zealand, you should be aware of the alternatives. One way to do this is to send either a personal cheque or a bank draft (cashier's cheque), which should both be sent by registered post. Money shouldn't be treated as having been paid until the cheque or draft has cleared the system, which is usually within seven days of receipt. Note, however, that a bank draft shouldn't be treated as cash, and you cannot be sure that payment has been made until it has cleared. A safer method of transferring money is to make a direct transfer or a telex or electronic transfer between banks. A direct transfer involves a process similar to sending a cheque or bank draft and usually takes at least seven days (but can take much longer). A telex or electronic transfer can be completed within a few hours. However, bear in mind that (because of the time difference) banks in New Zealand close for the day before they open in Europe or the USA, so it will be at least the next day before funds are available in New Zealand. The transfer process is usually faster and less likely to come unstuck when it's between branches of the same or affiliated banks (in any case, delays are more likely to be overseas than in New Zealand). The Commonwealth Bank of Australia, which has branches in Europe and the USA, can transfer funds almost instantaneously to its branches in New Zealand, although its branch network there (around 130) isn't the most extensive.

NZ Post can transfer, send and receive money within New Zealand and to and from overseas. For domestic transactions, money order certificates costing $3 are available for amounts up to $1,000 and for larger amounts electronic money orders can be purchased for $5. For the transfer of money to and from overseas, NZ Post uses the services of Western Union, which charges around $74 for sums up to $1,000. Further information is available on ☎ freephone 0800-005 253.

The cost of transfers varies considerably – not only commission and exchange rates, but also transfer charges (shop around and compare rates). Usually the faster the transfer, the more it will cost. Transfer fees also vary with the amount being transferred, and there are usually minimum and maximum fees. For example, banks in the UK charge from £5 to process a cheque for up to £50, and up to £40 for a cheque worth the equivalent of £10,000 (most banks in the UK charge in the region of £10 to £45 for electronic transfers). In emergencies, money can be sent via American Express offices by Amex card holders.

When you have money transferred to a bank in New Zealand, ensure that you give the name, account number, branch number and the bank sort code.

Bear in mind that the names of some New Zealand banks (and towns) are strikingly similar, so double check your instructions. If you plan to send a large amount of money to New Zealand or overseas for a business transaction such as buying property, you should ensure that you receive the commercial rate of exchange rather than the tourist rate. Check charges and rates in advance and agree them with your bank (you may be able to negotiate a lower charge or a better exchange rate). If you send a cheque or bank draft to New Zealand, it should be crossed so that it can only be paid into an account with exactly the same name as shown on the cheque.

Most banks in major cities have *bureaux de change*, and there are banks and *bureaux de change* with extended opening hours at both Auckland and Wellington international airports, plus other airports when international flights arrive (which may be just a few times a week). At *bureaux de change* you can buy and sell foreign currencies, buy and cash travellers' cheques, cash personal cheques, and obtain a cash advance on credit and charge cards. There are private *bureaux de change* in the major cities and tourist resorts with longer business hours than banks, particularly at weekends, e.g. they open on Saturdays from 9.30am to 12.30pm when banks are closed, and there are 24-hour, automatic, money-changing machines in some major cities (e.g. outside the Downtown Airline Terminal, Auckland). Most *bureaux de change* offer competitive exchange rates, low or no commission (but always check) and are easier to deal with than banks. If you're changing a lot of money, you may be able to negotiate a better exchange rate. Note, however, that the best exchange rates are usually provided by banks. The New Zealand dollar exchange rate against most major international currencies is displayed in banks and listed in daily newspapers.

If you're visiting New Zealand, it's safer to carry travellers' cheques than cash. Travellers' cheques in major currencies, including US$ and £ sterling, are easily exchanged in New Zealand but aren't usually accepted by businesses, except perhaps some luxury hotels, restaurants and shops, which usually offer a poor exchange rate. You can buy travellers' cheques from any New Zealand bank, which charge a minimum commission fee of $5 or 1.25 per cent. Shop around, as fees can vary, particularly on larger amounts. Some banks exchange travellers' cheques free of commission, although their charges are usually built into the (inferior) exchange rate, so always compare the net amount you will receive. Keep a separate record of cheque numbers and note where and when they were cashed. American Express provides a free, three-hour replacement service for lost or stolen travellers' cheques at any of their offices worldwide, provided you know the serial numbers of the lost cheques. Without the serial numbers it can take three days or longer. Most companies provide freephone telephone numbers for reporting lost or stolen travellers' cheques in New Zealand, e.g. American Express (☎ freephone 0800-442 208).

Note that there isn't a lot of difference in the cost between buying New Zealand currency using cash, travellers' cheques or using a debit or credit card. However, many people simply take cash when travelling overseas, which is asking for trouble, particularly if you have no way of obtaining more cash locally, e.g. with travellers' cheques or a debit or credit card. **One thing to bear in mind when travelling anywhere, is *never* to rely on only one source of funds!**

SURVIVAL TIP
If you plan to send a large amount of money to Australia or New Zealand or abroad for a business transaction such as buying property, you should ensure you receive the commercial rate of exchange rather than the tourist rate.

OBTAINING CASH

There are various methods of obtaining cash for everyday use, including the following:

- **Banks:** Most banks in major cities have foreign exchange windows, where you can buy and sell foreign currencies, buy and cash travellers' cheques, and obtain a cash advance on credit and charge cards.

- **Bureaux De Change:** Bureaux de change often have longer business hours than banks, particularly at weekends. Most offer competitive exchange rates and low or no commission (but check). They're easier to deal with than banks but generally offer worse exchange rates. There are many private exchange bureaux at airports, main railway stations and major cities. However, airport bureaux de change and change machines usually offer the worst exchange rates of all and charge the highest fees (e.g. handling charges). Never use unofficial money changers, who are likely to short change you.

- **Credit & Debit Cards:** If you need instant cash, you can draw on debit, credit or charge cards (but there's usually a daily limit). Exchange rates are better when obtaining cash with a credit or debit card as you're given the wholesale rate, although there's usually a 1.5 per cent charge on cash advances and ATM transactions in foreign currencies (although some UK banks provide clients with a no-fee debit card for overseas cash withdrawals). Some ATMs may reject foreign cards – if this happens try again and if necessary try another ATM.

- **Telegraphic Transfer:** One of the quickest (it takes around ten minutes) and safest methods of transferring cash is via a telegraphic transfer, e.g. Moneygram (☎ UK 0800-666 3947, 🖥 www.moneygram.com) or Western Union (☎ UK 0800-833 833, 🖥 www.westernunion.com), but it's also one of the most expensive, e.g. commission of 7 to 10 per cent of the amount sent! Western Union transfers can be picked up from a post office in Australia and New Zealand just 15 minutes after being paid into an office abroad. Money can be sent via American Express offices by Amex cardholders.

- **Travellers' Cheques:** If you're visiting Australia or New Zealand, it's safer to carry travellers' cheques than cash (although unnecessary if you have a Mastercard or Visa debit card). Always keep a separate record of cheque numbers and note where and when they were cashed. American Express provides a free, 24-hour replacement service for lost or stolen travellers' cheques at any of their offices worldwide, provided you know the serial numbers of the lost cheques. Without the serial numbers, replacement can take three days or longer. All companies provide local numbers for reporting lost or stolen travellers' cheques.

BANKS & BUILDING SOCIETIES

Australia

The major Australian banks with branches in cities and large towns throughout Australia are the Australia & New Zealand (ANZ) Bank, the Commonwealth Bank of Australia (majority owned by the Australian government), the National Australia Bank, and WBC (often called Westpac), collectively referred to as the big four. These banks also have the widest representation overseas. In addition to the national banks, there are also many city, regional and state banks (including drive-in banks).

The major banks offer over 200 products, ranging from current and savings accounts to home insurance and personal superannuation schemes. If you do a lot of travelling overseas, you may find the comprehensive range of travel and other services provided by the major banks advantageous. Many services provided by Australian banks are also

© Vivienne Peters

Photography by Tourism Queensland

Courtesy Tourism New South Wales

Photography by Tourism Queensland

Photography by
Tourism Queensland

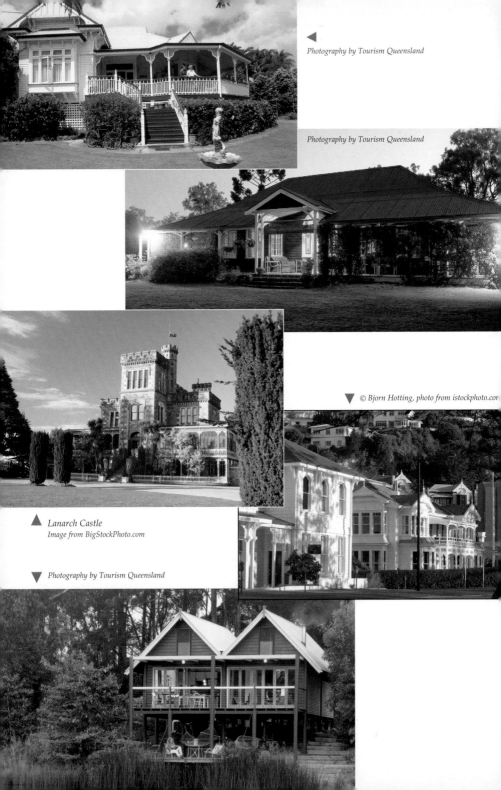

© Vivienne Peters

© Jonathan Ling,

© Joe Gough,
photo from istockphoto.com

© Dougal Robertson

© Andrew Dean,
photo from www.istockphoto.com

offered by Building Societies (see below). Banks are keen to attract migrants as customers and offer a range of special services to newcomers. The major banks (e.g. the Commonwealth Bank of Australia) provide financial advice and assistance to migrants in a number of countries, and also operate a network of Migrant Service Centres in Australia's capital cities.

Australian banking made huge losses in the '80s, and the first half of the '90s was spent cost cutting and recovering. The second half of the '90s saw strong growth and a stable credit environment, leading to higher profit margins. Australian banks are currently highly profitable and in 2004 paid over $5 billion in Australian company tax (around 17 per cent of the total), more than any other industry. Nevertheless, many regional (bush or country) banks have closed in recent years (over 2,000 branches have closed in the last decade or so) as banks have slimmed their branch networks. The proliferation of electronic banking (see below) has meant that banks require a much smaller workforce, and they've shed thousands of jobs (bank is a four-letter word with many people in Australia, where they're generally held in low esteem). Consequently, many communities have been left without a local bank, although some towns have successfully fought closures by threatening to withdraw $millions in assets from a bank. In some areas, building societies and credit unions have stepped in to fill the void, but in a small rural town or village, there's likely to be a post office agency, but no bank. A post office account is handy for travellers in rural areas or an account with one of the banks that allow withdrawals to be made from post offices.

The major banks have also established low-cost 'kiosk' branches in supermarkets and shopping centres operated by just one or two people and open seven days a week. After initial indifference, supermarket bank kiosks have proved popular and have increased in number to over 500.

Building Societies & Credit Unions

Building societies (or permanent building societies to give them their full name) were established in the 19th-century to cater for people saving to buy a home. Customers saved a deposit of 5 or 10 per cent of the cost of a home with the building society, who then lent them the balance. A building society would rarely lend to anyone who wasn't a regular saver, although this policy changed some years ago. Today, Australian building societies have some 3 million members and nearly $13 billion in assets, although this represents just 5 per cent of the national financial services market. Added competition in the financial sector in recent years (particularly from mortgage originators) has made life difficult for building societies, many of which are struggling to survive in their present form. Like banks, building societies have also been raising their fees to offset smaller margins on home loans.

Building societies and credit unions can now compete with banks on a more even footing and, after a long battle, they recently won the right to issue cheques in their own name (previously all cheques had to be issued by and cleared through banks). Nowadays, building societies offer many of the services provided by banks, including cash cards, credit cards, current and savings accounts, insurance, personal loans and travel services. However, building societies don't all offer the same services, types of accounts or rates of interest. If you're looking for a long-term investment, the number of branches may not be of importance, as members of most building societies are linked with the major banks and customers can use their ATM networks.

Electronic Banking

Australian banks are in the forefront of electronic banking and over half of all bank transactions are made through electronic banking methods, some banks recording three-quarters of their transactions electronically. Electronic banking includes automated bill payment (BPAY), automated computer banking through dial-up services, automatic teller machines (ATMs), of which there were around 460,000 in Australia in 2004, electronic funds transfer, internet banking, smart cards, stored debt cards, telephone banking, and touch-screen customer service terminals. In future, banks will have even fewer branches and it's expected that almost all banking transactions will be done via an ATM, computer or telephone. Video telephone banking will soon allow customers to do business via a video link with centralised bank staff.

Telephone banking (or telebanking) and internet banking are offered by most Australian banks as well as by building societies and credit unions, usually 24 hours a day, seven days a week. Calls may be answered by a recorded message rather than a real person. Services provided include obtaining account balances, obtaining interest rates earned/charged, obtaining mortgages and other loans, ordering statements and cheque books, paying bills, providing details of the last five (or more) cheques cleared or the last five transactions, and transferring funds between accounts.

Business Hours

Normal bank and building society opening hours are from 9am or 9.30am until 4pm, Mondays to Thursdays, and from 9.30am until 5pm on Fridays, with no closure over the lunch period in cities and most towns. Some city branches open from 8am until 6pm, Mondays to Thursdays, and until 8pm on Fridays, while in rural areas banks may open on only one or two days a week. Some banks and building societies open on Saturday mornings, e.g. from 9am until noon. There are bank branches with extended opening hours at international airports and in an increasing number of supermarkets and shopping centres (some open seven days a week). All banks are closed on public holidays. Most banks, building societies and main post offices in Australia have 24-hour Automatic Teller Machines (ATMs) at branches for cash deposits and withdrawals, and checking account balances.

New Zealand

There are officially just two kinds of financial institution in New Zealand: registered banks and what are euphemistically known as 'other financial institutions'. The main exception is the Reserve Bank of New Zealand (🖥 www.rbnz.govt.nz), which doesn't fit into either of these categories and is the country's central bank, performing a role similar to the Bank of England or the Federal Reserve Bank in the USA. It has a range of functions, including managing the money supply, supervising commercial banks, implementing the government's financial policy, controlling the exchange rate, providing a banking service to the government and acting as a registrar for government stocks.

Savings banks in New Zealand were traditionally mutual organisations owned by their members or investors, which concentrated on accepting personal savings and granting mortgages for residential property. In this respect they were much like building societies in the UK and savings and loan organisations in the USA. However, deregulation in the financial sector during the '80s allowed commercial banks to enter this market. With their greater financial clout and marketing expertise they've managed largely to take it over, and as a result many savings banks have either converted to commercial or registered banks or been taken over by them.

Changes in the banking system over the last few years have meant that most individuals and businesses in New Zealand carry out their banking, including savings, loans, mortgages and day-to-day transactions, with one of the registered commercial banks (there were 16 in 2005). Banks operating in this sector include: Australia New Zealand Bank (ANZ, 🖥 www.anz.com/nz) and ASB (🖥 www.asbbank.co.nz), formerly the Auckland Savings Bank, which has its strongest presence in Auckland but is also popular throughout the rest of the country. (In 2004, for the fifth consecutive year, ASB was rated New Zealand's number one major bank in terms of customer satisfaction in a University of Auckland survey of bank customers.) Other major banks include the Bank of New Zealand (BNZ, 🖳 www.bnz.co.nz), which is New Zealand's largest bank in terms of asset and, despite its name, wholly Australian-owned; the National Bank (🖳 www.nationalbank.co.nz); and Westpac NZ (🖳 www.westpac.co.nz), which probably has the biggest market share in the country (with 1.3 million customers in 2005) and is also the government's banker.

It's estimated that only around 12 per cent of the New Zealand banking market is operated by indigenous banks. Note that the New Zealand banking operations of Australian banks are completely separate, therefore customers of Australian Westpac, for example, cannot access their Australian accounts at Westpac in New Zealand, or vice versa.

Some banks are mainly telephone and internet-based, e.g. TSB (🖳 www. tsb.co.nz). PSIS is a financial institution owned by its customers, which offers banking services administered by the Bank of New Zealand, although it isn't a bank and as such isn't a member of the Banking Ombudsman scheme nor subject to supervision by the Reserve Bank. The large insurance group AMP (🖳 www.amp.co.nz) also offers banking services, and the New Zealand Post Office offers banking services at post shops under the name Kiwibank.

In addition to locally registered banks, there are also many international banks in New Zealand, which are mainly located in the financial district of Wellington and don't have extensive branch networks around the country. Other financial institutions that aren't registered banks include merchant banks and leasing companies, which mainly serve the business sector. They aren't authorised to accept deposits from the public and, in any case, registered banks offer a more comprehensive range of services to the public and business community. Finance companies aren't registered banks, but provide consumer credit such as loans and hire purchase (or time purchase as it's also known in New Zealand).

All New Zealand banks are efficient and highly automated. You will find that staff, who are generally friendly and informal, work behind low counters or desks rather than armoured glass. This isn't to say that banks in New Zealand aren't robbed (they most certainly are), but the transition towards cash-less banking has done much to reduce the amount of cash shuffled across bank counters (or used in shops and other businesses).

Normal banking hours in New Zealand are from 8.30 or 9am until 4.30pm, Mondays to Fridays, although banks may stay open for half an hour later one evening a week (which is the exception rather than the rule). Banks don't open at weekends and are also closed on public holidays, although *bureaux de change* open longer at weekends.

Opening an Account

You can open a New Zealand bank account from outside the country or after your arrival, although given the widespread use of cash-less transactions in New Zealand, it's better to open an account before you arrive. To open an account while overseas, you need to find the nearest office of a New Zealand bank, e.g. by looking in the telephone directory or asking your bank for assistance. You probably won't find a great deal of choice, but there are branches of the major New Zealand banks in most major cities in Europe, North America and Asia. You don't usually need to visit a branch in person, as an account can be opened by telephone or post. Note that most banks require an opening balance of at least $200 and up to $500 in some cases.

To open a bank account in New Zealand, simply choose any of the registered banks. Different banks require different documentation, so you should check exactly what's required beforehand; typically you will need two forms of identification, your IRD number (see page 248) and possibly statements from your current or previous bank. Note that if you don't have an IRD number when you open an account, you will be charged resident withholding tax (RWT) at 39 per cent. If you think that you might need an overdraft, loan or mortgage in New Zealand in the future, you should obtain a reference from your overseas bank manager to the effect that your account has been maintained in good order.

MORTGAGES

Australia

Mortgages (home loans) in Australia are available from over 100 sources, including banks, building societies, credit unions, finance and insurance companies, mortgage managers, mortgage originators/providers, motoring organisations and state housing authorities. The Commonwealth Bank is the largest lender (with mortgage loans totalling some $102 billion in 2004) followed by the Westpac Banking Corporation. Competition to lend you money is fierce and homebuyers in Australia have a wider variety of home loan finance than is available in many other countries. However, despite the increased competition, banks still handle around 80 per cent of new home loans. The usual home loan period is 25 years, although it can be anything from 5 to 30 years (or up to the age at which a state pension is paid), while the maximum term for land loans is usually 20 years. Around half of all homeowners have a mortgage, the average loan being $218,000

(2004). Many lenders offer additional benefits such as free home insurance and life assurance.

The Commonwealth and state governments provide funds for housing loans through the Commonwealth/State Housing Agreement, with loan repayments linked to the borrower's income. Interest subsidies provided during the early years of the loan are generally recovered when the borrower's income permits. In most states, the loans are made through co-operative building societies, a list of which is maintained by the state Registrar of Co-operative Societies. Housing commissions and state banks in some states also provide loans, although eligibility is restricted to low and moderate-income families and there are often long waiting lists.

The interest rate for variable-rate mortgages in mid-2005 was 6.5 to 7 per cent. In recent years, loans have become cheaper thanks to increased competition between the banks and other lenders. The major banks have been savaged by smaller, non-bank rivals offering better deals, which has resulted in some excellent offers for borrowers. Banks have been forced to cut their margins (the difference between what they pay on deposits and the home loan rate) from 4 or 5 per cent to around 3 per cent in order to compete with some mortgage originators who charge borrowers only a couple of per cent above the cost of obtaining funds. Banks also offer lower interest rates to selected customers such as professionals and other 'high net-worth' individuals.

However, low rates also have their down side, as they encourage people to borrow more than they can afford and, according to surveys, a high percentage of Australian families are burdened by their loan repayments. The average size of a home loan has risen from $136,000 in 1999 to $218,000 in 2004, and home loan defaults have increased, owing partly to a decline in the quality of lending, particularly by mortgage providers, who tend to market loans more aggressively and lend to people that banks reject. There are fears that the number of defaulters will soar if interest rates increase again.

You shouldn't rush into taking out a mortgage, particularly if your income isn't secure. Many people are denied mortgages because of bad credit ratings or insecure employment, which may include the self-employed, who usually need to produce a number of years' tax returns (usually two). It's possible to take out a mortgage protection policy in case you fall ill, have an accident or are made redundant and are unable to pay your mortgage, although it can be expensive and there are many loopholes. Most lenders offer a 'home loan protection plan' which guarantees repayments in case of death or permanent disability.

Your monthly mortgage repayments mustn't usually be more than 30 per cent of your gross basic income – a couple's incomes are combined (some

60 per cent of families paying off a home loan in Australia have two or more wage earners). Sydney owner-occupiers are generally more highly geared than Melbourne families. It's usually necessary to have a high income and a secure job to get into and remain in homeownership in Australia, and only some 40 per cent of buyers pay over 30 per cent of their wages towards a mortgage. Interest is calculated on the daily loan balance and charged monthly. Repayments can be paid fortnightly (which can save a considerable amount over the term of a loan) or monthly. Some lenders allow you to reduce your payments by up to 50 per cent for up to six months when taking maternity or paternity leave.

Although it's possible to obtain a loan for the whole cost of a property (i.e. a 100 per cent mortgage) from some developers, particularly if you're a first-time buyer, most lenders expect borrowers to pay a deposit of 5 to 25 per cent of the purchase price. The average deposit paid is around a third of the value of a property in Sydney and some 40 per cent in Melbourne. Housing loan insurance is payable when a loan is greater than 75 or 80 per cent of the value of a property. The insurance premium is usually between $250 and $500 or 1 per cent of the loan value, and is normally added to the loan amount. Expensive 'captive' mortgage insurance is offered by some lenders, when you pay around 20 per cent above the market rate (shop around for independent mortgage insurance). Mortgage insurance contracts cover the lender and not the borrower.

You can usually choose between a fixed-rate and a variable-rate mortgage. With the latter, the interest rate goes up and down in line with fluctuations in the bank base rate. Those who cannot afford an increase in their mortgage repayments are usually better off with a fixed-rate mortgage, where the interest rate is fixed for the term of the loan or a number of years (e.g. one to ten), irrespective of what happens to bank lending rates in the meantime. The longer the fixed-rate period, the lower the interest rate offered. If interest rates go down, you may find yourself paying more than the current mortgage rate, but at least you know exactly what you must pay each month. To judge whether a fixed-rate mortgage is worthwhile, you must estimate in which direction interest rates are heading (a difficult feat). Most variable-rate loans offer borrowers the option to fix the rate at any time, e.g. when interest rates are rising, and some mortgages combine fixed and variable-rate loans (split fixed/variable rate), which some analysts recommend as the best compromise. However, this means taking out two loans and incurring higher fees. Homebuyers have shunned fixed-rate loans in recent years as rates have tumbled, although the number is now increasing ahead of fears of interest rate rises.

Types Of Loan

There are few different types of home loan in Australia, where most are repayment mortgages (endowment, pension and other types of mortgages are rare). Standard home loans often include extra flexibility, including additional payments, fixed-variable splits, offset accounts, redraw facilities and variations to payment frequency. However, many lenders offer basic variable-rate loans with fewer features than standard loans (such as no offset account or redraw facility, see below). Most lenders offer low-start (honeymoon-rate) loans, which reduce your mortgage payments for a number of years (usually one or two). Around a third of all complaints against banks concern home loans, in particular honeymoon-rate loans, on which banks levy high fees.

A new type of loan introduced in recent years is an equity overdraft loan (called current account mortgages in the UK). It works like a standard overdraft bank account, where the higher the balance of your account the lower the amount owed (and hence less interest is payable), and you can borrow money whenever you wish (usually up to your original mortgage limit) at the same rate of interest as your mortgage (it isn't recommended for spendthrifts).

Variable-rate mortgages usually allow extra payments to be made. For example, paying an extra 10 per cent each month can knock five or six years off the repayment term of a 25-year mortgage. One of the advantages of standard bank loans is that they usually have greater flexibility than other loans and offer additional features, such as redraw facilities and offset accounts. If you make extra payments, a redraw facility allows you to 're-borrow' the money later if the need arises. An offset account enables you to deposit money in a special account and receive interest in the form of a reduction in the interest payable on your loan. This means that a larger part of your repayments goes towards reducing the principal, resulting in significant interest savings and the loan being paid off quicker. An example of an offset account is the Commonwealth Bank's 'mortgage interest saver account' (MISA). Money lodged in a MISA is available on call, and you don't pay bank fees on deposits and withdrawals (each of which must be a minimum of $1,000), although no interest is paid. A minimum balance of $2,000 must be maintained. Making payments fortnightly instead of monthly also helps you pay off a loan quicker.

Fees & Charges

Various fees are associated with mortgages, including legal fees, a loan registration fee, maintenance fees, a mortgage application or establishment fee, and a valuation fee. The mortgage establishment fee is usually between $300 and $800 (e.g. in 2005, Australia and New Zealand Banking Group's fee was $600). Some banks (e.g. the Commonwealth Bank and WBC) have cut or eliminated fees for setting up mortgages, although they may be clawed back by administrative or maintenance fees. Some lenders don't charge a valuation fee, which can be up to $275. Legal fees are sometimes waived. Some mortgages have a maintenance fee, e.g. $60 to $100, which may apply only to certain types of loans. Loan registration costs vary from state to state, from around $10 to $100. Stamp duty is also payable on mortgages in all states except the ACT, Northern Territory and Victoria (the average is around $425 on a $100,000 mortgage and $850 on a $200,000 mortgage).

Some mortgages carry crippling discharge (redemption) or exit fees if they're repaid early, although most now charge $100 to $650 plus a state fee ranging from around $50 to $110. While most borrowers never change their lenders, some homeowners re-mortgage every two or three years after shopping around for the best deal available. However, you must do your sums carefully, as changing lenders can be expensive. Some banks offer lower 'loyalty rates' of interest for customers who have maintained a loan for five years or more. While mortgage interest rates have generally fallen in recent years, fees have risen. Always make sure that you receive a list of all costs associated with a loan, including discharge fees.

New Zealand

Mortgages (home loans) are available from New Zealand banks, mortgage brokers and some direct response (i.e. via telephone or internet) lenders. Generally, there's little difference between the interest rates charged, although there's a wide variety of mortgage plans with different repayment methods, terms (i.e. periods) and fees (see below), so it's worth shopping around for the best deal. Mortgage brokers are increasing in popularity and in 2005 accounted for 30 per cent of the market, compared with 17 per cent in 1999 and a mere 1 per cent in 1991. If you decide to use the services of a mortgage broker, ensure that he's a member of the New Zealand Mortgage Brokers Association, whose members must have professional indemnity insurance and work with at least six different lenders. You can contact the Association at PO Box 303-353, Takapuna, Auckland (☎ 09-912 1000, 🖳 www.nzmba.co.nz).

Generally, New Zealand financial institutions are accommodating when it comes to granting mortgages and put a great deal of effort into gaining your business. Banks are keen for you to take out a mortgage with them and many offer competitive deals. Some banks don't even require you to attend an interview at their local branch but offer mortgages by telephone or via the internet. All you need to do is telephone a freephone number (or complete an online questionnaire) and provide details of the property you wish to purchase and your personal details, and you will receive an 'in principle' decision virtually immediately. The main direct response mortgage companies are BankDirect and AMP Banking. Telephone mortgage companies are highly competitive (although they offer a 'no frills' service) and are particularly suitable if you know exactly what kind of mortgage you require. If you don't, you'd be wise to visit your local bank, where staff will explain the different types of mortgage on offer.

There are no fixed lending criteria in New Zealand, although generally the maximum mortgage you can obtain is where the repayments are no more than 30 per cent of your net income (which is combined for a couple). It's sensible, however, to take out a mortgage on which the repayments constitute no more than 20 to 25 per cent of your income. The most you can usually borrow is 90 per cent (some lenders set the limit at 80 per cent) of the value of a property, although a high percentage mortgage may be based on the lender's own valuation (rather than what you're actually paying for the property) and you may be required to take out mortgage guarantee insurance (which guarantees that the lender gets his money back if you default on your repayments). It's customary in New Zealand for a property to be held as security for a loan taken out on it, i.e. the lender takes a first charge on the property.

Mortgages can be obtained for any period up to 25 years, although the trend nowadays is for people to take 20 or even 15-year mortgages. The reason for this is that many New Zealanders take out a second mortgage in order to pay for their children's education or a holiday home before they retire. Although the repayments on a shorter mortgage are higher, you pay much less interest in the long term.

Types Of Mortgage

The two main kinds of mortgage offered are a 'table mortgage' (equivalent to a repayment mortgage in other countries), where you make equal repayments of capital and interest throughout the period of the loan, and an interest-only mortgage, where you pay only the interest on the sum borrowed and are required to repay the original capital sum at the end of the term. Most lenders require you to take out an insurance policy to guarantee repayment of the loan, and in this way an interest-only mortgage is similar to an endowment mortgage offered in some other countries. Some lenders allow you to take out an interest-only mortgage without insurance, which makes the repayments temptingly low, but unless you make lots of money (or win the lottery) during the period of the mortgage, you may need to sell your home at the end of the term in order to repay the capital! A third kind of mortgage that's sometimes offered is a 'straight line' mortgage, where you repay capital and interest throughout the term and repayments reduce over the years as the amount of capital owed reduces.

The interest rate on a New Zealand mortgage is either 'floating', so that it varies with interest rates generally, or fixed for the period of the loan, the repayment period being adjusted accordingly. A recent trend is for lenders to offer mortgages that are fixed (usually at a 'bargain' rate) for a period, such as one to five years, and then revert to a floating rate. These offer a temptingly cheap opportunity to get a foot on the property ladder, provided you budget for the fact that your repayments are likely to increase after the fixed rate period expires, depending on how interest rates change in the meantime. A New Zealand mortgage usually provides a high degree of flexibility. Many lenders allow you to convert from one type of mortgage to another, increase or decrease your payments, take a payment 'holiday' for a few months, or repay part of the capital early (thus reducing your repayments or the term of the mortgage). It's even possible to transfer your mortgage to another property. In fact, provided you keep making repayments, you're likely to find your lender accommodating. In 2005, floating mortgage interest rates ranged from 7.25 to 7.45 per cent and fixed mortgage rates for the first year ranged from 6.75 to 7.25 per cent.

As you work your way through the mortgage maze, you should bear in mind that banks and financial institutions in New Zealand are experts at dressing up mortgages in a user-friendly way and creating a variety of seemingly too-good-to-be-true packages. Your mortgage can, however, only be either a table, straight line or interest-only mortgage, with either a fixed or floating rate – no matter what fancy marketing name may be given to it. Make sure that you compare interest rates and calculate how much you're going to have to repay.

Should you need to, it's usually quite easy to remortgage your property and gain access to some of the equity capital you've built up in it (assuming that property prices have risen since you purchased it!). It's also possible to have a mortgage linked to a revolving loan facility, where the difference between the capital borrowed and the value of your property can be advanced for other uses, such as home improvements, a car purchase or a holiday. This is a cheap way of borrowing, as the mortgage interest rate is usually much lower than that for a loan, although interest on a mortgage cannot be claimed as a tax allowance in New Zealand. Many New Zealanders use one of these methods to finance the purchase of a holiday home (bach or crib), which, because of their often flimsy construction, don't qualify for a full mortgage.

Conditions & Fees

Once a loan has been agreed in principle, a lender will provide you with a conditional offer of a loan outlining the terms. You need to provide proof of your income and outgoings, such as other mortgage payments, rent, other loans and regular commitments (e.g. bills). Proof of income includes three months' pay slips for employees; if you're self-employed, you require an audited copy of your trading accounts for the past three years. If you decide to accept the offer, you must usually pay a deposit (likely to be at least $500) to your mortgage lender. If the sale doesn't go ahead for any reason, the deposit should be refundable, although many lenders charge a 'discontinued application fee' which is deducted from the deposit, so it isn't wise to accept a mortgage offer unless you're certain you want to go ahead with a property purchase.

There are various fees associated with mortgages. All lenders charge an application fee for setting up a loan, usually 1 per cent of the loan amount or from $150 to $600 (you won't be charged all of this sum if your application is rejected). There's usually a minimum fee and there may also be a maximum, although many mortgage lenders will negotiate the fees. In addition, there's a land transfer registration. It isn't usually necessary to have a survey unless you're borrowing over 80 per cent of the value of a property.

If you fail to maintain your mortgage repayments, your property can be repossessed and sold at auction, although this rarely happens in New Zealand, as most lenders are willing to arrange lower repayments when borrowers get into financial difficulties. It's best to contact your lender immediately if you have repayment problems, rather than wait until a huge debt has accumulated. You may be offered the chance to transfer to another type of mortgage or may be able to remortgage entirely and gain access to some of the equity in your property.

Foreign Currency Mortgages

It's possible to obtain a foreign currency mortgage, e.g. in Japanese yen, Swiss francs or US dollars, all currencies which, with their historically low interest rates, have provided huge savings for some borrowers in the last few decades. However, you should be cautious about taking out a foreign currency mortgage, as interest rate gains can be wiped out overnight by currency swings. In the '80s many Australians (and not a few New Zealanders) took out Swiss franc loans and were unable to maintain their payments when the value of the A$ and NZ$ plummeted against the Swiss franc in later years. Most mainstream lenders advise against taking out foreign currency home loans unless you're paid in a foreign currency.

The conditions for foreign currency loans are much stricter than for local currency loans, e.g. they're generally granted only to high-rollers (e.g. those earning a minimum of $100,000 a year) and are usually for a minimum of $200,000 and a maximum of 60 per cent of a property's value. When choosing between a local currency loan and a foreign currency loan, be sure to take into account all costs, fees and possible currency fluctuations. If you have a foreign currency mortgage, you must usually pay commission charges each time you transfer money into a foreign currency to meet your mortgage repayments, although some lenders do this free of charge.

Whatever type of home loan you choose, take time to investigate all the options and bear in mind that mortgage advice offered by lenders can be misleading and isn't to be trusted. One way of finding the best deal is to contact an independent mortgage broker. One such company is Mortgage Choice in Sydney (☎ freecall 13-1462, 💻 www.mortagechoice.com.au), a one-stop shop for those seeking the best mortgage deal and offering hundreds of home loan deals from which to choose. You should note, however, that brokers earn their living from fees paid by lenders and therefore may not always be impartial. Wherever you obtain advice, always ensure that it's impartial (ask whether an adviser is being paid a commission by a lender). Invaluable independent advice and comparative tables of lenders are published in specialist magazines such as *Your Mortgage* (quarterly) in Australia.

5.

THE PURCHASE PROCEDURE

This chapter details the purchase procedures for buying a home in Australia and New Zealand. They are generally straightforward, although (as in all countries) there are possible pitfalls for the unwary. It's wise to employ a lawyer before paying any money or signing a contract and, if necessary, have him check anything you're concerned about regarding a property that you're planning to buy.

PURCHASE PROCEDURE

Australia

Once a suitable property has been found and a price has been agreed, the estate agent completes a Contract of Sale, which is signed by both parties. Contracts are published in standard form by the Law Society and the Real Estate Institute. Since July 2001, all contracts have carried a government statement bringing to your attention important matters such as the recommendation to seek legal advice and information on cooling-off periods (see below) and the payment of deposits. The client as well as the estate agent must sign this statement in front of a witness. **You should never sign a contract without having it checked by a legal adviser.** It's important to check that a property's particulars are complete in every detail and have been entered correctly and that the terms of sale are correct, including any changes made to the standard terms. A deposit (typically 10 per cent of the purchase price) is paid by the buyer to the agent and deposited in the agent's escrow (trust) account until completion, which is usually around a month later. **The deposit is forfeited if you pull out of a purchase after signing a contract and aren't covered by a clause in the contract.** However, a holding deposit paid before signing a contract (as a sign of 'good faith') is refundable if you change your mind.

Only after the contract has been signed do the searches and checks (see **Conveyance** below) take place and, when all searches have been satisfactorily completed, the sale is completed. After signing and exchanging contracts, called simply 'exchange', both parties are legally obliged to go through with the deal, subject to cooling-off rights in some states, e.g. NSW, SA and Victoria, of two to five working days. For example, buyers in NSW have a cooling-off period from the day of exchange until 5pm on the fifth working day following, during which they can withdraw from the purchase without penalty other than forfeiting 0.25 per cent of the purchase price. Cooling-off rights don't apply when buying at public auction. Any conditions attached to a sale must either be dealt with before the exchange or during the cooling-off period, otherwise they *must* be included as a specific provision (conditional clause) in the contract. Note that vendors sometimes refuse to sell unless a certificate waiving the cooling-off period is signed.

Conditional Clauses

Contracts often contain conditional clauses, such as the sale being conditional on a clear survey. Conditions usually apply to events out of control of the vendor or buyer, although almost anything agreed between the buyer and vendor can be included in a contract. If any conditions aren't met, the contract can be suspended or declared null and void and the deposit returned. However, if you fail to go through with a purchase and aren't covered by a clause in the contract, you forfeit your deposit or might even be compelled to complete a purchase. If you're buying anything from the vendor such as carpets, curtains or furniture which are included in the purchase price, you should have them listed and attached as an addendum to the contract. Any fixtures and fittings present in a property when you view it (and agree to buy it) should still be there when you take possession, unless otherwise stated in the contract.

When signing a contract to buy a home or land on which you require a loan, you should complete the clause regarding your ability to obtain finance. This makes the contract 'subject to finance'; if you cannot obtain finance within the time specified in the contract, e.g. 7 to 14 days, it becomes null and void and you won't have to proceed. Without a finance clause, you could be sued by the vendor for failing to buy the property. If you cannot arrange finance in the specified time, you can ask for an extension to the settlement date.

Most properties in Australia are owned freehold, where the owner receives a copy of the certificate of title (deeds) or the strata title. A certificate of title is usually issued by the state lands title office (land registry), where land and property ownership is recorded. Mortgages are also recorded at the lands title office.

Conveyance

Conveyance (often improperly called conveyancing) is the legal term for the process of buying and selling properties and transferring the deeds of ownership. A conveyance is a deed (legal document) that conveys a house from the vendor to the buyer, thereby transferring ownership. There are two main stages when your conveyancer becomes involved. The first stage takes you up to the exchange of contracts and the second leads to the completion of the sale, when you become the new owner.

Conveyance includes ensuring that proper title is obtained, arranging the necessary registration of the title, checking whether the land has been registered and the existence of any restrictive covenants, enquiring about any planned developments that may affect the value of the property (like a new airport runway or motorway at the bottom of your garden), and drawing up a contract of sale. However, conveyance duties and laws in Australia vary according to the state or territory where the property is situated. Searches should include a building inspection report, drainage or sewerage service diagram, enquiries with the local council and utility companies as to whether the property is clear of any debts, identifications survey (to identify the rightful owner), pest certificate, property certificate, strata inspection (for a strata title unit – see page 163), technical report and zoning certificate. Land tax, council and water rates are a charge on the property and, if they haven't been paid by the previous owner, the new owner must pay them.

Property conveyance in Australia is usually done by a solicitor (lawyer) or a conveyancer (also called land brokers, land agents and settlement agents), although you can also do it yourself. In the ACT, Queensland and Tasmania, solicitors have a monopoly on conveyance, and in Victoria a conveyancer must work with a solicitor, but in other states you can engage a conveyancer. In some states (such as South Australia and Western Australia), the majority of settlements are handled by conveyancers, which helps reduce costs. Some lenders carry out conveyance as a free service to borrowers. Separate conveyance fees are usually paid by both the buyer and the vendor (in some states the buyer's costs are higher, as there's more work involved).

There isn't a fixed fee for conveyance, which can range from around $500 to $1,700. Shop around for the lowest rate, as some solicitors and conveyancers negotiate. Conveyance companies are generally cheaper than solicitors and usually levy fixed fees with no hidden charges. Always check what is included in the fees and whether a quoted fee is 'full and binding' or just an estimate. A low basic rate may be supplemented by much more expensive 'extras' (called disbursements). Ask your colleagues, friends and neighbours whether they can recommend a solicitor or conveyancer and try to obtain a binding quotation in writing. **It isn't wise to use a solicitor or conveyancer who is acting for both the borrower and the lender, as conflicts of interest could arise.**

It's possible and perfectly legal to do your own conveyance, and there are a number of DIY kits available. However, you will need to do at least ten hours' work and you require a good grasp of details plus a good measure of patience. **Conveyance isn't recommended for most people, as it's complex, risky and time-consuming.** If you miss a mistake in the lease, you could be left with an unsellable property – if a solicitor or licensed conveyancer is at fault, you can at least sue him!

New Zealand

When you find a house you wish to buy, you need to make a formal offer in writing, and most estate agents have a standard form for this purpose. A formal offer has to be made even if you wish to pay the advertised price. The offer is conditional and conditions may include the approval of finance (e.g. a mortgage), a satisfactory independent valuation, a satisfactory title search, the sale of another home, etc. Unless you've agreed to pay the asking price, there then follows a bargaining process which concludes when both parties have agreed a price for the property. As soon as you agree the price, you must sign a sales contract, which commits you to go through with the purchase. There are usually exclusions to this commitment (e.g. you aren't obliged to go ahead with the purchase if you find out that a new road is about to be built through the living room), but you cannot back out because you decide that you don't like the house or cannot afford it, unless you pay compensation. You also cannot subsequently reduce the price you've agreed to pay.

Many estate agents try to insist that purchasers sign a contract as soon as a sale is agreed, i.e. the day you view the property and say that you want it. **However, you shouldn't sign a contract before taking legal advice and confirming that the title is clear.** If you feel obliged to sign a contract before the conveyance checks are complete, you should ask your lawyer to insert a clause in the contract to the effect that the contract is null and void if any problems arise. However, there's no legal requirement to sign a contract immediately, provided it's done within a reasonable time, so don't allow yourself to be pressured into signing. It's usually better to pass up a property if, for example, the agent says that another party is keen to sign (which may in any case be a bluff), rather than buy a property that you aren't really sure about. The advantage of this system is that the seller cannot accept a higher offer after he has signed a contract with you, although most estate agents will try to push up the price to the highest possible level before pressing the highest bidder to sign a contract.

A deposit of 10 per cent is required when a sales contract is signed. This is usually non-refundable, but most contracts include a clause requiring its return if the title to the property isn't clear or the land is subject to government requisition (compulsory purchase). When buying a property in New Zealand, it's the exception rather than the rule to have a structural survey carried out. The main exception is if you're borrowing more than 80 per cent of the value of the property, when the lender usually insists that a survey and valuation is carried out to protect their interests.

Because the time between viewing a property and being required to sign a contract can be short, you should have your finances arranged before you start looking. Most banks will give you an 'in principle' decision on a mortgage before you've found a suitable property and issue you with a mortgage guarantee certificate. This allows you to make an offer in the knowledge that, assuming the property is in order and your financial circumstances haven't changed, you will be lent the money to buy the property.

Conveyance

Transferring the ownership of property (conveyance) is relatively straightforward in New Zealand, as it's easy to establish whether the title to a property is clear. As a result, it isn't mandatory to use a lawyer to do your conveyance, although given the thousand-and-one other things to be done when buying a house it's unlikely you would want to do it yourself. Conveyance by a lawyer, who's the only professional permitted to charge for conveyance, normally costs between $600 and $2,000. The fee may include the land transfer registration fee of $128. There's no fixed scale of conveyance charges, as this was abolished in 1984, so it's worth shopping around and haggling over the cost. It's possible to find a lawyer who will do the job for as little as $400.

Once you've instructed your solicitor to act on your behalf in a property purchase, his main task will be to conduct a title search, i.e. to establish that the person selling the property is in fact entitled to sell it. This is usually carried out swiftly (Land Information New Zealand is efficient) and it's rare to discover hidden horrors in New Zealand, such as dozens of relatives laying claim to a property. One peculiarly local concept in property purchase is cross leasing (also known as X-leasing). This usually applies in a situation where the previous owner of a section has leased part of it for the construction of another home (e.g. the one you're planning to buy). In this case your ownership of the land is leasehold rather than freehold, usually for the balance of a period such as 100 years, at a nominal rent. To all intents and purposes your title to an X-leased section is as secure as freehold. Your lawyer will explain if there are any particular conditions that you need to be aware of.

You should also ask your lawyer to obtain a Land Information Memorandum (LIM) report from the local council, which describes the title of the land, outlines the official boundaries and buildings, the changes allowed to these buildings and flood risks. This useful document (particularly for future reference) can cost anything from $2 to $1,500 depending on the property and the details included, therefore you should check the cost in advance. Application for a LIM must be made in writing to the local council and is usually issued within ten working days.

6.

MOVING HOUSE

This chapter contains information about shipping your belongings, immigration and customs, plus checklists of the tasks to be completed before or soon after arrival in Australia or New Zealand, and suggestions for finding local help and information.

SHIPPING YOUR BELONGINGS

The cost of removing the contents of an average three-bedroom property from Europe or North America to the Antipodes is usually from around GB£7,500 (US$10,000 to $15,000), depending on the country or region. Removal companies usually take care of the paperwork and ensure that the correct documents are provided and properly completed (see **Customs** on page 221). Major international moving companies generally provide a wealth of information and can advise on a wide range of matters regarding an international relocation. It's also wise to check the procedure for shipping your belongings to Australia or New Zealand with the relevant embassy or consulate in the country where you live.

It's wise to use a major shipping company with a good reputation. For international moves it's best to use a company that's a member of the International Federation of Furniture Removers (FIDI) or the Overseas Moving Network International (OMNI), with experience in Australia or New Zealand. Members of FIDI and OMNI usually subscribe to an advance payment scheme providing a guarantee: if a member company fails to fulfil its commitments to a client, the removal is completed at the agreed cost by another company or your money is refunded. Some removal companies have subsidiaries or affiliates in Australia and New Zealand, which may be more convenient if you encounter problems or need to make an insurance claim.

You should obtain at least three written quotations before choosing a company, as costs can vary considerably. Moving companies should send a representative to provide a detailed quotation. Most companies will pack your belongings and provide packing cases and special containers, although this is naturally more expensive than packing them yourself. Ask a company how fragile and valuable items are packed and whether the cost of packing cases, materials and insurance (see below) is included in a quotation. If you're doing your own packing, most shipping companies will provide packing crates and boxes. Shipments are charged by volume, e.g. the square metre in Europe and the square foot in the USA.

If you're flexible about the delivery date, shipping companies will quote a lower fee based on a 'part load', where the cost is shared with other deliveries. This can result in savings of 50 per cent or more compared with an individual delivery. Whether you have an individual or shared delivery, obtain the maximum transit period in writing, otherwise you may need to wait months for delivery!

Be sure to fully insure your belongings during removal with a well established insurance company. Don't insure with a shipping company that carries its own insurance, as its rates are usually high and it may fight every penny or cent of a claim. Insurance premiums are usually 1 to 2 per cent of the declared value of your goods, depending on the type of cover chosen. It's prudent to make a photographic or video record of valuables for insurance purposes.

Most insurance policies provide cover for 'all risks' on a replacement value basis. Note that china, glass and other breakables can usually be included in an all-risks policy only when they're packed by the removal company. Insurance usually covers total loss or loss of a particular crate only, rather than individual items (unless they were packed by the shipping company). If there are any breakages or damaged items, they must be noted and listed before you sign the delivery bill (although it's obviously impractical to check everything on delivery).

If you need to make a claim, be sure to read the small print as some companies require clients to make a claim within a few days, although seven is usual. Send a claim by registered post. Some insurance companies apply an 'excess' of around 1 per cent of the total shipment value when assessing claims. This means that if your shipment is valued at $30,000 and you make a claim for less than $300, you won't receive anything.

If you're unable to ship your belongings direct to Australia or New Zealand, most shipping companies will put them into storage and some allow a limited free storage period before shipment, e.g. 14 days, after which you may be charged between $60 and $100 per month for an average container, excluding insurance, although prices (and the quality of storage facilities) vary greatly.

 If you need to put your household effects into storage, it's imperative to have them fully insured, as warehouses have been known to burn down!

Make a complete list of everything to be moved and give a copy to the removal company. Don't include anything illegal (e.g. guns, bombs or drugs) with your belongings, as customs checks can be rigorous and penalties severe.

Provide the shipping company with detailed instructions of how to find your Antipodean address from the nearest main road and a telephone number where you can be contacted. If your Antipodean home has poor or impossible access for a large truck, you must inform the shipping company (the ground must also be firm enough to support a heavy vehicle). Note also that, if furniture needs to be taken in through an upstairs window, you may need to pay extra. You should also make a simple floor plan of your new home with rooms numbered and mark corresponding numbers on furniture and boxes as they're packed, so that the removal company will know where everything is to go and you can leave them to it.

After considering the shipping costs, you may decide to ship only selected small items of furniture and personal effects, and buy new bulky items of furniture Down Under. If you're moving abroad permanently, take the opportunity to sell, give away or throw out at least half of your possessions. It will cut down your removal bill, clear your mind and make life simpler, plus you will have the added pleasure of buying new furniture locally that really suits your new house.

Bear in mind when moving home that everything that can go wrong often does, so allow plenty of time and try not to arrange your move from your old home on the same day as the new owner is moving in; that's just asking for fate to intervene! See also **Pets** on page 51, **Customs** on page 221 and the **Checklists** on page 231.

PRE-DEPARTURE HEALTH CHECK

If you're planning to take up residence in Australia or New Zealand, even for part of the year only, it's wise to have a health check (including general health, eyes, teeth, etc.) before your arrival, particularly if you have a record of poor health or are elderly. If you're already taking medicine regularly, you should note that the brand names of drugs and medicines vary from country to country, and you should ask your doctor for the generic name.

IMMIGRATION

Australia

All arrivals must complete an Incoming Passenger Card (IPC), distributed by airlines and shipping companies (one per family), before their arrival in Australia. The IPC contains your personal details such as your address in Australia, name and passport number, and used by immigration officials to record the reason for your visit. The card is also for customs and quarantine purposes, and contains questions regarding plants and animals and whether you've exceeded the duty-free allowances. A married couple and their children under 18 years need complete only one statement. If you (or anyone over 12 months of age who's travelling with you) have stayed overnight or longer in a yellow fever infected country or area (e.g. Africa or South America) in the 6 days prior to your arrival in Australia, a yellow fever vaccination certificate is required.

When you disembark, you proceed to the Entry Control Point where you present your passport and IPC. You may be asked to verify the reason for your visit and provide evidence that you have sufficient funds for your trip and a return or onward ticket. Your IPC is returned to you and must be presented when you arrive at the customs checkpoint (see below). Australia operates an Advanced Passenger Processing (APP) system at major airports (e.g. Sydney) where passengers can be cleared in the 'express' lane in as little as 20 seconds. It also allows passengers on certain flights (Air New Zealand, Cathay Pacific, Japan Airlines and Qantas) to complete their immigration and customs processing at check-in and be issued with an Express card, which is simply passed through an immigration card reader on arrival.

When you receive your visa from an Australian mission overseas, you usually get a stamp in your passport stating that the visa is valid 'subject to an entry permit on arrival'. This means that you must satisfy the immigration official that you won't infringe the terms of your visa. If you have a visitor's visa, you should present it along with evidence that you have sufficient funds (or access to funds) to last you throughout your stay (e.g. $1,000 per month) and enable you to leave Australia when your visa expires. An airline ticket, bank statements, cash, credit cards and travellers' cheques all help convince immigration officials. If you're staying with friends or relatives in Australia, you usually require less funds, but the immigration officer may check with them to verify your statement. Generally, the onus is on you to *prove* that you're a genuine visitor and won't infringe the immigration laws. The immigration authorities aren't required to establish that you will violate the immigration laws, and in cases where they believe that you plan to work illegally or overstay your visa, they can refuse you entry or restrict your entry to a shorter period than that permitted by your visa.

The treatment of foreigners by immigration officers varies, but young people in particular may be liable to close scrutiny, especially those travelling light and 'scruffily' dressed or coming from notorious drug areas such as Asia or South America. Like any other visitor, you should carry evidence of your funds (or access to funds) and proof of why you're entering Australia and why you need to leave (e.g. to return to work or study overseas). Take care how you answer seemingly innocent questions (immigration officials *never* ask innocent questions) from immigration officials, as you could find yourself being refused entry if you give incriminating answers. Whatever the question, never imply that you may remain in Australia longer than the period permitted or for a purpose other than that for which you've been granted permission. For example, if you aren't permitted to work in Australia, you could be asked, "Would you like to work in Australia?" If you reply, "Yes", even if you have no intention of doing so, you could be refused entry.

When all is in order and the immigration official is satisfied, he will stamp your passport with the official entry permit stating the period that you're permitted to remain in the country. If you decide that this isn't long enough, some visas (e.g. visitor's visas) can be extended, but it's an expensive procedure and you need to convince the authorities that you should be granted an extension. You may find that it's easier to leave the country, e.g. by travelling to New Zealand or Indonesia, and re-apply for a new visa from there.

New Zealand

When you arrive in New Zealand, your passport and other papers will be inspected by an immigration officer and (provided everything is in order) you will be given permission to enter and remain for the purpose and the period for which you've applied. It's worth noting that visitors can be refused entry (even with a valid visa) if an immigration officer believes that they could be a threat to public security or health, i.e. a visa doesn't automatically grant right of entry. Visitors arriving from countries that come under the visa waiver scheme can apply for a visitor permit on arrival using the form that's provided on aircraft and ships. Bear in mind that you may be expected to produce other documents to support your claim for entry, such as a return ticket and/or evidence of funds. New Zealand immigration officials are usually fairly amiable, although certain Asian visitors and young people on working holidays (who rank highly as potential illegal immigrants) may be subjected to greater scrutiny.

If you arrive in New Zealand at a location which isn't an authorised customs airport or seaport, you're required to report to an immigration officer within 72 hours of your arrival and must meet the usual visa requirements. The harbour master or airfield owner will tell you where to report. Special arrangements apply to yachts which arrive for the purpose of undertaking essential repairs or to wait out bad weather during the hurricane season (October to April), in which case a visitor permit may be granted for a longer period than usual.

CUSTOMS

Australia

After you've cleared immigration, you proceed to the baggage claim area to collect your bags. When you have all your bags, you go to the customs checkpoint, where you hand your Traveller's Statement to a customs officer. All airports in Australia use a system of red and green 'channels'. Red means you have something to declare and green means you have nothing to declare, i.e. no more than the duty or tax-free allowances, no goods to sell, and no prohibited or restricted goods. **If you're *certain* that you have nothing to declare, go through the 'green channel', otherwise go through the red channel.** Customs officers make random checks on people going through both red and green channels and there are stiff penalties for smuggling.

When you enter Australia to take up temporary or permanent residence, you can usually import your belongings duty and tax-free. Personal and household goods that you've owned and used overseas for over 12 months can be imported free of duty and sales tax, although proof of the length of ownership may be required and this concession doesn't apply to alcohol, motor vehicles or tobacco products. Any goods not owned and used overseas for over 12 months may be subject to duty and tax at varying rates, depending on where you've come from, where you purchased the goods, how long you've owned them, and whether duty and tax have already been paid in another country. If you need to pay duty or tax, it must be paid at the time goods are brought into the country. Payment may be made in cash, by travellers' cheque in Australian currency or by American Express, Bankcard, Diners Club, Mastercard or Visa.

There's no limit to the amount of Australian or foreign currency (banknotes and coins, not travellers' cheques or other monetary instruments) that can be brought into Australia, but a sum of $10,000 or more (or the equivalent in foreign currency) must be declared on arrival. **If you're caught trying to smuggle any goods into Australia, they can be confiscated and, if you attempt to import prohibited items (see page 227), you may be liable to criminal charges and/or deportation.**

Australian Customs publish a variety of information for travellers, including a booklet entitled *Customs Information for Travellers*, available from Australian customs offices (see **Appendix A** for a list). General inquiries should be directed to the Australian Customs Service, PO Box 148, Fyshwick, ACT 2609 (☎ 1300-363 263 within Australia and 02-6275 6666 outside Australia, 🖳 www.customs.gov.au).

Temporary Residents & Visitors

In addition to the usual duty-free concessions (see page 223), temporary residents and visitors coming to Australia for a limited period may bring most articles into the country duty and tax free, provided customs is satisfied that they're for your personal use and will be taken out of Australia on your departure. However, you may be required to lodge a cash or bank security with customs to the value of the duty and tax assessed. Customs determine the form of security acceptable in each case and, if you don't take the articles with you when you leave Australia, you must pay the duty and tax assessed. Before shipping any articles to Australia which you think will qualify for this concession, you should contact a customs office for advice (see **Appendix A**). This concession isn't available if you're migrating to Australia or a returning resident.

Tourists and temporary residents may bring a caravan, motor vehicle, trailer, yacht or other craft to Australia for up to 12 months (or longer under certain circumstances) without paying duty or tax on it. However, you may be required to lodge a cash or bank security with customs equal to the amount of duty or tax assessed.

Migrants & Returning Residents

If you're coming to Australia to take up permanent residence for the first time or returning to resume permanent residence, you may import duty and tax free belongings, furniture and household articles that you've owned and used overseas for at least 12 months before your departure for Australia. Migrants may also bring machinery, plant and other equipment to Australia duty and tax free, provided certain conditions are met. Commercial equipment imported tax and duty free mustn't be hired, mortgaged, sold or otherwise disposed of during your first two years in Australia.

Unaccompanied Effects: The Australian Customs Service is responsible for the clearance of all unaccompanied effects from overseas. Unaccompanied personal effects can be cleared by the owner, a nominee appointed by the owner or a customs broker (a list of brokers, who charge a fee for their services, is published in the yellow pages). If you don't use a broker, you need to contact the local state or territory customs office to arrange clearance and must produce your passport and complete an *Unaccompanied Effects Statement* (form B534). Your effects can be cleared through customs before your arrival, provided you're arriving in Australia within six months of the arrival of your belongings. If you employ an international company (see page 216), they handle the associated paperwork and customs clearance for you. Household effects are inspected on arrival in Australia for possible illegal and quarantine risk items. A list of all the items you're importing is required if you pack the goods yourself. Duty-free concessions don't apply to goods arriving in Australia as unaccompanied effects. Australian Customs publish an *Unaccompanied Effects* leaflet.

Duty-free Allowances

Visitors or migrants coming to Australia are permitted to import the following goods duty-free:

- 2,250ml (2.25 litres) of alcoholic drinks, including beer, wine or spirits, per person over 18 years of age;

- 250g of tobacco products (for customs purposes, 250 cigarettes are equal to 250g) per person over 18 years of age;

- all personal clothing and footwear (excluding furs);

- articles for personal hygiene/grooming such as toiletries, but excluding perfume concentrate;

- articles taken out of Australia on departure, but excluding articles purchased duty and/or sales tax-free in Australia (any duty/tax-free goods are counted against your duty-free allowance);

- any other articles (except alcohol and tobacco) obtained overseas or duty and sales tax-free in Australia, up to a total purchase price of $900 per person aged 18 or over ($450 for under 18s) – this includes goods intended as gifts or received as gifts, whether personal or carried on behalf of others.

Members of the same family travelling together may combine their individual duty-free allowances. Duty and/or sales tax must be paid on any goods above the duty-free allowance, excess articles being valued for duty/tax on the price paid for them, converted to Australian dollars. However, duty and/or sales tax up to $50 is waived on goods in excess of duty-free concessions, provided that the goods are declared as excess to concessions and aren't for commercial purposes. If purchase receipts aren't available, alternative methods of valuation may be used. Some items (such as jewellery) are subject to high rates of duty and/or sales tax. Payment of duty and tax can be made in cash, by international credit card and by travellers' cheque (in

A$). Information can be obtained from state customs offices (see **Appendix A**) or the Australian Customs Service (💻 www.customs.gov.au).

One unusual feature at Australian airports is in-bound, duty-free shops where you can buy alcohol and tobacco products and a limited range of perfumes and cosmetics before you reach immigration and customs. There are also city duty-free shops where you can buy duty-free goods (upon presentation of a valid international air ticket) before going to the airport to catch your flight. Check the prices here first as they're usually lower than at airports. Purchases must usually be taken from the shop in a sealed bag (marked 'Important – Duty-Free Goods in Possession') that you must keep intact until you've boarded your flight. Alcohol, cigarettes, jewellery and perfume must be purchased within ten days of your departure and kept sealed until you've left Australia. However, some goods such as cameras, most electronic goods, film and watches can be used as soon as they're purchased. The maximum permitted value of purchases is $900, which are listed on your ticket and must be shown to customs officers at airports, so you must take them with you as hand baggage when leaving the country (so don't buy a life-size toy kangaroo!).

Prohibited & Restricted Goods

There are strict laws prohibiting or restricting the entry of drugs, firearms, steroids, weapons and certain articles subject to quarantine into Australia. If you're carrying any goods which you think may fall into any of the following categories, you must declare them to customs on your arrival in Australia.

If you're carrying any prescribed drugs of dependence, including medicines containing amphetamines, barbiturates, hallucinogens, narcotics, tranquilisers or vaccines, you must declare them to customs on arrival. It's wise to carry a doctor's prescription with you, and Australian Customs recommend that you declare all medicinal products when you arrive. If you're uncertain about any drugs or medicines that you're carrying, check with the customs officer on your arrival. Penalties for drug offences in Australia are severe and can result in imprisonment (see **Crime** on page 292).

The importation of anabolic steroids, androgenic substances, natural and manufactured growth hormones, and certain other pharmaceutical substances is prohibited unless prior written approval has been obtained from the Department of Health and Ageing, Therapeutic Goods Administration, Canberra (☎ 1800-020 653 within Australia or 02-6232 8610 outside Australia, 💻 www.tga.gov.au).

Many weapons and firearms are prohibited in Australia, while others require a permit and safety testing to import them. You should contact

Australian Customs before you travel if you intend to import any weapons or firearms. There are strict rules about carrying firearms and dangerous goods such as fireworks and flammable liquids on aircraft. If you wish to do so, contact your airline for advice before you travel.

Quarantine

Australia is free from many of the world's worst animal and vegetable diseases and from pests that afflict many other regions of the world, and it has strict quarantine regulations to ensure that it remains that way. All food or goods of plant or animal origin must be declared on your Traveller's Statement. This includes gifts and souvenirs that are made from plants or animals, or that contain plant or animal material (such as feathers, seeds or skin). If you have prohibited or unwanted items that you don't wish to declare, you can drop them in the quarantine bin on the way to collect your baggage. Food includes any bottled, dried, fresh or cooked, packaged or tinned food products, e.g. beans, confectionery, eggs and egg products, herbal medicines, herbs and spices, honey and bee products, jams, meat and meat products, milk and dairy products, nuts, sauces, and teas and beverages. Any food from meals you were served on the aircraft or ship must be left on board or put in the quarantine bin. Animal products include bee products, bones, feathers, hair, hunting trophies, rawhide, shells, skins and hides, and wool. Plants and plant products include bamboo, cane and rattan items, fresh and dried flowers, pine cones, potpourri, seeds, straw objects such as corn dollies, wood carvings and wreaths. Live animals can be imported only with prior permission and a valid import permit. There are also restrictions on taking fruit and vegetables (produced in Australia) between certain states.

Declared goods won't automatically be confiscated and in most cases they're simply inspected by a quarantine officer and returned to you, although some items may require treatment (e.g. fumigation). Quarantine inspections have been strengthened in recent years and on-the-spot fines of up to around $250 are imposed for minor offences. For further information contact the Australian Quarantine and Inspection Service (AQIS), PO Box 858, Canberra, ACT 2601 (☎ freecall 1800-020 504 within Australia or 02-6272 3933 outside Australia, 🖳 www.affa.gov.au). AQIS publishes information leaflets about what can and cannot be taken into Australia.

Protected Wildlife

Australia strictly regulates the import and export of wildlife and products made from the bones, feathers, shells, skins, etc. of protected species.

Wildlife or any accessories, clothing, handbags, ornaments, shoes, souvenirs, trophies, etc. made from protected species are seized by customs on arrival. Travellers are particularly warned of restrictions on items made from alligators and crocodiles (including gavials and caiman), big cats (jaguars, leopards, tigers, etc.), elephants (especially ivory and hide products), giant clam shells, hard corals (including black coral), lizards and monitors (goannas), orchids (including live orchids), rhinoceros, snakes, turtles, whales and zebras. Antiques made from protected species (such as ivory or tortoiseshell) require a CITES certificate (🖳 www.cites.org).

Some overseas retailers provide certificates and other guarantees stating that their products are made from protected animals specially bred in captivity and legally farmed for by-products, such as their skins. Such certificates aren't recognised by Australia and the only document recognised by customs is an import permit from the Department of the Environment and Heritage, PO Box 787, Canberra, ACT 2601 (☎ 02-6274 1111, 🖳 www. deh.gov.au). Import permits may be issued by this Department, provided that export approval has been obtained from the relevant wildlife authority in the country where you made the purchase, and where Australian wildlife import requirements have been met.

Telephones & CB Radios

The importation of cordless telephones and citizenband (CB) radios is prohibited unless they're approved by the Australian Spectrum Management Agency (SMA). Only importers authorised by the SMA and the Australian Telecommunications Authority (AUSTEL) who comply with strict conditions may import cordless telephones into Australia. Approved cordless telephones must display an approval number and an AUSTEL 'permit to connect' authorisation number. Cellular mobile telephones and facsimile machines can be imported.

New Zealand

New Zealand customs carry out checks at all points of entry into the country to enforce customs regulations, which apply to everyone entering the country, whether residents, visitors or migrants. There are no special concessions, even for visitors from Australia, despite the 'closer economic agreement' with New Zealand (apparently they're not that close!). Prior to your arrival in New Zealand you will be given a New Zealand Passenger Arrival Card, which you must complete and give to customs when you arrive.

This card includes a declaration stating whether you have any banned, restricted or dutiable goods (i.e. above your duty-free allowance – see below). Most ports of entry operate a red (goods to declare) and a green (nothing to declare) channel system. If you know (or think) you may have goods that must be declared, you should declare them on arrival. If you don't make a declaration, you may be subject to a random check.

Duty-free Allowances

Apart from personal effects (such as clothing) everyone aged over 17 entering the country is allowed certain duty-free allowances which include:

- 200 cigarettes *or*

- 250g of tobacco *or*

- 50 cigars *or*

- a mixture of all three of the above not weighing more than 250g;

- 4.5 litres of wine or beer;

- a 1.125 litre bottle of spirit or liqueur.

You may also import other goods valued up to $700. New Zealand law allows you to purchase duty-free goods at a New Zealand airport on arrival, although if you exceed your allowance you can be charged customs duty plus goods and services tax (GST) at 12.5 per cent. If you're entering the country to take up residence, you can also import used household effects and a car, although it's unlikely you will be bringing these when you arrive at the airport! New Zealanders are entitled to the same allowances if they've been out of the country and living abroad for at least 21 months.

Restricted & Prohibited Goods

In addition to the usual items such as drugs, pornography, guns and explosives (which you cannot import without special permission), New Zealand customs (like Australian customs) are particularly sensitive about the import of anything with plant or animal origins. Breaches of the strict New Zealand Biosecurity laws result in an instant $200 fine as well as the prospect of an additional fine of up to $100,000 for an individual ($200,000 for a corporation) and of up to five years in prison. Food, plants, dried flowers, seeds and potpourri mustn't be imported into New Zealand under any circumstances. You can be fined for importing an apple or kiwi fruit, even if it came from New Zealand in the first place!

There are also special regulations governing the following:

- animals or items made from animal feathers, fur, horns, skin, tusks, etc;
- equipment used with animals, including riding tackle;
- biological specimens;
- garden tools, furniture and ornaments;
- garden tools, furniture and ornaments;
- lawn mowers, strimmers, etc;
- tents and camping equipment;
- golf clubs;
- vacuum cleaners, brooms and brushes;
- wicker and cane items;
- bicycles;
- walking/gardening boots.

It isn't recommended to import any of the above listed items into New Zealand. If you wish to you should obtain advice from customs in advance and declare them on arrival. Special inspection, cleaning and fumigation procedures are often required, for which you may be charged a fee.

On your arrival card you're asked to declare whether you've been camping or hiking in forest or parkland in the previous 30 days, and whether you have been in contact with animals other than domestic cats and dogs. You must also list the countries you've visited within the previous 30 days.

Pets and other animals shouldn't be imported into New Zealand without prior authorisation from customs. Should you wish to take your pet to New Zealand, you should entrust the job to a specialist pet shipping service. You require a health certificate provided by a vet in your home country and your pet must undergo a period of quarantine after it arrives in New Zealand (limited exemptions apply to pets imported from Australia, Hawaii, Norway, Singapore, Sweden and the UK). The good news is that you won't be charged duty on your pet.

If you bring prescribed medicines with you, you should carry a prescription or letter from your doctor stating that the medicine is being used under a doctor's direction and is necessary for your physical well being. You should carry medicines in their original containers.

You must also declare amounts of cash in any currency to the value of $10,000 or more.

Information

If you have any doubts about whether anything you wish to import into New Zealand is banned or restricted, then you should make inquiries with a New Zealand embassy, consulate or high commission, or directly to New Zealand customs (☎ freephone 0800-428 786 or 04-473 6099). Customs also have a comprehensive website that you can visit for more information (🖳 www. customs.govt.nz) or alternatively you can contact the New Zealand customs office at your point of entry (see the list in **Appendix A**),

EMBASSY REGISTRATION

Nationals of some countries are required to register with their local embassy or consulate after taking up residence in Australia and New Zealand, and most embassies like to keep a record of their country's citizens who are resident in Australia or New Zealand (it helps to justify their existence).

FINDING HELP

One of the biggest difficulties facing new arrivals in Australia and New Zealand is how and where to obtain help with day-to-day problems. For example, finding a home, insurance requirements, schools and so on. This book will go some way towards answering your questions – as will our sister books, *Living and Working in Australia* and *Living and Working in New Zealand* – although you will also need detailed local information. How successful you are in finding help depends on your employer, the town or area where you live (e.g. those who live and work in a major city are much better served than those living in rural areas), your nationality and English proficiency, even your sex.

Obtaining information isn't a problem, as there's a wealth of information available in Australia and New Zealand on every conceivable subject (from astronomy to zoology). The problem is sorting the truths from the half-truths, comparing the options available and making the right decisions. Much information isn't intended for foreigners and their particular needs. You may find that your acquaintances, colleagues and friends can help, as they're often able to proffer advice based on their own experiences and mistakes. **But beware!** Although they mean well, you're likely to receive as much false and conflicting information as accurate data (not always wrong, but possibly invalid for your particular area or situation).

The governments of Australia and New Zealand provide basic post-arrival facilities and there's a wealth of settlement programmes for migrants. For example, in Australia government programmes for immigrants include an adult migrant English programme, a grant-in-aid scheme (mainly for refugees), migrant resource centres, telephone interpreter services, translation services and welfare assistance. Migrant resource centres (over 30) are located in all major cities and towns and provide newcomers with counselling and contacts to help them overcome initial problems. Telephone interpreter services are available 24 hours a day throughout the country for the cost of a local telephone call (☎ 13-1450). Operators speak several languages and can provide information on accommodation, education, health, insurance, legal and police matters, social welfare and a wide range of other topics. There are also translation units in Canberra, Melbourne and Sydney, and translations can be obtained via the telephone interpreter service (a fee may be charged for documents other than migrant settlement documents).

Citizens' Advice Bureaux (CABs), libraries, local council offices and tourist offices are excellent sources of reliable information on a wide range of subjects. Some companies may have a department or staff whose job is to help new arrivals, or they may contract this job out to a local company. If a woman lives in or near a major town, she's able to turn to many women's clubs and organisations for help (single men aren't so well served). There are numerous expatriate associations, clubs and organisations in the major cities and large towns (including 'settlers' or 'friendship' associations) for immigrants from most countries, providing detailed local information regarding all aspects of life, including health services, housing costs, schools, shopping and much more. Women living in country areas will find there's a good network of support provided by Country Women's Institutes.

Many organisations produce booklets, data sheets and newsletters, operate libraries, and organise a variety of social events, which may include day and evening classes ranging from cooking to English classes. For a list of local clubs, look under 'Clubs and Associations' in the yellow pages. The Department of Immigration or local authorities can put you in touch with clubs and societies in the city or area where you plan to live. Most embassies and consulates provide information bulletin boards (accommodation, jobs, travel, etc.) and keep lists of social clubs and societies for their nationals, and many businesses (e.g. banks and building societies) produce books and leaflets containing useful information for newcomers. Libraries and bookshops usually have books about the local area (see also **Appendix B**).

MOVING IN

One of the most important tasks to perform after moving into a new home is to make an inventory of the fixtures and fittings and, if applicable, the furniture and furnishings. When you've purchased a property, you should check that the previous owner hasn't absconded with any fixtures and fittings that were included in the price or anything that you specifically paid for, e.g. carpets, light fittings, curtains, furniture, kitchen appliances, garden ornaments, plants or doors. It's common to do a final check or inventory when buying a new property, which is usually done a few weeks before completion.

When moving into a long-term rental property it's necessary to complete an inventory of its contents and a report on its condition. This includes the condition of fixtures and fittings, the state of furniture and furnishings, the cleanliness and state of the decoration, and anything that's damaged, missing or in need of repair. An inventory should be provided by your landlord or agent and may include every single item in a furnished property (even the number of teaspoons). The inventory check should be carried out in your presence, both when taking over and when terminating a rental agreement. If an inventory isn't provided, you should insist on one being prepared and annexed to the lease. If you find a serious fault after signing the inventory, send a registered letter to your landlord and ask for it to be attached to the inventory.

It's wise to obtain written instructions from the previous owner (agent or current owner if you're renting) regarding the operation of appliances, heating and air-conditioning systems, maintenance of grounds, gardens and lawns and swimming pool, care of special surfaces such as wooden or marble floors, and the names of reliable local maintenance men who know the property and are familiar with its quirks. Check with your local town hall regarding local regulations of such things as rubbish collection, recycling and on-road parking.

CHECKLISTS

Before Arrival

The following list contains a summary of the tasks that should (if possible) be completed before your arrival in Australia or New Zealand:

- Obtain a visa (if applicable) for all your family members (see **Chapter 1**). Obviously this *must* be done before your arrival.

- If possible, visit Australia or New Zealand before your move to arrange schooling for your children, compare communities and find a job.

- Arrange temporary or permanent accommodation.

- Arrange for the shipment of your personal effects (see page 216).

- Arrange health insurance for your family (see page 265). This is essential if you won't be covered by Medicare on your arrival in Australia or by New Zealand's public healthcare scheme.

- Open a local bank account and transfer some funds (you can open an account with most Australian and New Zealand banks from overseas). You should also obtain some local currency before your arrival, which saves you having to change money immediately on arrival.

- Obtain an international driving license, if necessary.

- Obtain an international credit card (or two), which will prove invaluable during your first few months Down Under.

- Collect and update your records, including those relating to your family's educational, employment (including job references), insurance (e.g. car insurance), medical and professional history.

Don't forget to bring the above documents with you if relevant, plus bank account and credit card details, birth certificates, death certificate (if a widow or widower), divorce papers, driving licenses, educational diplomas and professional certificates, employment references, insurance policies, marriage certificate, medical and dental records, receipts for any valuables you're bringing with you and student ID cards. You also need any documents that were necessary to obtain your visa, plus a number of passport-size photographs.

After Arrival

The following list contains a summary of tasks to be completed after your arrival in Australia or New Zealand (if not done before arrival):

- On arrival at the airport or port, have your visa cancelled and passport stamped, as applicable.

- If you don't own a car, you may wish to rent one for a week or two until you buy one locally. It's difficult or impossible to get around in rural areas without a car.

- Register with your local embassy or consulate (see page 229).

- If you plan to work in Australia, obtain a tax file number as soon as possible. This is necessary to open a bank account and before (or soon after) starting work, if applicable. In New Zealand, you will need to obtain an Inland Revenue Department (IRD) number from your local Inland Revenue office.

- Open an account at a local bank and give the details to your employer (if applicable) and other local businesses such as your landlord or utility companies.

- Do the following within the next few weeks:

  - Apply for a Medicare Card at a Medicare office in Australia or join New Zealand's public healthcare system. This also applies to temporary residents if their home country has a reciprocal agreement.

  - Arrange schooling for your children.

  - Find a local doctor and dentist.

  - Arrange whatever insurance is necessary (see **Chapter 8**), including health insurance (see page 265) and home contents insurance (see page 263).

7.

TAXATION

An important consideration when you're buying a home in Australia or New Zealand, even if you don't plan to live there permanently, is taxation, which includes property tax, wealth tax, capital gains tax (CGT) and inheritance tax. You will also have to pay income tax if you live permanently Down Under or earn an income from a property there.

INCOME TAX

Australia

As in many countries, there's a two-tier tax system in Australia: first class for the self-employed and companies and a second class system, called pay-as-you-go (PAYG), for employees. The self-employed pay their tax in arrears, whereas an employee's income tax is deducted at source from his salary by his employer. There's no state income tax in Australia, although it may be introduced under wide-ranging tax reforms currently under consideration. The income tax year in Australia runs from 1st July to 30th June of the following year (for reasons known only to the tax office). Tax is calculated on taxable income derived during the income tax year, although in certain circumstances a substitute accounting year beginning on a different date may be used. Changes in federal taxation are usually announced in the annual budget in May. Australian income tax law recognises the following general types of taxpayer: companies, individuals, partnerships and trusts. Specific provisions apply to insurance companies, mining operations, minors, primary producers, superannuation funds and certain other businesses.

Domicile

Residents of Australia are taxed on their worldwide income and non-residents only on Australian income. An individual is resident in Australia for tax purposes if he:

● normally resides in Australia *or*

● is domiciled in Australia and doesn't have a permanent place of abode outside the country *or*

● spends at least 183 days per financial year in Australia (unless he doesn't intend to take up Australian residence and has a usual place of abode outside Australia).

Double-taxation Agreements

Australia has double-taxation agreements with many countries, including Argentina, Austria, Belgium, Canada, China, the Czech Republic, Denmark, Fiji, Finland, France, Germany, Hungary, India, Indonesia, Ireland, Italy, Japan, Kiribati, the Republic of Korea, Malaysia, Malta, the Netherlands, New Zealand, Norway, Papua New Guinea, the Philippines, Poland, Romania, Singapore, the Slovak Republic, South Africa, Spain, Sri Lanka, Sweden, Switzerland, Thailand, the UK, the USA and Vietnam. Despite their name, double-taxation agreements are designed to prevent you paying double taxes and not to ensure that you pay twice! Under double-taxation agreements, certain categories of people are exempt from paying Australian tax. If part of your income is taxed overseas in a country with a double-taxation treaty with Australia, you won't be required to pay Australian tax on that income.

Foreign employees working in Australia for Australian companies or organisations are subject to Australian tax on their earnings. However, if your stay is less than six months, you aren't considered an Australian resident and are subject to Australian tax at the rates applicable to non-residents. However, double-taxation agreements contain particular articles dealing with directors, entertainers, government services, professors and teachers, which may alter this position. If you stay in Australia for longer than six months, you may be considered an Australian resident and therefore pay tax at the same rates as residents. Salary and wage income earned by residents from services performed overseas is exempt if the taxpayer has been employed outside Australia for a continuous period of at least 91 days, provided the income has been taxed overseas.

In addition to Australian taxes, you may also be liable for taxes in your home country. Citizens of most countries are exempt from paying taxes in their home country when they spend a minimum period overseas, e.g. one year. One exception is citizens of the USA. It's usually your responsibility to familiarise yourself with the tax procedures in your home country or country of domicile. If you're in doubt about your tax liability in your home country, contact your embassy or consulate. American citizens can obtain a copy of a brochure entitled *Tax Guide for US Citizens and Resident Aliens Abroad* from American embassies.

Tax Evasion & Avoidance

Tax evasion in Australia is a criminal offence, for which you can be heavily fined or even imprisoned. Nevertheless, most Australians don't consider it a crime to cheat the tax office – an attitude that has spawned a nation of tax fiddlers (it's a national sport). Australia has a flourishing black economy, which the ATO estimates costs around $16 billion per year in unpaid tax on undeclared income.

Tax avoidance, i.e. legally paying as little tax as possible, if necessary by finding and exploiting loopholes in the tax laws, is a different matter altogether from tax evasion. It's practised by most companies, self-employed people and wealthy individuals. Unfortunately there are few (legal) ways an individual paying PAYG tax can reduce his income tax bill (dying is one of them), although it's possible to appeal against your tax bill or anything connected with your tax affairs which you believe is incorrect.

If you own a company or are self-employed, you can delay paying your tax for a period by appealing against a tax demand. As in many countries, the wealthiest Australians use elaborate schemes to avoid paying tax and take maximum advantage of low-tax investments. Many wealthy Australians avoid or minimise their income tax by establishing trusts, which cost the government $millions per year in 'lost' tax. However, the tax office is planning a crackdown on overseas tax shelters and trusts. Around two million Australians are estimated to use trusts in some form. Australian banks and other institutions paying interest and dividends must provide details to the tax office of all payments made (which is why some people invest their money overseas, although not declaring income earned overseas is illegal).

There are many books published annually about how to reduce your income tax bill, including the *Australian Tax Guide* and the *Australian Master Tax Guide* (Longman). Whether you're self-employed or an employee, you should always ensure that you don't pay any more tax than is necessary.

Accountants

If your tax affairs are complicated or you're unable to understand your own finances (like many people), you should consider employing an accountant or tax consultant (many banks also provide a personal tax service). This applies to most self-employed people, but very few who are on PAYG. However, don't pick an accountant simply by sticking a pin in the telephone book, but ask your business associates, colleagues or friends if they can recommend someone. If you're self-employed, you should choose an accountant who deals with people in your line of business and who knows exactly what you can and cannot claim.

Substantial tax savings can be made with regard to pensions, trusts and other tax-avoidance schemes, although some schemes apply only to the very rich, as the cost of using them is prohibitive to anyone else. As soon as the ATO closes one loophole, tax accountants usually find another. Accountant's fees vary from around $100 to $400 per hour, so ask in advance what the rates are (they're highest in the major cities) and avoid 'high-powered' accountants who cost the earth. You can reduce your accountant's fees considerably by keeping itemised records of all your business expenses (preferably on a computer), rather than handing your accountant a pile of invoices and receipts. A good accountant, however, usually saves you more than he charges in fees.

Australia has Byzantine tax regulations (the Income Tax Act runs to around 3,300 pages) and it's possible to receive conflicting information from different tax 'experts' and even from different branches of the tax office. Taxpayers constantly complain of inconsistency in the way the ATO makes its rulings and you should never trust the ATO to take only what it should or to credit you with all your allowances and deductions; although the ATO won't cheat you deliberately, it does make mistakes. If you pay PAYG tax, make sure that the tax deducted is correct and never hesitate to dispute a tax bill with which you disagree. A tax appeals system was introduced in 1997 and the ATO also has a problem resolution service (☎ local call rate 13-2870).

Information

Tax Help is a volunteer service to help certain people complete their tax returns, including Aborigines and Torres Strait Islanders, those on low incomes (including senior citizens), people from non-English speaking backgrounds, and those with disabilities. The translating and interpreting service (TIS) helps non-English speaking people with tax questions by setting up a three-way telephone conversation with an interpreter and the tax office (☎ local call rate 13-1450). The languages covered include Arabic, Chinese, Croatian, Greek, Indonesian, Italian, Japanese, Korean, Macedonian, Polish, Serbian, Spanish, Turkish and Vietnamese.

For general income tax enquiries, contact the Australian Taxation Office (ATO), Head Office, 2 Constitution Avenue, Canberra, ACT 2601 (☎ 13-2861). There's also a 'fax from a tax' information service where you can receive information via fax (☎ 13-2860). The ATO runs a comprehensive (if complicated and cumbersome) website where most information is accessible (💻 www.ato.gov.au). Australia's tax system was revised on 1st July 2000. The reforms included the introduction of a goods and services tax (GST, see page 252) and a $12 billion cut in personal income tax. Benefits such as family assistance and pensions were also increased – older Australians are also entitled to a one-off bonus. Most TAFE colleges

(Technical and Further Education colleges, Australia's largest providers of further education), in conjunction with the ATO, run courses explaining the tax system and how to complete tax returns.

There are various computer tax programs such as QuickTax (Reckon Intuit) and SmartTax (Mysterious Pursuit), although they're mainly for 'experts'. A better option for individuals is to join Taxpayers Australia, who for an annual fee of $312 provide you with 24 issues of the latest tax information, a telephone helpline and a 900-page booklet on the current year's tax return (⌨ www.taxpayer.com.au).

Taxable Income & Rates

Taxable income includes income derived directly or indirectly from all sources except where it's specifically exempted. It includes allowances and benefits, capital gains, dividends and bonuses, foreign income, income from partnerships or trusts, interest, lump sum payments, pensions, rental income, salary or wages, and termination payments. The tax law makes a basic distinction between income and capital receipts, and generally only income is assessable. However, capital gains made from the sale of assets acquired after 20th September 1985 are included in your assessable income. Some income is tax exempt, including defence and United Nations payments, education payments, certain pensions, and social security allowances and payments.

Other income that's exempt from income tax includes family payment, certain scholarships, bursaries and other educational allowances, and the income of certain non-profit organisations. Most government pensions are subject to tax, although a system of rebates ensures that no tax is paid by a pensioner who earns only a small amount of other income. Special provisions deal with other types of income, including lump-sum payments received on retirement, non-cash benefits, irregular income earned by artists, sportsmen and the like, and the income of farmers. Those with irregular income are permitted to average their earnings out over five years; the tax payable is calculated according to a complicated formula, taking into account 'normal' income and adding this to one-fifth of your 'abnormal' income over a five-year period. Special tax rules apply to those under the age of 18, when income is generally taxed at a higher rate.

Since the 2000 tax reform, Australia has had four income tax rates, from 17 to 47 per cent (excluding the Medicare levy), as shown below (effective 1st July 2005):

Taxable Income	Tax Rate (%)
Under $6,000	0
$6,001-$21,600	17
$21,601-$63,000	30
$63,001-$80,000	42
Over $80,000	47

Some 40 years ago the top rate of tax (47 per cent) was applied at 14 times average weekly; today it's payable at just one and a half times average earnings. However, it doesn't apply to most people and over 80 per cent of Australian taxpayers pay tax at 30 per cent or below. Anyone who isn't resident in Australia for a whole financial year receives a pro rata portion of the tax-free allowance ($6,000 per year), e.g. if you're resident in Australia for half the tax year, your tax-free allowance is $3,000. Your taxable income is your income after all allowances and deductions have been made from your gross income from all sources.

Non-residents: There's no tax-free allowance for non-residents, who are taxed as shown below. Note, however, that non-residents should have a tax file number and quote it to their employer (if applicable), otherwise they're taxed at the maximum rate of 47 per cent. Non-residents with business and trading income in Australia are taxed as below:

Taxable Income	Tax Rate (%)
up to $21,600	29
$21,601-$63,000	30
$63,001-$80,000	42
Over $80,000	47

Individual Taxation: The joint filing of returns by spouses isn't permitted in Australia, where the same tax rates apply to married and single individuals. There are three main systems of collecting tax from individuals in Australia:

● Pay-As-You-Go (PAYG);

- Prescribed Payments System (PPS);

- PAYG Instalments System.

Deductions & Rebates: All taxpayers can claim deductions and rebates in addition to credit for tax paid during the relevant financial year. The gross tax payable on taxable income is reduced by the relevant credits, deductions and rebates to obtain the net tax payable. There's a difference between a deduction and a rebate. Deductions reduce taxable income, but rebates are subtracted from the tax payable on your taxable income. Rebates are essentially available only to Australian residents whose dependants also live in Australia. There's no unified system of deductions or rebates that applies to all taxpayers. Full details of all deductions and rebates for individual taxpayers are contained in the free *Tax Pack*.

Deductions: Deductions are subtracted from your gross income to calculate your taxable income. Most deductions are occupation-specific and must be legitimate expenses incurred in earning your assessable income, provided they aren't capital, domestic or private. They're commonly claimed by employees and include car, self-education, travel and work expenses. Deductions are also allowed for certain non-business expenses such as gifts to approved charities. Deductions must usually be substantiated by documentation, and special documentation requirements must be met where employment-related expenses exceed $300 per year. Allowable deductions include:

- Car expenses relating to work;

- Travel expenses relating to work;

- Occupational clothing expenses (e.g. protective clothing and uniforms);

- Work-related self-education expenses;

- Other work-related expenses, including books, computer and office expenses, insurance premiums, journals, overtime meals, telephone, tools and union fees.

- Tax losses carried forward from previous years;

- Australian film industry incentives;

- Personal (non-employer sponsored) superannuation contributions;

- Interest and dividend expenses such as taxes and fees;

- Gifts or donations to recognised charities, funds, organisations and political parties;

- Expenses for managing your tax affairs;

- The deductible amount of the undeducted purchase price (UDP) of an Australian pension or annuity;

- The undeducted purchase price of a foreign pension or annuity;

- Non-employer sponsored superannuation contributions.

Rebates: Rebates (also called tax offsets) provide you with tax relief and are subtracted from the tax due on your taxable income. If rebates are greater than the tax due, you don't pay any tax. There are two exceptions to this: the private medical insurance rebate, where the excess is refunded; and the landcare and water facility rebate, where the excess is carried forward and used to reduce future tax liability. Rebates don't, however, reduce your Medicare levy. Rebates are made on tax due in respect of:

- savings income at 15 per cent with a maximum rebate of $450;

- private health insurance premiums at 30 per cent, provided insurance is from a registered health fund (you may choose to claim the rebate as a reduction in your insurance premium);

- net medical expenses (including dental, medical and optical aids) over $1,500 that aren't reclaimable from Medicare or private health insurance at 20 per cent.

There are also:

- zone rebates for people living in some remote or isolated areas of Australia (there are also special areas within these zones) – most apply to areas in northern and central Australia;

- rebates for beneficiaries, overseas forces personnel and pensioners;

- rebates for low-income taxpayers: if the sum of your assessable income and total reportable is less than $30,999, you may be eligible for a tax rebate of up to a maximum of $1,000;

- rebates for certain dependants, as follows:

Dependant	Rebate
spouse (including *de facto*)	$1,535
child-housekeeper	$1,535
child-housekeeper (with dependent child/student)	$1,841
invalid relative	$691
parent or parent-in-law	$1,381

Whether you can claim a rebate usually has nothing to do with the amount of taxable income you earned. However, some rebates, such as beneficiary and pensioner rebates and the rebate for low-income taxpayers, do depend on your income.

Family Tax Benefit: Under the tax reform in 2000, Family Tax Assistance was replaced by Family Tax Benefit. Family tax benefit can be paid either directly by the Family Assistance Office or through the tax system. Family tax benefit is subject to an income test, usually based on your tax return from the previous tax year. For further information contact the Family Assistance Office (☎ local call rate 13-6150, ▭ www.familyassist.gov.au).

Income Tax Returns: You must lodge a tax return in Australia if any of the following applied (with certain exceptions) during the previous financial year:

● You received a government benefit or allowance and had other income.

● You received a government pension or allowance which was reduced because you had other income.

● You received more than $6,000 in taxable income during the financial year.

● You received more than $772 in income other than salary and wages and you were under the age of 18 on 30th June of the financial year in question.

● You're a non-resident and earned more than $1 from which non-resident withholding tax had not been deducted.

● You stopped full-time education, became an Australian resident or stopped being an Australian resident and your income exceeded the part-year threshold amount.

- You paid tax during the previous tax year (with certain exceptions).

- You were liable for child support under the Child Support (Assessment) Act 1989.

- You made a loss or can claim for a loss made in a previous year.

- You carried out business in Australia.

- You were entitled to a distribution from a trust or had an interest in a partnership which carried out a business of primary production.

- You were an Australian tax resident and any of your income came from overseas.

If you don't need to lodge a return for the financial year in question but lodged one for the previous financial year, you must complete a *Non-lodgement Advice* and send it to the ATO (one is provided in the *Tax Pack* – see below).

Returns must be lodged by 31st October for the previous tax year, e.g. the tax return for the 2005/06 tax year ending 30th June 2006 must be lodged by 31st October 2006. If you're expecting a refund, the earlier you lodge your return, the sooner you're likely to receive it. If you're unable to meet the deadline because of circumstances beyond your control, you should request permission to lodge at a later date in writing to the office where you last lodged, **before the deadline**.

Tax Pack: The ATO provides a comprehensive free *Tax Pack* (almost 150 pages) for individual taxpayers, which is available from newsagents, post offices and tax offices (it's also available overseas in some countries). A copy is also delivered to all households just before the end of the financial year (30th June). The pack contains two 'long form' tax returns (consisting of six pages) at the back, one of which is to be completed and sent to the ATO (the other is in case you make a mistake or wish to make a copy for your records). A 'short form' tax return is available for those with simple tax affairs and is sent to you automatically if you answered a relatively small number of questions on your previous tax return. If applicable, attach statements (group certificates or tax stamp sheets) issued by your employer to your tax return. If you don't have them, you should obtain a statement from your employer showing salary and income tax payments; otherwise, you must complete a statutory declaration for missing or lost group certificates or tax stamp sheets.

Don't forget to sign and date the return on the last page before posting it. If you use the *Tax Pack* to complete your return and make a mistake, you won't be subject to any penalties, although you may be required to pay interest on any tax owed unless the mistake was due to misleading information contained in the *Tax Pack*.

The tax office where you lodge your return is determined by your postcode, a list of which is given in the *Tax Pack*. You can post your tax return or lodge it personally in the box provided at a tax office. You can also lodge your tax return electronically by using e-tax, a free service provided by the tax office. In 2003, over 800,000 Australians lodged their tax return using e-tax. Taxpayers have been able to lodge their returns over the internet since 1997/98.

Keep a copy of your tax form and anything else you send to the ATO. This is useful if your tax form is lost in the post or there are any queries. You should also keep a copy of all documentation (invoices, receipts, statements, etc.) which substantiate claims made in your tax return. Records must be kept for three and a half years for salary and wage earners, and five years for the self-employed (seven years for car and travel-related expenses). Selected tax returns are audited, and you may be penalised if the information provided is found to be incorrect. As in most countries, the self-employed are *much* more likely to be audited than employees.

New Zealand

Generally speaking, income tax in New Zealand is below average for a developed country. During the '90s most people saw their income tax reduced, but in the 21st century income taxes have increased. Most New Zealanders are resigned to paying taxes (tax evasion isn't a national sport as it is in some countries) and in any case the country has a system of pay-as-you-earn (PAYE) that ensures that tax is deducted at source from employees' salaries. The tax system in New Zealand isn't particularly complicated. It's designed so that most people can prepare and file their own tax returns, although if your tax situation is complicated you may need to seek help from an accountant.

The Inland Revenue Department (IRD) provides a comprehensive help service and publishes numerous factsheets and brochures for taxpayers. The following helplines are available:

● Income tax and general enquiries: ☎ freephone 0800-227 774 or 04-801 9973;

● Overdue tax and returns: ☎ freephone 0800-227 771;

● Student loans: ☎ freephone 0800-377 778;

- Family Assistance: ☎ freephone 0800-227 773;

- INFOexpress: ☎ freephone 0800-257 999;

- Forms and stationery: ☎ freephone 0800-101 035.

The IRD (PO Box 3754, Christchurch, PO Box 1535, Hamilton or PO Box 39-050 Wellington) also has a comprehensive website (⌨ www.ird.govt.nz) which includes downloadable factsheets and forms.

Liability

Your country of domicile determines whether you're liable to pay New Zealand income tax. New Zealand residents are taxed on their worldwide income, while non-residents are subject to income tax only on income derived from New Zealand. To determine 'domicile' the tax authorities apply what's known as the 'permanent place of abode test', although this is arbitrary and isn't enshrined in New Zealand tax law. Usually anyone who's present in New Zealand for more than 183 days in a 12-month period is considered resident there and liable to pay taxes. You don't need to be a permanent resident to be liable, and the existence of financial and social ties (including bank accounts and club memberships) may be taken as evidence of domicile. You can usually be considered exempt from New Zealand taxes only if you aren't present in New Zealand for 325 days in a 12-month period. However, if you maintain a home in the country, you cannot be considered non-resident, no matter how brief your stay. If you decide to leave New Zealand, you should inform your local IRD office. Note that the 325-day time limit doesn't start until the IRD has confirmed that you've ceased to become a resident.

Income that's subject to tax in New Zealand includes commissions, dividends, interest, profits or gains from a business, rents, royalties, salary and wages, and trust distributions.

Double-taxation Agreements

New Zealand has double taxation treaties with 29 countries: Australia, Belgium, Canada, China, Denmark, Fiji, Finland, France, Germany, India, Indonesia, Ireland, Italy, Japan, Korea, Malaysia, the Netherlands, Norway, the Philippines, the Russian Federation, Singapore, South Africa, Sweden, Switzerland, Taiwan, Thailand, the UAE, the UK and the USA. Double taxation treaties are designed to ensure that income which has been taxed in one treaty country isn't taxed again in another. A treaty establishes a tax credit or exemption on certain kinds of income, either in the taxpayer's country of residence or in the country where the income is earned. Where applicable, a double taxation treaty prevails over local law.

Tax Code

Every taxpayer in New Zealand is required to complete a Tax Code Declaration (form IR330) when they start employment and if there are any changes in their employment circumstances, e.g. if working hours are reduced. You should be given the form by your employer, who returns the completed form to the IRD. The tax code for most employees is M. It's important that you fill in the form correctly, as the amount of tax you pay is based on the information provided.

Tax Return & Tax Bill

When you start work in New Zealand, you should register with your local IRD office, who will issue you with an IRD or tax file number, which must be quoted on tax documents and enquiries. To apply for your IRD number you need to complete an IRD form and send a copy of your passport (☎ freephone 0800-227 774, 💻 www. ird.govt.nz). IRD numbers are usually issued within five working days.

Recent changes in tax legislation have made tax calculations simpler and more accurate, and tax returns easier to complete. Until recently, everyone who earned an income in New Zealand had to file an income tax return annually with the Commissioner of the Inland Revenue Department. However, under new tax legislation tax returns have been eliminated for individuals who receive income from employment subject to PAYE or from interest and dividends subject to Resident Withholding Tax (RWT). All individuals who derive income that isn't taxed at the time of payment or who are in business must file an annual return. The return, known as an IR3, is sent to you automatically each year. The New Zealand tax year runs from 1st April to 31st March of the following year, and returns must be filed by 7th July. The IRD then issues a tax assessment (i.e. a tax bill) showing the amount of income tax payable.

Payments for due tax can be made in a variety of ways, including by cheque, by electronic payment or direct debit from your bank, by cash or cheque at any branch of the Westpac Trust bank, or online through the internet banking facility at any major New Zealand bank.

Employees whose income tax is deducted at source by their employer under PAYE and who don't have any other income, receive a Personal Tax Summary from the IRD based on information provided by employers and shouldn't have any more income tax to pay. The Personal Tax Summary states your tax code and you should check with the IRD that you're using the correct tax code (see above).

You will also receive a Personal Tax Summary if you receive family assistance payments from IRD; if you receive family assistance payments from Work and Income and earn over $20,000; if you have a student loan and qualify for an interest write-off; and if you have paid too little or too much tax. The Personal Tax Summary shows whether you're entitled to a tax refund or have tax to pay. If you have tax to pay, you must pay it by the 7th February for people without a tax agent or by the 7th April for those with an agent and a time extension. If you're entitled to a refund it will be paid when you've confirmed your Personal Tax Summary or within 30 days if the amount owing is less than $200. If you wish to claim certain rebates, such as a child or low income earner rebate (see **Rebates** below), or if you earn under $38,000 but your dividend income was taxed at 33 per cent, you should request a Personal Tax Summary.

Tax Rates

It has become common practice in recent years for the rate of income tax to be adjusted annually in the July budget. There are three tax rates in New Zealand, which are currently as follows:

Taxable Income ($)	Tax Rate (%)	Cumulative Tax ($)
0-38,000	19.5	7,410
38,001-60,000	33	14,670
over 60,000	39	

Under recent tax changes, if you receive a lump sum payment (e.g. bonuses, back pay or retirement payment) and your annual income is over $60,000, you can elect to pay the higher tax rate of 39 per cent on the lump sum and therefore avoid 'squaring up' your tax at the end of the year. If you receive a redundancy payment which together with the annual value of your income for the previous four weeks is less than $38,000, you will pay a flat rate of 21 per cent tax on the redundancy payment.

Rebates: Before you're liable for income tax, you can deduct certain allowances (known as rebates) from your gross salary, which reduce your tax bill. Some income rebates, such as the low earner rebate, are built into the PAYE rates but others, such as the housekeeper, childcare and donations rebates, must be claimed from the IRD on separate forms. Key rebates include:

- **child taxpayer rebate** ($156), available for children under 15 or still at school;

- **housekeeper rebate** ($310), which generally includes childcare costs for working parents;

- **donations rebate** ($630), on charitable donations of $1,890 or more;

- **low income earner rebate** (4.5 per cent of net income up to $9500 and 1.5 per cent of income above $9,500);

- **transitional tax allowance** ($728, reduced by 20¢ per $1 of earnings over $6,240), which is available to full-time earners working at least 20 hours per week.

Tax rebates must be claimed by 30th September following the end of the relevant tax year. Expenses associated with employment (such as clothing or travel to work) cannot usually be claimed as a tax allowance in New Zealand. However, the self-employed can claim legitimate business expenses. Interest on a mortgage cannot be claimed as a tax allowance in New Zealand.

Resident Withholding Tax: Interest on bank and other savings accounts is paid after deduction of resident withholding tax (RWT) at a rate equivalent to the standard rate of income tax (19.5 per cent). If, however, you don't provide your IRD or tax file number (see page 248) to a bank when opening an account, it's taxed at the higher rate (39 per cent).

Businesses & Self-employment: Income tax for the self-employed and small businesses is broadly similar to wage and salary earners. You're sent a tax return (form IR3) at the end of your financial year, which you must complete and return by the 7th day of the fourth month following the end of your financial year. If your financial year is the same as the tax year (April to March), your tax return must be filed by 7th July each year. You can apply to have a financial year that differs from the tax year. The self-employed are required to pay a proportion of their estimated tax on a monthly basis, which is based on their previous year's liability. When your tax return is submitted, the IRD reconciles the tax due with the sum already paid and issues a tax assessment for any tax payable or a refund if you've over-paid. Company tax is levied at a flat rate of 33 per cent, whether a company is resident or non-resident.

OTHER TAXES

Australia

Property & Land Taxes

Property taxes (called council rates in Australia) are levied by councils on homeowners to pay for local services. These include community and welfare services, footpaths, health inspections, libraries, parks and recreational facilities, roads, rubbish collection and disposal (which may be charged separately), and town planning and building control. In some states there's a swimming pool levy to ensure compliance with safety standards. Rates are based on the 'rateable value' of a property, officially called the 'unimproved capital value', which is reassessed every few years by the Valuer General's Department. Rates are levied annually but are usually paid quarterly. Check the current rates before buying a property, as in some areas they can be very high (pensioners may receive a concession). Rates usually also increase when land valuations go up, although there's a limit on what councils can charge.

　　Land tax is levied on the ownership of land in all states and territories except the Northern Territory. It's based on the unimproved value of land (i.e. excluding the value of any buildings or capital improvements) at a prescribed date, e.g. 31st December in NSW, which is determined by a state's Valuer General. There's sometimes a threshold, below which no land tax is payable. For example, in ACT land tax is levied at 0.65 per cent on land valued at up to $50,000, at 1 per cent on land valued between $50,001 and $125,000, at 1.25 per cent on land valued at between $125,001 and $225,000, and at 1.5 per cent on land valued at over $225,000. In NSW, land tax is payable on investment property holdings (not principal residences) at 0.4 per cent for properties valued at up to $400,000, 0.6 per cent on those valued at between $400,000 and $500,000, and for those worth above $500,000, the tax is $2,200 plus 1.4 per cent of the value above $500,000. In Queensland land tax is only payable if the land is worth over $275,997 and if you've been awarded a deduction claim (as most people are); primary residences are exempt.

Goods & Services Tax

Australia originally levied a wholesale tax, which was applied at varying rates on a limited range of 'new' goods. In July 2000, as part of a major tax reform, a goods and services tax (GST) was introduced. GST is a broad-based tax (similar to VAT in western European countries) and is levied at a flat rate of 10 per cent on most goods and services. GST is included in the price you pay, and an 'easy' way to calculate the amount of GST on goods and services is to divide the price by 11. Some items are exempt from GST, such as basic foods, cars for the disabled, and certain medical aids and appliances.

The introduction of GST has been a logistical and public relations disaster for the government. Large and small businesses have had tremendous problems in the interpretation and implementation of GST rules, which for a single item may run into several paragraphs! The government has also had to introduce compensatory measures such as an Educational Textbook Subsidy, which was offered to students when they objected to the ten per cent increase in the price of books.

In mid-2001, on the first anniversary of the introduction of GST, statistics were released showing that bankruptcies were at a record high and consumer spending at an all-time low, although it wasn't clear whether these were caused by GST or other economic factors. Large groups, including pensioners and the self-employed, claim that GST has made them significantly worse off. On the other hand, some groups such as fresh food retailers (unaffected by GST) have seen sales grow strongly. The general impression is that GST is a negative, time-comsuming tax that has generally made Australians poorer and has done little to combat the black market.

Most businesses are required to register for GST and most must lodge a quarterly return to pay or claim GST, although if a company's annual turnover exceeds $20 million, a monthly return must be made.

Fringe Benefits Tax

Fringe benefits tax (FBT) was introduced in 1986 in order to reduce the amount of non-cash, non-taxable benefits (or 'perks') offered to employees by employers as part of their salary package. It includes children's private education, company cars for employees' private use, free or subsidised accommodation, free holiday travel, low interest or interest-free loans, and private health insurance. The level of taxation on company cars depends on the business 'mileage' and is from 7 to 26 per cent. However, leases of luxury cars as part of executive salary packages are exempt. FBT also applies to: airline transport provided free or at a discount to employees in the airline travel industry; discounted goods or services provided by an employer in excess of a specified threshold; entertainment expenses; payment or reimbursement of private expenses on behalf of employees; and the waiver of employee loans or debts. A portion of a living-away-from-home allowance paid to employees may also be subject to FBT, although 'reasonable' costs for food and accommodation aren't. Staff canteens, employee share acquisition schemes and employer superannuation schemes are exempt from FBT. Frequent-flyer schemes aren't taxable, even when your employer pays the membership fees, and childcare provided on 'business premises' or a building controlled by your employer is also exempt (including employer-sponsored/leased places at childcare centres).

FBT is paid at the rate of 48.5 per cent. The FBT tax year is different from the financial year (just to confuse you even further) and runs from 1st April to 31st March. Payments are made quarterly, by the 28th of July, October, January and April, each payment being equal to 25 per cent of the previous year's liability, the balance being payable when your annual tax return is filed. An employer must usually file an annual fringe benefits tax return by 28th April each year and fringe benefits are recorded on the employee's payment summary.

Capital Gains Tax

Australia doesn't have capital gains tax as such, but provides for the inclusion in assessable income of any profits made on certain assets during the financial year. The part of a gain that's subject to income tax, i.e. the proceeds of a sale less the purchase cost after being reduced by indexation and any losses, is treated as ordinary income and subject to the same income tax rates. However, the amount of tax you pay is calculated by adding 20 per cent of the total gain to your other income, calculating the extra tax due on this portion, and then multiplying it by five (the ATO *never* makes anything simple).

Tax is payable on the sale of certain assets, including equipment and plant, goodwill on the sale of a business, personal use assets, real estate (other than your principal home), shares, and trust distributions. What are termed 'listed personal use assets', such as works of art and antiques, are also taxable if the purchase price was over $100. Listed personal use assets include money or property received other than as gifts or loans, but don't include an inheritance arising from the death of an asset-holder. Exemptions from tax include bonds, debentures and other loans without a deferred interest element, motor vehicles (whether acquired for personal or business use), your principal residence and up to two hectares of attached land, superannuation and insurance policies, and certain personal use goods with a disposal value of less than $10,000 and any assets acquired before 20th September 1985.

Any realised capital gain from the disposal of assets acquired after 19th September 1985 is taxable. There are two methods of calculating a taxable gain: indexation or the discount system. Under indexation, the excess of the sale price over the indexed cost base is the taxable capital gain, which is added to your other taxable income. The discount system consists of a 50 per cent discount on the amount of capital gain being taxed provided the assets have been owned for at least 12 months by an individual or jointly with others. If the item was purchased after 21st September 1999, the discount system applies. Capital losses can be used to offset gains, either in the current year or in future years without a time limit, but cannot be used to offset other income.

New residents are deemed to have acquired non-Australian assets for their fair market value at the time they became resident (except for assets acquired prior to 20th September 1985, which are exempt). Upon ceasing to be a resident, you can choose to treat all non-Australian assets as 'taxable Australian assets', thereby deferring payment of tax until the assets are disposed of or you resume resident status. Overseas employees who become residents during their Australian assignments are subject to complex tax rules that may affect their assets located outside Australia. If you're in this position, you should obtain expert advice regarding capital gains.

Gains made on the sale of your principal residence in Australia are usually exempt from tax. However, tax is payable on capital gains made on the sale of an investment property or a second home. There's a federal government taxation incentive for those who let a property for less than their mortgage repayments, when the loss can be offset against other income. There's a qualifying period of two years for exemption from tax on an inherited home and, if you choose not to live in an inherited home and sell it after two years, no tax is payable.

There are four capital gains tax concessions available for small businesses: a 15-year exemption from capital gains tax; a 50 per cent active asset reduction; a retirement exemption, where you're entitled to a lifetime tax-free amount of $500,000 (if you retire before the age of 55, the amount must be paid into a superannuation or similar fund); and a 'roll-over'. All these concessions are subject to certain conditions and you should seek advice from a professional tax adviser. Tax complications can occur when a business undergoes re-organisation or re-structuring, when you should seek advice from an accountant or tax consultant.

The ATO publishes a number of booklets (also available online), including *Capital Gains Tax – What You Need to Know, Capital Gains Tax and Your*

Home, Capital Gains Tax and Investments in Shares and Units, Capital Gains Tax after Divorce or Involuntary Disposal of Assets, Capital Gains Tax and the Assets of a Deceased Estate, and *Capital Gains Tax and Small Businesses.*

New Zealand

There are no local income taxes, wealth tax, capital gains tax or estate taxes (inheritance taxes) in New Zealand. However, income tax may be levied on income derived from any undertaking or scheme entered into or devised for the purpose of making a profit. For example, income from the sale of property and land if the principal purpose of purchasing it was to resell it or if your business is dealing in property. In addition, gains resulting from certain investments, such as debentures and some preference shares, options and leases, may be taxable irrespective of whether the nature of the gain is capital or income.

Goods & Services Tax

A goods and services tax (GST) is levied in New Zealand, which is essentially the same as the value added tax levied in European Union countries but isn't a sales tax as in the USA. GST is the second largest component of tax revenue and is levied at a single rate of 12.5 per cent on most goods and services, although some are exempt (e.g. the letting of residential accommodation). When you import goods into New Zealand, GST (and in some cases also customs duty) is assessed on their value, unless they're exempt or imported under a tax-free arrangement. Immigrants can import their personal possessions free of duty and tax, provided they've been owned and used prior to their arrival. This also applies to used cars, provided you meet the import criteria.

All businesses with a turnover of $40,000 or more within a 12-month period must register for GST with the Inland Revenue Department and must levy GST on goods and services supplied (unless they're exempt). Similarly, businesses can reclaim GST paid on goods and services used in their business. A GST return must usually be filed every two months, although businesses with a turnover of less than $250,000 per year can choose to file a return every six months, and those with an annual turnover of over $24 million must file monthly. A penalty of 1 per cent of the tax due is levied if a return isn't filed by the due date, plus a further 4 per cent if there's still unpaid tax a week later. Thereafter, a further 1 per cent per month is added to any unpaid amount. For further information on GST contact the Inland Revenue on ☎ freephone 0800-377 776.

Property Taxes

Property taxes (rates) are levied by local authorities and are based on the rateable value (valuation) of properties. Bills are sent out at the beginning of the financial year and are payable by whoever occupies the property, whether it's the owner or a tenant. If you occupy a property for just part of a year, then only a proportion of the tax is payable. The annual bill for an average family house is between $1,000 and $2,000. It isn't uncommon for residents, either individually or collectively, to appeal against their property valuation in order to obtain a tax reduction.

Property taxes pay for local services such as street cleaning, lighting and subsidies paid to local public transport companies. They usually include rubbish collection (although an extra charge is levied in some areas), recycling collection and water, although in some areas such as Auckland, water is billed separately. Auckland residents have been protesting against water charges and rates for the last few years, because although water charges were recently excluded from their rates, they weren't reduced! As a result, Auckland residents pay more or less the same as before in rates as well as expensive water charges (most households pay more than $800 per year).

Gift Tax

Gift tax (known as gift duty) is imposed at fixed rates on certain gifts, including property in New Zealand or elsewhere if the donor was domiciled in New Zealand at the time of the gift. Gifts that aren't dutiable include those made to charities, gifts for the maintenance or education of your immediate family and gifts of up to $2,000 per year to an individual if they're made as part of the donor's normal expenditure, e.g. birthday and Christmas presents. The rates of gift duty range from 5 per cent on amounts above $27,000 to 25 per cent plus $5,850 on amounts in excess of $72,000.

Fringe Benefits Tax

FBT is payable by employers on the value of most fringe benefits paid to employees in New Zealand. The rate varies between 49 and 64 per cent (except as below). Examples of fringe benefits are:

- vehicles, which are subject to FBT at 24 per cent of their cost or market value, although there's a proposal to reduce this to 20 per cent;

- subsidised or low-interest loans or mortgages, which are subject to FBT at rates revised quarterly (in the third quarter of 2005 the rate was 9.01 per cent);

- employer contributions to medical insurance, which are subject to FBT for the whole amount of the contribution.

For further information, see the *Fringe benefit tax return guide* (IR425).

It's important to note that income such as interest, rents, dividends and royalties are taxable under income tax in New Zealand, rather than separately as is the case in some other countries.

8.

INSURANCE

An important aspect of owning a home in Australia or New Zealand is insurance, not only for your home and its contents, but also for your family when visiting.

SURVIVAL TIP
It's vital to ensure that you have sufficient insurance when visiting your home abroad, including building and contents insurance, third party liability insurance, health insurance and travel insurance.

It's unnecessary to spend half your income insuring yourself against every eventuality from the common cold to being sued for your last cent, but it's important to insure against any event that could precipitate a major financial disaster, such as a serious illness or accident or your house falling down.

When buying insurance, shop till you drop! Obtain recommendations from friends, colleagues and neighbours (but don't believe everything they tell you!). Compare the costs, terms and benefits provided by a number of companies before making a decision. Simply collecting a few brochures from insurance agents or making a few telephone calls could save you a lot of money. Note also that insurance premiums are often negotiable.

BUILDING INSURANCE

For most people, buying a home is the biggest financial investment they will ever make. When buying a home, you're usually responsible for insuring it before you even move in. If you take out a mortgage to buy a property, your lender usually insists that your home (including most permanent structures on your property) has building insurance from the time you sign the contract and legally become the owner. Even when it isn't required by a lender, you'd be extremely unwise not to have building insurance.

Building insurance usually includes loss or damage caused by aircraft impact, animals, earthquake, explosion, falling trees or aerials, fire, flood, malicious damage, oil leakage from central heating systems, riot, storm and lightning, subsidence or landslide, theft, vehicles, or water leakage from pipes or tanks, and may also include cover for temporary homelessness. Some insurance companies also provide optional cover to include trees and shrubs damaged maliciously or by storms. Building insurance must be renewed each year, and insurance companies are continually updating their policies, so you must ensure that a policy still provides the cover you require when you receive a renewal notice.

Lenders fix the initial level of cover when you first apply for a mortgage and usually offer to arrange the insurance for you, but you're usually free to make your own arrangements. If you arrange your own building insurance, your lender will insist that the level of cover is sufficient. Many people take the easy option and arrange insurance through their mortgage lender, which is generally the most expensive option.

Most lenders provide index-linked building insurance, where premiums are linked to inflation and building costs (premiums are usually added to your monthly mortgage payments). It's your responsibility, however, to ensure that your level of cover is adequate, particularly if you carry out improvements or extensions which substantially increase the value of your home. All lenders provide information and free advice. If your level of cover is too low, an insurance company is within its rights to reduce the amount it pays when a claim is made, in which case you may find that you cannot afford to have your house rebuilt or repaired should disaster strike.

SURVIVAL TIP
If you're insuring a second or holiday home,
you must inform your insurance company, otherwise
your insurance (including your contents insurance
– see below) could be null and void.

The amount for which your home must be insured isn't the current market value but the cost of rebuilding it if it's totally destroyed. This varies according to the type of property and the area, and is calculated per $1,000 of insurance, e.g. from around $3 to $4 per $1,000 of cover (per year) in an inexpensive area to $10 or more per $1,000 in the most expensive high-risk areas. Therefore insurance on a property costing $150,000 to rebuild costs from around $450 to $1,500 per year. There's usually no deduction for wear and tear, and the cost of redecoration is usually met in full. Building insurance doesn't cover structural faults that existed when you took out the policy, which is why it's important to have a full structural survey carried out when you buy a property.

Insurance for 'non-standard' homes such as those with thatched roofs or timber construction is usually higher. The highest level of cover usually includes damage to glass (e.g. windows and patio doors) and porcelain (e.g. baths, washbasins and WCs), although you may have to pay extra for accidental damage, e.g. when your son blasts a cricket ball through the patio window. Always ask your insurer what *isn't* covered and what it costs to include it (if required).

Premiums can usually be paid monthly (although there may be an extra charge) or annually. There may be an excess, e.g. $50 or $100, for some claims, which is intended to deter policyholders from making small claims. Some policies have an excess only for certain claims, e.g. subsidence or landslip (when your house disappears into a hole in the ground or over a cliff), which is usually $2,000 or $4,000. Owners of houses vulnerable to subsidence and those living in flood-prone areas are likely to pay higher premiums.

Many insurance companies provide emergency telephone numbers for policyholders requiring urgent advice. Should you need to make emergency repairs, e.g. to weather-proof a roof after a storm or other natural disaster, most insurance companies allow work up to a certain limit (e.g. $2,000) to be carried out without an estimate or approval from the insurance company, but check first. Building insurance is often combined with home contents insurance (see below), when it's called home or household insurance, which is usually cheaper than taking out separate policies.

Earthquake Insurance

New Zealand is within an earthquake zone and minor (usually unnoticeable) tremors occur almost monthly, although records show that serious earthquakes occur, on average, only once every 210 years. As the consequences of a major earthquake would be catastrophic and no insurance company could possibly cover them, the New Zealand government assumes the responsibility of providing earthquake insurance. The Earthquake Commission operates an insurance scheme, which is funded through a small levy on property insurance policies. In the event that an earthquake devastates your property, the Earthquake Commission will pay you compensation up to a maximum of $100,000 for a property and $20,000 for contents. If your property is insured for less, you will receive only the sum insured. The Earthquake Commission pays no compensation for boats, jewellery, money, vehicles or works of art. This scheme ensures that, in the event of an earthquake, most property owners are compensated, even if the government goes bust as a result! Because $100,000 is unlikely to be sufficient to rebuild anything other than a very modest home, most insurance companies offer top-up insurance to cover the difference between the $100,000 paid by the government and the value of your home, which is a must for owners of valuable properties. Further information is available from the Earthquake Commission, PO Box 311, Wellington (☎ 04-499 0045, 🖥 www.eqc.govt.nz).

HOME CONTENTS INSURANCE

Home contents insurance is recommended for anyone who doesn't live in an empty house. Burglary and house-breaking is a major problem in Australia, particularly in the major cities, and also in some urban areas of New Zealand. Although there's a lot you can do to prevent someone breaking into your home, it's usually impossible or prohibitively expensive to make your home completely burglar proof without turning it into a fortress. However, you can ensure you have adequate contents insurance and that your most precious possessions are locked in a safe or safety deposit box.

Types Of Policy

A basic home contents policy covers your belongings against the same sort of 'natural disasters' as building insurance (see above). You can optionally insure against accidental damage and all risks. A basic contents policy doesn't usually include items such as bicycles, cash, credit cards (and their fraudulent use), jewellery, musical instruments, sports equipment and certain other valuables, for which you may need to take out extra cover. You can usually insure your property for its secondhand value (indemnity) or its full replacement value (new for old), which covers everything except clothes and linen (for which wear and tear is assessed) at the new cost price. The most popular form of contents insurance in Australia is replacement value, and it's best to take out an index-linked policy, where the level of cover is automatically increased by a percentage or fixed amount each year. Most policies have a maximum amount they pay per item and/or a maximum amount per claim, e.g. $1,500 for each item of jewellery or work of art, or a total claim of $7,500.

A basic policy doesn't usually include accidental damage caused by your family to your own property (e.g. putting your foot through the TV during a political party broadcast) or your home freezer contents (in the event of a breakdown or power failure). A basic policy may include garden contents, loss of oil and metered water, personal liability insurance (see below), replacement locks and temporary accommodation.

If they aren't included, these items can usually be covered for an additional premium. Some policies include legal expenses cover (e.g. up to $100,000) for disputes with employers, neighbours, shops, suppliers and anyone who provides you with a service (e.g. a plumber or builder). Most contents policies include public liability cover, e.g. up to $2 million. Items such as computers and mobile telephones may need to be listed individually on your policy, and computers and other equipment used for business aren't usually covered (or may be covered only for a prohibitive extra payment). If you have friends or lodgers living in your home, their personal property won't be covered by your policy.

Premiums

Your premium depends largely on where you live and your insurer. All insurance companies assess the risk by location, based on your postcode. **Check before buying a home, as the difference between low and high-risk areas can be considerable.** Annual premiums, which start at around $400 per annum in low-risk areas, can be several times this amount in high-risk areas. Many homeowners in high-risk areas would be willing to forego theft insurance, although insurance companies are reluctant to offer this option, as theft is a convenient excuse to load premiums.

As with building insurance, it's important to shop around for the lowest premium, as premiums vary considerably with the insurer. If you're already insured, you may find that you can save money by changing insurers. However, watch out for penalties when switching insurers. Combining your home contents insurance with your building insurance (see above) is a common practice and is usually cheaper than insuring each separately. Having your building and contents insurance with the same insurer also avoids disputes over which company should pay what, which can arise if you have a fire or flood affecting both your home and its contents. Those aged over 50 or 55 (and possibly first-time homeowners) may be offered a discount, and some companies provide special policies for students in college accommodation or lodgings (ask an insurance broker).

Security

Most insurers offer a no-claims discount or a discount (e.g. 5 or 10 per cent) for homes with burglar alarms and other high security features. In high-risk areas, good security is usually a condition of insurance. Beware of the small print in policies, particularly those regarding security, which insurers often use to avoid paying claims. You forfeit all rights under your policy if you leave doors or windows open (or the keys under a mat or flower pot), particularly if you've claimed a discount for impregnability. If there are no signs of forced entry, e.g. a broken window, you may be unable to claim for a theft. If you plan to leave your house empty for a long period, e.g. a month or longer, you may need to inform your insurer (you must also inform them if it's a second or holiday home).

Sum Insured

Take care that you don't under-insure your house contents (including anything rented such as a TV or video recorder) and that you periodically reassess their value and adjust your premium accordingly. Your contents should include everything that isn't part of the fixtures and fittings and which you could take with you if you were moving house. If you under-insure your contents, your claim may be reduced by the percentage by which you're under-insured. Some insurance companies offer policies called 'no-sum' or 'fixed-sum', where you aren't required to value all your possessions but are covered for a fixed amount depending on the number of bedrooms in your home. With this type of policy the insurance company cannot scale down a claim because of under-insurance. However, you're usually better off calculating the value of the contents to be insured. You can take out a special policy if you have high-value contents, which may be cheaper than a standard contents policy. **Always list all previous burglaries on the proposal form, even if nothing was stolen.**

Claims

Some insurers provide a 24-hour emergency helpline for policyholders and assistance for repairs for domestic emergencies, such as a blocked drain or electrical failure, up to a maximum amount for each claim. Take care when completing a claims form, as insurers have tightened up on claims and few people receive a full settlement. Many insurers have an excess of $50 to $100 per claim (see above). Bear in mind that, if you make a claim, you may need to wait months for it to be settled. Generally, the larger the claim, the longer you have to wait for your money, although in an emergency a company may make an interim payment. If you aren't satisfied with the final amount offered, don't accept it and try to negotiate a higher figure.

HEALTH INSURANCE

Health insurance is an important consideration for anyone planning to spend some time in Australia or New Zealand, whether a few weeks or months or permanently. If you make frequent trips a year for periods of up to three months, the cheapest insurance cover is usually to have an annual travel policy (see page 272), although you must ensure that it provides adequate cover. When comparing the level of cover provided by different health insurance schemes, the following points should be considered:

- Does the scheme have a wide range of premium levels and are discounts or special rates available for families or children?

- Is private hospital cover available and are private rooms available at local hospitals? What are the costs? Is there a limit on the time you can spend in hospital?

- Is dental cover included? What exactly does it include? Can it be extended to include extra treatment? Dental insurance usually contains numerous limitations and doesn't cover cosmetic treatment.

- Are there restrictions regarding hospitalisation, either in Australia or New Zealand or other countries?

- What is the qualification period for special benefits or services?

- What level of cover is provided outside Australia or New Zealand and what are the limitations?

- What is the cover regarding pregnancy, hospital births and associated costs? What is the position if conception occurred before joining the insurance scheme?

- Are medicines included?

- Are convalescent homes or spa treatments covered when prescribed by a doctor?

- What are the restrictions on complementary medicine, e.g. acupuncture, chiropractic, massage, naturopathy and osteopathy? Are they covered? Must a referral be made by a doctor?

- Is life insurance or a disability pension included, possibly as an option?

- Are possible extra costs likely, and if so, what for?

- Are spectacles or contact lenses covered, and if so, how much can be claimed and how frequently?

- Is the provision and repair of artificial limbs and similar health aids covered?

International Health Policies

It's also possible to take out an international health insurance policy, which may be of particular interest to people living in Australia or New Zealand temporarily, or those whose work involves a lot of travel or who work part of the time overseas. Some policies offer members a range of premiums, from budget to comprehensive cover. All policies offer at least two fee scales, one covering the whole world, including North America (and possible other high cost areas), the other excluding North America. Most policies include a full refund of ambulance, emergency dental treatment, home nursing (usually for a limited period), hospital, outpatient and repatriation charges. All policies include an annual overall claims limit, usually from $200,000 to $2,000,000 (the higher the better, particularly for North America).

Some comprehensive policies provide a fixed amount for general medical costs (including routine doctors' visits) and elective dental, maternity and optical expenses. Premiums range from around $1,750 to over $5,000 per year, depending on your age, level of cover and the areas covered (if North America is covered, premiums are much higher). If you don't require permanent international health insurance, you should consider a policy which provides limited or optional cover when you're overseas. All bills, particularly those received for treatment outside Australia, must include precise details of treatment received. Terms such as 'dental treatment' or 'consultation' are usually insufficient.

If you're living or working in Australia or New Zealand and aren't covered by the national healthcare scheme, it's risky or even foolhardy not to have private health insurance for you and your family. Whether you're covered by a local or foreign health insurance policy makes little difference (except perhaps in cost), provided you have the required level of cover, including international cover if necessary. If you aren't adequately insured, you could be faced with some extremely high medical bills. When deciding on the type of policy, ensure that the insurance scheme covers *all* your family's health requirements. If your stay in Australia or New Zealand is short, you may be covered by a reciprocal agreement or by a private health insurance scheme. **Make sure you're fully covered *before* you receive a large bill.**

When changing employers or leaving Australia or New Zealand, you should ensure that you have continuous medical insurance. For example, if you and your family are covered by a company health fund, your insurance probably ceases after your last official day of employment. If you're planning to change your health insurance company, ensure that no important benefits are lost. When changing health insurance companies, you should inform your old insurance company if you have any outstanding bills for which they're liable.

Australia

The Australian Medicare system provides free or subsidised medical treatment for all permanent residents. Anyone living or working in Australia (even temporarily) who isn't eligible for Medicare treatment and who doesn't like living dangerously should have private health insurance. Private health insurance in Australia is usually complementary insurance, so called because it complements (rather than replaces) Medicare. It's commonly used to pay the difference ('gap') between the Medicare schedule fee and what Medicare actually pays. The main reason most people have private health insurance in Australia is to circumvent Medicare waiting lists for specialist appointments and non-emergency hospital treatment (e.g. elective surgery). Patients are also usually free to choose their own doctor and hospital. **Private insurance ensures that you receive the medical treatment you need, when you need it.** However, despite what insurance companies may say, the quality of private treatment isn't better than that provided by Medicare, and you shouldn't assume that because a doctor (or any other medical practitioner) is in private practice, he's more competent than his Medicare counterpart. In fact, you're likely to see the same specialist or be treated by the same surgeon under Medicare as privately (but a lot earlier).

Most private health insurance in Australia is provided by health funds, which are regulated by the Commonwealth government and follow the principle of 'community rating' to determine premiums, i.e. premiums don't vary according to age, sex or your state of health. This ensures that high-risk members such as the elderly and the chronically sick aren't required to pay astronomical premiums as in some other countries. However, most health funds are eroding this principle and in recent years have introduced a variety of conditions to exclude expensive treatment (called exclusion policies) and surgery such as joint replacements; there may also be financial limits. Many analysts believe this could be the thin end of the wedge and that insurance companies will abandon 'community rating' by stealth.

Changes to private health insurance have been proposed by the government, although they're strongly contested by the Australian Medical Association, which fears that health funds will dictate clinical practices, i.e. the insurer rather than the doctor will decide the treatment.

Private health insurers are allowed to offer four categories of membership as follows:

- single person;

- couple;

- family, consisting of at least two adults and one or more others, which may include children and grandparents;

- single-parent, consisting of at least one adult (who's the contributor) and one or more dependent children.

When taking out family or single-parent membership, always carefully check what constitutes a dependent child, as your children may not be covered.

Each state has its own private health insurers, the largest of which include the Hospital Contribution Fund (HCF), Medibank Private, the Medical Benefit Funds (MBF) and National Mutual Health Insurance. By far the largest insurer is Medibank Private (💻 www.medibank.com.au), a non-profit health benefits organisation (established in 1976) operated by the state-run Health Insurance Commission, covering some three million people (one third of all those with private health insurance), with some 100 customer service centres throughout the country. **Medibank Private also provides cover for temporary residents of Australia who aren't eligible for Medicare benefits.** It's possible to obtain health insurance from some banks, although they may insure only high earners. Compare the benefits and costs provided by a number of health insurers. Most provide a choice of basic, intermediate and comprehensive cover, with intermediate and comprehensive levels usually providing private rooms in private hospitals and ancillary cover.

Types Of Insurance

Health insurers offer two basic types of insurance: hospital and ancillary. Hospital cover contributes to the cost of in-hospital treatment and accommodation as a private patient in a private or public hospital. Ancillary cover contributes to the cost of out-patient medical services which aren't covered by Medicare, such as acupuncture, chiropractic and other alternative therapies, dental treatment, physiotherapy, and spectacles or contact lenses. Ancillary insurance may also include ambulance cover, home nursing and other services, although there's usually no refund for X-rays or prescriptions. There are payment limits for ancillary cover, both per visit and annual limits. Some funds (e.g. HCF) have a 'fit and well' policy which pays for gym membership or sports equipment such as running shoes.

Premiums

The average cost of 100 per cent hospital cover for a family in 2005 was around $1,600 and the average cost of 100 per cent ancillary cover around $1,150. Premiums vary considerably depending on the state or territory. The average cost of private health insurance per year for a single person is: basic (private hospital expenses, including choice of doctor) $750, comprehensive (covers 100 per cent private hospital expenses) $875, and ancillary (non-hospital expenses such as chiropractic treatment, dental, optical and physiotherapy) $575. Premiums vary little between couples, families and single-parent families, who all pay around double the single premium. Premiums can usually be paid monthly, quarterly or annually, and a discount may be given for prompt or annual payment. Alternatively, you can pay on a weekly or fortnightly basis through deductions from your pay packet.

Medicare automatically pays 85 per cent of the Medicare Benefits Schedule (MBS) fee for a doctor's services (100 per cent for some GP treatment), accommodation in a private hospital or for a private bed in a public hospital, and the insurer pays the balance. Health insurers have contracts with hospitals and doctors in order to maintain some control over costs and therefore reduce their premiums. You may need to choose a hospital and doctor contracted to your health insurer; otherwise you must pay the difference between what the insurer pays and what your doctor or hospital charges. Some insurers have agreements with relatively few private hospitals, outside which you're limited to a private bed in a public hospital, and you may not be covered outside your home state. You should receive a written quotation for non-emergency hospital treatment, including all costs and out-of-pocket expenses.

Extra Costs & Excess Charges

The benefits (rebates) provided by health insurers aren't usually 100 per cent and you normally need to make a contribution (an excess or co-payment) towards fees, called 'out-of-pocket' costs. These can be very high and can run into hundreds or even thousands of dollars (and can increase at short notice). If you want your own doctor to treat you in a public hospital, you must pay a daily accommodation charge, and some insurers levy a fee per night (e.g. $80) for private hospital patients. In addition to out-of-pocket costs, there's also usually an annual excess charge, which can be up to $2,000 for a family and may be applied per person for a couple. When you leave hospital, you're generally asked to pay the difference (if any) between your health insurer's refund and the hospital's fees. **High out-of-pocket expenses are the main reason people have abandoned private health insurance in recent years.**

People have been deserting private health insurance in their thousands as premiums and surcharges ('gap' fees) have soared. Before Medicare was introduced in 1984, over 50 per cent of Australians had private cover; this has since fallen to below a third – the system ceases to be viable at 30 per cent! After increasing premiums by 10 to 20 per cent in one year, insurers were losing around 1,000 members a day in the late '90s. The government is desperate to encourage people to return to (or remain in) private health cover, as Medicare is facing a funding crisis and its survival in its present form relies heavily on a strong private health sector. **If things go on this way, there could be a collapse of health funds AND Medicare (maybe you'd better insure with a foreign company).**

Private health insurance premiums increased vastly between the early '90s and 2000, although since then premiums have stabilised somewhat. However, despite the high premiums, health insurers are making very little (or no) money owing to the spiralling costs of hospital accommodation and operations; some are even on the verge of bankruptcy. The number of people cancelling their policies simply adds to the vicious circle of increasing premiums and the pressure on Medicare.

Incentives

In 2000, the federal government introduced a 30 per cent rebate on private health insurance premiums. Under the scheme, anyone who pays hospital and/or ancillary premiums to a registered health fund can obtain a 30 per cent reduction on the cost of their health insurance. The rebate isn't means tested but the private health insurance policy must cover people eligible for Medicare. The rebate can be claimed in three ways: from your health fund as a premium reduction, thereby reducing your premium costs; from a Medicare office, which reimburses you the 30 per cent; or from the Tax Office on your annual income tax form.

New Zealand

Everyone who's resident in New Zealand or a visitor from a country with which New Zealand has a reciprocal agreement is covered by the national healthcare scheme, which provides either free or reduced cost medical treatment. However, while treatment under the state health scheme is considered adequate, many people also have private health insurance. The main purpose of this is to pay the cost of doctor's consultations, prescriptions and dentistry (which aren't covered by the state healthcare system), and also to pay for treatment in private hospitals, thus circumventing public hospital waiting lists. Private health insurance schemes also provide other benefits, such as cover for loss of earnings due to illness. Nearly 50 per cent of New Zealanders have some form of private health insurance, which can be purchased from a variety of insurance companies of which the largest is Southern Cross Healthcare, Private Bag 99-934, Newmarket, Auckland (☎ freephone 0800-800 181, 🖳 www.southerncross.co.nz).

The cost depends on what's covered and which company you insure with. For a family of four a hospital-only policy costs from $500 to $1,500 per year and a comprehensive policy from $600 to $4,500 per year. Private health insurance costs have rocketed in recent years as more people make claims to avoid waiting for treatment at public hospitals, and they're likely to continue increasing at a rate well above inflation, particularly for the elderly. The Consumers' Institute (🖳 www.consumer.org.nz) publishes helpful information on health insurance, including advice on whether you really need it!

HOLIDAY & TRAVEL INSURANCE

Holiday and travel insurance is recommended for all who don't wish to risk having their holiday or travel ruined by financial problems or to arrive home broke. As you know, anything can and often does go wrong with a holiday, sometimes before you even get on the plane (particularly if you *don't* have insurance). Travel insurance is available from many sources, including airlines, banks, insurance brokers, motoring organisations, tour operators and travel agents.

Level Of Cover

Before taking out travel insurance, carefully consider the level of cover required and compare policies. Most policies include cover for accidents (including evacuation home if necessary), delayed or lost baggage, departure delay at both the start *and* end of a holiday (a common occurrence), loss of deposit or holiday cancellation, legal expenses, medical expenses (up to $4 million), missed flight, money (e.g. $500 to $1,000), personal effects (e.g. $3,000), personal liability ($2 million or $4 million), and a tour operator going bust. You should also insure against missing your flight after an accident or transport breakdown, as almost half of travel insurance claims are for cancellation (you should also be covered for transport delays at the end of your holiday, e.g. the flight home). With some policies, the amount you can claim for belongings may be limited to around $400 per item, which is insufficient to cover your Rolex watch or Leica camera. Some home contents policies include cover for belongings worldwide. Your insurance company won't pay out if you're negligent, e.g. you leave your camera in a taxi or on a beach.

Medical Expenses

Medical expenses are an important aspect of travel insurance and you shouldn't rely on reciprocal health agreements, cover provided by charge and credit card companies, house contents policies, or private medical insurance, none of which usually provide the necessary cover. The minimum medical insurance recommended by experts is $500,000 for Europe and $2 million for North America and the rest of the world. Personal liability should be at least $2 million for Europe and $4 million for the rest of the world. **Many travel and holiday insurance policies don't provide the level of cover that most people need.** Always check any exclusion clauses in contracts by obtaining a copy of the full policy document, as all relevant information won't be contained in insurance leaflets.

Exclusions

Health or accident insurance included in travel insurance policies usually contains exclusions, e.g. dangerous sports such as crocodile wrestling, hang-gliding, kangaroo boxing, mountaineering, scuba-diving, skiing, white-water rafting, and even riding a motorbike in some countries. Check the small print and find out exactly what terms such as 'hazardous pursuits' include or exclude. Skiing and other winter sports should be specifically covered and *listed* in a travel insurance policy. Special winter sports policies are available, which are usually more expensive than normal holiday insurance.

Cost

The cost of travel insurance varies considerably according to your destination. Many companies have different rates for different areas, e.g. Australia, Europe, North America and worldwide (excluding North America).

Premiums for travel within Australia are around $28 to $40 per person for two weeks, European destinations are usually from $145 for two weeks, and North America (where medical treatment costs an arm and a leg) and a few other destinations cost from $200 for three weeks. The cheapest policies offer reduced cover, but may not be adequate for most people. Premiums may be higher for those aged over 65 or 70. Generally, the longer the period covered, the cheaper the daily cost, although the maximum period may be limited, e.g. six months. With some policies an excess (e.g. $50) must be paid for each claim.

Annual Policies

For people who travel overseas frequently, whether for business or pleasure, an annual travel policy is often an excellent idea, costing around $225 to $350 per year for worldwide cover for an unlimited number of trips. However, always carefully check exactly what is included and read the small print (some insist that travel is by air). Most annual policies don't cover you for travel within Australia and there's a limit on the length of a trip, e.g. one to three months. Some companies offer 'tailor-made' insurance for independent travellers (e.g. backpackers) for any period from a few days to a year.

Claims

Although travel insurance companies quickly and gladly take your money, they aren't so keen to pay claims, and you may need to persevere before they pay up. Fraudulent claims against travel insurance are common, so unless you can produce evidence to support your claim, insurers may think that you're trying to cheat them. Always be persistent and make a claim irrespective of any small print, as this may be unreasonable and therefore invalid in law. **Insurance companies usually require you to report any loss (or any incident for which you intend to make a claim) to the local police within 24 hours and to obtain a report. Failure to do this usually means that a claim won't be considered.**

Flight insurance and comprehensive travel insurance are available from insurance desks at most airports, including in-transit baggage, personal accident, travel accident and worldwide medical expenses. When you pay for your travel costs with some credit cards, your family (possibly including children under the age of 25) are provided with free travel accident insurance up to a specified amount, e.g. $300,000. **Don't rely on this insurance, as it usually covers only death and serious injury.**

9.

LETTING

Some people planning to buy a holiday or future retirement home Down Under are interested in owning a property that will provide them with an income to cover the running costs and help with mortgage payments (or to supplement a pension). The most common method of earning money from a property is to let all or part of it. If you're planning to let a property, it's important not to overestimate the income, particularly if you're relying on letting income to help pay the mortgage and running costs. If you have a mortgage on a property in Australia or New Zealand, you're highly unlikely to meet your mortgage payments and running costs from rental income alone. Most experts recommend that you don't purchase a second home if you need to rely heavily on rental income to pay for it.

SURVIVAL TIP
Bear in mind that if you use a
letting agent to let a property, your total costs
including agent's fees, cleaning, utilities, gardening,
pool cleaning, maintenance and repairs, could
swallow up to half of your rental income.

CONTRACTS

It's usual to have a written contract for all rentals. Most people who let a property for holiday accommodation draw up a simple agreement that includes the property description, the names of the clients, and the dates of arrival and departure. However, if you do regular letting, you may wish to check with a lawyer that your agreement is legal and contains all the necessary safeguards. For example, it should specify the types of damage for which the tenant is responsible. If you're letting through an agent, he will provide a standard contract. If you offer longer lets (e.g. from one to six months) outside the high season, you need to ensure that you or your agent uses an appropriate contract.

LOCATION

If letting income is a priority, you should buy a property with this in mind, in which case location is paramount. In particular, you should consider the following:

Climate

Properties in an area with a pleasant year-round climate have a greater rental potential, particularly outside the high season. Areas that *don't* have good weather all year round include parts of New Zealand's South Island and Tasmania, parts of New South Wales, South Australia and Victoria in Australia. This is also important should you wish to use the property yourself outside the high season; for example, you could let a property during the summer months, when rental rates are at their highest, and use it yourself in May or October and still enjoy fine weather.

Proximity To An Airport

A property should be situated within easy travelling distance of a major airport, as most holidaymakers won't consider travelling more than say one hour to their destination after arriving at the airport. Make sure you choose an airport with frequent flights from your home country. It isn't wise to rely on an airport served only by budget airlines, as they may alter or cancel routes at short notice.

Accessibility

It's an advantage if a property is served by public transport (e.g. buses or trains) or is situated in a town where a car is unnecessary. If a property is located in a town or development with a maze of streets, you should provide a detailed map. On the other hand, if it's in the country where signposts are all but non-existent, you will not only need to provide a detailed map with plenty of landmarks, but you may also need to erect signs (for which permission may be necessary). Holidaymakers who spend hours driving around trying to find a holiday home are unlikely to return or recommend it! Maps are also helpful for taxi drivers, who may be unfamiliar with the area.

Attractions

The property should be as close as possible to a major attraction (or more than one), e.g. a beach, theme park, area of scenic beauty or tourist town, although this will depend on the sort of clientele you wish to attract. If you want to let to families, a property should be within easy distance of leisure activities such as theme parks, water parks, sports activities (e.g. tennis, golf, water sports, fishing, etc.) and night-life. If you're planning to let a property in a rural area, it should be somewhere with good hiking possibilities, preferably near one of Australia or New Zealand's many natural parks. Proximity to one or more golf courses is also an advantage to many holidaymakers and is an added attraction outside the high season, where there may otherwise be little to attract visitors in the winter.

Swimming Pool

A swimming pool is desirable, particularly in warmer regions, as properties with pools are much easier to let than those without (unless a property is situated near a beach, lake or river). It's usually necessary to have a private pool with a single-family home, but a shared pool is sufficient for an apartment or townhouse. You can also charge a higher rent for a property with a pool and you may be able to extend the season even further by installing a heated or indoor pool. Some private letting agencies won't handle properties without a pool. Note that there are safety regulations regarding pools used by the public, which include pools at private homes that are let for holidays.

FURNISHINGS

If you let a property, don't fill it with expensive furnishings or valuable belongings. While theft is rare, items will be damaged or broken eventually. When furnishing a property that you plan to let, you should choose durable furniture and furnishings and hard-wearing, dark-coloured carpets that won't show the stains. Small, two-bedroom properties usually have a sofa-bed in the living room. Properties should be well-equipped with cooking utensils, crockery and cutlery, and you must also provide bed linen and towels. You may need a cot or high chair for young children. Depending on the price and quality of a property, your guests may also expect central heating, a washing machine, dishwasher, microwave, covered parking, a barbecue (compulsory!) and garden furniture. Some owners provide bicycles and sports equipment (e.g. badminton and table tennis). It isn't usual to have a telephone in rental homes, although you could install a credit card telephone or a phone that will receive incoming calls only.

KEYS

You will need several sets of spare keys, which will inevitably get lost at some time. If you employ a management company, their address should be on the key fob and not the address of the house. If you let a home yourself, you can use a 'keyfinder' service, whereby lost keys can be returned to the keyfinder company by anyone finding them. You should ensure that you get 'lost' keys returned, otherwise you may need to change the locks (in any case it's wise to change the external locks periodically if you let a home). You don't need to provide clients with keys to all the external doors, only the front door (the others can be left in your home). If you arrange your own lets, you can post keys to clients in your home country, or they can be collected from a caretaker in Australia or New Zealand. It's also possible to install a key-pad entry system, although this isn't as secure as a good lock.

USING AN AGENT

If you're letting a second home, the most important decision is whether to let it yourself or use a letting agent (or agents). If you don't have much spare time, you're better off using an agent, who will take care of everything and save you the time and expense of advertising and finding clients.

Take care when selecting a letting agent, as they sometimes go bust owing customers thousands of dollars. Make sure that your income is kept in an escrow account and paid regularly, or even better, choose an agent with a bonding scheme who pays you the rent before the arrival of guests (some do). It's absolutely essential to employ an efficient, reliable and honest company, preferably long-established. Ask a management company to substantiate rental income claims and occupancy rates by showing you examples of actual income received from other properties. Ask for the names of satisfied customers and check with them. It's also worthwhile inspecting properties managed by an agency to see whether they're well looked after.

Other things to ask a letting agent include the following:

- Who they let to;
- Where they advertise;
- What information they send to potential clients;
- Whether they have contracts with holiday and travel companies;

- Whether you're expected to contribute towards marketing costs;

- Whether you're free to let the property yourself and use it when you wish.

You should also check the type of contract you will have with the agency: whether, for example, you will receive a detailed analysis of income and expenditure and what notice you're required to give if you decide to terminate the agreement. Management contracts usually run for a year.

The larger companies market homes via newspapers, magazines, overseas agents, colour brochures and the internet, and have representatives in many countries. A management company's services should include the following:

- Arranging routine and emergency repairs;

- Reading meters (if electricity is charged extra);

- Routine maintenance of house and garden, including lawn cutting and pool cleaning;

- Arranging cleaning and linen changes between lets;

- Advising guests on the use of equipment;

- Providing guest information and advice (possibly 24-hours in the case of emergencies).

Agents may also provide someone to meet and greet clients, hand over the keys and check that everything is in order. The actual services provided usually depend on whether a property is basic one or two-bedroom apartment or a luxury four-bedroom detached house. A letting agent's representative should also make periodic checks when a property is empty to ensure that it's secure and that everything is in order. You may wish (or need) to make periodic checks on an agency to ensure that all bookings are being declared and that your property is being well managed and maintained.

DOING YOUR OWN LETTING

Some owners prefer to let a property to family, friends and colleagues, which allows them more control (and with luck the property will be better looked after). In fact, the best way to get a high volume of lets is usually to do it yourself, although many owners use a letting agency in addition to doing their own marketing.

Rental Rates & Deposits

To get an idea of the rent you should charge, simply ring a few letting agencies and ask them what it would cost to rent a property such as yours at the time of year you plan to let. They're likely to quote the highest possible rent you can charge. You should also check the advertisements in newspapers and magazines. Set a realistic rent, as there's a lot of competition. Add a returnable deposit (e.g. $200) as security against loss (e.g. of keys) or breakages, although this cannot be more than 25 per cent of the rental fee or be requested more than six months in advance. A deposit should be refundable only up to six weeks before a booking. It's normal to have a minimum two-week rental period in December and January. You will need to have a simple agreement form that includes the dates of arrival and departure and approximate times.

Advertising

You can advertise among friends and colleagues, in company and club magazines (which may even be free), and on notice boards in companies, stores and public places. The more marketing you do, the more income you're likely to earn. It also pays to work with other local people in the same business and send surplus guests to competitors (they will usually reciprocate). It isn't necessary to just advertise locally or stick to your home country and you can extend your marketing to other countries or internationally via the internet. Ideally you should have an email address and possibly also an answer-phone and fax machine.

Publications

There's a wide range of local and foreign newspapers and magazines in which you can advertise, e.g. newspapers such as the *Telegraph*, *Observer* and *Sunday Times* in the UK. You will need to experiment to find the best publications and days of the week or months to advertise.

Internet

Advertising on the internet is an increasingly popular option for property owners. There are two options: place an advertisement on an agent's site which will cost you between around $200 and $250 per year, or set up your own site. Although more expensive, a personalised website can include photographs, brochures, booking forms and maps of the area, in addition to comprehensive information about your property. You can also provide information about flights, car rental, local attractions, sports facilities and links to other useful websites. A good website should be easy to navigate (don't include complicated page links or indexes) and must include contact details, preferably via e-mail. It's also advisable to subscribe to a company that will submit your website to all the popular search engines, such as Altavista, Google and Yahoo. You can also exchange links with other websites.

Brochures & Leaflets

It's wise to produce a coloured brochure or leaflet containing the following:

- External/internal pictures (or a single colour brochure with coloured photographs glued to it, although this doesn't look so professional);

- Important details;

- The exact location;

- Local attractions; details of how to get there (with a small map);

- Your name, address and telephone number, and that of your local caretaker or letting agent.

Handling Inquiries

If you plan to let a home yourself, you will need to decide how to handle enquiries about flights and car rentals. It's easier to let clients make their own bookings, but you should be able to offer advice and put them in touch with airlines, travel agents and car rental companies. You will also have to decide whether you want to let to smokers or accept pets or young children (some people don't let to families with children under five years of age because of the risk of bed-wetting, breakages and the other chaos sometimes wrought by young children). It's usual to provide linen (some agents provide a linen hire service) and to include electricity in the rental fee.

You should enclose a stamped addressed envelope when sending out leaflets. It's necessary to make a home look as attractive as possible in a brochure without distorting the facts or misrepresentation. Advertise honestly and don't over-sell your property. Finally, keep detailed records and ensure that you never double book!

Information Packs

You should also provide information packs for clients who have booked: one to be sent to them before they leave home and another for them to use after they arrive.

Pre-arrival

After accepting a booking, you should provide guests with a pre-arrival information pack containing the following:

- Information about local attractions and the local area (available free from tourist offices);

- A map of the local area and instructions how to find the property;

- Emergency contact numbers in your home country (e.g. the UK) and Australia or New Zealand if guests have any problems or plan to arrive late;

- The keys (or instructions where to collect them on arrival).

Post-arrival

It's an advantage if you can arrange for someone to be on hand to welcome your guests when they arrive, explain how things work, and deal with any special requests or minor problems. You should also provide an information pack in your home for guests explaining the following:

- How things work, e.g. kitchen appliances, TV/video, heating and air-conditioning;

- Security measures;

- What not to do and possible dangers (for example, if you allow young children and pets, you should make a point of emphasising dangers such as falling into the pool);

- Local emergency numbers and health services such as a doctor, dentist, clinic and a hospital with an accident & emergency department;

- Emergency assistance such as a general repairman, plumber, electrician and pool maintenance (you may prefer to leave the telephone number of a local caretaker who can handle any problems);

- Recommended shops, restaurants and attractions.

Many people provide a visitor's book, in which guests can write their comments and recommendations regarding local restaurants and attractions, etc. Some owners also send out questionnaires.

If you really want to impress your guests, you may wish to arrange for fresh flowers, fruit, a bottle of wine and a grocery pack to greet them on their arrival. It's little personal touches like this that ensure repeat business and recommendations. If you go 'the extra mile', it will pay off and you may even find after the first year or two that you rarely need to advertise. Many people return to the same property each year and you should do an annual mail-shot to previous clients and send them some brochures. Word-of-mouth advertising is the cheapest and always the best.

Maintenance

If you do your own letting, you will need to arrange for cleaning and maintenance, including pool cleaning and a gardener if applicable. You should also allow for the consumption of electricity, gas, water, etc. by your tenants and the cost of additional equipment (e.g. cots and highchairs for children).

When letting a property, you should take care not to underestimate maintenance and running costs, which can be considerable.

Caretaker

If you have a second home Down Under, you will find it beneficial or even essential to employ a local caretaker, irrespective of whether you let it. You may also need to employ a gardener. You can have your caretaker prepare the house for your family and guests as well as looking after it when it isn't in use. If you have a holiday or future retirement home in Australia or New Zealand, it's wise to have your caretaker check it periodically (e.g. fortnightly) and give him authority to authorise minor repairs. If you let a property yourself, your caretaker can arrange for (or do) cleaning, linen changes, maintenance and repairs, gardening and the payment of bills. Ideally you should have someone on call seven days a week who can repair broken appliances or arrange any necessary maintenance or repairs.

Closing A Property For The Winter

Before closing a property for the winter, you should turn off the water at the mains and drain all pipes, remove the fuses (except the one for a dehumidifier if you leave it on while you're away), empty the food cupboards and the refrigerator/freezer, disconnect gas cylinders, bring in any outdoor furniture and empty dustbins. All exterior doors, large windows and shutters should of course be locked, but you should leave interior doors and a few small windows (with grilles or secure shutters), as well as wardrobes, open to provide ventilation. Many people keep their central heating on a low setting during the winter when they're absent to prevent pipes from freezing, which can occur in parts of southern Australia and New Zealand. In humid areas you may wish to leave the air-conditioning on in order to prevent mildew and have someone check your property periodically.

If your property is in an area liable to flooding, move valuable and easily damaged items to an upper floor, raise the fridge, washing machine and other apparatus off the floor (e.g. on pallets) and, if necessary, fit flood boards across external doors and lay sand bags against them.

Secure anything of value against theft or leave it with a neighbour. Check whether any essential work needs to be done before you leave and if necessary arrange for it to be done in your absence. Most importantly, leave a set of keys with a neighbour and have a caretaker check your home periodically (e.g. once a month). It's worth making yourself a checklist of things to be done each time you leave a property unattended.

Security

Note that most people aren't security conscious when on holiday and you should provide detailed instructions for guests regarding security measures and emphasise the need to secure the property when they're out. It's also important for them to be security-conscious when in the property, particularly when having a party or in the garden, as it isn't unusual for valuables to be stolen while guests are outside.

SURVIVAL TIP
Security is of paramount importance when buying a home Down Under, particularly if it will be left empty for long periods. Obtain advice from local security companies and neighbours and take note of what they tell you. However, bear in mind that no matter how good your security, a property is rarely impregnable, so you should never leave valuables in an unattended home unless they're kept in a safe.

When leaving a property unattended, it's important to employ all the security measures available, including the following:

- Storing valuables in a safe (if applicable) – hiding them isn't a good idea, as thieves know ALL the hiding places;

- Closing and locking all doors and windows;

- Locking grilles on patio and other doors;

- Closing shutters and securing any bolts or locks;

- Setting the alarm (if applicable) and notifying the alarm company when you're absent for an extended period;

- Making it appear as if a property is occupied through the use of timers for lights and a television or radio.

Bear in mind that prevention is always better than cure, as stolen property is rarely recovered. If you have a robbery, you should report it to your local police station, where you must make a statement. You will receive a copy, which is required by your insurance company if you make a claim.

INCREASING RENTAL INCOME

It's possible to increase rental income outside the high season by offering special interest or package holidays, which can be done in conjunction with other local businesses in order to broaden the appeal and cater for larger parties. These may include the following:

- Activity holidays, such as golf, tennis, cycling, hiking, fishing or skiing;

- Cooking, gastronomy and wine tours/tasting;

- Arts and crafts such as painting, sculpture, photography and writing courses.

You don't need to be an expert or conduct courses yourself, but can employ someone to do it for you.

10.

MISCELLANEOUS MATTERS

This chapter contains miscellaneous, but nevertheless important, information for homeowners in Australia and New Zealand, including facts about crime, heating and air-conditioning, home security, the internet, postal services, shopping for household goods, radio and television, telephone services, utilities and selling your home.

CRIME

Australia

Australia is a safe country by international standards, and you can walk almost anywhere at any time of the day or night in Australian cities without the risk of being mugged or murdered. However, it's important to take the usual safety precautions that you would in any country and to bear in mind that Australia has become a more violent society in the last decade. Crime rates vary from state to state: the ACT and the Northern Territory are the most dangerous places to live, while Tasmania and Victoria are the safest. House-breaking and burglary are rampant in Australian cities, particularly Sydney, and nearly 500,000 cases are reported a year. Car theft is also widespread in cities, although the incidence is decreasing. Beware of pickpockets and opportunist thieves such as bag snatchers in major cities and crowded places, and keep a close eye on your belongings when travelling on public transport and when staying in hotels or hostels.

Although basically honest, many Australians delight in 'beating the system', including cheating their employers (bludging), fiddling their income tax (e.g. by not declaring income) and not paying motoring fines – unpaid fines total $millions annually. Many people take their lead from officials, the police and politicians, among whom corruption is widespread. Organised crime is rife in Australia's major cities, where much crime is linked to Asian gangs, including Chinese, Thais and Vietnamese. It's estimated that crime costs Australia some $32 billion annually, including white-collar crime (e.g. forgery and fraud), which is the country's largest crime cost (it's also the biggest crime growth area and the hardest to prosecute). Around $13 billion (of the $32 billion mentioned above) per year is spent on public and private crime prevention.

Violent crime is still relatively rare in Australia, although it has increased considerably in the last decade or so (along with most other western countries). There's been a huge increase in armed robbery in the last decade, and assaults, murders and rapes have all increased dramatically, although muggings are still relatively rare. Violent crimes by the young have soared (many children and youths are totally out of control) and gun (see below) and knife culture is widespread. Armed robbery is becoming fairly common in Australia, where banks, petrol stations and retail outlets are the most common targets (particularly all-night shops and petrol supermarkets). As a result, some outlets have stopped accepting cash and many are considering closing at night. Women should avoid travelling alone at night, and hitchhiking can be dangerous for both sexes (there have been a number of murders of backpackers in recent years).

Central government, local authorities, police forces and security companies all publish information and provide advice on crime prevention. Police forces have local crime prevention officers whose job is to provide free advice to businesses, homeowners and individuals.

New Zealand

New Zealand has a reputation as a low-crime country and is safe by international standards, although serious crime (such as murder) and petty crime (such as burglary) have risen considerably in the last few decades. The only real 'no-go' areas are certain parts of Auckland, where residents of the more affluent parts of the city dare not venture. (The North Shore area of Auckland has experimented with New York-style 'zero tolerance' policing.) In reality, although strangers wandering into high-crime areas are at risk of being mugged, knifed or even murdered, the risk is much lower than, for example, in most American cities. A worrying trend, however, is that an increasing number of violent attacks and rapes are racially inspired, particularly against Asians and Pacific Islanders. However, it should be noted that, overall, race relations in New Zealand are good and the envy of many other countries.

There's a huge difference between crime levels in the major cities and in rural areas: in the latter it's still common to find communities where people never lock their homes or their cars when leaving them unoccupied, a practice which used to be common throughout New Zealand. In urban areas, however, decent door and window locks and an alarm system are considered essential. Car theft is also a problem in cities and it's wise to have an immobiliser and alarm system fitted to your car (although little notice may be taken of it when it's triggered).

A Crime and Safety Survey carried out among the New Zealand population revealed that 1 in 14 houses had been burgled in the previous year and one in five people had been the victim of some kind of assault. In the light of these worrying findings and the general rise in crime, the government has introduced a series of measures designed to reduce the rate of crime (such as the DNA testing of criminals, including burglars, and greater police funding) and provide increased support for the victims of crime. For example, a Sentencing and Parole Bill passed in 2001 sets out sentencing guidelines for judges and juries. Future initiatives include a task force on youth offending, which is a particular problem in some cities. Crime statistics show that these measures have been at least partially successful: burglary and car theft rates are down by nearly 15 per cent and the resolution of crime is the highest for a decade. Violent crime, however, is still on the increase, and convictions for domestic violence have risen significantly, although it's believed that this may be due to greater public awareness of the problem and the fact that more domestic violence is reported to the police.

Despite the statistics, you can safely walk almost anywhere at any time of the day or night in most parts of the country. However, it's important to take the same precautions as you would in any country. Beware of pickpockets and bag-snatchers in cities and keep a close eye on your belongings in shops and when using public transport, particularly trains and the Interislander ferry. If your luggage is stolen on public transport, you should make a claim to the relevant authority, as they may make an ex-gratia payment for lost, stolen or damaged baggage.

Most New Zealanders are law-abiding and their 'criminal' activities amount to little more than speeding, 'pulling a sickie' (i.e. taking a day off work to go to the beach), or exaggerating a road or workplace accident in order to secure a more generous payout from the ACC. (Insurance companies recently reported that genuine insurance claims were believed to be inflated by at least $50 million annually by otherwise law-abiding citizens.) White collar fraud and corruption have become a more serious problem in recent years and a number of respected companies have been rocked by financial scandals, which were previously unknown in New Zealand.

HEATING & AIR-CONDITIONING

Australia

Central heating isn't common in eastern, northern and western Australia, as the climate doesn't usually warrant it. In these regions, a portable electric fan heater, an electric fire or radiator/column heater, or a gas fire is sufficient to heat most rooms during the wet or winter seasons. Both gas and electric heaters and hot water systems have an energy efficiency rating. Central heating, double glazing and good insulation are more common in new homes in southern states, where many people consider them essential. Central heating systems may be powered by electricity, gas, oil or solid fuel, and luxury homes may have a combined, thermostatically controlled heating and cooling (air-conditioning) system. Many homes have storage heaters, which store heat from electricity supplied at a cheaper, off-peak rate overnight and release it to heat homes during the day. In country and remote areas, where open fires and stoves are fairly common, solid fuels such as coal and wood are often used (and may also provide hot water). Whatever form of heating you use, you should ensure that your home has good insulation, without which up to 60 per cent of heat is lost through the walls and roof.

Solar Heating

Solar heating is popular in Australia and is most commonly used to provide hot water, although dual solar hot water and heating systems (with a hot-air solar radiator) are available. These are usually combined with an electric booster or gas heating system, as solar energy cannot be relied upon year-round for hot water and heating requirements, e.g. on overcast days. The use of solar energy is most common in remote areas. Some 5 per cent of Australian homes use solar energy for heating water, including around 25 per cent of homes in WA and 60 per cent in the Northern Territory (average savings are around $225 a year compared with electricity). Although currently relatively expensive to install, breakthroughs in solar cell technology are set to increase its efficiency and reduce the cost dramatically in the next decade. Solar energy can meet up to 90 per cent of normal household heating needs. In mid-2004, the Australian Government announced an investment of $75 million to support the establishment of 'solar cities' trials in urban areas and the trial results will be monitored for at least five years before deciding whether to implement or expand the scheme nationwide.

Humidity

Central heating dries the air and may cause your family to develop coughs and other ailments. Those who find dry air unpleasant can increase the humidity by adding moisture to the air with a humidifier, steam generator, vaporiser or even a water container made of porous ceramic. These range from simple water containers hung from radiators to electric or battery-operated devices. Humidifiers that don't generate steam should be disinfected occasionally with a special liquid available from pharmacies (to prevent nasty diseases). In regions where high humidity is a problem, you can buy a dehumidifier to re-circulate room air and reduce humidity.

Air-conditioning

In most regions of Australia, air-conditioning is a blessed relief in summer, while in northern and western Australia it's considered essential at almost any time of the year (also in cars). It's still considered something of a luxury in southern states such as Victoria and New South Wales, where it's usually confined to luxury properties, although you won't consider it a luxury when the temperature soars above 40°C (104°F)! Most business premises are air-conditioned throughout Australia. Modern homes in tropical areas often have a ducted air-conditioning system powered by electricity. You can choose between a huge variety of air-conditioners, fixed or moveable, indoor and outdoor installations, with high or low power. An air-conditioning system with a heat pump provides cooling in summer and heating in winter.

Most window-mounted air-conditioning units have a choice of fan speeds and the fan can usually be switched on separately from the cooling system. The cooling system can be adjusted for temperature and units often have a vent that can be opened to allow air into the room when they aren't in use. When using air-conditioning, all windows and outside doors should obviously be closed. Note, however, that if you suffer from asthma or respiratory problems, air-conditioning can exacerbate your condition. Many homes have electric pedestal and/or ceiling fans to provide cooling during the summer.

You can have a study made of your home's heating and cooling requirements and the cost, taking into account the climate and the current insulation and equipment installed. An engineer will produce a report detailing the most-effective means of cooling, heating and insulating your home, and provide a number of cost estimates. The Australian Consumers Association publish an excellent book entitled *Warm House Cool House* by Nick Hollo.

New Zealand

Although the weather in New Zealand is generally mild in summer, you shouldn't assume that you won't need heating at other times of the year; there are few areas of New Zealand where you won't need effective heating and good insulation (older properties aren't usually well insulated). Only a few areas, such as Northland (the northernmost tip of the North Island), are warm enough to manage without good heating all year round, although you may want an air-conditioning system instead. Most newer homes (and many older homes) have central heating systems, consisting of heated water systems or ducted air. These are powered by electricity or mains/bottled gas and often double as air-conditioning in summer. Many homes also have a fireplace, as much for show as for effect. Older properties often have free-standing electric or gas heaters rather than a central heating system, and some may have a wood burner, which is essentially a stove that heats the room but also provides hot water. Note, however, that although it's attractive, a wood burner requires a good deal of care and attention, and wood is relatively expensive.

HOME SECURITY

Security is obviously an important consideration for anyone buying a home in Australia or New Zealand (or anywhere else), particularly if it's a holiday home that will be unoccupied for long periods. While it's important not to underestimate security risks, even in rural areas, where crime rates are generally low (see **Crime** on page 292), you should avoid turning your home into a fortress, which will deter visitors as well as would-be thieves! Bear in mind that your home is generally more at risk from fire and storm damage than from burglary.

Generally, the minimum level of security required by insurance companies is fairly basic, e.g. security locks on external doors and shutters on windows (small windows generally have bars rather than shutters). Some owners fit additional locks on external doors, alarm systems (see below), grilles on doors and windows, window locks, security shutters and a safe for valuables, although such systems are rarely required by insurance companies. The advantage of grilles is that they allow you to leave windows open without inviting criminals in (unless they're *very* slim). You can also install UPVC (toughened clear plastic) security windows and doors, which can survive an attack with a sledge-hammer without damage, and external steel security blinds (that can be electrically operated), although these are expensive. A policy may specify that all forms of protection on doors must be employed when a property is unoccupied, and that all other protection (e.g. shutters) must also be used after 10pm and when a property is left empty for two or more days.

When moving into a new home, it's often wise to replace the locks (or lock barrels) as soon as possible, as you have no idea how many keys are in circulation for the existing locks. This is true even for new homes, as builders may give keys to sub-contractors. In any case, it's wise to change the external locks or lock barrels periodically if you let a home. If they aren't already fitted, it's best to fit high security (double cylinder or dead bolt) locks. Modern properties are usually fitted with special high security locks that are individually numbered. Extra keys for these locks cannot be cut at a local hardware store and you need to obtain details from the previous owner or your landlord. Many modern developments and communities have security gates and caretakers.

You may wish to have a security alarm fitted, which is usually the best way to deter thieves and may also reduce your household insurance (see page 260). It should include external doors and windows, internal infra-red security beams, and may also include an entry keypad (whose code can be frequently changed and is useful for clients if you let) and 24-hour monitoring. With a monitored system, when a sensor (e.g. smoke or forced entry) is activated or a panic button is pushed, a signal is sent to a 24-hour monitoring station. The duty monitor will telephone to check whether it's a genuine alarm (a code must be given); if he cannot contact you, someone will be sent to investigate. Note, however, that an insurer may require you to have a particular alarm fitted; check before buying one that may be unacceptable. More sophisticated security systems using internet technology are now available, including cameras and sound recorders that can be monitored via a computer or mobile phone.

You can deter thieves by ensuring that your house is well lit at night and not conspicuously unoccupied. External security 'motion detector' lights (that switch on automatically when someone approaches); random timed switches for internal lights, radios and televisions; dummy security cameras; and tapes that play barking dogs (etc.) triggered by a light or heat detector, may all help deter burglars. A dog can be useful to deter intruders, although it should be kept inside where it cannot be given poisoned food. Irrespective of whether you actually have a dog, a warning sign with a picture of a fierce dog may act as a deterrent. If not already present, you should have the front door of an apartment fitted with a spy-hole and chain so that you can check the identity of a visitor before opening the door. Remember, prevention is better than cure, as stolen property is rarely recovered.

Holiday homes are particularly vulnerable to thieves and in some areas they're regularly ransacked. No matter how secure your door and window locks, a thief can usually obtain entry if he's determined enough, often by simply smashing a window or even breaking in through the roof or by knocking a hole in a wall! In isolated areas thieves can strip a house bare at their leisure and an unmonitored alarm won't be a deterrent if there's no-one around to hear it. If you have a holiday home, it isn't wise to leave anything of great value (monetary or sentimental) there. If you vacate your home for an extended period, it may be obligatory to notify a caretaker, landlord or insurance company, and to leave a key with someone in case of emergencies. If you have a robbery, you should report it immediately to your local police station, where you must make a statement. You will receive a copy, which is required by your insurance company if you make a claim.

When closing up a property for an extended period, e.g. over the winter, you should ensure that everything is switched off and that it's secure (see **Closing A Property For The Winter** on page 286). Another important aspect of home security is ensuring that you have early warning of a fire, which is easily accomplished by installing smoke detectors. Battery-operated smoke detectors can be purchased for around $15 and should be tested weekly to ensure that the batteries aren't exhausted. You can also fit an electric-powered gas detector that activates an alarm when a gas leak is detected.

THE INTERNET

Australia

Australia was ranked ninth out of the top 50 countries for per capita internet use in 2005, with over 500 users per 1,000 people. There are internet service providers in all the major cities and many regional towns, where the main internet service providers (ISPs) include Bigpond (Telstra) and OzEmail. Competition has driven down fees in recent years and you should shop around for the best deal. Telstra's Bigpond internet service (🖳 www. bigpond.com) offers a range of pre-paid plans, with six hours for $9.95, 20 hours for $19.95, 35 hours for $34.95 and 60 hours for $54.95. ADSL monthly rates range from $29.95 to $129.95 for various packages.

New Zealand

The internet is popular in New Zealand, where most companies and all government bodies are online, and internet time is free if you have free local calls and your service provider has a local access number. There are numerous internet service providers (ISPs), mainly based in the large cities, including Telecom's Jetstream and Jetstream Xtra, and TelstraClear's clear.net, while smaller ISPs include ihug (🖳 www.ihug.co.nz) and Paradise (🖳 www.paradise.net.nz). Most companies also offer a broadband service, although it isn't available in all areas. Prices are competitive and limited free access (e.g. two hours per month) is available from a few dollars per month or unlimited access from around $30 per month. The monthly magazine *NZ PC World* publishes a comparison of rates and packages, which can also be viewed online (🖳 www.pcworld.co.nz), and the Consumers' Institute provides an online comparison of ISP rates (🖳 www.consumer.org.nz).

Internet Telephony

If you have a broadband internet connection, you can make long-distance and international phone 'calls' for free (or almost-free) to anyone with a broadband connection. Voice over internet protocol (VOIP) is the latest technology which is reshaping the telecoms landscape and will eventually (some say within five years) make today's telephone technology (both land lines and mobile networks) obsolete. The leading company in this field is Skype (💻 www.skype.com), recently purchased by Ebay, which has over 50 million users worldwide. There are numerous other companies in the market – a search on 'internet phone' on Google will throw up many other internet phone providers. All you need is access to a local broadband provider and a headset (costing as little as $10) or a special phone, and you're in business. Calls to other computers anywhere in the world are free, while calls to landlines are charged at a few cents a minute.

POSTAL SERVICES

Australia

Australia Post (AP) handles over five billion articles of post per year (a large percentage of which is junk mail) and provides one of the best services in the world in terms of cost, reliability and speed. AP underwent deregulation in 1994, when parts of the post business were opened to private competitors. However, it has since gone from strength to strength and is a highly profitable and well-run business. (There are plans to completely deregulate AP, but no date has been fixed.) There's a post office in most main towns in Australia (a total of around 4,500), offering a wide range of services. In country and outback towns, post services are provided by an Australia Post agency (e.g. a café/restaurant, general store or petrol station) licensed to provide most of the services offered by a main post office.

The post office provides a wide range of services, which, in addition to the usual services provided in most countries, include a number of unique services. These include bill payment, faxpost, gifts (e.g. at Christmas from AP shops or by mail order), giroPost, money orders, passport applications, poste restante mail, stamps, telegrams, stationery and office products (a catalogue is published for the latter). AP also operates the country's largest bill payment service (council rates, electricity, gas, insurance, Medibank, Telstra and water rates) and some 25 per cent of consumer bills are paid at AP's retail outlets. It handles over 170 million financial transactions a year through its electronic retail network and provides one of the country's largest banking services (giroPost).

Post boxes in Australia are red with a white stripe and modern post boxes look like litter bins, although there are still some Victorian 'receiving pillars' around, while in cities and large towns there are express 'gold' post boxes. However, post boxes are scarce in rural areas and you may need to take your post to a post office or agency. In major towns and metropolitan areas there are daily mail deliveries on Mondays to Fridays, while in remote areas there may be just one a week (although a twice-weekly service has been introduced in some areas). Deliveries in remote areas can be affected by the weather, as post is usually delivered by air, and in the outback mail must usually be collected from a local post office or agency. There are no weekend deliveries anywhere in Australia.

The post office parcel delivery and courier services have been privatised in recent years, although AP maintains a monopoly on letters weighing up to 250g. Private operators must charge a minimum of $1.80, which is nearly four times the AP rate for a standard letter. There's a thriving courier business in Australia, particularly in the major cities, where 24-hour domestic and international courier services are provided by many companies, including Allied Express, DHL, FedEx, Mayne Nickless and TNT. AP also operates a domestic courier service, Australia Air Express, via Qantas. Many more companies (such as Salmat and Streetfile) just deliver locally, e.g. within a particular city. In major cities, there are companies such as Mail Boxes Etc. which provide a wide range of post services (e.g. post boxes), as well as business services, courier, fax and telephone.

The post office produces a wealth of free brochures regarding postal rates and special services, most of which are available from all post offices. A general *Post Charges* booklet contains details of most services and rates, and a comprehensive *Post Guide* ($50) is available for businesses. Information about Australia Post's services is also available on the internet (🖥 www.auspost.com.au).

New Zealand

The New Zealand Post Office (known as NZ Post) is a national institution and has a rich past, similar to the American 'Pony Express'; tales abound of how postmen in bygone days struggled through forests and mountains to ensure that the mail was delivered are legendary. Today the postal service remains a mainstay of New Zealand life, particularly for those living in remote regions. The spirit of private enterprise extends to rural postmen, who aren't NZ Post employees but self-employed individuals with a concession to deliver mail, and who offer various other delivery and collection services to supplement their income. In addition to delivering (and collecting) letters and parcels, rural postmen deliver a variety of goods, including bread, milk, newspapers and even animals. They also offer a haulage service and, in some cases, carry passengers in their trucks and post buses to and from villages and isolated farms. A lot of sorting is still done by hand and postmen need to rely on their geographical and personal knowledge of who lives in their area. Nevertheless, the system is efficient enough, and NZ Post manages to deliver even poorly addressed letters on time (most of the time).

There are over 1,000 post offices throughout the country, known as post shops and are operated by NZ Post in major towns and cities. In small towns, post shops are run by private individuals who also run another business (such as a grocery or dairy) and are paid either a salary or a commission by NZ Post. Some 80 per cent of New Zealand post shops are operated in this way. Post shops offer a friendly, personal service as well as providing a range of other goods and services, such as bill payment (BillPay) and national lottery (Lotto) tickets, and acting as a focal point for the local community. Some post shops provide cheque cashing and deposit services (there's usually a sign indicating the services available).

Information about NZ Post services is available from post shops in a variety of leaflets, and also via Customer Service (☎ freephone 0800-501 501) or on NZ Post's website (💻 www.nzpost.co.nz), which has numerous *Step by Step* guides to using the postal service.

SHOPPING

Australia

Australia isn't one of the world's great shopping countries, either for variety or for bargains. Although the choice and quality of goods provided has improved considerably in the last decade, it's still limited compared with Europe and North America, and many new products aren't available in Australia or cost a fortune. However, there's a reasonable choice of chain, department and international stores in the major cities, and exclusive boutiques and chic stores abound in arcades and shopping centres. In stark contrast to the cities, small country towns are likely to have only a general store and a few other shops. Prices are also higher in rural areas due to freight costs and most people who live in the country stock up on goods (and buy expensive items) when visiting a city or large town, or shop by mail-order or on the internet.

Furniture

Furniture is usually good value in Australia, where there's a wide choice of modern and contemporary designs in every price range, although (as with most things) you generally get what you pay for. Exclusive imported furniture is available (with matching exclusive prices), although imports also include reasonably priced quality leather suites and a wide range of cane furniture from Asia. Among the largest furniture chain stores in Australia are Freedom Furniture and Harvey Norman, plus the major department stores, all of which offer a wide range of top quality Australian-made and imported furniture. The Swedish giant Ikea has six outlets in Australia, with more planned. It costs around $10,000 to furnish an average three-bedroom home, although secondhand furniture is widely available. Furniture can also be rented for around $225 to $300 per month for an average home.

Note that when ordering furniture, you may have to wait weeks or months for delivery. Try to find a shop that has what you want in stock or one that can give you a guaranteed delivery date (after which you can cancel and receive a full refund if you wish). A number of manufacturers sell direct to the public, although you shouldn't assume that this will result in huge savings and should compare prices and quality before buying. There are also shops specialising in beds, leather, reproduction and antique furniture, and a number of companies manufacture and install fitted bedrooms and kitchens. Fitted kitchens are an extremely competitive business in Australia and you should be wary of 'cowboy' companies who are specialists in shoddy workmanship.

If you want reasonably priced, quality, modern furniture, there are a number of companies (e.g. Ikea, see above) selling furniture for home assembly, which helps keep down prices. Assembly instructions are generally easy to follow (although some people think that Rubik's cube is easier) and some companies print instructions in a number of languages. Retailers often assemble furniture for you, although this increases the price. All large furniture retailers publish catalogues, which are generally distributed free of charge. Some shops offer you $100 or $200 for your old suite when you buy a new one from them. This may not be much of a bargain, however, particularly if your suite is worth more than the amount offered, and you should shop around for the best price and quality.

Furniture and furnishings is a competitive business in Australia, and you can often reduce the price by some judicious haggling, particularly if you're spending a large amount of money. Some shops will match a competitor's price rather than lose a sale. Another way to save money is to wait for the sales. If you cannot wait and don't want to (or cannot afford to) pay cash, look for an interest-free credit deal. Check the advertisements in local newspapers and national home and design magazines such as *Australian Interiors, Better Homes and Gardens* and *Home Beautiful.* See also *The Bargain Shoppers* guides to Melbourne and Sydney.

Household Goods

Large household appliances such as cookers and refrigerators are usually provided in rented accommodation and may also be fitted in new homes. Many homeowners include fitted kitchen appliances such as a cooker, dishwasher, refrigerator and washing machine when selling their house or apartment, although you may need to pay for them separately. Dishwashers (the mechanical type, not the wife or husband) are still something of a luxury item in Australia and aren't usually found in rented accommodation. There's a wide range of household appliances available in Australia, from Australian and foreign manufacturers. Some makes of certain appliances, e.g. refrigerators, cost twice as much to run as others (choose those with a high energy efficiency rating), and refrigerators/freezers in Australia are normally 'tropicised' or fan-assisted to cope with the high average temperatures.

If you wish to bring large appliances with you, such as a dishwasher, refrigerator or washing machine, the standard Australian unit width isn't the same as in other countries. Check the size and the latest Australian safety regulations before shipping these items to Australia, as they may need expensive modifications. On the other hand, if you already own small household appliances, it's worth bringing them to Australia, as usually all that's required is a change of plug (but check first). If you're coming from a country with a 110/115V electricity supply (e.g. the USA), you need a lot of expensive transformers. Don't bring a TV to Australia (other than from New Zealand) as it won't work. A huge choice of home appliances is available in Australia, where smaller items such as electric irons, grills, toasters and vacuum cleaners aren't expensive and are of good quality. It pays to shop around, as prices, quality and reliability vary (the more expensive imported brands are usually the most reliable).

Before buying household appliances, whether large or small, it may pay to check the test reports in *Choice* magazine at your local library. If you need kitchen measuring equipment and cannot cope with decimal measures, you must bring your own cups (American and Australian recipe cups aren't the same size), jugs, measuring scales and thermometers (see also **Appendix D**). Australian pillows and duvets aren't the same size or shape as in many other countries.

New Zealand

New Zealand isn't noted for offering a very interesting or exciting shopping experience. Traditionally, many New Zealanders were almost self-sufficient and shopped only for the basic necessities that they couldn't grow or make themselves (they still have a strong preference for making or growing things themselves wherever possible, particularly in rural areas). Fortunately, the situation has improved considerably in recent years, with an influx of international chain stores and designer shops in towns and cities. Naturally, you won't find the same choice of shops or merchandise on offer in New Zealand that you will in the USA, the UK or even Australia, as the market is so much smaller. However, a shopping trip in New Zealand is now a much more rewarding experience than previously.

Furniture

The average New Zealand home is furnished much as it would be in Europe or North America. The staple items of furniture are the three-piece suite (usually called a lounge suite) and the dining table with four or six chairs. All kinds of furniture are available, from antique or reproduction to modern, and quality ranges from bargain-priced flat-pack or secondhand furniture to exclusive handmade and designer items. Most properties in New Zealand have large fitted wardrobes in the American style, which are often walk-in rooms fitted with shelves and rails, thus rendering bedroom furniture other than a bed and a dressing table unnecessary. Fitted kitchens are also standard in new properties and basic appliances (oven, hob and refrigerator, and possibly also a washing machine and dishwasher) are included in the price.

Household Goods

New Zealand used to be notorious for the high cost of domestic appliances, which were a result of swingeing import taxes designed to protect local industries. In the '80s, however, the government decided to allow imports on more favourable terms and as a result New Zealanders have been able to replace their ageing home appliances with modern equipment at more reasonable prices. A huge choice of home appliances is available in New

Zealand, and smaller appliances such as electric irons, grills, toasters and vacuum cleaners aren't expensive and usually good quality. All electrical goods sold in New Zealand must conform to local safety standards. It pays to shop around, as quality, reliability and prices vary considerably (the more expensive imported brands are usually the most reliable). Before buying household appliances, whether large or small, it may pay you to check the test reports in consumer magazines.

It isn't usually worthwhile shipping bulky domestic appliances to New Zealand, such as a dishwasher, refrigerator or washing machine, which, irrespective of the shipping expense, may not meet local safety regulations or fit into a New Zealand kitchen. However, if you own good quality small household appliances it's worth bringing them to New Zealand, as all that's usually required is a change of plug, provided you're coming from a country with a 220/240V electricity supply (see page 320). Don't bring a TV to New Zealand (other than from Australia), as it won't work.

Secondhand Bargains

There's a lively secondhand market in Australia and New Zealand for almost everything, from antiques to motor cars, computers to photographic equipment. You name it and somebody is selling it secondhand. With such a large secondhand market there are often bargains to be found, particularly if you're quick off the mark. Many towns have a local secondhand or junk store and charity shops (e.g. Salvation Army or Vincent de Paul), selling new and secondhand articles for charity, where most of your money goes to help those in need. There are a number of national and regional weekly newspapers devoted to bargain hunters, such as the *Trading Post* in Sydney.

If you're looking for a particular item, such as a boat, camera or motorcycle, you may be better off browsing the small ads. in specialist magazines rather than those in more general newspapers or magazines. Classified ads. in local newspapers are also a good source of bargains, particularly for furniture and household appliances. Shopping centre (mall) and newsagent bulletin boards and company notice boards may also prove fruitful. Expatriate club newsletters are a good source of household items, which are often sold cheaply by those returning home. Another place to pick up a bargain is at an auction, although it helps to have specialist knowledge about what you're buying (you will probably be competing with experts). Auctions are held in the major cities in Australia and New Zealand throughout the year for everything from antiques and paintings to motorcars and property.

There are antique shops and centres in most towns, and street markets and fairs are common in the major cities (where you can pick up interesting local artifacts – but you must get there early to beat the dealers to the best buys). Ask at your local tourist office or library for information about local markets. Car boot (trunk) sales are gaining popularity in Australia, and yard sales, where people sell their surplus belongings at bargain prices, are also popular. Sales may be advertised in local newspapers and signposted on local roads (they're usually held at weekends).

TELEPHONE SERVICES

Australia

Most Australian homes (some 97 per cent) have a telephone, and Australia also has one of the highest (per capita) numbers of mobile telephones in the world. Because of its huge size, communications in Australia have always been a priority and today it has one of the highest standards of communications in the world, employing the latest broadband cable, digital technology, fibre optics and satellite systems. Wireless and radio-based communication is used in rural and remote areas, where in future residents will receive their telecommunications services via satellite links and enjoy the same services that are available in metropolitan centres. There are also solar-powered public telephone boxes in outback areas requiring no mains electricity.

The Australian telecommunications market was deregulated on 1st July 1997 and around 30 companies now operate in the country, although the market is still dominated by Telstra (🖥 www.telstra.com.au, formerly Telecom Australia and two-thirds government-owned), which has some 10.3 million fixed line customers and over 7.6 million mobile customers. Its main rival Optus (🖥 www.optus.com.au, established in 1992 and owned by Cable & Wireless) has around a third as many customers. AAPT and Primus are other large telecommunications companies. Not surprisingly, the lack of competition (prior to deregulation) led to Australians paying some of the highest telephone charges in the world, with Telstra and Optus charging customers an average of five times the actual cost of providing international call services.

However, since deregulation many new companies have entered the market, including BT Pty Ltd., Satellite Cowboys and WorldxChange, and users can now choose from a number of companies when making long-distance and international calls. Long-distance telephone charges have been slashed by up to 70 per cent, the price of mobile telephone calls has fallen by 50 per cent and that of local calls by 12 per cent in recent years. In the first six months of deregulation, there were tens of thousands of defections from Telstra and Optus. However, despite the increased competition, deregulation has failed to deliver all the expected benefits to consumers, although it's generally agreed that the situation has vastly improved in recent years.

In 1998, Telstra lost its monopoly on local calls worth $4 billion per year, and most other telephone companies now offer local calls. However, Telstra still has around 75 per cent of the local call market. Local number portability (LNP), which allows users to switch between telephone companies without changing their number, has been introduced. However, if you sign up with a company you may have a prefix assigned to your telephone number in order that your calls are handled by your chosen company.

Before signing up with a telephone company, check the competition and compare rates. If you make a lot of long-distance and international calls, you can save a lot of money by using one of the new companies whose call rates are sometimes below those charged by Telstra and Optus (or make calls via the internet – see page 300). However, you should continually monitor the market, as new deals are constantly being introduced and what was the best offer last month (or week) is unlikely to remain so for long. Many companies offer a range of services, which may include high speed access to on-line and interactive services such as the internet, local and long-distance telephone services and pay TV. This may be beneficial, as many companies offer attractive package deals if you buy two or more services, such as telephone and pay TV.

The telecommunications industry in Australia is regulated by the Australian Communications Authority (ACA), PO Box 13112, Law Courts PO, Melbourne, VIC 8010 (☎ 03-9963 6800, 🖳 http://internet.aca.gov.au) and has its own ombudsman (☎ freecall 1800-062058, 🖳 www.tio.com.au).

There's only one national emergency number in Australia, the 000 service, which is for ambulance, cave and mountain rescue services, coastguard, fire and police. Emergency calls are free from all telephones, including payphones.

Installation

Before moving into a new home, check whether there's a telephone line and that the number of lines or telephone points is adequate (most homes already have telephone lines and points in a number of rooms). If a property has a cable system or other telephone network, you don't require a Telstra telephone line. However, if you move into a house or apartment where you aren't the first resident, a telephone line will almost certainly already be installed, although there's usually no telephone. If you're moving into a house or apartment without a telephone connection, e.g. a new house, you must usually apply to Telstra for a line to be installed or connected.

To have a telephone line installed or re-connected, call at any Telstra shop or dial the Telstra Customer Service Centre (☎ local call rate 13-2200) between 8am and 5pm, Mondays to Fridays, and 9am to 5pm on Saturdays. Telstra will arrange a suitable date and time with you to connect your telephone service. If you live in a metropolitan area, your telephone should be connected within seven days at the latest. Connection often takes longer if you live in a rural or remote area, e.g. from two weeks to two months. If you simply need an existing Telstra service reconnected, this can usually be done on the day and time requested, or at least within three working days. If you're moving house within the same exchange area and call-charging zone, you may retain your old number; otherwise your old number is typically re-allocated to the incoming customer at your old address. You may request an unlisted number ('silent line'), for which an unlisted number fee applies.

Line installation costs $209, although this depends on the amount of work involved, and you're required to pay an advance of around $300 from which the fee is deducted. If a line already exists, connection costs $59, which is deducted from an advance payment of around $150. Credit assessments are made for all customers and your billing period may depend on your credit assessment. Payment of a security bond may be required or you may be given only restricted access, e.g. no international calls (but see **Internet Telephony** on page 300). Interest is paid on a bond, which is generally repaid after 12 months when you've established a satisfactory payment record. Generally, a $250 bond is necessary if you wish to make interstate calls and a $500 bond if you want to make international calls.

If your telephone or line has a fault, you must report it to Telstra on ☎ 13-2203. If your health, life, safety or shelter may be at risk without a telephone, you can register for a priority repair service (24 hours, seven days a week) and take out a maintenance contract with Telstra to maintain equipment and cabling. If you need help in using a Telstra product or service ☎ 13-2200.

International Calls

International fax, telephone and telex links are provided by the Overseas Telecommunications Commission (OTC) using undersea cables and satellites (Australia has telephone connections with around 200 countries via

Intelsat). All private telephones in Australia are on International Direct Dialling (IDD), allowing calls to be dialled direct to over 250 countries. To make an international call, dial ☎ 0011, the country code, the area code without the first zero, and the subscriber's number. Dial ☎ 0101 for the international operator (☎ 0107 from payphones) to make credit card calls, non-IDD calls, person-to-person and reverse charge calls (which aren't accepted by all countries). Dial ☎ 1225 for international directory enquiries. The international code for most countries is listed at the back of the white pages under 'Telstra 0011 International and Telstra Faxstream 0015 International', and includes the time difference (one sure way to upset most people is to wake them at 3am). You can also obtain dialling codes, world time information and a time converter for over 220 countries via the internet.

As with all types of telephone calls, customers in most regions and major cities can choose the carrier they use. Since deregulation, there's been a huge reduction in the cost of international calls (see also **Internet Telephony** on page 300). However, if you make a lot of international calls it may be beneficial to sign up with a number of companies and 'cherry pick', using the one that offers the lowest rate to the country you're calling. To use a particular carrier, you must open an account with them and may either pre-select that company or dial an access code before an STD or overseas number.

Telstra currently offers a range of international call options, depending on which HomeLine plan you subscribe to (see **Local Calls** above). You can call a static line in New Zealand for between 21¢ and 39¢ per minute, and a mobile telephone there from 61¢ per minute. Ten-minute calls cost from $1 and half hour blocks cost from $5.25 (under the 0018 HalfHours scheme). Calls to a UK fixed line aren't much more expensive than those to New Zealand, ranging from 21¢ to 47¢ per minute, and the same price, 61¢, to a mobile.

Mobile Telephones

Mobile telephones were introduced in Australia in 1987 and it's estimated that by 2007 some 85 per cent of the population will own one. Mobile telephone services are operated by Telstra (46 per cent of the market), Optus (30 per cent), Vodaphone (almost 20 per cent), and other smaller companies. The analogue network was phased out in 2000 and Australia now has an all-digital network, although telephones in some rural areas without a digital service still have access to the analogue service. The digital network covers some 90 per cent of the population, including all the major population centres and corridors (all operators provide coverage maps). If you live or work in a remote area, you should ensure that a company's coverage includes that area.

In addition to services in the major metropolitan areas, Telstra mobile satellite and radio services provide mobile communications to the aeronautical, marine and remote land area markets. MobileSat allows you to plug a computer, fax machine or satellite navigation equipment into a terminal in an aircraft, boat or car and receive crystal clear communication wherever you are in Australia or up to 200km/124mi off the coast. Australia subscribes to the GSM digital network, which allows the same telephone to be used in around 170 countries worldwide, including most of western Europe and parts of Asia, the Middle East, the Pacific, and central and South Africa (referred to as international roaming).

Buying a mobile telephone is a mine-field, as not only are there three networks from which to choose, but numerous call charges, connection fees, insurance, monthly subscriptions and tariffs. Before buying a mobile, shop around and compare telephone charge rates, installation and connection charges, prices and features, and rental charges.

Mobile phones are sold by specialist dealers, Telstra shops, and department and chain stores which have arrangements with service providers or networks to sell airtime contracts (along with telephones). Don't rely on getting good or impartial advice from retail staff, some of whom know little or nothing about telephones and networks (it's said that the difference between Clint Eastwood and a mobile telephone seller is that Clint isn't a real cowboy). Retailers advertise in magazines and newspapers, where a wide range of special offers is promoted.

The most important point is where you're going to use a telephone, followed by when, how often, and whether you intend to make mostly local, long-distance or international calls. Don't be influenced by an inexpensive telephone when the real costs lie in high call and line rental charges. Generally, the higher the connection and line rental charges, the lower the cost of calls. If you make a lot of calls, select a tariff with low call charges. Conversely, if you make few calls or need a telephone mostly for incoming calls, choose a tariff with low monthly costs. You can obtain pre-paid cards (e.g. from post offices) that avoid the need to sign a long-term contract or produce a credit card. If you have a telephone with a pre-paid card, there's no charge for receiving calls, which is an ideal solution for someone who wants a telephone mostly for incoming calls.

New Zealand

New Zealanders are enthusiastic telephone users, and telephone ownership in New Zealand ranks 26th out of 209 countries surveyed, with over 1,000 fixed line and mobile telephones per 1,000 people. This is largely because local fixed line calls are free or inexpensive, long distances (or at least long travelling times) separate many communities, and many New Zealanders are immigrants with family members and friends overseas. The telephone system in New Zealand has been extensively modernised in the last decade and all areas are now served by modern digital exchanges (the last exchange on which subscribers could make calls only via the operator was closed in 1991).

The New Zealand telecommunications industry has been extensively deregulated in recent years. The main telecommunications operator is Telecom New Zealand (TCNZ), known simply as Telecom (💻 www. telecom.co.nz), which used to be state owned (and part of the post office) but became a separate company in 1987 and was then privatised. In the early 21st century, the largest individual shareholder in Telecom is Bell Atlantic, with around 25 per cent of shares. Although Telecom is essentially a private company, in effect it remains the national telephone company and maintains 1.8 million fixed lines and 1.3 million cellular telephone connections.

The deregulated environment has allowed Telecom to become more than a telephone company and it maintains a number of other telecommunications services, including cable networks. After deregulation, other telecommunications companies such as TelstraClear (💻 www.telstra clear.co.nz, and WorldxChange (💻 www.wxc.co.nz) entered the marketplace, although they remain small compared with Telecom.

The only emergency number you need to know in New Zealand is 111, which can be dialled free from any telephone and connects you to the emergency operator.

Installation

Many New Zealand households have two or more telephone lines, which enable them to connect a fax machine or modem or to remain contactable when teenage children spend hours (and hours) gossiping to their friends. In Auckland and Wellington, you can receive your telephone service via fibre optic cables (owned by First Media, yet another offshoot of Telecom), which also deliver TV signals. The easiest way to find out whether there's a choice of telephone companies in your area is to ask your neighbours. If a Telecom line and telephone are already installed in your property, you can usually take over the connection, but you aren't obliged to if an alternative is available.

To have a telephone connected, simply call your chosen telephone company (the number will be in your local telephone directory). Before connecting your line, Telecom (or another operator) will need your name and address, date of birth, proof of your address (e.g. driving licence), details of your previous address (and proof) and employer, and the address of a relative or friend in New Zealand (if applicable) whom you can use as a reference (plus six pints of blood or your first-born as security!). If you've just arrived in New Zealand, your immigration documents should be acceptable as proof of identity; otherwise ask your employer (if you have one) to confirm your identity. Once your application has been approved, your telephone will be connected within 24 hours if your home has an existing line, or within 48 hours if it hasn't but there are lines nearby. The fee is $45 to reconnect an existing line. If you need a line installed or you live in a remote area, you will be quoted a price for the labour costs and materials involved. You can call ☎ 123 for a quote.

Although you will probably need to rent your telephone line from Telecom, you can no longer rent a telephone from them. However, you can choose from a wide variety of telephones of all shapes and sizes (plus answering machines and other equipment) at telephone and electrical shops, with prices starting at around $20, which is a cheaper option than renting anyway. Make sure that the telephone you buy is a touch-tone (DTMF) telephone (most are). Although touch-tone telephones purchased abroad usually work perfectly well in New Zealand, you aren't supposed to connect them unless they're Telecom approved.

International Calls

You can direct dial international calls from private and public telephones in New Zealand through the ISD (International Subscriber Dialling) system. A full list of country codes is shown in the information pages of your telephone directory. To make an international call, dial the international access code of 00, followed by the country code (e.g. 1 for the USA, 44 for the UK) and number you want, usually omitting the initial 0. For international operator assistance dial 0170.

International telephone calls via Telecom are charged according to the time of day and the part of the world (zone), Australia being in the cheapest zone and the UK in one of the most expensive. Other companies usually charge a separate rate for each country. It's sometimes cheaper to use a company other than Telecom to make international calls (or the internet – see page 300). Telecom does, however, have periodic special offers, e.g. a Weekends and Weeknights plan offering a call lasting up to two hours made during the weekend (between 6pm Friday and 8am Monday) and during weeknights (6pm to 8am, Monday to Thursday) for $3 to Australia and $6 to Canada, Ireland, the UK and the USA.

If you're travelling overseas, you can use Telecom's Direct service to call New Zealand. By dialling the relevant local access number you can speak to an operator in New Zealand and charge the call to your Telecom account or a calling card or credit card, or place a reverse charge (collect) call. For information and access numbers contact Telecom.

It's possible to make Home Country Direct (HCD) calls in New Zealand by dialling 0009 followed by the country code of the country you wish to call. You will then be connected directly to an operator in the country you're calling, who will place the call for you and charge it either to the number you're calling or your bill, assuming you have a telephone account in that country. It's quite expensive, however, much more expensive than paying for the call yourself. Travellers visiting New Zealand from the USA and holding a calling card from an American telephone company can use HCD and have the cost charged to their account. If you have an MCI calling card in the USA (or a card issued by a company with which MCI has an agreement), simply dial 000 912 from any telephone; if you have an account with BT in the UK, you can dial 000 944. You can then dial the number yourself and no operator intervention is necessary.

Mobile Telephones

Given the remoteness of many parts of New Zealand, mobile (cellular) telephones are popular and there are well over two million mobiles in use. Coverage is surprisingly good despite the difficult terrain in many places. Recently, however, there have been scare stories about the risks to health from mobile telephones and the antennae towers (one garage owner who planned to mount a tower on his land adjacent to a primary school received death threats!).

The cellular market is dominated by Telecom Mobile and Vodafone, which operate the only cellular networks in the country. Vodafone became the leader in terms of the number of mobile subscribers in late 2004 and has around 56 per cent of the market. Competition for business is fierce, prices are keen, it's no longer necessary to have a contract, and both firms offer a (sometimes bewildering) range of payment plans. Telecom has a complex selection of Prepaid plans (the 027 range), Onebill plans, Monthly plans and Multi-phone plans. Vodafone has a similar range, including Mobilise, Motormouth and Prepay.

Pre-pay ('pay as you talk') telephones are increasingly popular in New Zealand, as elsewhere, and you can buy cards for $20, $30 and $50 in many shops, including post shops. You can buy a mobile telephone directly from Telecom or Vodafone or from a mobile telephone shop, where you can be connected to a network. It's also possible to rent mobiles by the day or week, starting at around $20 per day. Calls to and from mobile telephones are generally expensive, but vary according to the many payment plans on offer.

RADIO

Australia

Radio reception in Australia is excellent in most parts of the country, including stereo radio, which is clear in all but the most remote or 'mountainous' areas (not that Australia has many mountains). Radio is very popular, particularly among the young – three out of four teenagers listen daily. Local stations broadcast on the FM wave band in stereo or on the medium wave (MW) band. High-quality FM radio can also be received via cable or satellite, which provides dozens of stations. The short wave (SW) band is useful for receiving foreign radio stations. Digital radio was introduced in 2001 and allows stations to transmit several channels of sound simultaneously, as well as text and pictures to a small screen attached to receivers. Australian radio is regulated by the Australian Broadcasting Authority (ABA) and there are no radio licence fees in Australia.

There are literally hundreds of radio stations in Australia, including ABC, commercial, ethnic, community and university-based stations (operated on a shoe-string and run by volunteers). In the last few decades, dozens of public (community) radio stations have sprung up around Australia, supported by the government and various educational institutions. They often have a limited transmission range and cater for specific community groups within their areas, e.g. there are around 16 public radio stations in Sydney, which although amateurish are diverse and original.

New Zealand

Radio broadcasting in New Zealand follows the model established for the TV industry: there are state-operated and commercially run stations. Radio New Zealand (RNZ, 🖳 www.radionz.co.nz) runs three national stations, Concert FM and National Radio, which are similar to the BBC's Radio 3 and 4, and the AM Network, which relays Parliamentary proceedings. They have a good reputation for the quality of their broadcasting, although they're rather staid and have a mainly older (and declining) audience. The stations are entirely state-funded and don't broadcast advertising. RNZ also operates a network of local radio stations throughout the country, which are partly state-funded and partly funded from advertising. They broadcast mainly rock, pop and easy listening music, local and regional news, and sport. CanWest (the owner of TV3 and C4) runs RadioWorks, the second largest national radio network, which broadcasts mainly pop music.

BBC World Service

The BBC World Service (the insomniac's station) broadcasts worldwide, in English and around 35 other languages, with a total output of over 750 hours per week (a *very* long week). The BBC World Service is the most famous and highly respected international radio service in the world, with regular listeners estimated at some 120 million (give or take a few). Its main aims are to provide unbiased news, project British opinion, and reflect British culture, life and developments in science and industry. News bulletins, current affairs, political commentaries and topical magazine programmes form the bulk of its output, supported by drama, general entertainment, music and a comprehensive sports service. A programme guide is also listed on the internet (🖳 www.bbc.co.uk/worldservice/programmes).

TELEVISION

Australia

Australian television (TV, the 'electric goldfish bowl') is among the best (or least worst) in the world and much better than the rubbish dished up in many other countries, e.g. the USA, but not as good as British TV. However, over half the programmes are purchased from the UK and the USA, most local content consisting of current affairs, game shows, soaps and sport. Free-to-air (or terrestrial) TV includes both government-owned and commercial stations. In addition, pay (cable) TV is provided in most major cities, and satellite TV is also available in country and outback areas. WebTV was introduced in 1998, where customers can purchase a set-top box (for around $200) with a built-in modem for internet access (no computer is required), a pay-TV decoder and a CD-ROM drive for games. Digital TV started in early 2001 in Adelaide, Brisbane, Melbourne, Perth and Sydney, and by 2005 was available in many metropolitan areas, but there's still no timetable for its start in remote areas. Digital TV allows hundreds of channels to be received via satellite and cable. Australian radio includes both state-owned ABC and commercial stations and is generally excellent.

The standards for TV reception in Australia aren't the same as in many other countries. TVs and video recorders manufactured for use in North America (NTSC Standard) and for the European PAL B/G or PAL-I systems won't function in Australia. Some foreign TVs can be converted to operate under Australia's PAL-D system, although it usually isn't worth the trouble and expense of shipping a TV (or VCR) to Australia.

There are five national terrestrial or free-to-air (FTA) networks in Australia: ABC, Nine, SBS, Seven and Ten. ABC (Australian Broadcasting Corporation) and SBS (Special Broadcasting Service) are government-owned, while Nine, Seven and Ten are commercial networks. There are also a number of regional commercial stations (including NBN, Prime, Seven Network, Southern Cross, Ten Network and Win), Imparja Television (an Aboriginal commercial station), plus community, local and student TV. Not all areas receive all the national networks: most state capitals can receive between three and five, while in some remote areas ABC may be the only free-to-air station you can receive. Overall control of Australia's TV and radio services is exercised by the Australian Broadcasting Authority (ABA).

Pay Television

Pay TV was introduced in Australia in 1995 and shouldn't be confused with pay-per-view, where subscribers pay on a per programme basis (e.g. for a live concert or sports event). With pay TV, viewers pay a monthly fee for a package of stations, delivered via cable or satellite. There are two major pay TV operators in Australia, Foxtel (50 per cent owned by Telstra) and Optus Vision, plus some smaller operators.

The installation of cables for pay TV in Australia was one of the largest and fastest cable installation programmes undertaken anywhere in the world. Both Telstra and Optus laid their cables in the same streets in Brisbane, Melbourne and Sydney, afraid that their rivals would steal a march on them (Optus laid its cables above ground, to the revulsion of residents, rather than burying them as Telstra did). Cable currently reaches over three million homes, mostly in major cities. Most homes in Brisbane, the Gold Coast, Melbourne and Sydney are cabled, plus parts of Adelaide and Perth. The broadband cable is used to deliver FM radio, high-speed internet access, pay TV, telephone, and other interactive services such as community information systems. It also enables operators to offer pay-per-view films and other broadcasts on demand.

Some 20 per cent of households in Australia subscribe to pay TV, although the biggest fans are children; many families have tried it and quit. Unlike satellite and cable TV in Europe and North America, pay TV in Australia doesn't have sufficient big exclusive sports or entertainment specials to attract the average viewer (Australia's climate also means that many people have better things to do than watch TV). Foxtel (💻 www.foxtel.com.au) provides over 100 channels, including BBC World, the cartoon network, Fox Children's Network, Fox Sports, Sky, the world movie channel and world news. Optus provides around 50 channels, including community broadcasts, Disney and Warner Bros, education, films, general entertainment, music, news and sport. However, critics claim that most output consists of boring documentaries, old films, banal local news and minor sports. Pay TV operators have been allowed to broadcast advertisements since 1997.

Foxtel and Optus both charge an installation fee of around $72 (which may be much higher for homes with difficult access) plus a monthly subscription of between around $49.95 and $97.95, depending on the programme package. You can choose from a range of packages depending on your preferred viewing, e.g. sport or films. Subscriptions can be paid by cash at ANZ branches and post offices and by cheque, credit card, direct debit or money order. Some cable companies offer inexpensive telephone services, in some cases including free local off-peak calls, and it's possible to save enough money on your telephone bill to pay for your cable TV. Optus offers customers who use its pay TV and long-distance telephone services a discount on their monthly TV bill, or an equal discount on their long-distance telephone bill.

Although Brisbane, Melbourne and Sydney have been 'cornered' by Optus and Telstra, the rest of the country is wide open and being exploited by small companies (such as Northgate Cable in Ballarat and Neighbourhood Cable in Mildura (VIC)) who have encroached on Telstra's market share by offering internet, telephone and TV services at lower prices, e.g. between $10.95 and $54.95 per month for various packages. Subscribers usually receive free monthly programme guides, which are also available from newsagents. However, most Australian newspapers and TV guides virtually ignore pay TV and don't list any programmes, while some list only selected channels (e.g. Showtime and Foxtel highlights). The Australian PayTV website (💻 www.auspaytv.com) offers comprehensive information on the current state of the market as well as links to all pay TV companies.

New Zealand

Television is popular in New Zealand, where over 1.25 million households have at least one television set and it's estimated that the vast majority of the population watches some television every day. There are three terrestrial, national free TV stations in New Zealand, imaginatively named TV One, TV2, and TV3. There used to be a fourth (you guessed it, TV4), but that's now a youth music based channel called C4. TV One and TV2 are state owned, while TV3 and C4 are privately owned by the Canadian company, CanWest. All stations, even those that are state owned, carry advertising, although the amount of revenue the state-funded channels can raise from advertising is limited. There are also state and privately owned regional TV stations in some areas (e.g. Triangle TV in Auckland, Channel 7 in Wellington, Canterbury TV and Channel 9 in Dunedin), although TVNZ, the state broadcasting company, has closed its five Horizon Pacific regional channels.

Cable & Satellite TV

Cable: Cable television has made slow but steady progress in New Zealand, and is available in certain areas, including Wellington and Kapiti Coast, Greymouth, Gisborne and several suburbs of Auckland. The main operators are Pacific Satellite Cable TV and TelstraClear Limited. Cable TV is the poor relation of satellite TV and, despite initial optimistic predictions, isn't very popular; the sparse population in many parts of the country means that universal cable coverage is unlikely. The easiest way to find out whether cable TV is available in your area is to ask your neighbours. The presence of cable 'pillars' (junction boxes) and unsightly, subsiding trenches in the roads and pavements of Auckland and Wellington's smartest suburbs are also a good indication!

Cable TV provides exclusive cable channels as well as terrestrial TV broadcasts and satellite channels such as CNN. TelstraClear Limited operates a pick-and-choose menu pricing system, with a basic package costing around $59.95 per month, increasing with various film and sports channels. It's also possible to choose which channels you wish to receive and the days on which you wish to receive them, paying as little as $1.50 per day for one channel, which works out cheaper if (for example) you just want to watch films at weekends. If you subscribe to cable TV, you can also obtain your telephone and internet service via cable.

Satellite: Sky satellite TV is well established in New Zealand, where it's owned by a consortium of international communications and media companies (TVNZ also has a stake in the enterprise). Foreign investors have pumped millions of dollars into satellite TV, confident that it's the way ahead in a country where long distances and a sparse population have slowed the sprawling trenches of cable networks. Sky TV had a 13.6 per cent audience share in 2004.

You can take out a subscription by calling your nearest dealer and have a dish installed within a few days. If you live in a remote or mountainous area, you may need a large dish in order to receive transmissions. A start-up package to receive Sky TV, including a large dish, receiver/decoder and installation, costs around $300, although Sky have occasional special offers, with installation from around $99. Sky viewers pay a monthly subscription fee of $43.40, although an increasing number of programmes, such as arts, films and top sporting events, are on a pay-per-view basis, which is in addition to the basic cost, e.g. $12.78 for the Arts Channel, $15.15 for Sport and $23.77 for Platinum Sport. Sky Sports' trump card has been to secure exclusive broadcasting rights to many top sporting events in New Zealand, including rugby matches. As sport, particularly rugby and especially the All Blacks, is something which few New Zealanders can live without (literally), it may account for the impressive following of satellite TV.

UTILITIES

Utilities is the collective name given to electricity, gas and water supplies.

Electricity

The electricity supply in Australia and New Zealand is 240/250 volts AC, with a frequency of 50 Hertz (cycles). If you move into a new home, the electricity supply may have been disconnected by the local electricity company. You must contact your local electricity company and complete a registration form and should allow at least two days to have the electricity reconnected and the meter read. There's usually a charge for connection and a security deposit may be payable. You need to contact your electricity company to get a final reading when you vacate your home.

Power Rating

Electrical equipment rated at 110 volts (for example, from the USA) requires a converter or a step-down transformer to convert it to 240 volts, although some electrical appliances (e.g. electric razors and hair dryers) are fitted with a 110/240 volt switch. Check for the switch, which may be located inside the casing, and make sure it's switched to 240 volts *before* connecting it to the power supply. Converters can be used for heating appliances but transformers, which are available from most electrical retailers, are required for motorised appliances (they can also be bought secondhand). Add the wattage of the devices you intend to connect to a transformer and make sure that its power rating *exceeds* this sum.

Generally, all small, high-wattage, electrical appliances such as heaters, irons, kettles and toasters need large transformers. Motors in large appliances such as cookers, dishwashers, dryers, refrigerators and washing machines will need replacing or fitting with a large transformer. In most cases it's simpler to buy new appliances in Australia, which are of good quality and reasonably priced. The dimensions of Australian and New Zealand cookers, dishwashers, dryers, microwave ovens, refrigerators and washing machines differ from those in some other countries. All electrical goods sold in Australia and New Zealand must conform to local safety standards. If you wish to buy electrical appliances such as a cooker or refrigerator, you should shop around, as prices vary considerably (choose those that have a high energy efficiency rating, which are cheaper to run). Refrigerators/freezers in Australia are normally 'tropicised' or fan assisted to cope with the high average temperatures, which is why it isn't usually worthwhile bringing one with you.

Frequency Rating

A problem with some electrical equipment is the frequency rating, which in some countries, e.g. the USA, is designed to run at 60 Hertz and not Australia's and New Zealand's 50 Hertz. Electrical equipment *without* a motor is generally unaffected by the drop in frequency to 50Hertz (except TVs). Equipment with a motor may run with a 20 per cent drop in speed, but clocks, cookers, record players, tape recorders and washing machines are unusable if they aren't designed for 50 cycle operation. To find out, look at the label on the back of the equipment. If it says 50/60 Hertz, it should be okay. If it says 60Hertz, you can try it anyway, **but first ensure that the voltage is correct as outlined above**. If the equipment runs too slowly, seek advice from the manufacturer or the retailer. Bear in mind that the transformers and motors of electrical devices designed to run at 60Hertz run hotter at 50Hertz, so make sure that equipment has sufficient space around it for cooling.

Fuses

Most apartments and all houses have their own fuse boxes, which are usually of the circuit breaker type in modern homes. When a circuit is overloaded, the circuit breaker trips to the OFF position. When replacing or repairing fuses of any kind, if the same fuse continues to blow, contact an electrician and **never fit a fuse of a higher rating than specified, even as a temporary measure**. When replacing fuses, don't rely on the blown fuse as a guide, as it may have been wrong. If you use an electric lawnmower or power tools outside your home or in your garage, you should have a Residual Current Device (RCD) installed. This can detect current changes of as little as a thousandth of an amp and in the event of a fault (or the cable being cut) it switches off the power in around 0.04 seconds.

Plugs

Unless you've come to Australia from New Zealand (or vice versa), all your plugs will require changing, or you'll need a lot of expensive adapters. Australian and New Zealand plugs have three pins: two diagonally slanting flat pins above one straight (earth) pin. Plugs aren't fused. Some electrical appliances are earthed and have a three-core flex* – you must *never* use a two-pin plug with a three-core flex. **Always make sure that a plug is correctly and securely wired, as bad wiring can prove fatal**. For maximum safety, electrical appliances should be turned off at the main wall point when not in use.

Bulbs

Electric light bulbs (called globes) in Australia are of the Edison type with a bayonet, not a screw fitting. In New Zealand they may have a bayonet or screw fitting. Low-energy light bulbs are also available and are more expensive than ordinary bulbs, although they save money due to their longer life and reduced energy consumption. Bulbs for non-standard electrical appliances (i.e. appliances not made for the local market) such as lamps, refrigerators and sewing machines may be unavailable locally, therefore you should bring spares with you. Plug adapters for imported lamps and other electrical items can be difficult to find locally, therefore you should bring a number of adapters and extension cords with you, which can be fitted with local plugs.

Safety

Only a qualified electrician should install electrical wiring and fittings, particularly in connection with fuse boxes. Always ask for a quotation for any work in advance and check the identity of anyone claiming to be an electricity company employee (or any kind of 'serviceman') by asking to see an identity card and checking with his office. Special controls can be fitted to many appliances to make their use easier for the disabled and the blind or partially sighted (e.g. studded or Braille controls).

Australia

Electricity and gas are used for cooking and heating in cities and towns throughout Australia, and it's common for homes to have both electricity and gas. Each state and territory has its own Energy Commission, which used to be owned and administered by local governments, but are now mostly privatised. There are a number of electricity generating and distribution companies in most states. Australia has a non-nuclear policy and has no nuclear power stations, despite being a major producer of uranium.

Suppliers, Cost & Bills: Energy Australia (🖥 http://energyaustralia. com.au) is one of Australia's larger electricity and gas suppliers, providing energy to over 1.5 million Australian homes and businesses in the ACT, NSW, South Australia and Victoria. Integral Energy (🖥 www.integral. com.au) is the second-largest, state-owned energy corporation in NSW, distributing electricity to 800,000 customers or some 2.1 million people. Power & Water (🖥 www.powerwater.com.au) is the Northern Territory's major provider of electricity, sewerage and water services, with over 70,000 customers and Aurora Energy (🖥 www.auroraenergy.com.au) is Tasmania's electricity supplier, where it's connected to almost every home. Western Power (🖥 www.westernpower.com.au) is Western Australia's leading energy corporation, with around 800,000 customers, while ETSA Utilities (🖥 www. etsautilities.com.au) is South Australia's electricity distributor, with some 750,000 customers. Ergon Energy (🖥 www.ergon.com.au) is Queensland's electricity supplier (it also operates in the ACT, NSW and Victoria) and has over half a million customers. Actew AGL (🖥 www.actewagl.com.au) is based in the ACT, where it supplies electricity, gas and water.

Electricity charges vary considerably depending on the state and local competition, e.g. Integral Energy charges 11.777 cents (excluding GST) per kilowatt hour (kWh) for the first 1,750 kWh per quarter, plus an access charge of 30 cents (excluding GST) per day and a $38.20 'establishment fee' for a new contract. Some companies offer a range of tariffs which may include peak, off-peak and weekend rates (some tariffs require a special meter to be installed). The biggest savings can be made when using a night rate with electric storage water heaters. Many metropolitan households use gas for cooking and heating, and some 5 per cent of Australian homes use solar energy for heating water. Electricity bills usually show meter readings, the kWh used, charges and a daily energy/cost comparison. There's no tax on electricity bills. Customers are billed quarterly and payment can be made at certain banks, by post (by cheque), at post offices and by telephone (with a credit/debit card).

New Zealand

The electricity supply in New Zealand is mostly generated by hydroelectric power plants, therefore conservationists can consume energy to their heart's content. The energy market in New Zealand is completely privatised and most major areas have at least two electricity suppliers, so you can shop around. The main companies are Bay of Plenty/King County Energy (🖥 www.bopelec.co.nz), Empower Ltd. (Contact Energy Ltd., 🖥 www.contactenergy.co.nz), Energy Online (Genesis Power Ltd, 🖥 www.energyonline.co.nz), Genesis Energy (🖥 www.genesisenergy.co.nz), Meridian Energy Ltd. (🖥 www.meridianenergy.co.nz), Mighty River Power Ltd. 🖥 www.mightyriverpower.co.nz), Mercury Energy (🖥 www.mercury.co.nz) and Trustpower Ltd. (🖥 www.trustpower.co.nz). The supply is usually reliable, despite the catastrophic and well publicised cable failures in Auckland in 1998, which left the centre of the city without full power for several weeks.

Connection & Payment: To have the electricity supply connected (or the bill transferred to your name when moving into a new home), simply call a local electricity company. Connection charges are around $40, although if the electricity hasn't been disconnected you won't be charged. You may need to pay a bond if you don't own your home, which can be around $250 if you don't meet the company's credit criteria or $100 if you rent a property. You're billed every two months – most people pay by direct debit from a bank account. The typical bill for an average house is around $200 for two months.

Gas

Australia

Australia has vast natural gas reserves and it's available in all of Australia's major cities from companies such as Australian Gas Limited (AGL, 🖥 www.

agl.com.au), which also sells electricity, and has three million customers across Australia. The gas industry is deregulated in most of the country. Gas is popular for cooking (it costs less than electricity), although it's less commonly used to provide heating and hot water (but gas heaters are becoming more popular). There may be no gas supply in older homes and some modern houses are all electric. If you're looking for a rental property and want to cook by gas, make sure it already has a gas supply (some houses have an unused gas service pipe). In country areas without piped gas, you can buy a cooker that uses bottled gas. If you buy a house without a gas supply, you can arrange with your local gas company to install a line between your home and a nearby gas main (provided there's one within a reasonable distance, or the cost will be prohibitive).

If a home already has a gas supply, simply contact your local gas company to have the gas supply reconnected or transferred to your name (there's a connection charge). Usually a security deposit (e.g. $120) is payable and there may also be a payment to establish an account (e.g. $25). You must contact your local gas company to get a final reading when vacating a property. If you need to purchase gas appliances, such as a gas cooker or fire, you should shop around as prices vary considerably. Special controls can be fitted to many appliances to make them easier to use by the disabled and the blind or partially sighted (studded or Braille controls). Gas tariffs vary but are around 1.5 cents per megajoule and there's a quarterly supply maintenance fee of around $30. Rates vary from city to city (or even its suburbs) and region to region, and are more expensive in remote areas. There's no tax on gas bills. Customers are billed quarterly and payment can be made at certain banks, by post (by cheque), at post offices and by telephone (with a credit/debit card.

Gas central heating boilers, fires and water heaters should be checked annually. **Gas installations and appliances can leak and cause explosions or kill you while you sleep. If you suspect a gas leak, first check to see if a gas tap has been left on or a pilot light has gone out. If not, there's probably a leak, either in your home or in a nearby gas pipeline. Ring your local gas service centre immediately and vacate your home as quickly as possible.** Gas leaks are extremely rare and explosions caused by leaks even rarer (although often spectacular and therefore widely reported). Nevertheless, it pays to be careful. You can buy an electric-powered gas detector which activates an alarm when a gas leak is detected.

New Zealand

Natural gas is available in most cities, towns and villages in the North Island, with the exception of a few remote corners, but not in the South

Island. Liquefied petroleum gas is distributed nationally. Natural gas is used by around 200,000 commercial, industrial and residential customers, and despite not being available in the South Island, it's become one of New Zealand's most important energy sources. This is a recent development, dating back to the '70s, when natural gas production took off in local fields. By the mid-'90s, natural gas was supplying a third of the country's energy needs.

As with electricity, gas is supplied by local companies, the largest of which include Contact Energy and NGC. Gas is popular for cooking and costs less than electricity, although it's less commonly used to provide heating and hot water (gas heaters are, however, becoming more popular). There may be no gas supply in older homes, and modern properties may also be all-electric. If you're looking to rent a property and want to cook by gas, make sure it already has a gas supply (some houses have an unused gas service pipe). In country areas without mains gas, you can buy appliances that operate on bottled gas. On payment of a deposit for the bottle and regulator, a local supplier will provide you with gas bottles and replace them when they're empty. Large users can also have a storage tank installed and have gas delivered by tanker. If you need to purchase gas appliances, such as a cooker or fire, you should shop around, as prices vary considerably.

If you buy a home without a gas supply, you can usually arrange with a local gas company to install a line between your home and a nearby gas main (provided there's one within a reasonable distance, otherwise the cost will be prohibitive). If a home already has a gas supply, simply contact a local gas company to have it reconnected or transferred to your name (there's a connection charge of around $40). A security deposit (e.g. $100) is usually payable if you're renting. You must contact your gas company to obtain a final reading when vacating a property. In areas where mains gas is unavailable, some properties are plumbed for bottled gas. A 45kg bottle costs around $150 per year to rent and around $60 for each refill, although prices are higher in rural areas. Alternatively, you can buy 9kg gas bottles and refill them at most petrol stations for around $20.

Water

Australia

Each city and major region in Australia has a water board operated by the local government. Water, or rather the lack of it, is a major concern in Australia and the price paid for all those sunny days. Australia is the world's driest country, and country areas are hit by frequent droughts. Many country homes have a bore (well) that comes in handy when there are water restrictions, which may restrict homeowners to watering their gardens once every three days before dawn or after dusk (to reduce evaporation). Many homes also have rainwater tanks that can be used to water gardens and for baths and showers. In some states there are frequent water restrictions, such as sprinkler bans during the day, e.g. between 9am and 6pm or from 8am until 8pm, although there may be no restriction on hand held hoses. To reduce water consumption, many people plant native Australian plants requiring little water and use wood chips or gravel as an alternative to lawns. **In Australia, water is a precious resource and not something simply to pour down the drain!**

When moving into a new home, you should ask where the main stopcock is, so that you can turn off the water supply in an emergency. If the water stops running for any reason, you should turn off the supply to prevent flooding from an open tap when the supply starts again. Contact your local water company if you have a problem reconnecting your water supply, as it could have been turned off by them. If you need a plumber, e.g. as a result of a burst pipe, you may be able to get a recommendation or a list of names from your local water company. Before calling a plumber, always ask the minimum call-out charge. In some states (e.g. Victoria), water companies no longer inspect work carried out by plumbers, who certify their own work. Plumbers must be licensed and have indemnity insurance, and work valued at over $500 must have a certificate of compliance. New sewerage systems have been installed in many areas, the bulk of the cost being paid for by residents, irrespective of whether they want or need the improvements.

Charges & Bills: There was traditionally a fixed charge for water in Australia based on the gross rental or rateable value of a property. However, water is now metered in metropolitan areas, and most households pay for their actual consumption rather than a flat fee. When consumption is metered, you may be charged around $1.10 per 1,000 litres (kl). Bills also contain a water service charge, e.g. $25 per quarter. Water bills may include drainage, water and sewerage, and may show your average daily use in litres. In some areas, however, e.g. Sydney and coastal districts, sewerage and drainage are charged separately, and quarterly charges can be high, e.g. $120. Bills can usually be paid in a number of instalments, e.g. two or four per year, and can be paid at certain banks (in cash or by cheque), by post (by cheque),at post offices and by telephone (with a credit/debit card).

Quality: Although Australian drinking water is among the cleanest and safest in the world, the quality varies and it can taste terrible in areas with high mineral deposits. It's possible to have a water purifier fitted to a drinking water tap to improve the taste. Fluoride is added to water in some cities. Australian water doesn't usually contain limescale, so it isn't necessary to use a decalcification liquid to keep your iron, kettle and other apparatus and utensils clean. Contaminated water in garden hoses and domestic swimming pools can cause amoebic meningitis, so it's important to clean pools and hoses thoroughly and frequently.

New Zealand

Although much of New Zealand usually has an abundant supply of water (see **Climate** on page 22), the country suffers from recurring droughts. The first half of 2005 saw some very dry months, for example April had less than 25 per cent of the normal rainfall. Mains water is available everywhere in New Zealand except in the most remote areas (where it sometimes shoots up in boiling form directly out of the ground!). All tap water is drinkable, although it's heavily chlorinated in towns (as in many other countries). Water is supplied and billed by a local water company, which may be a division of your local council.

Usually, you pay an annual water rate, which is set according to the size and value of your property. In most areas, water rates are included in local property taxes (see page 256), but in some areas water is billed separately, e.g. in Auckland some households pay several hundred dollars per year. In some areas, properties (generally newer homes) have a water meter and you're charged according to use. Usually, it's cheaper to pay for your water on the rated system, although modest users living in large properties find it cheaper to have a meter fitted. Mains drainage is found throughout New Zealand with the exception of remote rural areas, where properties usually have a septic tank.

SELLING YOUR HOME

Although this book is primarily concerned with buying a home in Australia and New Zealand, you may wish to sell your home at some time in the future. Before offering your home for sale, you should investigate the state of the property market. For example unless you're forced to sell, it definitely isn't recommended during a property slump when prices are depressed. It may be wiser to let your home long-term and wait until the market has recovered. It's also unwise to sell in the early years after purchase, when you will probably make a loss unless it was an absolute bargain (and you may have to pay capital gains tax as well).

Having decided to sell, your first decision will be whether to sell it yourself or at auction or use the services of an estate agent (see below). Although most properties in Australia and New Zealand are sold through estate agents, thousands of homes are also sold at auction (around a quarter of all homes in Melbourne and Sydney) and many owners sell their own homes. If you need to sell a property before buying a new one, this must be included as a conditional clause in the purchase contract for a new home.

Price

It's important to bear in mind that (like everything) property has a market price, and the best way of ensuring a quick sale (or any sale) is to ask a realistic price. If your home's fairly standard for the area, you can find out its value by comparing the prices of other homes on the market, or those that have recently been sold. Most agents will provide a free appraisal of a home's value in the hope that you will sell it through them. However, don't believe everything they tell you, as they may over-price it simply to encourage you. You can also hire a professional appraiser to determine the market value.

If you're marketing your property abroad, e.g. in the UK, take into account the prevailing exchange rate: if the dollar is strong, this will deter foreign buyers; if it's weak, you may even be able to increase the price.

You should be prepared to drop the price slightly (e.g. 5 or 10 per cent) and should set it accordingly, but shouldn't grossly over-price a home, as this will deter buyers. Don't reject an offer out of hand unless it's ridiculously low, as you may be able to get the prospective buyer to raise his offer. When selling a second home in Australia or New Zealand, you may wish to include the furnishings (plus major appliances) in the sale, particularly when selling a relatively inexpensive property with modest furnishings. You should add an appropriate amount to the price to cover the value of the furnishings, or alternatively you could use them as an inducement to a prospective buyer at a later stage, although this isn't usual practise.

Presentation

The secret to selling a home quickly lies in its presentation (assuming that it's competitively priced). First impressions (both exteriors and interiors) are vital when marketing your home and it's important to make every effort to present it in its best light and make it as attractive as possible. It may pay to invest in new interior decoration, new carpets, exterior paint and landscaping. A few plants and flowers can do wonders. Note that when decorating a home for resale, it's important to be conservative and not to do anything radical (such as install a red or black bathroom suite); white is a good neutral colour for walls, woodwork and porcelain (garish patterned carpets are also out).

It may also pay you to do some modernisation, such as installing a new kitchen or bathroom, as these are of vital importance (particularly kitchens) when selling a home. Note, however, that although modernisation may be necessary to sell an old home you shouldn't overdo it, as it's easy to spend more than you could ever hope to recoup in the sale price. If you're using an agent, you can ask him what you should do (or need to do) to help sell your home. If your home is in poor repair, this must be reflected in the asking price and, if major work is needed that you cannot afford, you should obtain a quotation (or two) and offer to knock this off the asking price.

Selling Your Home Yourself

While certainly not for everyone, selling your own home is a viable option for many people and is particularly recommended when you're selling an attractive home at a realistic price in a favourable market. Saving estate agent's fees may allow you to offer the property at a more appealing price, which could be an important factor if you're seeking a quick sale. Even if you aren't in a hurry, selling your own home saves you an agent's fees.

How you market your home will depend on the type of home you have, the price, and the country or area from where you expect your buyer to come. For example, if your property isn't of a type and style and in an area desirable to local inhabitants, it's usually a waste of time advertising it in the local press.

Advertising is the key to selling your home. The first step is to get a professional looking 'for sale' sign made (showing your telephone number) and to erect it in a prominent position. Do some research into the best publications for advertising your property, and place an advertisement in those that look the most promising. If you own a property in an area popular with foreign buyers, it may be worthwhile using an overseas agent or advertising in foreign newspapers and magazines.

You could also have a leaflet printed (with pictures) extolling the virtues of your property, which you could drop into local letter boxes or have distributed with a local newspaper (many people buy a new home in the vicinity of their present home). You may also need a 'fact sheet' printed if your home's vital statistics aren't included in the leaflet mentioned above and could offer a finder's fee (e.g. $1,000) to anyone who finds you a buyer. Don't omit to market your home around local companies, schools and organisations, particularly if they have many itinerant employees. Finally, it may help to provide information about local financing sources for potential buyers. With a bit of effort and practice you may even make a better job of marketing your home than an agent! Unless you're in a hurry to sell, set yourself a realistic time limit for success, after which you can try an agent.

Using An Agent

Most owners prefer to use the services of an agent, either locally or in their home country (which may not be feasible if you live in the UK or USA), particularly when selling a second home. If you purchased the property through an agent, it's often wise to use the same agent when selling, as he will already be familiar with it and may still have the details on file. You should take particular care when selecting an agent, as they vary considerably in their professionalism, expertise and experience (the best way to investigate agents is by posing as a buyer). Note that many agents cover a relatively small area, so you should take care to choose one who regularly sells properties in your area and price range.

APPENDICES

Appendix A: USEFUL ADDRESSES

Australia

Embassies & Consulates (Canberra)

A full list of embassies and consulates in Australia is contained in two booklets (*Diplomatic List* and *Consular List*) published by the Department of Foreign Affairs and Trade, and available from the Australian Government Publishing Service. Business hours vary considerably and all embassies close on their national holidays as well as on Australian public holidays. Always telephone to check opening hours before visiting. A selection of embassies in Canberra is listed below:

Austria: 12 Talbot Street, Forrest, ACT 2603 (☎ 02-6295 1533).

Belgium: 19 Arkana Street, Yarralumla, ACT 2600 (☎ 02-6273 2501).

Canada: Commonwealth Avenue, Canberra, ACT 2600 (☎ 02-6270 4000).

China: 15 Coronation Drive, Yarralumla, ACT 2600 (☎ 02-6273 4780).

Finland: 12 Darwin Avenue, Yarralumla, ACT 2600 (☎ 02-6273 3800).

France: 6 Perth Avenue, Yarralumla, ACT 2600 (☎ 02-6216 0100).

Germany: 119 Empire Circuit, Empire Cct, Yarralumla, ACT 2600 (☎ 02-6270 1911).

Greece: 9 Turrana Street, Yarralumla, ACT 2600 (☎ 02-6273 3011).

Indonesia: 8 Darwin Avenue, Yarralumla, ACT 2600 (☎ 02-6250 8600).

Ireland: 20 Arkana Street, Yarralumla, ACT 2600 (☎ 02-6273 3022).

Israel: 6 Turrana Street, Yarralumla, ACT 2600 (☎ 02-6273 1309).

Italy: 12 Grey Street, Deakin, ACT 2600 (☎ 02-6273 3333).

Japan: 112 Empire Circuit, Yarralumla, ACT 2600 (☎ 02-6273 3244).

Malaysia: 7 Perth Avenue, Yarralumla, ACT 2600 (☎ 02-6273 1543).

Netherlands: 120 Empire Circuit, Yarralumla, ACT 2600 (☎ 02-6220 9400).

New Zealand: Commonwealth Avenue, Canberra, ACT 2600 (☎ 02-6270 4211).

Norway: 17 Hunter Street, Yarralumla, ACT 2600 (☎ 02-6273 3444).

Papua New Guinea: 39-41 Forster Crescent, Yarralumla, ACT 2600 (☎ 02-6273 3322).

Philippines: 1 Moonah Place, Yarralumla, ACT 2600 (☎ 02-6273 2535).

Portugal: 23 Culgoa Circuit, O'Malley, ACT 2606 (☎ 02-6290 1733).

Russia: 76 Canberra Avenue, Griffith, ACT 2603 (☎ 02-6295 9033).

Singapore: 17 Forster Crescent, Yarralumla, ACT 2600 (☎ 02-6273 3944).

South Africa: Corner State Circle and Rhodes Place, Yarralumla, ACT 2600 (☎ 02-6273 2424).

Spain: 15 Arkana Street, Yarralumla, ACT 2600 (☎ 02-6273 3555).

Sweden: 5 Turrana Street, Yarralumla, ACT 2600 (☎ 02-6270 2700).

Switzerland: 7 Melbourne Avenue, Forrest, ACT 2603 (☎ 02-6162 8400).

Thailand: 111 Empire Circuit, Yarralumla, ACT 2600 (☎ 02-6273 1149).

United Kingdom: Commonwealth Avenue, Canberra, ACT 2600 (☎ 02-6270 6666).

USA: Moonah Place, Yarralumla, ACT 2600 (☎ 02-6214 5600).

Australian Customs Service

Australian Capital Territory: Australian Customs Service, 5 Constitution Avenue, Canberra, ACT 2601 (☎ 02-6275 6666).

New South Wales: Regional Director of Customs, 10 Cooks River Drive, Sydney International Airport, NSW 2020 (☎ 02-8339 6147).

Northern Territory: Regional Director of Customs, 21 Lindsay Street, Darwin, NT 0800 (☎ 08-8946 9999).

Queensland: Regional Director of Customs, Terrica Place, 140 Creek Street, Brisbane, QLD 4000 (☎ 07-3835 3444).

South Australia: Regional Director of Customs, 220 Commercial Road, Port Adelaide, SA 5015 (☎ 08-8847 9211).

Tasmania: Regional Director of Customs, Imports/Exports, Level 1, 25 Argyle Street, Hobart, TAS 7000 (☎ 03-6230 1201).

Victoria: Regional Director of Customs, Lexington Building, 414 Latrobe Street, Melbourne, VIC 3001 (☎ 03-9244 8000).

Western Australia: Regional Director of Customs, 2 Henry Street, Freemantle, WA 6160 (☎ 08-9430 1444).

Motor Vehicle Registration Authorities

Australian Capital Territory: Transport Regulation, PO Box 582, Dickson, ACT 2602 (☎ 02-6207 7000).

New South Wales: Registrar of Motor Vehicles, Roads and Traffic Authority, PO Box K198, Haymarket, NSW 1238 (☎ 02-9218 6888).

Northern Territory: Motor Vehicle Registry, PO Box 2520, Darwin, NT 0820 (☎ 08-8999 3111).

Queensland: Queensland Transport, Registration Division, PO Box 2451, Brisbane, QLD 4701 (☎ 07-3834 2011).

South Australia: Vehicle Standards, Transport SA, PO Box 2526, Regency Park, SA 5942 (☎ 08-8348 9599).

Tasmania: Registrar of Motor Vehicles, PO Box 1002, Hobart, TAS 7001 (☎ 03-6233 5201).

Victoria: Vic Roads, 60 Denmark Street, Kew, VIC 3101 (☎ 1800-814762).

Western Australia: Department of Transport, Licensing Division, 21 Murry Road South, Welshpool, WA 6101 (☎ 08-9351 1680).

Miscellaneous

Australian American Association, PO Box 1717, Neutral Bay, NSW 2089, Australia (🖥 www.aaafed.asn.au).

Australian-Britain Society, National Office, PO Box 9088, Deakin, ACT 2600, Australia (🖥 www.aust-britsociety.org.au).

Australian-British Chamber of Commerce, Level 16, The Gateway Building, 1 Macquarie Place, Sydney, NSW 2000, Australia (☎ 02-9247 6271, 🖥 www.britishchamber.com).

Australian Embassy, 1601 Massachusetts Ave., NW, Washington, DC 20036, USA (☎ 202-797 3000, 🖥 www.austemb.org).

Australian High Commission, Australia House, Strand, London WC2B 4LA, UK (☎ 020-7379 4334, 🖥 www.australia.org.uk).

Australian Taxation Office, Ground Floor, Ethos House, 28-36 Ainslie Ave, Civic Square, ACT 2600, Australia (☎ Excise Inquiry Line 13-28 61, 💻 www.ato.gov.au).

Department of Industrial Relations, Employment, Training & Further Education, 1 Oxford Street, Darlinghurst, NSW 2010, Australia (☎ 13-16 28, 💻 www.industrialrelations.nsw.gov.au).

Foreign Investment Review Board, Department of the Treasury, Langton Crescent, Canberra, ACT 2600, Australia (☎ 02-6263 3795, 💻 www.firb.gov.au). Provide information about buying property in Australia for non-residents and retirees.

Tourism Australia, PO Box 2721, Sydney, NSW 2001, Australia (☎ 02-9360 1111, 💻 ww.tourism.australia.com).

United Kingdom Settlers' Association (UKSA), PO Box 707, South Yarra, Victoria 3141, Australia (☎ 03-9787 3112, 💻 www. geocities.com/endeavour_uksa/).

New Zealand

Embassies & Consulates

Most foreign embassies in New Zealand are located in the capital Wellington, although some countries have their missions in Auckland. Note that business hours vary considerably and embassies close on their national holidays as well as on New Zealand's public holidays. Always telephone to check the business hours before visiting. A selection of embassies in Wellington is shown below:

Argentina: Level 14, 142 Lambton Quay, Wellington (☎ 04-472 8330).

Australia: 72-76 Hobson Street, Thorndon, PO Box 4036, Wellington (☎ 04-473 6411).

Austria: 57 Willis Street, Wellington (☎ 04-499 6393).

Belgium: 12th Floor, 1-3 Willeston Street, PO Box 3841, Wellington (☎ 04-472 9558).

Brazil: 10 Brandon Street, Wellington (☎ 04-473 3516).

Canada: 3rd Floor, 61 Molesworth Street, PO Box 12-049, Wellington (☎ 04-473 9577).

Chile: 19 Bolton Street, PO Box 3861. Wellington (☎ 04-471 6270).

China: 2-6 Glenmore Street, Kelburn, Wellington (☎ 04-472 1382).

Finland: Simpson Grierson Building, 195 Lambton Quay, PO Box 2402, Wellington (☎ 04-499 4599).

France: 34-42 Manners Street, Wellington (☎ 04-384 2555).

Germany: 90-92 Hobson Street, Thorndon, PO Box 1687, Wellington (☎ 04-473 6063).

Greece: 5-7 Willeston Street, PO Box 24–066, Wellington (☎ 04-473 7775).

India: 180 Molesworth Street, PO Box 4045, Wellington (☎ 04-473 6390).

Indonesia: 70 Glen Road, Kelburn, PO Box 3543, Wellington (☎ 04-475 8699).

Iran: 151 Te Anau Road, Roseneath, Wellington (☎ 04-386 2976).

Ireland: 6th Floor, 18 Shortland Street, PO Box 279, Auckland (☎ 09-977 2252).

Israel: 13th Floor, Equinox House, 111 The Terrace, PO Box 2171, Wellington (☎ 04-472 2368).

Italy: 34-38 Grant Road, Thorndon, PO Box 463, Wellington (☎ 04-473 5339).

Japan: Level 18-19, Majestic Centre, 100 Willis Street, Wellington (☎ 04-473 1540).

Korea: Level 11, ASB Bank Tower, 2 Hunter Street, PO Box 11–143, Wellington (☎ 04-473 9073).

Malaysia: 10 Washington Avenue, Brooklyn, PO Box 9422, Wellington (☎ 04-385 2439).

Mexico: Level 8, 111 Customhouse Quay, PO Box 110-510, Wellington (☎ 04-472 0555).

Netherlands: Investment House, Corner Ballance & Featherstone Streets, PO Box 840, Wellington (☎ 04-471 6390).

Papua New Guinea: 279 Willis Street, PO Box 197, Wellington (☎ 04-385 2474).

Peru: Level 8, Cigna House, 40 Mercer Street, Wellington (☎ 04-499 8087).

Philippines: 50 Hobson Street, Thorndon, PO Box 12-042. Wellington (☎ 04-472 9848).

Poland: 51 Granger Road, Howick, Auckland (☎ 09-534 4670).

Russia: 57 Messines Road, Karori, Wellington (☎ 04-476 6113).

Singapore: 17 Kabul Street, Khandallah, PO Box 13-140, Wellington (☎ 04-470 0850).

Sweden: 13th Floor, Vogel Building, Aitken Street, Thorndon, Wellington (☎ 04-499 9895).

Switzerland: Panama House, 22 Panama Street, Wellington (☎ 04-472 1593).

Thailand: 2 Cook Street, Karori, PO Box 17-226, Wellington (☎ 04-476 8616).

Turkey: 15-17 Murphy Street, Thorndon, Wellington (☎ 04-472 1292).

United Kingdom: 44 Hill Street, Wellington (☎ 04-924 2888).

USA: 29 Fitzherbert Terrace, PO Box 1190, Wellington (☎ 04-462 6000).

Selected Government Departments

Citizenship Office, PO Box 10-526, Wellington (☎ freephone 0800-225 151, 🖳 www.citizenship.govt.nz).

Department of Building & Housing, PO Box 10-729, Wellington (☎ 04-494 0260, 🖳 www.dbh.govt.nz).

Department of Child, Youth and Family Services, PO Box 2620, Wellington (☎ 04-918 9100, 🖳 www.cyf.govt.nz).

Department of Internal Affairs, PO Box 805, Wellington (☎ 04-495 7200, 🖳 www.dia.govt.nz).

Department of Labour, PO Box 3705, Wellington (☎ 04-915 4400, 🖳 www.dol.govt.nz).

Department of the Prime Minister & Cabinet, Parliament Building, Wellington (☎ 04-471 9743, 🖳 www.dpmc.govt.nz).

Land Information New Zealand (LINZ), Private Bag 5501, Wellington (☎ 04-460 0110, 🖳 www.linz.govt.nz).

Ministry for the Environment, PO Box 10-362, Wellington (☎ 04-917 7400, 🖳 www.mfe.govt.nz).

Ministry of Agriculture & Forestry, PO Box 2526, Wellington (☎ 04-474 4100, 🖳 www.maf.govt.nz).

Ministry of Foreign Affairs & Trade, Private Bag 18-901, Wellington (☎ 04-439 8000, 🖳 www.mft.govt.nz).

Ministry of Health, PO Box 5013, Wellington (☎ 04-496 2000, 🖳 www.moh.govt.nz).

Ministry of Transport, PO Box 3175, Wellington (☎ 04-472 1253, 🖳 www.transport.govt.nz).

New Zealand Customs, PO Box 2218, Wellington (☎ freephone 0800-428 786, 🖳 www.customs.govt.nz).

New Zealand Immigration Service, PO Box 3705, Wellington (☎ 0508-558 855, 🖳 www.immigration.govt.nz).

Customs Offices

Auckland: Customhouse, 50 Anzac Avenue, PO Box 29 (☎ 09-359 6655).

Auckland International Airport: PO Box 73-003 (☎ 09-275 9059).

Christchurch: Drury Street, PO Box 14-086, (☎ 03-358 0600).

Dunedin: 32 Portsmouth Drive, Private Bag 1928 (☎ 03-477 9251).

Invercargill: Business Centre, Ground Floor, Menzies Building, 1 Esk Street, PO Box 840 (☎ 03-218 7329).

Napier: 215 Hastings Street, PO Box 440 (☎ 06-835 5799).

Nelson: 10 Low Street, PO Box 66 (☎ 03-548 1484).

New Plymouth: 54-56 Currie Street, PO Box 136 (☎ 06-758 5721).

Tauranga: Nikau House, 27-33 Nikau Crescent, PO Box 5014 (☎ 07-575 9699).

Wellington: Head Office, The Customhouse, 17-21 Whitmore Street, PO Box 2218 (☎ 04-473 6099).

Miscellaneous

Archives New Zealand, PO Box 12-050, Wellington (☎ 04-499 5595, 🖳 www.archives.govt.nz).

National Library of New Zealand, PO Box 1467, Wellington (☎ 04-474 3000, 🖳 www.natlib.govt.nz).

Statistics New Zealand, PO Box 2922, Wellington (☎ 04-931 4600, 🖳 www.stats.govt.nz).

TeachNZ, PO Box 1666, Wellington (☎ freephone 0800-832 246, 🖳 www.teachnz.govt.nz).

Appendix B: FURTHER READING

Australia

There are many useful reference books for those seeking general information about Australia, including the *Year Book Australia* published annually by the Australian Bureau of Statistics. The Australia Government Publishing Service (AGPS, PO Box 84, Canberra, ACT 2601) publishes and distributes a wealth of useful publications for businessmen, prospective migrants and visitors. A selection of books about Australia is listed below (the publication title is followed by the name of the author and the publisher's name in brackets). Books prefixed with an asterisk (*) are recommended by the author. Some of the books listed are out of print, but you may still be able to find a copy in a bookshop or library.

Living & Working

The Australian Immigration Book (Made-To-Measure)

*The Cost of Living and Housing Survey Book (Commonwealth Bank of Australia)

**Living and Working in Australia, David Hampshire (Survival Books)

Tourist Guides

*Australia (Lonely Planet)

*Australia: Insight Guide (Insight Guides)

*Australia: The Rough Guide, Margo Daly et al (The Rough Guides)

*Australia & New Zealand Travel Planner (TNT Magazine – See **Magazines & Newspapers**)

Berlitz Pocket Guide to Australia (Berlitz)

*Discover Australia, Ken Bernstein (Berlitz)

Essential Australia (Automobile Association)

Explore Australia: 2002 (Viking Australia)

*Frommers Australia from $50 a Day (Macmillan Travel)

*Insider's Australia Guide, Harry Blutstein (MPC)

Let's Go Australia (Pan)

*Maverick Guide to Australia, Robert W. Bone (Pelican)

*Sydney Time Out Guide (Penguin)

Lonely Planet (💻 www.lonelyplanet.com) and Rough Guides (💻 www.roughguides.com) also publish numerous activity, city and state guides to Australia.

Travel Literature

Australia: True Stories of Life Down Under (Traveler's Tales)

Daisy Bates in the Desert, Julia Blackburn (Minerva)

*Down Under, Bill Bryson (Doubleday)

*In The Land Of Oz, Howard Jacobson (Penguin)

Outdoor Traveller's Australia (Stewart, Tabori, Chang)

A Ride in the Neon Sun, Josie Dew (Little, Brown & Company)

*The Ribbon and the Ragged Square, Linda Christmas (Penguin)

*Sean and David's Long Drive, Sean Condon (Lonely Planet)

*Sydney, Jan Morris (Penguin)

Tracks, Robyn Davidson (Vintage)

The Great Outdoors

Australian Bushcraft, Richard Graves (Taylor-Type)

Bicycle Touring in Australia, Leigh Hemmings (Mountaineer Books)

***Bushwalking in Australia**, John Chapman (Lonely Planet)

Bush Tucker: Australia's Wild Food, Tim Low (Angus & Robertson)

Cycling Australia, Nicola Wells (Lonely Planet)

Discover Australia by 4WD (Hema Maps Pty Ltd.)

How to Survive Australia, Robert Treborlang (Major Mitchell Press)

***Outback Australia** (Lonely Planet)

Outback Australia? No Worries!, Peter Wearing Smith (Omni Travel)

***Safe Outback Travel**, Jack Absalom (Five Mile Press)

***Stay Alive, A Handbook on Survival**, Maurice Dunlevy (AGPS)

Australians

12 Edmondstone Street, David Malouf (Penguin)

The Australians, In Search of an Identity, Ross Terrill (Bantam)

***The Australian People**, Craig McGregor (Hodder & Stoughton)

Christina Stead, Hazel Rowley (William Heinemann)

Contemporary Australians (DW Thorpe)

***A Fortunate Life**, Albert Facey (Viking)

***From Strength to Strength**, Sara Henderson

***More Please**, Barry Humphries (Penguin)

***Patrick White: A Life**, David Marr (Vintage)

***Robert J Hawke**, Blanche D'Alpuget (Penguin)

*Unreliable Memoirs, Clive James (Picador)

Wild Card, Dorothy Hewett (Virago)

History/Culture

Australia's Immigrants 1788-1978, Geoffrey Sherington (Allen & Unwin)

*The Fatal Shore, Robert Hughes (Pan)

*The Lucky Country: Australia in the Sixties, Donald Horne (Angus & Robertson)

*The Penguin History of Australia, John Malony (Penguin)

*The Road to Botany Bay, Paul Carter (Faber & Faber)

*A Secret Country, John Pilger (Vintage)

A Short History of Australia, Manning Clarke (Penguin)

Aboriginal Australia

Aboriginal Art, Wally Caruana (Thames & Hudson)

Aboriginal Australians, K. Suter, K. Stearman (Minority Rights Group)

Charles Perkins, Peter Read (Viking)

Mutant Message Down Under, Mario Morgan (Thorsons)

*My People, Kath Walker (Jacaranga Wiley)

*My Place, Sally Morgan (Virago)

Seeing the First Australians, Ian & Tamsin Donaldson (Allen & Unwin)

*The Songlines, Bruce Chatwin (Picador)

*Triumph of the Nomads, Geoffrey Blainey (Macmillan)

*Wandering Girl, Glenys Ward (Virago)

Magazines & Newspapers

The Advertiser – Adelaide (💻 www.theadvertiser.news.com.au). Adelaide's leading daily newspaper.

The Age – Melbourne (💻 www.theage.com.au). Mebourne's quality newspaper.

The Australian – National (💻 www.theaustralian.news.com.au). Australia's only national newspaper and the most respected.

The Australian Financial Review – National (http://afr.com). Australia's daily financial newspaper.

Australian News, Outbound Publishing, 1 Commercial Road, Eastbourne, East Sussex, BN21 3XQ, UK (☎ 01323-726040, 💻 www.outboundpublishing.com). Subscription newspaper for prospective migrants.

Australian Outlook, Consyl Publishing, 3 Buckhurst Road, Bexhill-on-Sea, East Sussex TN40 1QF, UK (☎ 01424-223111, 💻 www.consylpublishing.co.uk). Subscription newspaper for prospective migrants.

The Bulletin (💻 http://bulletin.ninemsn.com.au). Australian news magazine affiliated with the American *Newsweek* magazine.

The Canberra Times – ACT (💻 http://canberra.yourguide.com.au). Canberra's leading daily.

The Courier Mail – Brisbane (💻 www.thecouriermail.news.com.au). Brisbane's best-selling daily newspaper.

The Daily Telegraph – Sydney (www.dailytelegraph.news.com.au). A leading Sydney newspaper.

The Herald-Sun – Melbourne (www.heraldsun.news.com.au). Melbourne's best-selling newspaper.

The Mercury – Hobart (🖳 www.themercury.news.com.au). Tasmania's leading newspaper.

National Library of Australia (🖳 www.nla.gov.au/npapers). Provides a comprehensive list of all Australia's national, state and local newspapers.

The Sydney Morning Herald (🖳 www.smh.com.au). Sydney's best-selling newspaper.

TNT Magazine, 14-15 Child's Place, Earls Court, London SW5 9RX, UK (☎ 020-7373 3377, 🖳 www.tntmagazine.co.uk). Free weekly magazine for expatriate Australians in the UK, but of interest to anyone planning to live in Australia.

The West Australian – Perth (🖳 www.thewest.com.au). Western Australia's best-selling newspaper.

Miscellaneous

The 100 Things Everyone Needs to Know About Australia, David Dale (Pan McMillan)

Australia (Commonwealth of Australia)

*Australia & New Zealand by Rail, Colin Taylor (Bradt)

*The Book of Australia (Watermark Press)

*The Great Barrier Reef (Readers Digest)

How to Be Normal in Australia, Robert Treborlang (Major Mitchell Press)

The Little Aussie Fact Book, Margaret Nicholson (Penguin)

*The Penguin Australian Encyclopaedia, Sarah Dawson (Penguin)

Traditional Australian Cooking, Shirley Constantine (McPhee Gribble/Penguin)

*The Wines of Australia, Oliver Mayo (Faber & Faber)

New Zealand

There are many useful reference books for those seeking general information about New Zealand, including the *New Zealand Official Year Book* published annually by Statistics New Zealand. A selection of books about New Zealand is listed below (the publication title is followed by the name of the author and the publisher's name in brackets). Books prefixed with an asterisk (*) are recommended by the author. Some of the books listed are out of print, but you may still be able to find a copy in a book shop or library.

Living & Working

**Living and Working in New Zealand, ed. Graeme Chesters (Survival Books)

The Small Business Book: A New Zealand Guide, Robert Hamlin & John English (Bridgit Williams)

Your Successful Small Business: A New Zealand Guide to Starting Out and Staying in Business, Judith Ashton (Viking Pacific)

Tourist Guides

*AA/Baedeker's New Zealand (AA Publishing)

*Australia & New Zealand Travel Planner (TNT Magazine)

Berlitz Pocket Guide to New Zealand (Berlitz)

*Berlitz Travellers Guide New Zealand (Berlitz)

*Blue Guide New Zealand (A & C Black)

Destination New Zealand, Hildesuse Gaertner & Sue Bollans (Windsor)

Essential New Zealand (Automobile Association)

Fielding's New Zealand, Zeke & Joan Wigglesworth (Fielding)

*Fodor's Gold Guides: New Zealand (Fodor)

*Frommers New Zealand from $50 a Day, Elizabeth Hanson & Richard Adams (Macmillan)

Insider's New Zealand Guide, Harry Blutstein (MPC)

*Landmark Visitor's Guide: New Zealand, Korner-Bourne (Landmark Publishing)

*Let's Go New Zealand (Macmillan)

*Lonely Planet New Zealand (Lonely Planet)

*Maverick Guide to New Zealand, Robert W. Bone (Pelican)

Nelles Guide: New Zealand (Verlag Nelles)

New Zealand 2001: Budget Travel Guide, V. Jacquemont (Thomas Cook Publications)

New Zealand Handbook, Jane King (Moon)

*New Zealand Insight Guide, J. Hollis (Insight Guides)

*New Zealand: A Travel Survival Kit, Tony Wheeler & Nancy Keller (Lonely Planet)

*New Zealand: The Rough Guide, Laura Harper (The Rough Guides)

Visitor's Guide to New Zealand, Grant Bourne & Sabine Korner-Bourne (Moorland)

Food & Wine

Fine Wines of New Zealand, Keith Stewart (Grub Street)

New Taste in New Zealand, Lauraine Jacobs & Stephen Robinson (Ten Speed Press)

*Pocket Guide to the Wines of New Zealand, Michael Cooper (Mitchell Beazley)

*Rough Guide to Auckland Restaurants, Mark Graham (Rough Guides)

Weekends for Food Lovers, Kerry Tyack (Charles Letts Publishing)

Weekends for Wine Lovers in North Island (New Holland Publishers)

Weekends for Wine Lovers in South Island (New Holland Publishers)

Wines of New Zealand, Michael Cooper (Millers)

*The Wines of New Zealand, Rosemary M. George (Faber & Faber)

Magazines & Newspapers

The Dominion Post – Wellington (⌨ www.dompost.co.nz).

Migrant News (⌨ www.migrantnews.co.nz). New Zealand's primary resource for migrants.

The National Business Review (⌨ www.nbr.co.nz).

The New Zealand Herald – Auckland (⌨ www.nzherald.co.nz).

New Zealand News UK, South Bank House, Black Prince Road, London SE1 7S6 (☎ 020-7476 9704, ⌨ www.nznewsuk.co.uk). Subscription newspaper for prospective migrants.

New Zealand Outlook, Consyl Publishing, 3 Buckhurst Road, Bexhill-on-Sea, East Sussex TN40 1QF, UK (☎ 01424-223111, ⌨ www.consylpublishing.co.uk). Subscription newspaper for prospective migrants.

The Opinion (⌨ www.theopinion.co.nz). National monthly newspaper that examines and analyses in depth, the performance of government, its bureaucracy and political system

TNT Magazine New Zealand, 14-15 Child's Place, London SW5 9RX, UK (☎ 020-7373 3377, ⌨ www.tntmagazine.com). Free weekly magazine for expatriate New Zealanders in the UK, but of interest to anyone planning to live in New Zealand.

Online Newspapers (⌨ www.onlinenewspapers.com/nz.). Provides a comprehensive list of all New Zealand's national and local newspapers.

The Otago Daily Times – Dunedin (⌨ www.odt.co.nz).

The Waikato Times – Hamilton (⌨ www.waikatotimes.co.nz).

Miscellaneous

Australia and New Zealand Contact Directory, Sheile Hare (Expat Network)

*Australia & New Zealand by Rail, Colin Taylor (Bradt)

Back Country New Zealand (Hodder)

Beautiful New Zealand, Peter Morath (Hale)

Culture Questions: New Zealand Identity in a Transitional Age, Ruth Brown (Kapako)

*Dictionary of New Zealand English, H. W. Oarsman (Oxford University Press)

National Parks & Other Wild Places of New Zealand, K. Ombler (New Holland Publishers)

New Zealand – A Visual Celebration, Graeme Lay & Gareth Eyres (New Holland Publishers)

New Zealand in Pictures (Paperboards)

New Zealand Ways of Speaking English, Allan Bell & Janet Holmes (Multilingual Matters)

*Oxford Illustrated History of New Zealand, Keith Sinclair (Oxford University Press)

Politics in New Zealand, Richard Mulgan (Auckland UP)

Smooth Ride Guide to Australia & New Zealand (FT Publishing)

Truth About New Zealand, A. N. Field (Veritas)

Wild New Zealand, B. Coffey (New Holland)

Wild New Zealand: Reader's Digest (Reader's Digest)

APPENDIX C: USEFUL WEBSITES

The websites listed below provide information for expatriates in general and about Australia and/or New Zealand in particular. Websites relevant to specific aspects of buying a home in Australia and New Zealand are listed in the appropriate section. Websites generally offer free access, although some require a subscription or payment for services. A particularly useful section found on most expatriate websites is the 'message board' or 'forum', where expatriates answer questions based on their experience and knowledge, which offer an insight into what living and working in Australia and New Zealand is really like (these are also provided by some magazine websites). Websites (below) are listed under headings in alphabetical order and the list is by no means intended to be exhaustive.

Expatriates

ExpatBoards (🖳 www.expatboards.com). The mega site for expatriates, with popular discussion boards and special areas for Britons, Americans, expatriate taxes, and other important issues.

Escape Artist (🖳 www.escapeartist.com). An excellent website and probably the most comprehensive, packed with resources, links and directories covering most expatriate destinations. You can also subscribe to the free monthly online expatriate magazine, *Escape from America*.

Expat Exchange (🖳 www.expatexchange.com). Reportedly the largest online community for English-speaking expatriates, provides a series of articles on relocation and also a question and answer facility through its expatriate network.

Expat Forum (🖳 www.expatforum.com). Provides interesting cost of living comparisons plus seven EU country-specific forums and chats (Belgium, the Czech Republic, France, Germany, the Netherlands, Spain and the UK).

Expat World (🖳 www.expatworld.net). 'The newsletter of international living.' Contains a wealth of information for American and British expatriates, including a subscription newsletter.

Expatriate Experts (🖳 www.expatexpert.com). A website run by expatriate expert Robin Pascoe, providing invaluable advice and support.

Expats International (🖳 www.expats2000.com). The international job centre for expats and their recruiters.

Real Post Reports (🖳 www.realpostreports.com). Provides relocation services, recommended reading lists and plenty of interesting 'real-life' stories containing anecdotes and impressions written by expatriates in just about every city in the world.

Travel Documents (🖳 www.traveldocs.com). Useful information about travel, specific countries and documents needed to travel.

World Travel Guide (🖳 www.wtgonline.com). A general website for world travellers and expatriates.

British Expatriates

British Expatriates (🖳 www.britishexpat.com). This website keep British expatriates in touch with events and information about the UK.

Trade Partners (🖳 www.tradepartners.gov.uk). A government sponsored website whose main aim is to provide trade and investment information on just about every country in the world.

Worldwise Directory (🖳 www.suzylamplugh.org/worldwise). This website run by the Suzy Lamplugh charity for personal safety, providing a useful directory of countries with practical information and special emphasis on safety, particularly for women.

American Expatriates

Americans Abroad (🖳 www.aca.ch). This website offers advice, information and services to Americans abroad.

USA Government Trade (🖳 www.usatrade.gov). A huge website providing a wealth of information principally for Americans planning to trade and invest abroad, but useful for anyone planning a move abroad.

Women

Family Life Abroad (🖥 www.familylifeabroad.com). A wealth of information and articles on coping with family life abroad.

Foreign Wives Club (🖥 www.foreignwivesclub.com). An online community for women in bicultural marriages.

Third Culture Kids (🖥 www.tckworld.com). A website designed for expatriate children living abroad.

Travel For Kids (🖥 www.travelforkids.com). Advice on travelling with children around the world.

Women Of The World (🖥 www.wow-net.org). A website designed for female expats anywhere in the world.

Travel Information & Warnings

The websites listed below provide daily updated information about the political situation and natural disasters around the world, plus general travel and health advice and embassy addresses.

Australian Department of Foreign Affairs and Trade (🖥 www.dfat.gov.au/travel).

British Foreign and Commonwealth Office (🖥 www.fco.gov.uk).

Canadian Department of Foreign Affairs (🖥 www.dfait-maeci.gc.ca). They also publish a useful series of free booklets for Canadians moving abroad.

New Zealand Ministry of Foreign Affairs and Trade (🖥 www.mft.govt.nz).

SaveWealth Travel (🖥 www.savewealth.com/travel/warnings).

The Travel Doctor (🖥 www.tmvc.com.au). Contains a country by country vaccination guide.

US State Government (🖥 www.state.gov/travel). US government website.

World Health Organization (💻 www.who.int).

Australia-specific Websites

About Australia (💻 www.about-australia.com). One of Australia's longest established information portals, with masses of information about business, lifestyle, towns, regions and what's on.

Adult Learning Australia (💻 www.ala.asn.au). A body concerned with all aspects of adult education.

Australia Council for the Arts (💻 www.ozco.gov.au). The Australian government's arts funding and advisory body.

Australian Broadcasting Corporation (💻 www.abc.net.au). Information about the government owned television and radio stations.

Australian Bureau of Statistics (💻 www.abs.gov.au). Provides a wide range of statistics on Australia's economy, environment and energy, industry, population and regions.

Australian Government (💻 www.australia.gov.au). Useful information for, among others, jobseekers, migrants, seniors, students and women.

The Australian National University (💻 www.anu.edu.au). ANU (Canberra) is one of the world's foremost research universities and attracts leading academics and outstanding students from Australia and across the world.

Australian Property (💻 www.australianproperty.com). A UK-based company that holds property 'info sessions' in London for prospective Australian property buyers.

Bureau of Meteorology (💻 www.bom.gov.au). Information about all aspects of Australia's climate.

Charles Sturt University Guide to Australia (💻 www.csu.edu/au/australia). A useful selection of links on many topics, including culture, education, geography, tourism, towns and cities, trade and commerce, and travel and communications.

Crikey ( www.crikey.com.au). Australia's leading independent online news service.

Department of the Treasury (www.treasury.gov.au). Responsible for the budget and economic policy and forecasts.

The Emigration Group (www.emigration.uk.com). The website for The Emigration Group Ltd. and Taylor & Associates Ltd., who together provide a comprehensive service for migrants to Australia and New Zealand.

Greenpeace Australia Pacific (www.greenpeace.org.au). Environmental information, news and resources.

Home Site (www.homesite.com.au). Australia's leading home and garden website.

Indigenous Australia (www.dreamtime.net.au). Information about Australia's indigenous peoples.

Insurance Council of Australia Limited (www.ica.com.au). The representative body of the Australian general insurance industry.

Invest Australia (www.investaustralia.gov.au). Australia's national inward investment agency.

Law Council of Australia (www.lawcouncil.asn.au). The representative body of 40,000 legal practitioners.

National Gallery of Australia (www.nga.gov.au). Details of collections, events and exhibitions.

National Library of Australia (www.nla.gov.au). A journey through centuries, continents and civilisations using the NLA's collections, services, exhibitions and publications.

National Museum of Australia (www.nma.gov.au). Details of collections, events and exhibitions.

National Wine Centre of Australia (www.wineaustralia.com.au). Part of the University of Adelaide, provides information about winemaking and Australia's vibrant wine industry.

News.com.au (🖥 www.news.com.au). The latest news about Australia.

Picture Australia (🖥 www.pictureaustralia.org). A service hosted by the National Library of Australia, providing access to the picture collections of a range of cultural institutions.

Refugee Council of Australia (🖥 www.refugeecouncil.org.au). Provides advocacy, legal advice, protection and support to asylum seekers and refugees.

Reserve Bank of Australia (🖥 www.rba.gov.au). Australia's central bank.

Special Broadcasting Service (🖥 www20.sbs.com.au/sbs_front/index.html). Good news website with more of a global rather than local outlook on news. Aims to reflect the multicultural nature of Australian society.

Study in Australia (🖥 http://studyinaustralia.gov.au). A government site with advice on studying in Australia.

Sydney Morning Herald (🖥 www.smh.com.au). A useful source of Australian and international business, entertainment, news, sport and technology.

Tourism Australia (🖥 www.australia.com). The organisation responsible for marketing Australia, providing extensive information about all aspects of visiting and living in the country.

Yellow Pages (🖥 www.yellowpages.com.au).

Australian State Government & Tourism Offices

Australian Capital Territory

Government of the Australian Capital Territory (🖥 www.act.gov.au).

Tourism Canberra (🖥 www.canberratourism.com.au).

New South Wales

New South Wales Government Trade and Investment Office (🖥 www.nsw.gov.au).

Tourism New South Wales (🖥 www.tourism.nsw.gov.au).

Northern Territory

Government of the Northern Territory (🖥 www.nt.gov.au).

Northern Territory Tourist Commission (🖥 www.ntholidays.com).

Queensland

Agent-General for Queensland (🖥 www.qld.gov.au).

Tourism Queensland (🖥 www.Queenslanholidays.co.uk).

South Australia

Agent-General for South Australia (🖥 www.sacentral.sa.gov.au).

South Australian Tourist Commission (🖥 www.south australia.com).

Tasmania

Government of Tasmania (🖥 www.tas.gov.au).

Tourism Tasmania (🖥 www.discovertasmania.com.au).

Victoria

Agent-General for Victoria (🖥 www.vic.gov.au).

Tourism Victoria (🖥 www.tourism.vic.gov.au).

Western Australia

Government of Western Australia (🖥 www.wa.gov.au).

Western Australian Tourism Commission (🖥 www.western australia.net).

New Zealand-specific Websites

Aardvark (🖥 www.aardvark.co.nz). One of New Zealand's longest-running online news and commentary sites.

British Council New Zealand (🖥 www.britishcouncil.org). The UK's agency for international cultural relations.

Creative New Zealand (🖥 www.creativenz.govt.nz). New Zealand's premier body for developing and promoting the arts.

Destination New Zealand (🖥 www.destination-nz.com). An online travel guide.

Franchise Association of New Zealand (🖥 www.franchise. org.nz). The Association promotes and explains franchising.

MetService (🖥 www.metservice.co.nz). Comprehensive information about New Zealand's weather.

My Town (🖥 www.mytown.co.nz). Local news for Auckland, Wellington, Hamilton, Dunedin, and Christchurch, including weather and traffic reports.

National Library of New Zealand (🖥 www.natlib.govt.nz). Provides details of the National Library's collection of archives, books, newspapers, paintings and photographs.

New Zealand Archaeology (🖥 www.nzarchaeology.org). Information about New Zealand's archaeological heritage.

New Zealand Book Council (🖥 www.bookcouncil.org.nz). An organisation that promotes books and reading, and provides information about authors and publishers.

New Zealand Film Commission (💻 www.nzfilm.co.nz). Information about all aspects of film making and promotion in New Zealand.

New Zealand Geographical Society (💻 www.nzgs.co.nz). Information by and for geographers and also for schools.

The New Zealand Herald (💻 www.nzherald.co.nz). The website of one of the country's leading newspapers, covering jobs, motoring, news, real estate, travel, TV and much more.

New Zealand in History (💻 http://history-nz.org). A website dedicated to New Zealand's history, from the time the country was first settled.

New Zealand Institute of Management (💻 www.nzim.co.nz). A professional body for the managerial class.

New Zealand Law Society (💻 www.nz-lawsoc.org.nz). The governing body of New Zealand's legal profession.

New Zealand Museums (💻 www.nzmuseums.co.nz). This allows you to tour New Zealand's museums online (so you don't have to waste time going in person!).

New Zealand on the Web (💻 www.nz.com). Tourism and travel guide.

New Zealand Police (💻 www.police.govt.nz). The website of New Zealand's police force, including information about crime statistics.

New Zealand Wine (💻 www.nzwine.com). Information about all aspects of one of New Zealand's most dynamic industries.

One New Zealand (💻 www.onenz.co.nz). Modestly claims to be 'New Zealand's leading travel net guide.'

Prime Minister of New Zealand (💻 www.primeminister.govt.nz). The country's head of government has her own website.

Reserve Bank of New Zealand (💻 www.rbnz.govt.nz). The website of New Zealand's central bank, with information about all aspects of monetary policy.

The Royal Society of New Zealand (💻 www.rsnz.org). An independent, national academy of sciences.

Stuff (💻 www.stuff.co.nz). News and comment from many of New Zealand's national and regional papers.

Tourism Auckland (💻 www.aucklandnz.com). Extensive information about New Zealand's largest city.

Tourism New Zealand (💻 www.tourismnewzealand.com). New Zealand's international marketing organisation.

TV New Zealand (💻 www.tvnz.co.nz). Latest text and video news, sports, financial information and weather conditions from New Zealand's highest rated TV company.

The University of Auckland (💻 www.auckland.ac.nz). New Zealand's leading research-led university.

WhatsOnNZ (💻 www.whatsonnz.com). One of the better information websites.

APPENDIX D: WEIGHTS & MEASURES

Australia and New Zealand use the metric system of measurement. Those who are more familiar with the imperial system of measurement will find the tables on the following pages useful. Some comparisons shown are only approximate, but are close enough for most everyday uses. In addition to the variety of measurement systems used, clothes sizes often vary considerably with the manufacturer.

Women's Clothes

Continental	34	36	38	40	42	44	46	48	50	52
UK	8	10	12	14	16	18	20	22	24	26
US	6	8	10	12	14	16	18	20	22	24

Pullovers

	Women's						Men's					
Continental	40	42	44	46	48	50	44	46	48	50	52	54
UK	34	36	38	40	42	44	34	36	38	40	42	44
US	34	36	38	40	42	44	sm	med		lar		xl

Men's Shirts

Continental	36	37	38	39	40	41	42	43	44	46
UK/US	14	14	15	15	16	16	17	17	18	-

Men's Underwear

Continental	5	6	7	8	9	10
UK	34	36	38	40	42	44
US	sm	med		lar		xl

Note: sm = small, med = medium, lar = large, xl = extra large

Children's Clothes

Continental	92	104	116	128	140	152
UK	16/18	20/22	24/26	28/30	32/34	36/38
US	2	4	6	8	10	12

Children's Shoes

Continental	18	19	20	21	22	23	24	25	26	27	28	29	30	31	32
UK/US	2	3	4	4	5	6	7	7	8	9	10	11	11	12	13

Continental	33	34	35	36	37	38
UK/US	1	2	2	3	4	5

Shoes (Women's and Men's)

Continental	35	36	37	37	38	39	40	41	42	42	43	44
UK	2	3	3	4	4	5	6	7	7	8	9	9
US	4	5	5	6	6	7	8	9	9	10	10	11

Weight

Imperial	Metric	Metric	Imperial
1oz	28.35g	1g	0.035oz
1lb*	454g	100g	3.5oz
1cwt	50.8kg	250g	9oz
1 ton	1,016kg	500g	18oz
2,205lb	1 tonne	1kg	2.2lb

Length

Imperial	Metric	Metric	Imperial
1in	2.54cm	1cm	0.39in
1ft	30.48cm	1m	3ft 3.25in
1yd	91.44cm	1km	0.62mi
1mi	1.6km	8km	5mi

Capacity

Imperial	Metric	Metric	Imperial
1 UK pint	0.57 litre	1 litre	1.75 UK pints
1 US pint	0.47 litre	1 litre	2.13 US pints
1 UK gallon	4.54 litres	1 litre	0.22 UK gallon
1 US gallon	3.78 litres	1 litre	0.26 US gallon

Note: An American 'cup' = around 250ml or 0.25 litre.

Area

Imperial	Metric	Metric	Imperial
1 sq. in	0.45 sq. cm	1 sq. cm	0.15 sq. in
1 sq. ft	0.09 sq. m	1 sq. m	10.76 sq. ft
1 sq. yd	0.84 sq. m	1 sq. m	1.2 sq. yds
1 acre	0.4 hectares	1 hectare	2.47 acres
1 sq. mile	2.56 sq. km	1 sq. km	0.39 sq. mile

Note: An *are* is one-hundredth of a hectare or 100m^2.

Temperature

°Celsius	°Fahrenheit	
0	32	(freezing point of water)
5	41	
10	50	
15	59	
20	68	
25	77	
30	86	
35	95	
40	104	
50	122	

Notes: The boiling point of water is 100°C / 212°F.

Normal body temperature (if you're alive and well) is 37°C / 98.4°F.

Temperature Conversion

Celsius to Fahrenheit: multiply by 9, divide by 5 and add 32. (For a quick and approximate conversion, double the Celsius temperature and add 30.)

Fahrenheit to Celsius: subtract 32, multiply by 5 and divide by 9. (For a quick and approximate conversion, subtract 30 from the Fahrenheit temperature and divide by 2.)

Oven Temperatures

Gas	Electric	
	°F	°C
-	225–250	110–120
1	275	140
2	300	150
3	325	160
4	350	180
5	375	190
6	400	200
7	425	220
8	450	230
9	475	240

Air Pressure

PSI	Bar
10	0.5
20	1.4
30	2
40	2.8

Appendix E: MAPS

The maps on the following pages show the administrative divisions and main towns and cities of Australia and New Zealand, which are described in detail in **Chapter 2**.

Australia

Australia has six states and two territories, the latter administered by the Commonwealth government.

State/Territory	Capital
Australian Capital Territory (ACT)	Canberra
New South Wales (NSW)	Sydney
Northern Territory (NT)	Darwin
Queensland (QLD)	Brisbane
South Australia (SA)	Adelaide
Tasmania (TAS)	Hobart
Victoria (VIC)	Melbourne
Western Australia (WA)	Perth

AUSTRALIA

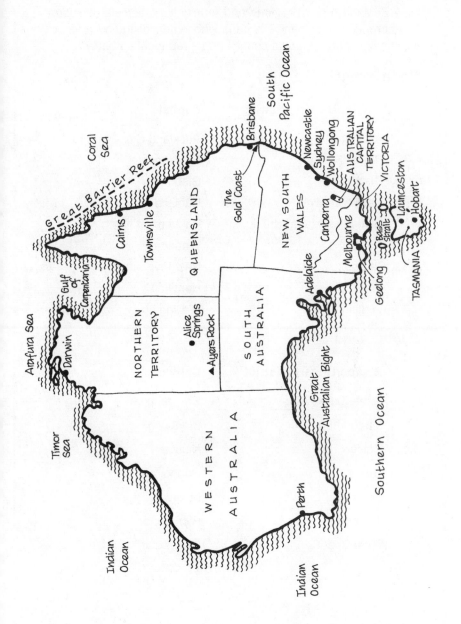

New Zealand

New Zealand has 12 regions and four unitary districts (Gisborne, Marlborough, Nelson and Tasman), whose administrations combine the functions of a regional council and a territorial authority.

North Island

Region/Unitary District	Capital
Auckland	Auckland City
Bay of Plenty	Tauranga
Gisborne	Gisborne
Hawke's Bay	Napier
Wanganui-Manawatu	Palmerston North
Northland	Whangarei
Taranaki	New Plymouth
Waikato	Hamilton
Wellington	Wellington

South Island

Region/Unitary District	Capital
Canterbury	Christchurch
Marlborough	Blenheim
Nelson	Nelson
Otago	Dunedin
Southland	Invercargill
Tasman	Richmond
West Coast	Greymouth

NEW ZEALAND

INDEX

Y

LIVING AND WORKING SERIES

Living and Working books are essential reading for anyone planning to spend time abroad, including holiday-home owners, retirees, visitors, business people, migrants, students and even extra-terrestrials! They're packed with important and useful information designed to help you **avoid costly mistakes and save both time and money.** Topics covered include how to:

- Find a job with a good salary & conditions
- Obtain a residence permit
- Avoid and overcome problems
- Find your dream home
- Get the best education for your family
- Make the best use of public transport
- Endure local motoring habits
- Obtain the best health treatment
- Stretch your money further
- Make the most of your leisure time
- Enjoy the local sporting life
- Find the best shopping bargains
- Insure yourself against most eventualities
- Use post office and telephone services
- Do numerous other things not listed above

Living and Working books are the most comprehensive and up-to-date source of practical information available about everyday life abroad. They aren't, however, boring text books, but interesting and entertaining guides written in a highly readable style.

Discover what it's *really* like to live and work abroad!

Order your copies today by phone, fax, post or email from: Survival Books, PO Box 3780, YEOVIL, BA21 5WX, United Kingdom (☎/🖨 +44 (0)1935-700060, ✉ sales@survivalbooks.net, 🖥 www.survivalbooks.net).

BUYING A HOME SERIES

Buying a Home books, including *Buying, Selling & Letting Property*, are essential reading for anyone planning to purchase property abroad. They're packed with vital information to guide you through the property purchase jungle and help you **avoid the sort of disasters that can turn your dream home into a nightmare!** Topics covered include:

- Avoiding problems
- Choosing the region
- Finding the right home and location
- Estate agents
- Finance, mortgages and taxes
- Home security
- Utilities, heating and air-conditioning
- Moving house and settling in
- Renting and letting
- Permits and visas
- Travelling and communications
- Health and insurance
- Renting a car and driving
- Retirement and starting a business
- And much, much more!

Buying a Home books are the most comprehensive and up-to-date source of information available about buying property abroad. Whether you want a detached house, townhouse or apartment, a holiday or a permanent home, these books will help make your dreams come true.

Save yourself time, trouble and money!

Order your copies today by phone, fax, post or email from: Survival Books, PO Box 3780, YEOVIL, BA21 5WX, United Kingdom (☎/▤ +44 (0)1935-700060, ✉ sales@survivalbooks.net, ▣ www.survivalbooks.net).

OTHER SURVIVAL BOOKS

The Alien's Guides: *The Alien's Guides to Britain and France* will help you to appreciate the peculiarities (in both senses) of the British and French.

The Best Places to Buy a Home in France/Spain: The most comprehensive homebuying guides to France and Spain, containing detailed profiles of the most popular regions for home-buying.

Buying, Selling and Letting Property: The most comprehensive and up-to-date source of information on buying, selling and letting property in the UK.

Earning Money From Your Home: Essential guides to earning income from property in France and Spain, including short- and long-term letting.

Foreigners in France/Spain: Triumphs & Disasters: Real-life experiences of people who have emigrated to France and Spain, recounted in their own words.

Lifelines: Essential guides to life in specific regions of France and Spain. See order form for a list of current titles in the series.

Making a Living: Essential guides to self-employment and starting a business in France and Spain.

Renovating & Maintaining Your French Home: The ultimate guide to renovating and maintaining your dream home in France.

Retiring Abroad: The most comprehensive and up-to-date source of practical information available about retiring to a foreign country.

Shooting Caterpillars in Spain: The hilarious experiences of an expatriate who sent to Spain in search of . . . she wasn't quite sure what.

Surprised by France: Even after living there for ten years, Donald Carroll finds plenty of surprises in the Hexagon.

Broaden your horizons with Survival Books!

Order your copies today by phone, fax, post or email from: Survival Books, PO Box 3780, YEOVIL, BA21 5WX, United Kingdom (☎/🖷 +44 (0)1935-700060, ✉ sales@survivalbooks.net, 🖳 www.survivalbooks.net).

Qty.	Title	Price (incl. p&p)			Total
		UK	Europe	World	
	The Alien's Guide to Britain	£6.95	£8.95	£12.45	
	The Alien's Guide to France	£6.95	£8.95	£12.45	
	The Best Places to Buy a Home in France	£13.95	£15.95	£19.45	
	The Best Places to Buy a Home in Spain	£13.95	£15.95	£19.45	
	Buying a Home Abroad	£13.95	£15.95	£19.45	
	Buying a Home in Australia & NZ	£13.95	£15.95	£19.45	
	Buying a Home in Cyprus	£13.95	£15.95	£19.45	
	Buying a Home in Florida	£13.95	£15.95	£19.45	
	Buying a Home in France	£13.95	£15.95	£19.45	
	Buying a Home in Greece	£13.95	£15.95	£19.45	
	Buying a Home in Ireland	£11.95	£13.95	£17.45	
	Buying a Home in Italy	£13.95	£15.95	£19.45	
	Buying a Home in Portugal	£13.95	£15.95	£19.45	
	Buying a Home in South Africa	£13.95	£15.95	£19.45	
	Buying a Home in Spain	£13.95	£15.95	£19.45	
	Buying, Letting & Selling Property	£11.95	£13.95	£17.45	
	Earning Money From Your French Home	£11.95	£13.95	£17.45	
	Earning Money From Your Spanish Home	£11.95	£13.95	£17.45	
	Foreigners in France: Triumphs & Disasters	£11.95	£13.95	£17.45	
	Foreigners in Spain: Triumphs & Disasters	£11.95	£13.95	£17.45	
	Costa Blanca Lifeline	£11.95	£13.95	£17.45	
	Costa del Sol Lifeline	£11.95	£13.95	£17.45	
	Dordogne/Lot Lifeline	£11.95	£13.95	£17.45	
	Normandy Lifeline	£11.95	£13.95	£17.45	
	Poitou-Charentes Lifeline	£11.95	£13.95	£17.45	
	Provence-Côte d'Azur Lifeline	£11.95	£13.95	£17.45	
	Living & Working Abroad	£14.95	£16.95	£20.45	
	Living & Working in America	£14.95	£16.95	£20.45	
	Living & Working in Australia	£16.95	£18.95	£22.45	
	Living & Working in Britain	£14.95	£16.95	£20.45	
	Living & Working in Canada	£16.95	£18.95	£22.45	
	Living & Working in the European Union	£16.95	£18.95	£22.45	
	Living & Working in the Far East	£16.95	£18.95	£22.45	
	Total carried forward (see over)				

ORDER FORM

Qty.	Title	Price (incl. p&p)			Total
			Total brought forward		
		UK	Europe	World	
	Living & Working in France	£14.95	£16.95	£20.45	
	Living & Working in Germany	£16.95	£18.95	£22.45	
	L&W in the Gulf States & Saudi Arabia	£16.95	£18.95	£22.45	
	L&W in Holland, Belgium & Luxembourg	£14.95	£16.95	£20.45	
	Living & Working in Ireland	£14.95	£16.95	£20.45	
	Living & Working in Italy	£16.95	£18.95	£22.45	
	Living & Working in London	£13.95	£15.95	£19,45	
	Living & Working in New Zealand	£16.95	£18.95	£22.45	
	Living & Working in Spain	£14.95	£16.95	£20.45	
	Living & Working in Switzerland	£16.95	£18.95	£22.45	
	Making a Living in France	£13.95	£15.95	£19.45	
	Making a Living in Spain	£13.95	£15.95	£19.45	
	Renovating & Maintaining Your French Home	£16.95	£18.95	£22.45	
	Retiring Abroad	£14.95	£16.95	£20.45	
	Shooting Caterpillars in Spain	£9.95	£11.95	£15.45	
	Surprised by France	£11.95	£13.95	£17.45	
				Grand Total	

Order your copies today by phone, fax, post or email from: Survival Books, PO Box 3780, YEOVIL, BA21 5WX, United Kingdom (☎/▤ +44 (0)1935-700060, ✉ sales@ survivalbooks.net, 🖥 www.survivalbooks.net). If you aren't entirely satisfied, simply return them to us within 14 days for a full and unconditional refund.

I enclose a cheque for the grand total/Please charge my Amex/Delta/Maestro (Switch)/MasterCard/Visa card as follows. (delete as applicable)

Card No. _ _ _ _   _ _ _ _   _ _ _ _   _ _ _ _   Security Code* _ _ _

Expiry date _____   Issue number (Maestro/Switch only) _____

Signature _____   Tel. No. _____

NAME _____

ADDRESS _____

_____

* The security code is the last three digits on the signature strip.